THE CITY OF POETRY

What did it mean to be a poet in fourteenth-century Italy? What counted as poetry? In an effort to answer these questions, this book examines the careers of four medieval Italian poets (Albertino Mussato, Dante Alighieri, Francesco Petrarch, and Giovanni Boccaccio) who wrote in both Latin and the Italian vernacular. In readings of defenses of poetry, speeches and letters on public laurel-crowning ceremonies, and other theoretical and poetic texts, this book shows how these poets viewed their authorship of poetic works as a function of their engagement in a human community. Each poet represents a model of the poet as a public intellectual – a poet-theologian – who can intervene in public affairs thanks to his authority within texts. *The City of Poetry* provides a new historicized approach to understanding poetic culture in fourteenth-century Italy which reshapes long-standing Romantic views of poetry as a timeless and sublimely inspired form of discourse.

DAVID G. LUMMUS is the co-director of the Center for Italian Studies and Devers Family Program in Dante Studies and a visiting assistant professor of Italian at the University of Notre Dame. He has published on fourteenth-century Italian poetry and poetics, especially Giovanni Boccaccio, and the reception of classical culture in medieval Italy. He is the co-editor of *A Boccaccian Renaissance* (2019).

T0364204

CAMBRIDGE STUDIES IN MEDIEVAL LITERATURE

Founding Editor
Alastair Minnis, *Yale University*

General Editor
Daniel Wakelin, *University of Oxford*

Editorial Board
Anthony Bale, *Birkbeck, University of London*
Zygmunt G. Barański, *University of Cambridge*
Christopher C. Baswell, *Barnard College and Columbia University*
Mary Carruthers, *New York University*
Rita Copeland, *University of Pennsylvania*
Roberta Frank, *Yale University*
Marissa Galvez, *Stanford University*
Alastair Minnis, *Yale University*
Jocelyn Wogan-Browne, *Fordham University*

This series of critical books seeks to cover the whole area of literature written in the major medieval languages – the main European vernaculars, and medieval Latin and Greek – during the period c.1100–1500. Its chief aim is to publish and stimulate fresh scholarship and criticism on medieval literature, special emphasis being placed on understanding major works of poetry, prose, and drama in relation to the contemporary culture and learning which fostered them.

A complete list of titles in the series can be found at the end of the volume.

THE CITY OF POETRY

*Imagining the Civic Role of the Poet in
Fourteenth-Century Italy*

DAVID G. LUMMUS

University of Notre Dame, Indiana

CAMBRIDGE
UNIVERSITY PRESS

Shaftesbury Road, Cambridge CB2 8EA, United Kingdom

One Liberty Plaza, 20th Floor, New York, NY 10006, USA

477 Williamstown Road, Port Melbourne, VIC 3207, Australia

314–321, 3rd Floor, Plot 3, Splendor Forum, Jasola District Centre, New Delhi – 110025, India

103 Penang Road, #05–06/07, Visioncrest Commercial, Singapore 238467

Cambridge University Press is part of Cambridge University Press & Assessment, a department of the University of Cambridge.

We share the University's mission to contribute to society through the pursuit of education, learning and research at the highest international levels of excellence.

www.cambridge.org
Information on this title: www.cambridge.org/9781108813174

DOI: 10.1017/9781108878050

First published 2020

A catalogue record for this publication is available from the British Library

Library of Congress Cataloging-in-Publication data
NAMES: Lummus, David, author.
TITLE: The city of poetry : imagining the civic role of the poet in fourteenth-century Italy / David G. Lummus.
DESCRIPTION: Cambridge, UK ; New York : Cambridge University Press, 2020. | Series: Cambridge studies in medieval literature | Includes bibliographical references and index.
IDENTIFIERS: LCCN 2020022981 (print) | LCCN 2020022982 (ebook) | ISBN 9781108839457 (hardback) | ISBN 9781108813174 (paperback) | ISBN 9781108878050 (epub)
SUBJECTS: LCSH: Political poetry, Latin (Medieval and modern)–History and criticism. | Latin poetry, Medieval and modern–Italy–History and criticism. | Italian poetry–To 1400–History and criticism. | Politics and literature–Italy–History–To 1500. | Poetry–Authorship–Social aspects. | Politics in literature. | Humanism.
CLASSIFICATION: LCC PA8065.P64 L86 2020 (print) | LCC PA8065.P64 (ebook) | DDC 871/.3093581–dc23
LC record available at https://lccn.loc.gov/2020022981
LC ebook record available at https://lccn.loc.gov/2020022982

ISBN   978-1-108-83945-7   Hardback
ISBN   978-1-108-81317-4   Paperback

Heu cineres bustumque petet qui, turbine quanquam
dilatus vario, multos absumpserit annos.
　　　　　— Petrarch, *Epystola metrica* 2.10.118–119

Contents

Acknowledgments

This book was written between three universities, where I was able to learn from mentors, colleagues, and students with a broad array of interests and expertise. To them goes my gratitude. I hope they are all able to recognize themselves here *etsi sine nomine*.

I have benefited from generous financial support of my research, without which I would not have been able to write this book: a Geballe Dissertation Prize from the Stanford Humanities Center at Stanford University, an A. Whitney Griswold Faculty Research Grant and a Morse Fellowship for Junior Faculty in the Humanities from Yale University, and a Junior Faculty Leave from Stanford University. I also acknowledge the Medieval Institute of the University of Notre Dame, which allowed me to use its rich library as a Visiting Scholar, as well as Notre Dame's Center for Italian Studies, which welcomed me first as a guest and then as a fellow citizen, and which gave me several opportunities to present my research for this book to groups of knowledgeable scholars.

My further thanks go to the numerous colleagues with whom I have been able to share ideas and work in progress, especially at meetings of the American Boccaccio Association, the Modern Language Association of America, and the Renaissance Society of America – I always walked away from these encounters richer in ideas.

The libraries I have used, along with the people who care for them, also deserve recognition here: the Cecil H. Green Library at Stanford, the Sterling Memorial Library at Yale, and the Theodore M. Hesburgh Library at Notre Dame, as well as the Biblioteca Angelica in Rome. A more specific debt is owed to the Biblioteca del Seminario and the Biblioteca Civica in Padua and the Biblioteca Civica Bertoliana in Vicenza, where I was granted access to archival materials during my preparation of the first chapter.

I should like to recognize the Modern Language Association of America for its contribution to the publication of this book, through the Aldo and

Jeanne Scaglione Publication Award for a Manuscript in Italian Literary Studies. Emily Hockley at Cambridge University Press could not have been more supportive, and I thank her together with the current and former editors of this series, Dan Wakelin and Alistair Minnis, for believing in the value of the project, and the editorial team for their work on producing the book, especially Natasha Burton, Sharon McCann, Ishwarya Mathavan, and Paul Smith. I am also grateful to the two anonymous readers for the Press who provided excellent feedback to which I hope to have responded adequately in my revision of the manuscript.

My warmest appreciation goes to Nicole M. Gounalis, James C. Kriesel, and Norman L. Whitman for the friendship, wit, and intelligence they have shared with me over the years. I offer my heartfelt thanks to Chris and Gladys Lummus for their unending and extraordinary love and support. To Aidan I can only begin to express my gratitude for so generously sharing his childhood – and so much more – first with my dissertation and then with this book.

Finally, I dedicate this book, with profound gratitude, to Sabrina Ferri, without whom it would not only be far poorer in expression and idea but it would also never have been written or published: *Car'amiga dols'e franca ... // Vos etz arbres e branca.*

Note on Translations

I have used widely available standard translations of primary texts when possible. If a dual-language edition or a translation is not cited, then the translation is my own. When I have occasionally changed the wording of a published translation for clarity or nuance, it is noted as "modified."

Introduction

adventum ipsum et huic urbi et illi de qua et universe Ytalie, ipsa saltem rei novitate, non inglorium futurum esse confido.

I trust that my coming, because of the novelty of the occasion if for no other reason, may serve to bring some glory to this city, to the city whence I come, and to all Italy.

Scire decet ... poete officium atque professionem [minime esse] quam multi, immo fere omnes opinantur.

You must know & that the office and profession of the poet are not by any means what they are commonly believed to be.

— Petrarch, *Collatio laureationis*

— Petrarch, *Coronation Oration*[1]

On April 8, 1341, when he addressed the Roman Senate on the Capitoline to accept the laurel crown as poet and historian, Petrarch asserted that poetry was a profession. Poets had an *officium*, or civic duty, and a *professio*, a declared occupation. He described that duty in terms of the figurative representation of history for the moral betterment of humankind. Petrarch's address was based on the exegesis of two lines from Virgil's *Georgica*, which were expanded into a commentary on history and on the present's relationship with the past. For Petrarch, the poet's role was based on a privileged understanding of the events of history and a calling to inspire others. The activities of the poet as interpreter and as inventor – as *auctor* – were the foundation of the poet's status and role in society. For all of its symbolic cultural value, Petrarch's performance of authority on the Capitoline indicates that in fourteenth-century Italy the conception of what a poet should be and do was linked to communities beyond the book. In order to carry out the poet's *officium*, the author needed to emerge from the text and enter the city. Petrarch was not alone in relating

---

[1] Petrarch 1988a, 38 and 42; Petrarch 1953, 1245 and 1246 (*Collatio laureationis* 6.34–36; 9.11–13).

the work of the poet to a social reality consisting of more than readers. Albertino Mussato, Dante Alighieri, and Giovanni Boccaccio all, in diverse ways, also situate the work of poetry in relation to the city. It is in view of this civic role of the poet that they all conceive of and defend poetry as theology. The production of meaning in their poetry according to the allegorical models of biblical exegesis forms the basis of these poets' status and reputation in diverse social realities.

In this book, I examine how these four Italian poets represent the role of the poet as a part of a civic context. The focus of my inquiry is the defense of poetry and the laurel crowning of the poet in the city (or its promise), though I also consider other texts that shed light on how these individuals perform their authority as poets in relation to the world beyond the book. I interpret this performance of authority primarily in view of their political concerns, but also in connection with their ideas about language and meaning. The central argument that I want to advance is that these poets viewed their authorship of poetic works as a function of their engagement in a human community, real or imagined. Indeed, as I hope to show, each poet creates a model of the poet as an intellectual who can intervene in public affairs thanks to their authority within texts.

Studies on medieval poetry and poetics tend to treat authorship as a phenomenon that inhabits books and schoolrooms, as if medieval poets considered their enterprises only in relation to other authors and other books. Indeed, ideas of authorship did develop out of the exegetical and pedagogical traditions, as the work of Alastair Minnis, Rita Copeland, and others has shown.[2] My inquiry in this book is possible thanks to the research on medieval exegesis and rhetoric that has taken place over the past several decades. Minnis' work on the commentary tradition has demonstrated, for example, that the literal or historical sense of a text's meaning increasingly became seen as the foundation for further allegorical interpretation.[3] The historical sense offered a level of certainty that the other senses could not provide. In interpretations of the Gospels and of classical poetry, exegetes as far afield as Hugh of St. Victor, Peter Abelard, and Nicholas of Lyre, on the one hand, and Arnulf of Orleans, Giovanni del Virgilio, and Giovanni Boccaccio, on the other, found the

---

[2] See Minnis 1988 and 2000; Minnis, Scott, and Wallace 1988; Copeland 1991 and 2002; and Copeland and Sluiter 2009. The question of the poetic employment of exegetical and rhetorical practices in the poetry of the Italian fourteenth century has focused on Dante and Boccaccio. See, e.g., Hollander 1969; Mazzotta 1979; Smarr 1986; Kirkham 1993; Barański 2000; Ascoli 2008 and 2010; Kriesel 2009 and 2018; Cornish 2011 and Lummus 2011a; 2012b; and 2015.

[3] See Minnis 1988, esp. 91–92, 152–153 and Minnis 2000, esp. 244–248.

intentionality of the writer key to the interpretation of a text's meaning. If the historical sense offered certainty to medieval exegetes, then their concern for it also demonstrates an awareness of the historicity of the creation of meaning. Copeland, furthermore, has demonstrated how literal and allegorical modes of reading were associated since antiquity with political disenfranchisement and agency respectively. In her study of the pedagogical practices surrounding the Lollard heresy, she shows how interpretation of the literal sense became the grounds for political dissent and for the promotion of intellectual activity beyond the university.[4] The poets considered in this study assimilate poetic and biblical modes of allegorical meaning and by so doing assert a political status in concomitance with the university. Applied to poetic strategies that make far-reaching truth claims, such as those of Dante, the attention given to the historical intention of the author reveals a related concern both to control allegorical modes of discourse and to locate the text's meaning in the world of history.

Similarly, the question of how a poet like Dante constructs for himself an authority that equals and even surpasses that of his classical models and contemporaries is often addressed as a phenomenon limited solely to the text. Teodolinda Barolini has argued that Dante constructed his own role as poet of the *Commedia* by self-consciously eroding the authority of his contemporaries and models – an authority that he assumes for himself as *poeta*.[5] Barolini shows how Dante restricts the notion of *poeta* across the poem so that it applies only to himself as the successor of Virgil. Albert R. Ascoli, furthermore, has shown the extent of Dante's unique obsession with constructing his own author-figure in the *Commedia*. As Ascoli notes about Dante, however, there is a disjuncture between being a *poeta* and being an *autore*.[6] As I hope to show in this book, to be a poet, while often a function of authorship, is not limited to asserting oneself as an *auctor*. Rather, it means to transfer and embody the writer's authority through the text and to reach beyond it. The poets considered in this study each build their sense of authorship out of exegetical and pedagogical practices, but their poetic strategies also intersect with their ideas about the function of the poet in the world of history.

By examining how these poets project themselves beyond their works, I also look past the material conditions of medieval reading and writing practices, such as the production of codices and their historical readership.

---

[4] See Copeland 2002, esp. 51–149.   [5] See Barolini 1984. See also Tavoni 2015a.
[6] See Ascoli 2008, 301–405, esp. 400–405.

My aim is not to examine the historical realities of the role that poets or poetry played in specific communities of readers but to understand how these poets imagined their roles in communities, whether through their works or with their physical presence. The material artifact of the books that contained works of poetry, however, did represent to a certain extent the status of the poet in society. For example, Justin Steinberg has shown how Dante's early attempts at anthologization and literary history, when viewed through the lens of the materiality of texts, demonstrate Dante's broader cultural and political concerns about his own reception.[7] Jonathan Usher, Jason Houston, and Martin Eisner have also demonstrated how Boccaccio's practices of compiling codices reflect a broader cultural vision about the status of poetry in society.[8] By examining the defenses of poetry and the historical or potential laurel crowning ceremonies of these poets, my aim is to add to this scholarship and to tell another part of the story, which escapes the materiality of the text. The poet's role is just as much a function of reputation as it is a result of being read. While discourses on poetic fame tend to be read as a poet's projection into the future, they are also indicative of a poet's engagement with the present.[9] The defense of poetry, like the rhetorical performance of the coronation ceremony, is a textual event that looks beyond itself onto the world of history and politics.

---

[7] See Steinberg 2007.   [8] See Usher 2007; Houston 2010; and Eisner 2013.

[9] In Book 15 of the *Genealogie deorum gentilium*, Boccaccio demonstrates the link between future and present in consideration of the poet's reputation. He contrasts the *auctoritas* earned by the ancients over time with the *gravitas* earned by modern individuals during their lifetime: "However new those authors who are now ancient once were, it seems that whatever has survived through many ages has been approved by a length of time, and thence gains most of its authority. But what one ought to think about all new men, whatever their merit, seems to many to be still in suspense. I am of the opinion that those whose novelty is not approved will not last in time, since the initial approval must be gained from their novelty. Thus, I have dared call forth in testimony those whom I call new, since I have known or know them by their merits to be exceptional men, worthy of approval. It is clear to me, about all of them, that for their entire lives they devoted themselves to sacred studies, frequented men famous for their learning and character, that they were praiseworthy in life, unmarked by any turpitude, and that both their writings and sayings have been approved by the most prudent men. I think for these reasons that novelty must be held as equal to antiquity" ("nam quantumcunque novi fuerint qui nunc ex autoribus veteres sunt, videtur quod per multa secula perseveratum est, a longitudine temporis approbatum sit, et inde plurimum autoritatis sumpsisse. Quod utrum de ominibus novis, quantumcunque bene sint meriti, arbitrari debeat, apud multos videtur in pendulo. Ego autem huius sententie sum, nunquam in evum duraturos hos quorum novitas approbata non sit, cum ab eorum novitate necesse sit exordium approbationis sumendum; et sic eos, quos ego novos invoco, cum vivos noverim aut noscam, meritis eorum agentibus, egregios esse viros atque probandos ausus sum in testimonium evocare. Hoc enim michi constat ex ominibus, eos fere per omne vite tempus studiis vacasse sacris, eos inter insignes scientia et moribus semper versatos homines, eos vita laudabiles, nec ulla turpi nota signatos, eorum scripta aut dicta a prudentioribus etiam approbata. Credo, his agentibus, equiparanda sit eorum novitas vetustati"). Boccaccio 1930, 111, modified Boccaccio 1998, 8.1528 (*Genealogie* 15.6.1–2). On the significance for Boccaccio's cultural ideology, see Lummus 2012a, 117–118.

My approach is based on a close rhetorical and intertextual analysis of verse and prose texts, which I place in the context of each poet's political ideas and activities. I see fourteenth-century defenses of poetry not only as emerging from distinct historical and political contexts but also as self-conscious responses to those contexts.

Much of the critical debate about poetic authority has traditionally concerned the question of how vernacular poetic culture emerged from and engaged with a dominant intellectual culture that used Latin. A great part of Dante's novelty resides, in fact, in his bold turn to the Florentine idiom as the language of the *Commedia*. To increase the status of the vernacular was also a major goal of Boccaccio's hybrid cultural project in Florence. For the other two poets, Mussato and Petrarch, however, the vernacular was either not under consideration or was discarded as the language of a publicly valuable poetry. The study of medieval Italian literature has inevitably gravitated toward poetic production in the vernacular and to a large extent has viewed these poets' Latin productions as minor works, which are valuable insofar as they shed light on their principal vernacular works. The result of this separation of the Latin and vernacular has been that the works of a Latin poet like Mussato have been all but eliminated from the history of Italian literature. It has also often rendered the Latin Petrarch a footnote to the study of his *Rerum vulgarium fragmenta*, a text that had an extremely limited circulation during his lifetime.[10] The eclogues of Dante, Boccaccio, and Petrarch have been pushed to the margins, even if for these last two poets, they were considered among their most important works during their lives.[11] With the exception of Dante's *Paradiso* and Boccaccio's *Vita di Dante*, this study looks primarily at the Latin production of each poet. When the question of the vernacular emerges, such as in Dante's correspondence with Giovanni del Virgilio or in Boccaccio's exchanges with Petrarch about the value of Dante's *Commedia*, it is addressed as a part of the larger question of the poet's role in the theater of the city. Fourteenth-century Italy was fundamentally diglossic, so by divorcing Latin from the vernacular, a significant element of its poetic culture is omitted. The emergence of vernacular poetry in Italy took place in intellectual environments that were predominantly Latinate. Thus, I try to avoid the characterizations of the relative

---

[10] For the complex history of the diffusion of Petrarch's *Rerum vulgarium fragmenta*, see Santagata 1996 and Eisner 2013, 74–94.

[11] These authors' eclogues have begun to elicit more critical interest of late. See, e.g., Allegretti 2004 and 2010; Lorenzini 2011; Lummus 2013a; Combs-Schilling 2015; and Zak 2016.

literary value of these poets' Latin and vernacular works that descend from the hierarchies of value embedded within the tradition of Italian literary history. My approach aims to reintegrate the Latin production of these poets with our understanding their vernacular works.[12]

Some explanation is due of the terms of my title – city and poetry – and of how I conceive of the question of the social and public worlds that these poets inhabited. Each poet in this study participated more or less actively as a member of a political body, whether in Padua, Florence, Rome, Avignon, or elsewhere.[13] In each case, however, the poet's ambitions for a political role are in excess of the real possibilities for political engagement. With the terms *city* and *civic*, thus, I mean to indicate not only the historical communities in which a poet lived but also the imagined communities that each poet projects in their efforts to individuate a place for poetic activity.[14] For Dante, the work of Claire Honess and Catherine Keen has demonstrated that the city is "the normative human community."[15] We can apply such a definition of the city also to Mussato and Boccaccio, and even to Petrarch, whose rhetoric of non-belonging and cosmopolitanism belies the political associations that he maintained in cities. The human community denoted by the term *city* is both metaphorical and historical in the works of the four poets here considered, just as their conception of their role in a community oscillates between an active presence and a projected ideal. Thus, when I refer to the city and to the poet's civic role, I mean above all to capture the poet's reconciliation of the historical reality of a place and its community with its counterpart in the realm of the imagination. Furthermore, I use the terms *poet* and *poetry* throughout to indicate what is essentially the author and the literary text, be it in verse or prose. Although these terms have come to mean something

---

[12] See Tavoni 2015b for a survey of the linguistic context in Dante's Italy, for example. On the importance of recuperating Latin in the study of the Renaissance, see Celenza 2004.

[13] Dante's political theories and practices have been by far the most studied. See, e.g., the classic studies by D'Entrevès 1952; Davis 1957; and Ferrante 1984. On Petrarch's political theories, see Furlan and Pittalunga 2016. See also Dotti 2001. For a recent study of Petrarch's political activities, see Caferro 2013. On the political Boccaccio, see Filosa 2014; Olson 2014; and Veglia 2015–16. For a study of the social world of the humanists who follow in the footsteps of these poets, see Martines 1963.

[14] While analogies may be made to Benedict Anderson's notion of imagined communities, his reflection on nationalism is based on post eighteenth-century political theory that does not find direct analogies in fourteenth-century Italy. My use of the turn of phrase here is in reference to the poet's projection of a community around himself, not to the stylized ideological communities of the modern nation. This should not hinder readers from reflecting on possible connections. See Anderson 2006. For a reconstruction of reading publics in medieval England, based on ideas of *habitus* surrounding virtue and language, see Breen 2010.

[15] Keen 2003, 15; Honess 2006, 5.

else that is far narrower, it is important to maintain them as historical terms that cover a broad semantic field in constant flux. For each of these poets, poetry indicated a meaningful and skillfully wrought creation through figurative language, including – at least for Boccaccio – prose fiction. While the form and language of a composition were important factors in determining the nature of poetry, it was meaning, communicated through allegory, that separated poetry from rhetoric and other forms of discourse.[16] In claiming a civic relevance for the work of poetry, each of these poets sought to expand the semantic field of the terms *poeta* and *poesis* to include an authority in the world. As authors of their texts, they would also be poets outside of them.

The Defense of Poetry and the Laurel Crown

In the intellectual culture of the late Middle Ages, poetry was not autonomous from other disciplines. It was associated with the lower arts of grammar and rhetoric, but was sometimes elevated to be considered a part

---

[16] While it was already common to trace the origin of the terms *poeta* and *poesis* to the Greek verb ποιέω, both Boccaccio and Petrarch explicitly reject this etymology and its association with the Latin verb *fingo*, as does Mussato implicitly. This is both because they did not want poetry to be associated with falsehood and because they wanted to dissociate poetry from the mechanical arts. Rather, both claim that the terms derive from the Greek ποιότης, which they understand as meaning exquisite discourse. Their etymology derives from Isidore of Seville's chapter on poets in the *Etymologiae* 8.7.2. The term ποιότης, which is transliterated as *poetés*, derives from the word ποιός, which was coined by Plato in the *Theaetetus* as indicating a certain quality. This etymology allows them to assert the sublime contemplative origins of poetry's function of communicating truth in beauty by means of allegory. Their definition seeks to represent poetry as a quality of discourse rather than as a fiction, precisely to avoid the negative connotations of fiction as weak form of knowledge. The other term that is employed for the poet is *vates*, which is sometimes translated as "bard." Like their etymology of *poeta*, that of *vates* links poetry with the speculative sciences and with religion, inasmuch as its etymology was traced to the Latin *vis mentis*, or power of the mind, and *vas Dei*, or vessel of God. The religious connotations of the term in relation to its employment as a term for the poet were readily available through Cicero, Virgil, Horace, and Ovid. Dante, aware of the links between poetry and making or inventing, self-consciously brings poetry and theological contemplation together in *Convivio* 2.1 and in the *Commedia*. At stake was the poet's ability to signify truth through linguistic inventions. In *Vita nova* XXV, even, Dante is interested in expanding the notion of *poeta*, typically used only for ancient poets, to include vernacular lyric poets (*dicitori per rima*). In *De vulgari eloquentia* 2.4, Dante defends this use of the term by insisting on the importance of style. Furthermore, Boccaccio associates poetry not only with a quality of discourse but also more simply with a discourse with a certain quality of meaning, so that when the aesthetic elements of a composition disappear (i.e., its meter and rhythm) it may still be considered poetry, even if it is in a prose form. The role of the poet in a social reality emerges from the status acquired from the connotations of this specific terminology. By calling poetry "literature" and poets "authors," the complexity of the terms' meanings are flattened. Even the Latin terms for these English words, *litterae* and *auctor*, bear connotations that are not easily transposed into a twenty-first-century idiom.

of ethical philosophy.[17] By the beginning of the fourteenth century, the
poets of the Italian peninsula began to claim that poetry, as a form of
knowledge, was not only superior to professional disciplines like medicine
and law but also equal to theology, the highest form of human inquiry to
which the study of the liberal arts ultimately led.[18] Their claims were
founded upon the conviction that poetry was able to communicate historical, moral, and higher truths hidden in verisimilar allegorical fictions.
Their defenses of poetry were oriented toward both salvaging the value of
ancient poetry and justifying their own poetic production. While they
were directed at poetry's attackers, real and imagined, more often than not
they were self-created contests and were often directed at other poets as a
way asserting a different role for poetry within a civic space. At stake for
them was the recognition of the status of poetry as a discipline or science to
which the study of the liberal arts would lead, but also the definition and
acknowledgment of the poet's task as a professional occupation.

   Ernst Robert Curtius listed among the commonplaces of medieval
literature the connection between poetry and theology made in Dante's
epistle to Cangrande and in the defenses of poetry of Mussato, Petrarch,
and Boccaccio.[19] Each poet, as he notes, links poetry to theology. For
Mussato poetry is "another theology" (altera ... theologia)[20] and for
Boccaccio theology and poetry are "almost the same thing" (quasi una
cosa) or otherwise poetry is "similar" (simigliante) to theology,[21] while for
Petrarch "theology is the poetry of God" (theologiam poeticam esse de Deo)[22]
and for Dante the Commedia is "consecrated" (sacrato) and "sacred" (sacro).[23]
Curtius traced the commonplace of the poeta theologus, or poet-theologian,
that appears in their defenses of poetry and that is implied by Dante's letter,
to Thomas Aquinas' commentary on Aristotle's Metaphysics, to Cicero's De
natura deorum, to Augustine's De civitate Dei, and to a series of patristic texts
that lead to Isidore of Seville's Etymologiae. He defined the source of the
debate in terms of the hierarchy of the sciences established by Aquinas.[24]

---

[17] See Minnis 1988, 56 and 182.
[18] On the relationship between the rise of humanism and professional identity, see Biow 2002, esp.
      27–44 on Petrarch and the "professionless profession" of being a poet.
[19] See Curtius 1953, 214–227.   [20] Mussato 2000, 39 (Epistola 7.21).
[21] Boccaccio 1974, 475 (Vita di Dante 1.154); Boccaccio 1974, 516 (Vita di Dante 2.91).
[22] Petrarch 1938–42, 2.301; Petrarch 1975–85, 2.69 (Familiares 10.4.1).
[23] Dante 2011, 460–461 (Paradiso 23.62); Dante 2011, 500–501 (Paradiso 25.1).
[24] The commonplace of the poeta theologus derives from the first book of Aristotle's Metaphysics (982
      b19; 983 b29), where he describes the story-lover (φιλόμυθος) as a kind of philosopher and goes on
      to mention that the first to discourse about the divine (θεολογήσαντας) did so in poetic terms
      (ἐποίησαν). Thomas Aquinas' commentary on Metaphysics 983 b29 links these poetic theologians to
      a series of pagan poets whom he notes were contemporaneous with the judges among the Hebrews,

Moreover, he found that, while each poet was in some way reacting to a Scholastic hierarchy of knowledge that saw poetry as the lowest of the sciences, these defenses of poetry were reactionary to the Thomistic modernity of the late Middle Ages and had "little to do with the Humanism of the *Trecento*."[25] Rather, what these poets were calling theology was not the theology of the Scholastics but was a part of ancient culture that had already been absorbed into Christianity by the Church Fathers; it was therefore old-fashioned. Much of the scholarship surrounding the defense of poetry has been a reaction to or expansion of Curtius' representation of the *poeta theologus* commonplace.

In an effort to connect the defense of poetry as theology to humanism, intellectual historians such as Eugenio Garin described the defenses of poetry of Mussato, Petrarch, and Boccaccio as part of a fundamental turning point in the secular appreciation of classical literature that would lead to the *studia humanitatis* of the next century.[26] Charles Trinkaus, seeking to reconcile the secular and the sacred, saw these defenses of poetry as leading "towards a greater universality in the conception of human culture by finding a means of bringing the vast world of ancient paganism within the frame of a Christian image of God and His works."[27] In her exhaustive survey of humanist and Scholastic poetics, influenced by Paul Oskar Kristeller, Concetta Carestia Greenfield places these three poets' defenses along with Dante's poetics squarely within a humanist tradition that developed out of medieval grammar and rhetoric in concomitance with the novel approaches of Scholastic logic.[28] Poets' claims to divine inspiration were, for her, linked to a neo-Platonic tradition of divine frenzy. For Ronald Witt, these defenses of poetry "tended to emphasize

an idea that he receives from Augustine *De civitate Dei* (18). The commonplace is further substantiated by the use of the term theologian (*theologi*) to refer to the creators and interpreters of myth in Cicero's *De natura deorum* and by Augustine's discussion of Varro's three types of theology in the *De civitate Dei*, one of which is a kind of poetic theology (*theologia fabulosa*). As Curtius 1953, 219 notes, once the idea finds its way into Isidore of Seville's *Etymologiae*, "it becomes the common property of the entire Middle Ages." While Aquinas recognized that theology and poetry shared a common use of metaphor and symbol in his commentary on Peter Lombard's *Sententiae*, he nevertheless characterized poetry as having the least amount of truth of all the sciences. In the *Summa theologiae*, Aquinas further classes poetry as the lowest of all the disciplines. It is clear that what is meant by theology in regard to poets is not the same as what is meant by theology in the Scholastic context. The equivocation, however, allowed poets to challenge not only the hierarchy of the sciences in Thomistic thought but also the status and privilege afforded to theologians within a social context.

[25] Curtius 1953, 220.   [26] See Garin 1957, 81 and 96–97.
[27] Trinkaus 1970, 2.689. For the full discussion of the *poeta theologus*, see Trinkaus 1970, 2.683–721. See also Trinkaus 1979, 90–113.
[28] See Greenfield 1981, 56–128, for her discussion of Dante, Mussato, Petrarch, and Boccaccio.

the natural character of ancient society and thus to secularize its history and achievements" and therefore represent an assertion of the aesthetic and stylistic value of ancient poetry and its modern imitations.[29] Each of these narratives seeks to explain how the truth value that these poets claimed either for their own poetry (Dante) or for the poetry of the ancients and their imitations of it (Mussato, Petrarch, and Boccaccio) was indicative of a future movement that would see the study of poetry and the other humanistic disciplines as foundational for the moral and political health of communities.

While these investigations tend to blend together the terms of the various defenses of poetry, as in Curtius' account,[30] Giuseppe Mazzotta has examined in different contexts the defenses of poetry of Mussato, Petrarch, and Boccaccio. As he has argued about Dante's poetry in the *Commedia*,[31] Mazzotta finds that their defenses of poetry intervene in the aesthetic–theological debates between Franciscans and Dominicans on the hierarchy of the arts within the medieval encyclopedic tradition, which saw theology as encompassing all the arts (Thomas Aquinas) or all of the arts as implying each other (Bonaventure). Mussato, for Mazzotta, sought to coopt this encyclopedic project through poetry "as a model for the ordering of institutions,"[32] while Boccaccio's defense was a justification of poetry's ability to reanimate history for the present.[33] Similarly, he sees Petrarch's defenses of poetry as indicative of an engagement with this same encyclopedic tradition, whose models of abstract knowledge Petrarch critiqued in favor of the more self-questioning form of knowledge that poetry represented.[34] Mazzotta's approach seeks to show how these poets tried to divorce poetry from its origins in grammar and rhetoric and to assert it as the organizing principle for all of the liberal arts, as a kind of theology, because of its capacity to harness the imagination and to communicate meaning in a stylistically compelling way, as opposed to the abstractions of neo-Aristotelian logic.

There is no doubt that medieval and humanistic conceptions of poetry evolved out of its origins in the study of grammar and rhetoric and in relation to contemporary intellectual debates about the status of the arts. What is missing from these studies, however, is an examination of the local circumstances within which these defenses of poetry emerged. On the one

---

[29] See Witt 1977, 538 and Witt 2000, 157–59. Witt argues that humanist ideas about poetry develop out of the medieval study of grammar, but that humanist poets demonstrate an increasing self-consciousness about being classical in their Latin style. More recently, see Witt 2015.

[30] See Curtius 1953, 226: "Petrarch and Boccaccio, then, follow the same line as Mussato."

[31] See Mazzotta 1993a.   [32] Mazzotta 2006a, 122.   [33] See Mazzotta 2000.

[34] See Mazzotta 1993b, 14–32.

hand, the historical context within which each poet defended poetry is elided in the service of a teleological intellectual history. Mazzotta, on the other, is less interested in tracing the origins of humanism and importantly contextualizes the debates on the status of poetry in terms of an intellectual tradition that is not teleological. Nevertheless, many of the local circumstances that produced these debates become absorbed within an account of a trans-historical intellectual tradition. By examining these defenses of poetry within their local historical and political contexts, we may better appreciate how poets' claims to link poetry with theology function in relation to the worlds that they inhabited. By so doing we may see, for example, that these debates on poetry were all initiated (or feigned) by poets themselves; any attack from the clergy or professional classes was already in response to their instigations. Many of these defenses of poetry were also directed at other poets, such as Boccaccio's revision of Petrarch's stance on poetry and Dante's angry response to del Virgilio. These defenses are self-created affirmations of the value of poetry that lay claim to an extra-textual authority for all poets, including ancient ones, but especially for themselves. The *poeta theologus* was not an esoteric notion of the poet as prophet or as divinely inspired; rather, it was a concept that allowed poets to claim moral and political authority within the civic sphere.

Dante's place in the story of the defense of poetry is an awkward one. He never overtly made a statement on the question of poetry's value as theology. He has been recognized as asserting obliquely the pairing of theology and poetry, both as a practice of reading allegory in *Convivio* 2.1, and as a practice of producing meaning allegorically in the *Commedia*.[35] If I am correct that the *poeta theologus* commonplace was specific to the assertion of a poet's role within a civic context, one of the reasons that Dante may have never felt inclined to defend poetry is that he was absent from the city in which he would have done so. Dante viewed himself and his poem as needing to have an impact on the city from which he was exiled. His only hope to return there was through the work itself, as the author of his poem, so it is only within the poem's narrative that Dante stages the conjunction between poetry and theology.[36]

---

[35] See, e.g., Hollander 1976; Mazzotta 1979; Barański 2000; Ascoli 2008; and Ascoli 2010.

[36] Hollander 1976 examines Dante's place in this tradition, arguing that Dante is a *theologus poeta* instead of a *poeta theologus*, because he does not admit that his poem is a fiction. Ascoli 2008, 357–405, esp. 393–394, provides a more complex understanding of how Dante relates to this context, suggesting that Dante constructs a "poetics of the theologian" in *Paradiso* 26.

The laurel crowning of poets is directly linked to the claims that poetry was equal to theology inasmuch as it publicly certifies the poet's status that is asserted in the defense of poetry. It has often been portrayed by scholars as an empty ceremony that demonstrates medieval humanists' admiration for Roman antiquity and their ambition to recreate it by imitation.[37] However, both of the poets who were crowned with the laurel, Mussato (1315) and Petrarch (1341), took away with them privileges and powers that secured their status in the political arena. Mussato, for example, who was prohibited from teaching at the university and who was not among the elite classes in Padua, was allowed to declaim his historical tragedy on Christmas Day for three years, during a period of political unrest and conflict with Verona when he was also named *defensor populi*, or defender of the people. Petrarch took away a diploma that granted him the right to read and teach poetry publicly as a *magister* and that gave him Roman citizenship. While these ceremonies certainly had symbolic value for both poets' intellectual enterprises of classical revival, they also and above all represent the acquisition of a certain status within the civic sphere.

While Dante was never crowned with the laurel for his efforts, he was offered the possibility toward the end of his life by Giovanni del Virgilio. This was the subject of their brief exchange between Bologna and Ravenna, in which del Virgilio criticized Dante's choice of the Florentine idiom and suggested he write a historical poem in Latin. Dante's refusal of the offer and his expression in *Paradiso* 25 of the hope to be crowned poet laureate in Florence have led many scholars to understand that Dante entertained hopes of returning to Florence at the end of his life. Boccaccio sorely desired to be recognized with the laurel crown, but he effaced his own aspirations in the service of championing Dante's posthumous repatriation as author of his poem. Linked to Boccaccio's ideas about the civic role of poetry was also Petrarch's promise as poet laureate of Rome, which he tried to bring to Florence on several occasions. Nevertheless, he also intimates at the end of his treatise on myth, the *Genealogie deorum gentilium*, that his work itself deserves to be crowned for his efforts.

The circumstances of the laurel crowning of poets also indicate the link between poetry and history. Both for Mussato and for Petrarch, the laurel was granted in their function not only as poets but also as historians. The conjunction of poetry and history is indicative of the authority that they wished to acquire. Both sought to demonstrate the poet's ability to interpret and pass judgment on the events of history and to apply them

---

[37] See, e.g., Picone 2005; and Sturm-Maddox 2009.

to the present. It was not only a question of the status of the arts in a hierarchy of learning, rather it was also and above all a question of the poet's authority to understand and communicate the myriad meanings of the world of creation. This was the privilege of theologians, whose superiority in the intellectual culture of the time had political repercussions as well. Mussato inscribes such an authority into his *Ecerinis* and Petrarch imagined the function of his *Africa* in much the same way. The texts in which Dante and Boccaccio assert their own laurel crowning also have to do with the poet's privileged vantage point over history. Before the end of Dante's journey in the *Commedia*, after a theological examination during which he is crowned, the pilgrim is given license to be the voice of Saint Peter in speaking the truth to the world. After the pilgrim briefly gazes back down on the path he has traversed, Beatrice pronounces a scathing diatribe against *cupidigia*, the source of all vice for Dante, and prophesies the coming of divine intervention to correct the course of history. Boccaccio's *Genealogie*, furthermore, is an encyclopedia that seeks to tell the history of the cosmos from chaos to civilization by interpreting ancient myths, which he sees as repositories of cultural memory. In different ways, the poet's task involves a figurative representation of history from the privileged perspective provided by poetry as theology.

Humanism and the City of Poetry

While my focus in this book is on the texts and contexts of these four individual poets, the question of humanism does not entirely escape its scope. The etiologies of the *studia humanitatis* mentioned above, along with others, represent the emergence of the appreciation of classical and modern letters as the foundation for moral and political education. Each participates in one way or another in qualifying or perfecting the thesis advanced by Hans Baron that civic humanism came about as a phenomenon between 1400 and 1402 as the Florentine response to aggression from Milan. For Baron, the civic humanists heroically defended against the threat of tyranny the values of republicanism, which were connected to their appreciation of classical texts.[38] The political underpinnings of Baron's thesis are grounded in the intellectual atmosphere that Baron himself experienced during his lifetime. His thesis was a response to Jacob Burckhardt's understanding of the Renaissance as the triumph of the individual, which was itself an effort to find the roots of his own modernity

---

[38] See Baron 1955 and Baron 1968.

in the past.[39] For Burckhardt, Dante was the great precursor to the Renaissance will to individual power, while for Baron it was Petrarch who embodied the man of letters who would come to fruition in the civic context of fifteenth-century Florence. Although Baron's ideas about civic humanism have been contested and revised over the years, especially concerning its origins and development and regarding the political or professional motivations of Leonardo Bruni,[40] they continue to exert force on the study of humanism in the Italian fourteenth century, especially on the study of Petrarch.[41]

As David Wallace has argued, Baron's thesis led him to "segregate the poetical and humanist Petrarch from the political conditions in which he worked ... Baron locates Petrarch in a mythical limbo that escapes definitions of time and place."[42] Although I do not entirely agree with the way that Wallace connects "a vatic, time-transcending Petrarch with the absolutist regimes he actually worked for,"[43] his point about Baron and about the historiographical foundations of civic humanism deserves to be addressed. In Burckhardt, Baron, and the historians of humanism discussed above, there is a tendency to divorce ideas about culture from the political and historical conditions in which they were born. Exceptions

---

[39] See Burckhardt 1929. On Baron and Burckhardt, see Hankins 1995, 310–312; and Wallace 1997, 57–62.

[40] For the challenges presented to Baron's thesis, see Hankins 1995, 314–330, esp. 319–330 on Bruni. With regard to the figures presented in this book, the principal challenges to Baron's thesis have to do with chronology. There has been an impulse to locate the advent of civic humanism in the early fourteenth century, with figures such as Mussato. See, e.g., Weiss 1949; Folena 1976, esp. 1–170; and Witt 2000. Witt, mediating between Kristeller's view of humanism as a part of the history of rhetoric bound to new professions and Baron's view of humanism as essentially republican, divides the humanists into generations, representing Mussato as secular and asserting that it was Petrarch's self-conscious merging of Christian and classical ideals that makes him the "father" of humanism.

[41] In particular, the portrait of Petrarch in Baron 1985 continues to shape the way in which Petrarch's spiritual life is interpreted vis-à-vis his political outlook. In it he revises his thesis on Petrarch in light of Rico 1974, but continues to see the move to Italy in terms of an Augustinian pessimism, ignoring the uncomfortable realities of Petrarch's association with the Visconti. See, e.g., Kircher 2006; and Zak 2010. This, in turn, shapes the over-arching narrative of Petrarch's turn to political life in northern Italy after 1353. For a reading of Petrarch's spiritual life and humanism in relation to Carthusian monasticism, see Yocum 2013.

[42] Wallace 1997, 57.

[43] Wallace 1997, 263. Wallace's ideological critique of Petrarch, whom he compares to Paul de Man inasmuch as both show an uneasiness with history that may derive from their associations with illegitimate forms of power (267–268), is historically accurate. However, it applies twentieth-century expectations about intellectual coherence and forthrightness that were alien to Petrarch. As Hankins 1995, 330 notes about fifteenth-century humanism: "it should be clearly recognized that the attempt to reform and revalorize the life of the city-state in accordance with ancient models ... was never a project confined to Renaissance republics." Ascoli 2011 provides a useful evaluation of Petrarch's association with power that takes into account the methodological difficulties of approaching the question.

occur when those conditions represent the *studia humanitatis* in a positive light – such as in the republican struggle against tyranny. This is the case not only for the study of Petrarch, which Wallace and others have partially undertaken in the form of a critique of the ethical and political foundations of his humanism.[44] Mussato's place in humanism is generally ascribed to his engagement with the classics, either in terms of style or in terms of imitative strategies, and either way in function of his status as pre-humanist, while the content of his poetry is often portrayed as political propaganda. With few exceptions, Dante's difficult politics tend to be treated aside from his universalizing poetic and theological strategies, which attenuate his reactionary political outlook. Boccaccio's political outlook, which may very well be the closest to the civic humanists of the early fifteenth century, has only recently begun to be considered in relation to his literary production. In response to this trend, I have done my best to show how each poet's ideas about poetry both emerge from and react to specific historical circumstances, without passing judgment on their respective ideologies or on their associations with power. It becomes clear that for each poet their *officium* was conceived in relation to the wielding of power in diverse political contexts – not only in republics.

My readings of fourteenth-century defenses of poetry and representations of the poet as theologian serve to demonstrate the fundamentally political role that poets saw themselves as filling. Essentially, I show how poets harnessed classical and biblical traditions of figurative speech in the service of truth in order to construct themselves as public intellectuals. This is not to say that the notions of publics or intellectuals as we understand them today have any place in fourteenth-century Italy. Nor is it the purpose of this book to attempt an etiology of the figure of the public intellectual that begins in the Italian fourteenth century.[45] The history of the public intellectual is a disjointed one, which often manipulates the past in the service of the present. While analogies can be made between the present and the past without an awareness of history, my hope is that by examining these poets' ideas about the role of the poet in their own world we might more fruitfully view the connections between that

[44] See, e.g., Wallace 1997 and Ginsberg 2002. Cf. Ascoli 2011.
[45] For the place of pre-modern and humanist intellectuals in the history of the public intellectual, see Copeland 2002 and Wallace 2002. Le Goff 1993 remains important for understanding the learning environments of the Middle Ages. See Copeland 2002 for a historicization of the term intellectual, as received through Le Goff, in relation to the Wycliffite–Lollard movement. See also Hobbins 2003, who considers the role of the late medieval schoolman in terms of the intellectual's public role.

world and ours. I would invite readers of this book, therefore, if they are so inclined, to reflect on how our own shifting notions of intellectuals and their publics can be enriched by the examples of these poets of medieval Italy.

*

The following chapters examine each poet's claims about poetry in their distinct civic contexts, with each chapter functioning both autonomously and in connection with the overall narrative of the book. The titles of the chapters express in terms of prepositions of relation – of, without, beyond, for – the model that each poet represents for understanding the place of the poet's civic duty. I proceed chronologically from Mussato and Dante to Petrarch and Boccaccio, concluding with a brief epilogue about the status of poetry in the city after Boccaccio, when poetry begins to be defended by a civil servant like Coluccio Salutati.

Chapter 1 examines Mussato's defenses of poetry in relation to his political role in Padua between 1309 and 1320 and to the poetry he composed during this period, a tragedy on the tyranny of Ezzelino da Romano, *Ecerinis* (1314), and a short epic poem on the siege of Padua by Cangrande della Scala, *De obsidione civitatis Padue* (1320). Challenging received notions that Mussato's defenses of poetry are not politically oriented, I argue that Mussato employs them to authorize his political role in the city. I describe Mussato as the poet of the city inasmuch as he establishes what he calls a *ministerium*, or institution, of poetry, which allows him to participate with increasing authority in the political debates of his city. This institution is formally recognized in the civic sphere with Mussato's crowning as poet laureate. In his efforts to defend poetry after his crowning, Mussato responds to those in the city who question the legitimacy of this new office, which also coincided with Mussato's appointment to the position of *defensor populi*, or defender of the people.

While his defenses of poetry have largely been viewed in terms of a humanistic appreciation for classical poetry in a Christian world, Mussato's poetry has long been described as political propaganda whose aesthetic value resides in its imitation of new classical models like Seneca. Instead, I argue that it functions in tandem with his defenses of poetry as the vehicle for the moral ideology of the poet. If in his defenses of poetry Mussato establishes the poet as equal to the theologian, then in his *Ecerinis* and *De obsidione*, which were both publicly declaimed, the poet performs that role by seeking to provide moral and political direction to the Latinate notaries and novices of the city. He assumes the role held by theologians of influencing the moral and political outlooks of the city's inhabitants. A Guelph notary, Mussato actively opposed both the incursions of Cangrande della Scala from Verona and the gradual ascension to power of the Carrara family in Padua. In his poetry he sought not so much to attack his political enemies as to demand that his audience view the events of the present in the light of the past. In readings of both works, I indicate how they demonstrate a complexity that is not reducible to propaganda any more than is Dante's *Commedia*. Like Dante, Mussato sees his poetry as providing a privileged historical perspective to the inhabitants of the city rather than recommending any one course of political action. Mussato's poetry reflects a profound engagement with the city's fate that is based on both classical and Christian ethics. While his assimilation of poetry and theology may emerge from Scholastic debates on knowledge, in practice it had a very different result.

In Chapter 2, I turn to Dante's representation of himself as a poet in relation to the civic sphere. At stake in this chapter is not Dante's theory of empire or his view of himself a poet of empire, a description which underestimates Dante's dedication to the city of his birth. Rather, I take as my point of departure the ways in which Dante figures himself as poet of exile in the *De vulgari eloquentia*, *Convivio*, and *Commedia*. Dante's poetics of exile forms the foundation of my description of him as a poet without a city. In a detailed analysis of the *Egloghe*, four Latin poems that form Dante's correspondence from Ravenna with Bolognese professor and poet Giovanni del Virgilio, I argue that Dante justifies his place in society as a poet. The exchange with del Virgilio has typically been read in terms of Dante's defense of his vernacular poem and his rejection of the humanist milieu of Bologna and Padua, where he would be offered the laurel crown should he write an epic poem in Latin. By focusing on the representation of place across the correspondence, I demonstrate that Dante's position on Latin and the vernacular is determined by the way he views his relationship to the cities in which he lives and to Florence. In these eclogues, Dante measures himself against a humanist paradigm for the role of the poet in the city. In his rejection of this role, he asserts himself as the poet of exile, who stands without a city. Yet, through the pastoral imaginary, he also imagines a space for poetry in the historical world, as marginal as it may be. Like Mussato and del Virgilio, he sees his role as poet in relation to a human community, but his authority as a poet depends upon remaining outside of it.

I conclude the chapter by applying this reading of Dante's humanism to the *Paradiso*. First, in an analysis of *Paradiso* 15–17, I establish that the human community of which Dante is poet sits in a non-place somewhere between the ideal of Cacciaguida's Florence of the past and a utopian Florence of the future. I then move to a reading of *Paradiso* 22–27, which I argue contains Dante's assertion of himself as *poeta theologus* together with a laurel crowning ceremony. This set of cantos is framed by the pilgrim turning his gaze down to the earth as he enters and exits the heaven of the fixed stars, where he is examined on the three theological virtues. The examination he undergoes establishes his authority to pronounce moral judgment on the world below as a poet-theologian. Furthermore, I suggest that the laurel crowning described by Dante at the beginning of *Paradiso* 25 is not, as is the common perception, an expression of Dante's desire to be crowned as poet in Florence before his death. Rather, I argue that Dante is inscribing the moment of his future recognition in Florence within the poem. That is to say, Dante as *poeta theologus* will become the poet of Florence through the text itself of his poem. In this way, Dante the poet can live as the poet without a city, while Dante the author is projected into the future civic space of a Florence ready to accept his poem.

While the first two chapters place poetic texts in relation to the performances of public authority of Mussato and Dante, the third and fourth chapters focus on the epistles, orations, and tractates in which Petrarch and Boccaccio reflect on their role as civic poets. Unlike Mussato and Dante, their vocations as poets did not necessarily coincide with a specific text or series of texts. Rather, the two used the defense of poetry, and the performance of poetic authority in the coronation ceremony, to assert a broader cultural paradigm founded on poetry.

Chapter 3 traces how Petrarch imagines the place of the poet in the period between 1341 and 1353. It begins, like the opening of this book, with Petrarch's coronation oration, which provides the basis for my understanding of Petrarch's representation of his relationship with the city as poet. Petrarch's coronation oration has long been recognized as representing the poet's status in an oscillation between past and present. I argue that this tension in Petrarch's self-representation is concomitant with Petrarch's ambiguous stance about appertaining to a city or being situated beyond it. This ambiguity will remain unresolved in Petrarch's view of his role as an intellectual, even after he discards the title of poet. In response to a challenge levied against his laurel crowning in 1343, Petrarch distances himself from any connection with the urban environment, as the place of the masses. With an ideal Rome as his city, he can claim a status that is above and beyond the vulgar concerns of the people of the city. Petrarch's language of vituperation against the common people (*vulgus*) in this letter will coincide years later with the language of his rejection of the vernacular. Yet, as his engagement as political adviser to Cola di Rienzo in 1347 shows, Petrarch was not above participating in political affairs from a distance.

I argue that the disappointment caused by di Rienzo's failed endeavor led not so much to an ideological shift in Petrarch as it did to a crisis of place. Petrarch further distances himself from the cityscape in his 1349 letter to his brother Gherardo, a Carthusian monk, in which he first links poetry to theology. In my reading of this letter, I show how Petrarch engages with Dante's representation of the poet's place through the pastoral imaginary. Instead of rejecting a humanist historical poetry for Dante's rough vernacular style, Petrarch invades the Dantesque pastoral space outside the city with his historical, classical poetics. In this way, he forcibly combines his civic poetry with Dante's marginal status vis-à-vis the city. He is able to combine the civic role of a poet like Mussato with the marginality of a poet like Dante. The chapter concludes with an analysis of Petrarch's most extended defense of poetry in the *Invective contra medicum*. Challenging the traditional view of the *Invective* as an assertion of the superiority of poetry as a discipline over medicine, I argue that it represents a power struggle between Petrarch and the physicians who advised the Curia in Avignon. Paying particular attention to its style and tone, my interpretation links Petrarch's poetics with his politics, showing how he associates vernacular stories with the city and an elite poetry of history with the solitary haunts of poets. Confident in his ability to attract political power to his location in solitude on the margins of the city, with the *Invective* Petrarch definitively abandons the city as the place of poetic authority. Soon afterward, when he takes up residence as a member of the court in Milan, he will continue to represent himself as an inhabitant of solitude, on the margins beyond the city.

Chapter 4 shows how Boccaccio manipulates the Petrarchan model for different ends. It is framed by a reassessment of the relationship between Boccaccio and Petrarch that focuses on the political differences between the two poets following Petrarch's move to Milan. In my analysis of the initial moment of their friendship, between 1351 and 1353, I show how Boccaccio moves from seeing Petrarch's presence in Florence as the condition for the repatriation of Dante's poem to trying to separate the two poets from one another in his first redaction of the *Vita di Dante*. After establishing the fundamental political and cultural differences between the two poets, I go on to analyze Boccaccio's extended defense of poetry in Book 14 of the *Genealogie deorum gentilium*, which has traditionally been understood as a reiteration of Petrarch's ideas. On the foundation of my initial arguments about their political and cultural divergence, I argue that Boccaccio undermines and at times reverses the terms of Petrarch's notion of the poet's relationship to the city, which also has implications for the value of vernacular poetry. In this way, I show his defense to be directed not only at those who attack poetry but also at Petrarch and his intellectual milieu.

The first part of my analysis centers on Boccaccio's representation of himself and of the opponents of poetry as the inhabitants of a city in the first five chapters of Book 14. I show how Boccaccio reverses the approach to the city that Petrarch had taken in the *Invective*. If, for Petrarch, the urban landscape represented a hierarchy of power, with a monarch at its center, for Boccaccio the center of urban reality was occupied by the university, which had an impact on the moral bearing of the city's inhabitants. Boccaccio subverts the ideal of solitude from Petrarch's *Invective* by establishing the poet as moving between solitary locales and the city, bringing the fruits of the contemplation of nature to the community at large. In the final part of this chapter, I analyze how Boccaccio's vision of the relationship between the poet and the city manifests itself in his poetics in the remaining chapters of his defense. I argue that Boccaccio creates a poetics of inclusion that is based on his vision for the poet's role in society, which I describe in terms of an ethics of engagement according to which the poet acts on behalf of the city. Throughout the chapter, I show how Boccaccio's *Decameron* in particular and vernacular poetry in general are often in the background of his considerations in the defense. I conclude by suggesting that Boccaccio insinuates his role as poet for the city by describing the laurel-crowning of the *Genealogie* itself at the end of the treatise.

In the Epilogue, I ask what becomes of the city of poetry after Boccaccio, when those who take up the case of poetry are no longer poets. A part of this book's story shows that these four poets sought to create an institution of poetry because other paths to recognition and power in the civic space were blocked to them. The defense of poetry and laurel crowning were modes of political empowerment. Mussato substantiated his local political role with the moral and intellectual value of poetry as theology. Dante, as exile, embedded in his poem the authority necessary to intervene in Florence, while avoiding associating the poem with any other city. Petrarch made himself poet laureate in order to engage with international political powers and carefully negotiated his relationship with civic centers by representing himself as a poet of solitude. Boccaccio, often caught between influence and impotence in Florentine affairs, intervened for other poets and for himself in an effort to create a space for the poet and poetry within a complex urban environment. The construction of poetic authority outside of the text was an effort to guarantee a high level of participation in the body politic.

By the end of the fourteenth century, with the increasing bureaucratization of cities like Florence, the intellectuals who take up the cause of poetry no longer do so to defend their own role in society. The authority of the poet is reabsorbed by the authors of the works read by these functionaries, who shared a similar training in grammar, rhetoric, and law with these poets, but whose effective authority in the city required no defending. The connection between these poets and the civic culture that came afterward can be found in the authority granted to poetry itself as a means of understanding history – which was at the basis of these four poets' ideas about the civic function of the poet. As a concluding example, I examine Coluccio Salutati's first defense of poetry in a series of private letters written to Bolognese Chancellor Giuliano Zonarini in 1378–79, near the beginning of Salutati's chancellorship. I suggest that the previous poets' concern for situating themselves vis-à-vis political power is translated into a role for poetry itself. Salutati, who has long been recognized as a pivotal figure between fourteenth- and fifteenth-century humanism, defends the reading of poetry as an aid to him in understanding a world that is increasingly difficult to interpret. His earliest defense of poetry represents the first in a series of developments of the fourteenth-century defenses that leads from poets' assertions of themselves as civic actors to defenses of poetry as a form of knowledge from which political leaders, bureaucrats, and citizens might benefit.

CHAPTER I

Albertino Mussato, Poet of the City

Mussato was one of the most politically driven poets of fourteenth-century Italy, but he was also a crucial figure in the revival of the classics in Padua.[1] A rough contemporary of Dante, Mussato is commonly referred to as a member of the pre-humanist circle of Padua (*cenacolo padovano*) that had begun in the generation before him with Lovato Lovati.[2] He was a notary and a member of the upper levels of the *popolo* – a socio-economic group of often affluent non-nobles – and was associated with the powerful money-lending family of the Lemici, of which he became the executor in 1310. He wrote two major histories on the events during and after the arrival of Henry VII in Italy,[3] and the first major classicizing tragedy since antiquity, the *Ecerinis*, for which he was crowned poet laureate of Padua in 1315;[4] he commented on the tragedies of Seneca, of whom he also wrote a

---

[1] The best introduction to Mussato and his life is Witt 2000, 117–173. See also Dazzi 1964 and Zabbia 2012. For a survey of his writings, see Lanza 2000.

[2] On Lovato dei Lovati and the *cenacolo padovano*, see Witt 2000, 81–116. See also (Guido) Billanovich 1958 and 1976. See also Beneš 2011 for a summary of the civic myth of Antenor fostered by this group.

[3] The sixteen books of his *De gestis Henrici VII Cesaris*, also known as the *Historia Augusta*, treat the movements of the emperor in Italy from 1311 to 1313, whereas the fourteen books of the *De Gestis Italicorum post Henricum VII Cesarem* chronicle the events following his death up until July 1321; a fifteenth book, which is now lost, would have covered up to 1325. Each book of these two histories has a conceptual unity that is autonomous from the whole, such as the book on Florence in the *Historia Augusta* (9) and the book on the Paduan Republic (10). Mussato's imitation of the classical historians Livy and Sallust is also visible in the many orations inserted within his histories. His work as a historian continued into his later exiles, such as with a treatise that recounts events leading to the treaty between Cangrande and the Carrara family of Padua in 1328 (*De traditione Padue ad Canem Grandem*, known as Book 12 of the *De gestis Italicorum*, 1328). On the links between the *De Gestis Henrici VII* and Mussato's laurel crowning, see Albanese 2016. On the classicizing orations of Mussato's histories, see Modonutti 2017.

[4] On Mussato's tragedy in the context of Neo-Latin theater in Italy, see Chevalier 2013. On Mussato's laurel crown, see Chevalier 2004. On the question of the laurel crown in Mussato's relation to the *tre corone*, see Sturm-Maddox 2009, 290–294.

biography and on whom he modelled himself as a moral philosopher;[5] and he wrote poetry (elegies, hexameters, and a cento, or patchwork poem).[6] Everything that survives was written in Latin, except for a single extant sonnet he wrote to a friend in Venice.[7] Politically, Mussato worked both locally and internationally, and like Dante, he was faced with exile, though it was not life-long. By supporting the emperor in the name of his city's freedom, uncannily like Dante, he also found himself at odds with the rising noble family of the Carrara, which would eventually take over Padua.[8] Mussato's poetic production and engagement with classical models was intricately connected with his political engagements in the city. As Mazzotta has noticed, Mussato "understood this [medieval encyclopedic] project, and here lies the novelty of his work, as a model for the ordering of institutions (the interests in the city-square, university, and the cloister/convent) within the political economy of the city."[9] Indeed, Mussato's role as poet provided him with an additional authority that underwrote his participation as a civic leader.

Scholarship on Mussato has tended to focus, on the one hand, on his innovations in poetics and in the understanding of classical models, and, on the other hand, on his chronicles and his political engagement. Since he defended poetry as a second theology and imitated the classics, he has earned a place in the narrative that leads to humanism, enlightenment, and modern secular education.[10] Politically, he is sometimes seen as a kind of proto-Petrarchan or even proto-Machiavellian civic humanist, with a combination of cynical and idealist historical perspectives.[11] He is often viewed as the provincial version of Dante, whose historical and theological vision and innovative vernacular poetics far exceed the scope of Mussato's

---

[5] Mussato wrote a dialogue and commentary on Seneca's tragedies and on the tragic form (*Evidentia tragediarum Senece* and *Argumenta tragediarum Senece*, *c*.1315). On Mussato's Seneca, see Megas 1969. Mussato also wrote a philosophical text, *De lite inter Naturam et Fortunam*. See Moschetti 1927; Billanovich and Travaglia 1942–54; and Facchini 2014.

[6] Mussato's Latin poetry has gone relatively unexamined, with the exception of his metrical letters on poetry. See, however, Chevalier 2006, 2010, and 2012; as well as Lombardo 2017, on the critical edition and Italian translation of all of Mussato's metrical letters currently in preparation. See also (Guido) Billanovich 1958. On Mussato's dream vision, *Somnium*, see Pastore Stocchi 1987 and Chevalier 2000, cxix–cxlviii.

[7] For Mussato's only surviving vernacular poem, see Novati 1881.

[8] On the rise of the Carrara in Padua and their subsequent reign, see Kohl 1998.

[9] See Mazzotta 2006a, 121–122.

[10] See, e.g., Garin 1957, 81–82 and 96–98 and Garin 1958, 2–19, but also Witt 2000, in which Mussato is presented within a teleological narrative that leads to the philology and Latinity of Renaissance humanism.

[11] See Witt 2000, 117–173.

local political and poetic ambitions.[12] This view of Mussato is connected to the circumstances of Dante's rejection of the laurel crown, which was offered to him by Giovanni del Virgilio were he to write a Latin epic poem about the fate of Italy after the death of Henry VII. Del Virgilio later turned to Mussato several years after his correspondence with Dante to offer him the crown.[13] While such recognition speaks to Mussato's importance, it has also served to relegate his status to provincial humanist circles like that of del Virgilio in Bologna. If Mussato has been seen as the poet that Dante refused to be, he has also been viewed in light of Petrarch's crowning as poet laureate of Rome. Again, Mussato's view of the poet's role within the city is portrayed as provincial when compared to Petrarch's more cosmopolitan view of the office of the poet.[14]

Little critical attention has been paid to the ways in which Mussato as a poet intersected with the politician, except insofar as to say that his poetry was propaganda. His poetry and defenses of poetry in the city of Padua, however, are far more complex in their relationship to his political ideology. As has long been recognized about Dante and Petrarch, Mussato sought to create and to harness the authority of the classical past and to meld it with a Christian authority, with the goal of guaranteeing his own moral and political ideology. His defenses of poetry and his laurel crowning are part of an effort to employ his learning to gain status in the city so that he could influence the political decisions being made. In his defenses

---

[12] See, e.g., Ronconi 1976, 48–49, where he describes Mussato's importance in relation to fifteenth-century humanists by placing him beneath Dante in a hierarchy of value: "the Florentine will make history for himself; the Paduan, however, precisely by means of his generous defense of the poetic art, begins a new chapter in literary history that will be continued by the Humanists" ("Il fiorentino farà storia per sé; il padovano invece, proprio attraverso la sua generosa difesa dell'arte poetica, inizia un nuovo capitolo di storia letteraria che sarà continuato dagli umanisti"). According to Ronconi, Dante's "conception of the universe and of history" was so "unitary and organic" that it "did not leave room for similar considerations" as those which Mussato addresses in his defense of poetry ("La sua concezione fortemente unitaria ed organica dell'universo e della storia non lascia spazi a simili considerazioni").

[13] In an eclogue written in 1327, years after his correspondence with Dante, Giovanni del Virgilio recognized him with reference to his laurel crown: "You, now crowned as poet with Pierian ivies, for whom the vine-bearing Eugan contends on behalf of your patriotic song" ("Tu modo Pyeriis vates redimite corimbis, / cui pugnat patrio pro carmine vitifer Eugan"). Del Virgilio 2011, 197 (*Ecloga* 1–2). On this eclogue, see Lorenzini 2011, 175–195.

[14] Petrarch recognizes Mussato on two occasions. First, in a defense of his own laurel crowning, he refers obliquely to Mussato: "Our times saw the Pergamean poet, whose firm hair was crowned by Paduan laurels" ("Secula Pergameum viderunt nostra poetam, / Cui rigidos strinxit laurus paduana capillos, / Nomine reque bonum"). Petrarch 2004, 164 (*Epistulae metricae*, 2.10.72–74). Second, he names him as a chronicler of current events: "The Paduan historian Mussato, a careful investigator of modern events" ("Muxatus patavinus historicus, novarum rerum satis anxius conquistator"). Petrarch 2014, 508 (*Rerum memorandarum libri*, 4.118).

of poetry as a different kind of theology, then, he was not only raising pagan artistic production to the level of Christian texts. He was also creating a genealogy of authority for the historical vision expressed in his poetry. In his crowning as poet laureate, he performed the acquisition of civic authority as poet, an invented professional office in the service of the city. In his Senecan tragedy, *Ecerinis*, and his Lucanian epic, *De obsidione civitatis Padue*, he puts into practice the historical and political vision that he had done so much to authorize. Mussato is, in every sense, the poet of the city.

In this chapter, I will address Mussato's letters in defense and praise of poetry in an effort to reconstruct their political import within the context of medieval Padua. I will further examine how his poetic practices enact his theories and emerge from his desire to participate in the political arena of the city by engaging with the citizenry's moral stance toward political unrest and historical change. The model of the poet that Mussato will be shown to represent is that of the intellectual who sees poetry as a discursive tool that will authorize his civic role. He constructs a history of poetry that places it on equal footing with theology, which in its various forms directed the city's moral stance. His combination of poetry, theology, and politics show him to be engaging with similar questions of poetic and political authority that we typically associate with Dante.

Albertino Mussato and Padua in the Early Fourteenth Century

Since Mussato's life and role in the city are so important for understanding his vision of the civic role of the poet, I would like to begin with a brief overview of his life and of the state of affairs in Padua at the turn of the fourteenth century.[15] The city's intellectual pole was its *Studium*, the university founded in 1222 and known for the teaching of law and later medicine, as well as the Dominican monastery of Sant'Agostino, also founded in 1222, where theology was taught and where, according to tradition, Albertus Magnus studied and was received into the Dominican order by Jordan of Saxony, and where Pietro d'Abano taught from 1311. Politically, the city was directed by a foreign *podestà* (executive official), a *consiglio maggiore* and *minore* (large and small assemblies), a college of elders (formed by election among the *popolo*) that could also elect a *capitaneus* (captain) when it felt threatened, and for a short time a *defensor*

---

[15] In addition to Mussato's own historical works, I have followed Zardo 1884; Hyde 1966; and Rippe 2003 for this brief portrait of Mussato and his city.

populi (defender of the people). Padua, like Florence and many Italian municipalities of the time, was defined by tensions between the old and new nobility, each of which manipulated the masses, and the *popolo*, which was often caught between the nobility and the masses, whose political allegiances were in constant transformation.

Ecclesiastically, Padua was a city with a thriving cult of a very recently confirmed saint, Anthony, who had died in 1231 and whose basilica had been completed with the help of large financial contributions from the city. Also present in and around the city were both reformed and old-rule Benedictines, Augustinians, and Dominicans, each of which were connected financially and ideologically with specific families among the old and new nobility. The factions of the city were often in conflict, especially in the years after the fall of Ezzelino da Romano, who had terrorized Padua between 1237 and 1256, not only stopping the business of the university but also quelling the voices of the clergy. In these years, the city took more control over the life of the university, prescribing books and paying the salaries of the professors of arts, selected by city officials. On account of this, as Nancy Siraisi has pointed out, "Paduan citizens were legally debarred from publicly salaried academic positions."[16] Also, the monasteries, especially that of the Dominicans, through the power of the Inquisition and by executing the wills and donations of property for decadent noble families, took on a political role that favored the rise of *signoria* (lordship) of the Carrara, who, with the promise of stability, took control of the city in 1318, 1324, and finally 1328. Mussato's Padua was a politically divided city, which soon came under attack by Cangrande della Scala, lord of Verona, whose ambitions for political domination were legitimated by his position, from 1311 onward, as vicar general of Henry VII.

Born in San Daniele d'Abano, in the territory of Padua, in 1261, Albertino Mussato attended Henry VII's coronation in Milan in 1311, after which he began an intense period of political involvement and literary production that led both to his coronation as poet laureate of the city and to various exiles. Mussato's ambition led him to rise from humble origins to become one of the leaders of the budding intellectual community in late thirteenth- and early fourteenth-century Padua known as the *cenacolo padovano*, which sought to construct a classical origin for the city in the myth of its founding by the Trojan Antenor. Politically, he was an ardent defender of the Paduan republic in a period of upheaval for the city that

---

[16] Siraisi 1973, 28. It was also the practice of the University of Bologna to exclude citizens from the university. See Rashdall 1936, 2.17.

fell between the end of Ezzelino da Romano's tyranny in the mid-thirteenth century and the beginning of Cangrande's takeover of the city and its territory in 1328. Although his compatriots did not always agree with his methods or ideas, when they were in need of an ambassador among other Italian communes or in the court of the Emperor, they called on Mussato to be their spokesman. As a poet, Mussato was an experimentalist and a reviver of long-forgotten genres, from tragedy to elegy to biography; he sought both to imitate and to renew the classical tradition within the intellectual and political context of medieval Padua. Although Mussato was born into the most modest caste of communal Padua, he was protected and brought up until 1277 by his godfather, Viviano Muso, a nobleman whose name Mussato eventually took. Upon Muso's death, which was quickly followed by that of Mussato's father, Mussato took on the responsibility of providing for his mother, two brothers, and a sister by copying books for students at the local university. In his autobiographical *De celebratione suae diei nativitatis* he writes of his poverty during this period: "Students and the sale of the letters made by my hand rendered little gains for my life. Oh, extreme labor! but the skill that secured my life! Oh the happy poor boy, with a double condition of life! I had only imminent hunger to fear, and although it was bitter, is was my only fear" ("Parva mihi victu prebebant lucra scolares / Venalisque mea lictera facta manu. / O labor extremus! sed vite tuta facultas! / O felix mixta condicione miser! / Sola fames nostro suberat ventura timori; / Ille licet mordax, sed timor unus erat").[17] Mussato was not born into a powerful position, but as he gained recognition in the city, he would seek through poetry an intellectual guarantee of his civic authority.

In the early 1280s, Mussato became a notary and by the beginning of the next decade he was well known as such among the local nobility – such as the Este family. In 1296, he became a member of the *consiglio maggiore* of the city and a *miles pro commune*, a knight or tactically appointed man-at-arms who could afford a horse and armor, most likely with the support of the powerful Lemici family. He was well known both within the city and without for his skills as an orator and a diplomat. From April 1 to September 30, 1309, he was given the position of *Esecutore degli ordinamenti di Giustizia* in Florence, the position of the guarantor of a series of laws meant to weaken Ghibelline noble families, and on January 6, 1311, he attended the coronation of Henry VII in Milan. His presence there on behalf of his city was intended as a gesture of courtesy, however, not of

---

[17] Mussato 2006, 162 (*De celebratione* 25–30).

allegiance. Whereas he believed that Henry had come to restore the peace between Guelphs and Ghibellines,[18] the arrival of the emperor in northern Italy soon became a threat both to Mussato's life and to the well-being of his city. As a result of the alliance between Cangrande della Scala and the new emperor, Verona was given a free hand in taking over many contested territories under Paduan influence, including Brescia and Vicenza. Mussato was sent a total of four times to negotiate the terms of Padua's position in Henry VII's empire. Each time Padua either directly refused the conditions of subjection to Henry or was reticent to follow through with the pacts due to its fear of falling into the hands of a local tyrant, such as Cangrande, who became the Imperial Vicar of Verona and Vicenza.

When Padua finally revolted against Henry in 1312, the city immediately tried to win back Vicenza from Cangrande, but failed. When the emperor died in 1313, the imperial restraints on Cangrande were released and he began attacking Padua. Although Mussato had fought in the wars against Cangrande both before and after the death of Henry, his association with the emperor – and thus with the imperially sanctioned Cangrande – caused him to be publicly attacked. His house was burned to the ground and he was subsequently exiled from the city in 1314, only to be called back after a few months' time to be honored for his patriotism by the *consiglio maggiore*. During this year Mussato finished the composition of the *Ecerinis*, a tragedy about Ezzelino da Romano's tyranny over Padua, in which the tyrant is portrayed as the son of the Devil. Its purpose was largely political, warning the Paduan people of the dangers of tyrants like Cangrande, although the moral underpinning of the tragedy is deeply ambiguous. Also during this year, he completed the *De gestis Henrici VII Cesaris*, which recounts the movements of the Emperor in Italian territory from his coronation in Milan in 1311 to his death at Buonincontro in 1313. On December 3, 1315, Mussato was crowned as poet laureate of Padua by order of the College of Artists, led by Rolando da Piazzola, another of the *cenacolo padovano*, both for his history and for his tragedy. As a result, the *Ecerinis* was read publicly in Padua on Christmas Day for three consecutive years between 1315 and 1317.[19]

Upon the death of the emperor, struggles for the imperial title left the lords of Northern Italy independent of imperial control and tensions again arose between Padua and Verona. In 1317, Padua tried unsuccessfully to take back Vicenza from Cangrande. On this occasion, Mussato was sent to Bologna and to Florence to ask for help. Between 1318 and 1319,

---

[18] See Mussato 2012, 295 (*Epistola* 5.76–78).   [19] See Chevalier 2000, clii.

however, he was again exiled upon the rise to power in Padua of Giacomo da Carrara, who took a more conciliatory attitude toward Cangrande, with whom he signed a peace treaty on March 14, 1319. When Cangrande besieged Padua again in late 1319, Mussato was called back from exile again to ask Bologna, Florence, and Siena for their help. During his visit to Florence, in August 1319, Mussato fell ill with a fever and was given hospice by Antonio d'Orso, Bishop of Florence. This fever was the occasion for the dream vision recounted in the *Somnium*, which is dedicated to d'Orso's hospitality and which praises the Florentines for their civility. Finally, when the Carrara family returned to power in 1325, Mussato found himself on the wrong side of a conspiracy against Marsiglio da Carrara that had been initiated by Mussato's brother, Gualpertino, and he was sent for a third time into exile. Never to return to his native city, he died in exile in Chioggia in 1329, secure in his belief that only a German emperor (this time Louis IV of Bavaria) could protect Padua.[20]

Poetry between Nature and History

Mussato's four letters on poetry, written in the years between 1309 and 1316, have been the center of interest in him for twentieth-century scholars of medieval poetics.[21] They have not been connected, however, to his engagement in the political life in Padua – as if he led a dual life as a notary and political leader, on the one hand, and as a classicizing poet, on the other. Each letter theorizes his poetics, and three of them defend poetry against its attackers. By doing so, each also situates Mussato as the inheritor of a tradition that underscores his own status as poet. Mussato first mentions that poetry was another theology (*altera theologia*) in his pre-1315 letter to fellow Paduan Giovanni di Vigonza, a local judge who sat on the college of judges.[22] In this defense of his classicizing Priapic

[20] On Mussato's support of Louis IV of Bavaria, see Lee 2018, 69, 253, and 377.

[21] On Mussato's letters on poetry, see Galletti 1912; Vinay 1949; Garin 1958, 77; Ronconi 1976, 17–59; Mésoniat 1984, 9–17; Cecchini 1985; Grassi 1988, 11–13; and esp. Chevalier 2000, xci–cxviii. See also Greenfield 1981, 79–94. In general, on his poetics and classicizing style, see (Guido) Billanovich 1958 and 1976, 67–82. From recent work on Mussato's poetics, it is clear that his concerns with poetry are not limited to these letters. See Facchini 2017 and Lombardo 2017.

[22] Mussato 2000, 39 (*Epistola* 7.22). In dating this letter, I have followed Calì's suggestion of 1309, which is also followed in Dazzi 1964. It is based on a possibly mistaken reading of verses by Lovato Lovati, who died in 1309, which sees a reference to Mussato's *Priapeia*. Guido Billanovich questioned the reading of Lovati's verses and suggested 1315 as an alternative. Neither dating is entirely satisfactory, as Billanovich bases his on the assumption that only a mature poet could have written the letter and so that it must have been written after Mussato's incoronation in 1315. As Cecchini has suggested, however, the seventh letter seems to be detached chronologically from the

poems – the *Priapeia* and *Cunneia* – Mussato claims that in the primitive world poets were the vessels of God and taught of a single, pious God:[23]

> Divine poets, throughout ancient centuries, have taught that there is a holy God in the heavens. In fact, they displayed to the first peoples hidden secrets that cannot be communicated except in well-arranged verses; and these poets began to be called by another name, *vates*. Whoever was a *vates* was a vessel of God. So we must contemplate that poetry, since it was once another theology.

> (Divini per secula prisca poete / Esse pium celis edocuere Deum. / Tecta quidem prime fudere enigmata genti / Non nisi compositis insinuanda metris; / Hique alio dici ceperunt nomine vates. / Quisquis erat vates, vas erat ille Dei. / Illa igitur nobis stat contemplanda poesis, / Altera que quondam theologia fuit.)[24]

Mussato's claim that poetry was once another theology and that the poet (*vates*) was a vessel of God is based on the allegorical reading of classical texts. This passage, however, shifts between the deep past (*secula prisca*) and the present (*nobis*). In this superimposition, Mussato – who is defending not just ancient poetry but his own rendition of ancient poetry – ascribes to himself the authority of those ancient poets, who hid ideas about the prime mover in their poetry.

After writing that Christ himself, in his parables, was a poet, like Job, Solomon, and the other prophets, Mussato points out that in the schools of the past poetry was also considered a second philosophy: "Poetry, once found in the studies of the gymnasium, was already previously another philosophy. At that time, it transmitted dogmas enclosed in certain figures, and verified them with its examples. Every great tradition approves our work: go around, mindful of what the letter holds" ("Ginnasiis olim studiis inventa poesis / Altera iam pridem philosophia fuit, / Dogmata sub certis que tunc inclusa figuris / Tradidit, exemplis verificata suis. / Traditio nostrum quevis probat optima fructum: / Circue nostra memor litera quicquid habet").[25] What is at stake here, again, is the relationship between present (*nostra*) and past (*olim; iam pridem*). Tradition (*traditio*)

---

others. I see the *Priapeia* as belonging to Mussato's participation in the *cenacolo padovano* under Lovati or shortly after Lovati's death. His production in the years following the incoronation seems to revolve around poetry of a moral and political kind, as would be natural given his intense political activity in the years following Henry VII's incoronation in 1311. See Calì 1893, 21–24; Dazzi 1964, 181; (Guido) Billanovich 1976, 75–76; and Cecchini 1985, 97 n. 8.

[23] On the *Priapeia*, see Dazzi 1964, 107–108. For the Latin text of the *Priapeia* and *Cunneia*, see Crescini 1885. For an Italian translation of the *Priapeia*, see Dazzi 1964, 178–180.
[24] Mussato 2000, 37–39 (*Epistola* 7.15–21).   [25] Mussato 2000, 39 (*Epistola* 7.41–46).

underwrites the function of poetry as that which transmits ideas (*dogmata*). Early on, Mussato is defending his use of poetry for the transmission of an ideology that makes claims to true discourse. Given the context of the Priapic poem that Mussato is defending, it is unlikely that Mussato was thinking about poetry's political purpose at this time. The *dogmata* that poetry transmits are here philosophical ideas linked to schools (*ginnasiis*). In the coming years of increasing political engagement, however, Mussato will expand his notion of the poet's role.

There are already allusions, however, that point to a possible political ideology behind Mussato's efforts. In the final lines of the poem, which he calls a "song without fault" ("carmen sine crimine") with an Ovidian turn of phrase, Mussato speaks in the first person as poetry itself, which had once inspired the voices of Statius, Ovid, and Lucan.[26] Poets, he says, do not just invent things, rather they confer meaning on what lies in nature. They recount and perpetuate what takes place in the natural world, which is the theater of history, without imposing their own ideas: "I took care to signify in various ways not what I made up, but what nature demanded" ("Non ego quid finxi, sed quod natura reposcit / curavi variis significare modis").[27] Underplaying the fictional aspect of poetry, Mussato aims to make the entirety of Nature the realm of poetic discourse, which is founded upon a principle of verisimilitude. Read alongside his efforts to justify his authority by linking his own poetry to that of the past, these lines suggest that Mussato already had a historically engaged poetry in mind. He goes on to say in the voice of poetry that:

> Through me the ages of the everlasting world are remembered, and in my meters lofty enterprises are recorded. I sang the fraternal battle lines, the wars of Cadmus, the blindness of Oedipus, and the slaughter of the Greeks. I transformed their forms, converting them into new bodies. This work has the right of lasting forever. Through me the Pergamon of the Trojan Teucer is recorded. I existed before Dardanus of Troy. Through me the civil wars on Macedonian fields and the glory of Caesar were made known to the people. By my law and norm poets are read in their song, and our music reaches the heights of God.
>
> (Per me perpetui memorantur tempora mundi, / Gestaque sunt numeris alta notata meis. / Fraternas acies cecini, Cadmeia bella, / Oedippode

---

[26] Mussato 2000, 40 (*Epistola* 7.77). By referring to the poem as "sine crimine," Mussato may be alluding to Ovid's love poetry, which he defends to Venus in the *Fasti* as "sine crimine." See Ovid 1931, 188 (*Fasti* 4.9). Ovid uses the phrase "sine crimine" other times in his works, such as *Amores* 1.3.13 and *Tristia* 5.21.

[27] Mussato 2000, 40–41 (*Epistola* 7.79–80).

tenebras Graiugenumque neces. / In nova conversas mutavi corpora formas, / Temporis eterni ius habet istud opus. / Per me Dardanii referuntur Pergama Teucri; / Quam fuerit Troie Dardanus ante fui. / Bella per Emathios per me civilia campos / Edita sunt populis Cesareumque decus / Lege mea vates cantu normaque locuntur, / Migrat ad excelsum musica nostra Deum.)[28]

This list of classical poetic subjects defines the role of poetry as a mode of transmitting historical events and of immortalizing them through tradition.[29] In the voice of poetry, Mussato invokes a law that stands outside the statutes of the city and that resides in the history of poetry that he describes in the letter – a history that places poetry beneath the aegis of God alone.

In this letter Mussato locates poetry's origins in the deep past, when reflecting on the natural world was the equivalent of reflecting upon God. Pagan poets, like Christ and the prophets, maintained the poetic mode of discourse in their works. While the Christian tradition spoke about God directly, the pagan poets' authority was underwritten by philosophy. The authority of the modern Christian poet, we can infer from the shifts in the adverbial timestamps across the poem, derives from both traditions and allows Mussato to pronounce himself on the most challenging of subjects. Mussato's reasoning in this letter to Giovanni di Vigonza will form the basis of his more sustained letter to the Dominican Fra Giovannino written after his incoronation in 1315. In the period between the two letters, however, Mussato focuses his notion of the poet's authority on the city in which he lives. Nature as the world of creation also includes political affairs.

The *Ecerinis*: Poetry and the Theater of History

Between 1309 and 1314, Mussato entered a period of intense political engagement in which he was the Paduan ambassador to the Imperial Court and a leader of Paduan forces against the encroachment of Cangrande della Scala in Vicenza, where he was imprisoned in 1314. After being freed, and before becoming the *defensor populi* between October and December 1315, Mussato wrote the *Ecerinis*, a 630-line Senecan tragedy about the rise and fall of the tyrant Ezzelino da Romano, who had held the Trevisan

---

[28] Mussato 2000, 41 (*Epistola* 7.85–98).
[29] Here Mussato alludes to Statius' *Thebaid*, Seneca's *Oedipus*, Ovid's *Metamorphoses*, and Lucan's *De bello civili*.

March and Padua in a reign of terror two generations earlier.[30] The
Ecerinis represents Mussato's efforts to enact poetically what he had
defended in his letter to Giovanni di Vigonza. The tragedy is a means of
engaging his fellow citizens in contemplating the present through the lens
of the past, so that the errors of the past are not made again.

Against the contemporary political background of Cangrande's threat to
Padua's territory, Mussato's tale of the horrors of tyranny was a vivid
commentary on the dangers of the present. It recounts the diabolical birth,
life of tyranny, and death of two brothers, Ezzelino and Alberico da
Romano. In it Ezzelino is characterized as the spawn of the Devil, whom
the tyrant calls upon for help in realizing his desire for destruction, and is
identified with tyrants of the biblical and classical traditions, whom God
had neglected to impede. The horrors of Ezzelino's campaign against
Padua are described in graphic detail throughout the poem. The chorus
in the play gives voice to the exaggerated fear of the people, which
amplifies the biblical version of Herod's slaughter of the innocents:[31]

> Ezzelino, witness to a thousand crimes, further exasperates cruelty and rage
> by ordering that babies have their genitalia mutilated, so that the seed of
> their future offspring may perish, and that screaming women should have
> their breasts cut off. Lying in their cradles a chorus of maimed innocents
> laments, though they have not yet learned to speak; devoid of light, they
> seek for light in the blind darkness.

> (Ille [Ecerinus] tantorum scelerum superstes / asperans saevas Ecerinus iras,
> / prolis ut semen pereat future, / censor infantum genital recidi, / feminas
> sectis ululare mammis. / Stratus in cunis chorus innocentum / luget indocto
> mutilates ore; / lumen in caecis tenebris requirit / lumine cassus.)[32]

In the final act, however, his crimes are neutralized by equally horrific
crimes enacted by the multitude, which breaks into Alberico's home and
murders his three sons, five daughters, and wife as he watches, before
finally killing him as well. The messenger announces:

---

[30] On Ezzelino da Romano and his rule over Padua, see Hyde 1966, 199–209. On Mussato's *Ecerinis*,
see Carducci 1900; Dazzi 1964, 82–96; Pastore Stocchi 1966; Raimondi 1970c; Galli 1974;
Gianola 1992; Schnapp 1995; Witt 2000, 124–129; Chevalier 2000, xliii–xc and 2013, 28–32;
and Locati 2006. Mussato's *Ecerinis* received two commentaries, one by Guizzardo da Bologna and
Castellano da Bassano, the other by Pace da Ferrara. On these texts, see Gianola 1992; Witt 2000,
130 n. 39. Around the same time as the composition of the *Ecerinis*, Mussato began a series of
studies of Seneca, in which he argued that Seneca was a poet-theologian as well. See Megas 1969 for
Mussato's commentaries on Seneca.

[31] Herod's massacre of the innocents was also depicted on the walls of the Scrovegni chapel in Padua.
See Frugoni 2008, 166–169. For the biblical source, see Matthew 2.

[32] Mussato 2011, 20–21 (*Ecerinis* 265–273).

First, the innocent children were put in a row on the fire. As the burning fire set the maidens' gowns ablaze and the hostile flame touched their golden tresses, they leapt back vainly, seeking their parents' protection, but embraces were denied to the criminals. ... With his [Albericus'] neck severed, his head fell with a thud, and for a long time the trunk of his body stood reeling, ready to drop, until the mob tore it apart, limb from limb, throwing the pieces to greedy dogs

(Ordo innocentum imponitur in ignem prius. / Incendit urens ut puellares sinus / tetigitque flavas ardor infestus comas, / retro resilient cassa quaerentes partum / praesidia: nocius his sed amplexus negant. ... // Cervice caesa, murmurat labens caput, / stetitque titubans truncus ad casum diu, / donec minutim membra dispersit frequens / vulgus, per avidos illa distribuens canes.)[33]

The representation of violence against the other as a form justice is central to the political vision of the *Ecerinis*. More than outright political propaganda, according to which Cangrande is demonized in the form of Ezzelino da Romano, son of the devil, as it has consistently been read,[34] the *Ecerinis* stages the existential and political concerns of the city, caught between the violent will of the tyrant and the uncontrollable rage of the masses. The play condemns the fury of the multitude just as much as it does the tyrant, giving voice to a deep cultural anxiety about the presence of a divine will in history and the difficulty of human agency in a chaotic vortex of changing fortunes. Mussato poses the problem of how evil can be present in history alongside the grace of a benevolent God, and how it can be eradicated without destroying the community – that is, without the people turning into a tyrant.

The primary protagonist of the play is the chorus, through which Mussato sought to give voice to the people's misgivings and fears. The chorus speaks in response to the superhuman will of Ezzelino, who is the embodiment of the chaotic elements of history that, left unchecked, could make life in the Trevisan March a literal hell on earth. Addressing his brother Alberico at the beginning of the play, Ezzellino describes the status of their family in terms of the supernatural origins of their political power:

We are born of gods. Mars did not exalt Romulus and Remus, once upon a time, by so great a lineage. This god is greater by far, a god of the widest realm, a king of vengeance, at whose command mighty princes, kings and leaders suffer punishment. We shall be judges worthy of our paternal tribunal if by our actions we lay claim to the kingdom of our father, who

---

[33] Mussato 2011, 44–45 (593–597; 612–615).   [34] See, e.g., Witt 2000, 124.

delights in wars, death, ruin, deceit, fraud and the perdition of the whole human race.

(Diis gignimur. Nec stirpe tanta Romulus / Remusque quondam Marte tolluntur suo. / Hic maior est, latissimi regni deus, / rex ultionum, cuius imperio luunt / poenas potentes principes reges duces. / Erimus paterno iudices digni foro, / si vindicemus operibus regnum patris, / cui bella mortes exitia frauds doli / perditio et omnis generis humani placent.)[35]

Far more ominous than Dante's Satan, the ruler of Mussato's hell is embodied by Ezzelino himself and is made real by the tyrant's will:

proud father, you who rule over the sad kingdom of deep Chaos, by whose command the shades of the dead atone for their crimes, accept from the deepest cavern, o Vulcan, the worthy prayers of your suppliant son; your true and unquestioned offspring calls upon you. Make me yours; test what the innate resolve burning in my breast can do.

(pater superbe, triste qui regnum tenes / chaos profundi cuius imperio luunt / delicta manes, excipe ex imo specu, / Vulcane, dignas supplicis gnati preces: / te certa et indubitata progenies vocat. / Potiare me; experiare, si quicquam potest / insita voluntas pectori flagrans meo.)[36]

Although the masses and even the semi-literate notary class would have had a hard time understanding the Latin in which the play was composed, the legendary quality of the events that it recounted, which had by this time become recorded in popular memory, made it possible for the public to identify with the chorus as it recounted and mimed the events.[37]

In response to the chaos that Ezzelino brings to the Paduans, both the chorus and the messenger respond by continually calling into question God's presence in history:

Exalted ruler of the world, Almighty God, do you dwell, perhaps, in the high heavens, far removed from our clime, and allow Mars alone to rule our region of earth? O dreadful feuds of the nobles! O madness of the people! The end of struggles you sought is at hand; at hand is the tyrant whom your rage created. I have seen unspeakable things.

(Excelse mundi rector, omnipotens Deus, / altos abhinc tu forsitan caelos colis / nostro remotos aethere, et Marti sinis / soli regendas climatis nostril

---

[35] Mussato 2011, 8–9 (*Ecerinis* 77–85).   [36] Mussato 2011, 9 (*Ecerinis* 92–98).
[37] See Witt 2000, 151, where the historian notes that Mussato sought to represent the citizenry as the chorus.

plagas? / O dira nobelium odia, o populis furor! / Finis petitus litibus vestris adest; / adest tyrannus, vestra quem rabies dedit. / Nefanda vidi.)[38]

Similarly to how the distance of God is used in the Psalms to explain the power of evil in the world, here the messenger indicates ironically what seems like the absence of God from human affairs.[39] Even more, however, he establishes the unrestrained desires of both the nobles and the masses as the principal cause of the tyrant's reign of terror. The messenger's vision of the current unholy events (*nefanda*) represents the present state of things as a kind of hell on earth. Later on, it is the chorus to question Christ's presence in the events of the world, almost accusing the Son of God of too much leisure as he sits immobile at the right hand of his father:

> O Christ, who dwells in heaven on high, at the right hand of his Father who sits upon his throne, can it really be that you are charmed completely by the allurements of high Olympus, delighting only in supernal joys, while neglecting what goes on beneath the stars? Doesn't the clamor of the human race send its cries through the air to your ears?

> (Christe, qui caelis resides in altis / patris a dextris solio sedentis, / totus an summi illecebris Olympi / gaudiis tantum frueris supernis, / negligis quicquid geritur sub astris? / Non tuas affert fremitus ad aures / rumor humani generis per auras?)[40]

After invoking the punishments of Abel and Sodom and Gomorrah, the chorus indicts Christ for not acting to change the Hell that the modern world has become: "Dispenser of justice, why do you not see men's sins of the present day in this way? A cruel overpowering tyranny dominates our age, a tyranny such as no age of the world can recall" ("Cur modo non sic, moderator aequi, / cernis errors hominum modernos? / Praepotens nostro dominator aevo / saeva tyrannis, / nulla quam mundo memoravit aetas").[41] A few lines later, trying to make sense of Ezzelino's mutilation of women and children, the chorus – not unlike Job – beseeches God for help and begins to doubt the very salvation narrative that underlies Christian universal history: "God, why do you allow such cruel madness, why do you not hurl down lightning as is your wont? Why does not the earth yawn beneath his feet so that this snake, destroyer of the human race, may go down to the darkness of hell? Your redeemed people, fallen once again, call

---

[38] Mussato 2011, 14–15 (*Ecerinis* 163–170).
[39] For the biblical parallel and a possible source for this attitude, see, e.g., Psalms 10 and 13 (9 and 12 in the Latin Vulgate).
[40] Mussato 2011, 18–19 (*Ecerinis* 228–234).   [41] Mussato 2011, 18 (*Ecerinis* 239–242).

upon you in supplication, Heavenly Father!" ("Quid Deus tantos pateris furores, / quos soles et non iacularis ignes? / Terra cur non sub pedibus dehiscit, / hic ut infernas subeat tenebras / anguis, humani generis peremptor? / Te Patrem caeli populus redemptus / invocate supplex, iterum relapsus").[42] While the chorus and the messenger give voice to their anxieties about the absence of the divine in the affairs of men, the central act of the *Ecerinis* strikes a blow against the clergy as mediator between that divine will and the progression of history.

The third act briefly stages a dialogue between Ezzelino and Friar Luca, a Franciscan in Ezzelino's court.[43] The friar seeks to convince the tyrant to change his ways and to accept the forgiveness of the just and gentle God, turning toward to the good:

> He [God] distributed fairly the works he has created using fair scales. And this sacred order is called justice. The just God ordained that justice be practiced by the mortal men he has created. Faith, hope, and charity, implanted in us by Nature herself, teach us that these things are so. Believe me, each man has these virtues innate within his breast, but error can lead anyone from the right path. I beg you, therefore, convert yourself to this species of the good, so that holy charity may spare your neighbor, so that you may hope for the grace of a merciful God, all of which a devout faith will cause you to follow.

> (Hic equus equa lance dispensat sua, / Que fecit, opera; dictus hic ordo sacer / Iustitia. Iustus hanc coli voluit Deus / A se creatis omnibus mortalibus. / Hos esse tales edocent primo insite / Natura ab ipsa, Caritas Spes et Fides. / Has, crede, quisque pectori innatas habet, / Traducat error devius quemquam licet. / Converte, queso, igitur ad has species boni, / Ut Caritas pia proximo parcat tuo, / Speresque gratiam misericordis Dei; / Que consequi omnia sancta te faciet Fides.)[44]

Friar Luca's words seem to be a parody of spiritual *naïveté*. His position is centered on the belief in the inherent goodness of humanity and in the power of reason to overcome evil. Ezzelino responds mockingly that God could stop him if He wished, following up with the claim that he is only a tool of the avenging God of the Old Testament, a punisher of sins, who wills a hell on earth: "I believe I have been given to the world on his orders to punish sins. . . . With how much blood did the deep sea redden on their orders? And your watchful God didn't want to stop them! He let it all

---

[42] Mussato 2011, 20–21 (*Ecerinis* 274–280).
[43] This character is probably based on Luca Belludi, a companion of Saint Anthony of Padua in Ezzelino's court. See Chevalier 2000, xlviii.
[44] Mussato 2011, 27–29 (*Ecerinis* 355–366).

happen willingly!" ("Me credo mundo, scelera ut ulciscar, datum, / illo [Deo] iubente. // Quantis cruoribus rubuit altum mare, / illis iubentibus? Nec inspector Deus / prohibere voluit, esse sic ultro sinens").[45] Although Friar Luca is portrayed as a character of dignity and honor within the play's poetic economy of horror and vice, his utter failure to convert Ezzelino enacts the clergy's inability to put to use the theological virtues against evil and for human life. The key term in his speech to Ezzelino is *convertere*, "to convert," which he uses in its spiritual meaning of a turning around of the spirit, from evil to good. As staged in the *Ecerinis*, the events of history defy the absolute kind of transfiguration that is required for a conversion. Things do change, however, and Ezzelino is represented as turning physically (*vertere*) several times. This turning, however, signals the movement of history according to the whims of fortune, the strong will of a proud man, and the frenzied rage of the masses.[46]

At the end of the play the chorus accepts the enactment of popular justice as it superficially restores balance to the divided city, praising it as an unchanging law:

> This rule of law endures forever. Just men, trust in it! If one day, fortune should happen to raise up some criminal, still the rule does not fail. Responsible for his works, each man gets what he deserves. The stern Judge, the mild Judge, is mindful of fair judgment; he rewards the just and punishes the unjust. This stable order never ends: virtue seeks the delights of heaven; misdeeds seek the darkness of hell. Therefore, be warned, and pay heed while you may to the stable law.

> (Haec perpetuo durat in aevo / regula iuris. Fidite, iusti: / nec, si quando forsitan ullum / quemquam nocuum sors extollat, / regula fallit. Consors operum / meritum sequitur quisque suorum. / Stat iudicii conscius aequi / iudex rigidus, iudex placidus; / donat iustos, damnat iniquos. / Haud hic stabilis desinit ordo: / petit illecebras virtus superas, / crimen tenebras expetit imas. / Dum licet ergo moniti stabilem / discite legem.)[47]

From the perspective of the popular chorus, the retributive justice of the Old Testament brings order back to the world with the death of Ezzelino

---

[45] Mussato 2011, 28–30 (*Ecerinis* 380–381; 395–397). The word "them" (*illis*) here refers to Nebuchadnezzar, the Pharaoh, Saul, Alexander the Great, and Nero, all of whom Ezzelino invokes in his rebuttal of Friar Luca.

[46] Mussato employs words with the root of *vertere* often in the tragedy (e.g., lines 32, 55, 208, 219, 301, 363, 445, 459, 461, 483, 488, 531). The term *convertere* is used three times, to refer to the literal turning of Ezzelino's army (363), to spiritual conversion (363), and to Ezzelino changing direction (488).

[47] Mussato 2011, 44–47 (*Ecerinis* 616–629), translation modified.

and his brother, and the murder of their families. This kind of justice, however, does not bring balance or stability. Rather, it promises future violence unless the cycle of retribution can be broken. The only stable order at the end is the continual turning of fortune's wheel, as the chorus had declared at the beginning: "So the wheel turns round and round forever; nothing endures" ("Sic semper rota volvitur, durat perpetuum nichil").[48] If we dissociate Mussato's intentions from the voice of the chorus, then his role as poet may be understood as more than just a political propagandist. The play enacts a dual fall from grace, both of the tyrant and of the people, from within a tragic, solitary vision of the universe.

In a letter to the College of Artists, written between December 3 and 25, 1315,[49] on the anniversary of the conferral of the laurel crown, Mussato mentions that the poetic purpose of a tragedy like the *Ecerinis* is to take on an ethical hortatory role among the people of Padua: "The voice of the tragic poet makes minds strong against chance, and cowardly fear is diluted" ("Vox tragici mentes ad contingentia fortes / efficit, ignavus diluitque metus").[50] He continues along the same lines, locating the political and economic domain of the poem outside of the influence of a single noble family and within the instability of the crowd: "This song is very useful and profitable to mortals, since it counts as nothing what we hold as property. There is no stable domain in any court, and certainty is in instability alone." ("Proficit hoc nimium mortalibus utile carmen, / cum nichil in nostris computet esse bonis. / Conspicitur nulla stabilis dominatus in aula, / certaque de sola est mobilitate fides").[51] Mussato's *Ecerinis* was not only a warning against the tyranny of Cangrande but also a condemnation of the blind rage of the mob, as it is manipulated by the powerful, and a denunciation of an ineffectual clergy, powerless to mediate between historical events and divine will. It was, in sum, a call to reflect on the human responsibility and ability to act within a historical world that lacked any apparent sense or direction.

Becoming Poet Laureate and the Politics of Defending Poetry

It was largely because of the success of the *Ecerinis* that Mussato was crowned poet laureate of Padua in 1315, even if in the ceremony he was

---

[48] Mussato 2011, 12–13 (*Ecerinis* 146–147).
[49] On the dating of this letter, see Albanese 2017, 16 n. 22.
[50] Mussato 2000, 33 (*Epistola* 1.93–94).   [51] Mussato 2000, 33 (*Epistola* 1.105–108).

also recognized for his history of Henry VII's expedition in Italy, known as the *Historia Augusta*, or *De gestis Henrici VII Cesaris*.[52] As we have seen with the *Ecerinis*, Mussato's role as poet was intricately connected to his interpretation of history.[53] The laureation ceremony, which Mussato had a hand in organizing,[54] was connected civically to the honors given to Rolandino of Padua a generation earlier, when the College of Artists had honored his chronicle with a public reading in 1262, which was itself based on the public reading and approval of Boncompagno da Signa's *Boncompagnus*, or *Rhetorica antiqua*, in 1226.[55] Mussato's crowning, however, was the first for a work of poetry and aimed at a higher level of classical imitation. Unlike the earlier laureates, Mussato was not associated with the city's university, since he could not teach there and had no formal advanced education. In his 1315 letter to the College of Artists, Mussato defines the role of the tragedian in terms of historical perspective, but he also connects that role to his political status. He reminds the authorities of the university about the local political role of poetry. Tragedy, he writes, "remembers the deeds of leaders and the generous names of kings, when great ruin overturns and grinds down their houses. Massive lightning strikes the highest towers but does not impetuously seize low-lying homes" ("Facta ducum memorat generosaque nomina regum, / cum terit eversas alta ruina domos. / Fulmina supremas feriunt ingentia turres / nec capiunt planas impetuosa casas").[56] In the story told by tragedy, the subject matter differentiates between the classes of society and memorializes the fall of the great for those who do not feel the grand historical movements of fortune. Mussato, in fact, limits his ambitions as poet to the local theater of history, even if his chronicle is more universal in scope. Unlike Petrarch, for whom Rome's past greatness will be of fundamental importance for his laureation, Mussato is content to be honored in Padua: "If Rome did not want to include me among her poets, then at least I will be read safely in this city

---

[52] On the circumstances surrounding Mussato's incoronation, see the detailed reconstruction in Albanese 2017, which includes a diplomatic edition of the deliberations of the Paduan College of Judges in which Mussato's "honorem maximum" was discussed (6–8). Albanese notes the political significance of Mussato's incoronation, which she sees as resembling a political celebration (13) and as recognizing Mussato's cultural and political accomplishments (14). Albanese also individuates two separate celebrations: the initial procession from his home to the municipal palace (*Palacium*) and the public readings that would take place on Christmas Day. See also Dazzi 1964, 67–68 and Chevalier 2004. For the importance of Mussato's chronicle of Henry VII for the incoronation, see Albanese 2016.

[53] On Mussato's "sense of history," see Bortolami 1995.   [54] See Albanese 2017, 26–27.

[55] On the precursors to Mussato's incoronation, see Chevalier 2000, xi n. 2. See also Weiss 1986.

[56] Mussato 2000, 33 (*Epistola* 1.87–90).

of Padua" ("Si me Roma suis nolet conferre poetis, / hac saltem Patava tutus in urbe legar").[57]

Following Mussato's official recognition as Padua's poet laureate, he defended himself in two separate letters. The first is an epistle to an otherwise unknown Venetian professor of grammar, Giovanni Cassio, who had asked him, in a letter dated December 6, 1315, about the nature of poetry and how to respond to those who devalue poetic fictions as lacking in truth,[58] whereas the second is an epistle to a Dominican professor of theology. In the first letter, Mussato tells his interlocutor that the man who attacks poetry does not know that the art of poetry is only for those who are divinely inspired and that it is a science sent down from heaven: "He ignores the greatness of this institution, my friend, he ignores it: the work of art does not take hold of anyone except divine men!" ("Grande ministerium nescit, carissime, nescit: / non nisi divinos hoc capit artis opus!").[59] Mussato situates poetry as a public office within the civic sphere, a *ministerium*, whose authority is founded upon the definition of poets as divinely inspired (*divinos*).[60] As he goes on to explain, the divine origins of poetry as another form of philosophy confirm the nobility of the poet's civic role: "This science was sent down from highest heaven; it has its right likewise with God on high" ("Hec fuit a summo demissa scientia celo; / cum simul excelso ius habet illa Deo").[61] Here he does not call poetry precisely theology, as he had earlier, but instead he defines it as a heavenly science and another philosophy. Its authority, however, is directly descended from a code of divine law (*ius*), according to which it has the right to fulfill its function in the world.

That these claims to poetic authority based on a transcendental origin for poetic inspiration are connected to his ideas about his own role in society becomes clear from the context of the letter. These lines are preceded by Mussato's reflections on the local political effect of his crowning ceremony:

---

[57] Mussato 2000, 31 (*Epistola* 1.43–44).
[58] See Onorato 2005 for a discussion of the identity of the addressee of this letter and the complete texts of their correspondence recently discovered in MS Vat. Lat. 6875. Mussato's response gives rise to a brief correspondence about the meaning of the birth of three lions in Venice, which Mussato interprets in a political key.
[59] Mussato 2000, 36 (*Epistola* 4.43–44). For the text of this letter, I have used the edition in Mussato 2000, which does not differ substantially from the edition provided in Onorato 2005, at least for the quotations in this chapter.
[60] See Mésoniat 1984, 14, where he mentions that Mussato's incoronation would have given him the privileges of a university professor. More recently, see also Albanese 2017.
[61] Mussato 2000, 36 (*Epistola* 4.45–46).

There are nevertheless some herdsmen in our territory: if they are not poets, they still resemble them. According to the ancient custom they made me their poet, and the vain crowd was eager enough to follow them; like on a holy day there was a complete lack of judicial argument and there were no elders in the court, nor did our market places sell any goods, and our artisans ceased their work.

(Sunt tamen hic aliqui per nostra suburbia fauni: / si non sint vates, at tamen instar habent. / Moribus antiquis sibi me fecere poetam, / hisque satis promptum vulgus inane, fuit; / utque die sacra nulla sub lite vacavit / iustitia et tenuit curia nulla patres / nec fora nostra dabant ullas venalia merces, / artifices operas destituere suas.)[62]

The honor given to Mussato is portrayed as completely displacing, even if for only a moment, the practical functions of the city, as if he were a kind of priest in a religious procession. In a city whose cult of Saint Anthony was rapidly growing, the significance of such a status given to a poet should not be underestimated, nor should the fact that the *Ecerinis* was given license to be recited on Christmas Day.[63] Mussato is highlighting in this letter the fact that the local sovereignty of the poet is underwritten by a higher transcendental power.

If his political role is based on the primitive divine origins of poetry, however, he goes on to explain that the importance of official recognition by the political structure of the city itself:

The bishop assented, the Duke [Albert] of Saxony applauded the celebrations: our laurel crown has two authorities; a number of learned men, the honor of our University, signed with their own titles both histories; and even more, the Senate along with the people established by law that it would hold faith to it for all time, and it sanctioned perpetual gifts, by way of eternal praise, and promised that I would always be read in our city

(Annuit antistes, plausit preconia Saxo / dux: habet auctores laurea nostra duos; / doctorum series, Studii reverentia nostri, / signavit titulis singula gesta suis; / et super his legem statuit cum plebe senatus, / observaturum tempus in omne fidem, / munera perpetua pro laude perennia nobis / sanxit et ut nostra semper in urbe legar).[64]

The intramoenial chain of authority that bolsters Mussato's status is located simultaneously within the secular and ecclesiastical realms of the

---

[62] Mussato 2000, 34 (*Epistola* 4.11–18).

[63] See Albanese 2017, 19 n. 23, where the critic notes the exceptionality of this honor with respect to other "normal" university celebrations of the *conventatio* (or diploma ceremonies), which could not take place on Sundays or other religious holidays.

[64] Mussato 2000, 36 (*Epistola* 4.31–38).

city. The doctors of arts and medicine who had crowned him were both secular and ecclesiastical members of the *Studium*, and his poetic text is legally inserted into public life for all time.

Although it was seconded by the bishop, Mussato's laurel crowning did not involve the mendicant orders of the city, which, according to Paolo Marangon, had gradually renounced direct institutional control in Padua for a broader engagement with the populous, seeking a cultural and moral influence over the city's inhabitants that went beyond the fate of their souls. In fact, in his definition of tragedy as providing people with the courage to face the events of history, Mussato seems to establish himself in a position parallel to the members of orders like the Dominicans, Franciscans, and reformed Benedictines, who, according to Marangon, were the pillars of Padua's civic identity during the years of Ezzelino da Romano's tyranny and in the subsequent reconstruction. Marangon elaborates on this cultural turn:

> The religious organizations renounce their institutional control on society and they aim at the evangelical formation of the faithful. In this way the reformed white Benedictines of the blessed Giordano Forzatè are born and thus are the new mendicant orders, the Franciscans and Dominicans, encouraged in every way. For some years [of the thirteenth century], Padua and the [Trevisan] March are maintained *de facto* by prestigious monks and friars such as the Dominican Giovanni of Vicenza and Giordano Forzatè, who is called "father of Padua" in the sources.[65]

The ceremony of receiving the laurel crown designated a local political authority that Mussato could use to influence the same faithful for his own ends. By the end of 1315, Mussato was one of the major political forces in the city with respect to the old aristocratic lines and the newer families of wealth, such as the Carrara and the Scrovegni respectively, and with his poetry he was publicly challenging the authority of the friars.[66]

---

[65] Marangon 1997, 59. "Le organizzazioni religiose rinunciano a un controllo istituzionale sulla società e puntano sulla formazione evangelica dei fedeli; nascono così i benedettini riformati albi del beato Giordano Forzatè e sono incoraggiati in tutti i modi i nuovi ordini mendicanti, francescani e dominicani. Per alcuni anni Padova e la Marca sono rette di fatto da figure prestigiose di monaci e di frati, come il domenicano Giovanni da Vicenza e il Forzatè, chiamato dalle fonti 'pater Padue.'" See also Marangon 1997, 428, where the historian mentions that local theologians "tenevano moltissimo alla supremazia e al controllo culturale," hypothesizing that "è forse proprio per realizzare questa forma di controllo ideologico, garantito anche dall'ufficio dell'inquisizione, riconosciuto dagli statuti comunali, che essi difendevano le 'libertates' del clero come 'vacacio salutifera in lege divina,' in accordo con una storiografia cittadina che accusa spesso il papa e l'imperatore di essere 'partiarii.'"

[66] On Mussato's complicated relationship with the Carrara family, into which the Scrovegni married, see Hyde 1966, 271–275.

Mussato's crowning publicly guaranteed the recognition of his voice among the members of both groups, whose public actions were linked. In the years after Ezzelino's fall, the clergy and the old nobility, once the two poles of civic life in Padua, had seen a dramatic loss of power. The magnates had tried to counterbalance the decentralization of power by participating in the life of the city through circles of clients. The bishop and the abbots of the most important monasteries did the same, often tying themselves to powerful families. Many of the political alignments between nobility and cloister dated back almost a century and became particularly important after the tyranny of Ezzelino. As Marangon notes, the rise of the reformed Benedictines and the mendicant orders in Padua was connected to this political shift. The Benedictines of the monastery of Santa Giustina had been staunchly opposed to Ezzelino and were also openly outspoken against Cangrande. The monastery had a tradition of political involvement in Padua going back at least to abbot Giordano Forzaté at the beginning of the thirteenth century. The Franciscans generally avoided open political associations, but they were in charge of the Inquisition until 1302–03, when they were accused of abuse of power and with accumulation of wealth.[67] The Dominicans, who took over the Inquisition from the Franciscans, had embedded themselves in the intellectual and political life of the city since they had arrived in Padua. The land on which they built their monastery of Sant'Agostino had been donated by Gnafo da Vo, ancestor of the Carrara line, and was the burial place of the Carrara family into the fifteenth century. The Dominican monastery was also the primary place in which theology was taught in Padua before the founding of the theological faculty of the *Studium* in 1363.[68] Marangon describes in general terms the relationship between politics and theology in thirteenth- and early fourteenth-century Padua: "Theology, which was studied in the convents and present in the cathedral [of Padua] ... allies itself with philosophy in the development of a global conception of reality, coherent with the common foundation of a 'respublica christiana' and supported by theories of balance expressed systematically in the thought of the friars, but managed politically by

---

[67] See Hyde 1966, 272. Mussato was involved in the effort to remove the administration of the Inquisition from the Franciscans.

[68] The formal foundation of the university in 1222, which was formed by a group of students and professors who migrated to Padua from the University of Bologna, seems also to be connected with the arrival of the Dominicans in Padua during the same period. See Brotto and Zonta 1922, 5. On Padua's university, see Gloria 1888; Arnaldi 1976; and Gallo 1998.

laymen."[69] Mussato's claim to a transcendent authority for his poetry, which is publicly recognized in his laureation ceremony and inserted into the moral life of the city with the public recitation of the *Ecerinis*, provides him with a sovereign voice within the city that challenges the hierarchical vision of reality of the friars and the nobility.

If Mussato's other letters were directed primarily toward rhetoricians, notaries, and judges in an effort to bolster the civic status of the poet within the scholarly and legal realms of the city, his most elaborate defense, addressed to a Dominican friar, actively engages the spiritual and intellectual backbone of the city. In this letter, Mussato addresses Fra Giovannino da Mantova, a professor of theology and natural and moral philosophy (*theologia et philosophia naturali et morali*) at the theological *studium* of the monastery of Sant'Agostino, where he had been since 1297.[70] Through the teaching of the friars at the convent and through their sermons, the Dominicans sought to reach and inform the Paduan people, both literate and non. In addition to the religious role that the Dominicans were leading in Paduan civic life, their intimate ties to the Carrara family placed them in direct opposition to Mussato's political interests, inasmuch as he was opposed to handing power over to Giacomo da Carrara.[71] From at least 1314, the Carrara were aiming to secure the *signoria* of Padua for themselves, at times openly and at others more indirectly. In their way stood the threat of Cangrande and his continual assaults on Paduan territory, and Mussato himself, who was wary of any single magnate family controlling the city and who disagreed with the terms according to which the Carrara would have brokered a peace with Verona.[72] Mussato had on his side the power of both the Benedictine Monastery of Santa Giustina, where his brother Gualpertino was abbot, and the wealthy Lemici family, of which he was the

---

[69] Marangon 1997, 64. "La teologia, studiata nei conventi e presente presso la cattedrale ... si allea con la filosofia nella elaborazione di una concezione globale della realtà, coerente con il sostrato comune di una 'respublica christiana', retta secondo teorie di equilibrio pensate sistematicamente dai frati, ma gestita politicamente da laici."

[70] See Gargan 1971, 8 and Marangon 1997, 378.

[71] Although there is no evidence to suggest that the Dominicans, or the friars of any other order for that matter, ever sided directly with the Carrara, there is abundant evidence that both of the mendicant orders had been in the business of administering land for the Carrara and their allies since the fall of Ezzelino. See Gargan 1971, 11, where he notes that the Carrara were among the most faithful to the Dominicans. On Mussato's own relationship with the Carrara, which can generally be described as cautious and suspicious, see Hyde 1966, 271–275. Mussato opposed Bartolomeo but tolerated Giacomo when necessary.

[72] On Mussato's cautious relations with Giacomo da Carrara in this light, see Hyde 1966, 273.

executor.[73] Each party had its own theological authority, the importance of which is attested by the protests of the Carrara against Gualpertino Mussato's abbacy and their avidity to assign that post to one of their own once they had taken over the *signoria* of the city.

The exchange between Fra Giovannino and Albertino Mussato is set against this complicated intersection of theological doctrine and political maneuvering. It began when Fra Giovannino, at the same time as the recitation of the *Ecerinis* in December 1315 or shortly afterward, delivered a sermon in which he praised the preeminence of theology over all the other sciences.[74] Since he had all together left out poetry from his list of sciences, as if not worthy of consideration, Mussato gathered all of the *doctores* of the sciences and complained about the friar's invectives, declaring that the Dominican could not say anything against poetry.[75] Giovannino was informed of Mussato's rant against him by notary Paolo da Teolo, a friend of Mussato, but also from a family of notaries that had served both the Carrara family and the friars of Sant'Agostino.[76] The friar immediately responded publicly to Mussato's remarks with an attack on poetry. At this point Mussato followed up with a metrical letter (now lost) that praised poetry for nine reasons, which can be reconstructed from Giovannino's response. Mussato's arguments to Fra Giovannino repeat some of his declarations from other letters and are listed in Fra Giovannino's response. Mussato wrote that poetry was the first kind of theology, that its object is divine or celestial, that poets (*vates*) are vessels of God, that poetry is a divine gift, that poetry's artifice and marvel capture the attention of listeners, that Moses was a poet, that the Bible, especially the Book of Revelation, is poetic, that poetry is everlasting (as symbolized by the laurel and the poet's fame),

---

[73] The abbacy of S. Giustina was worth £1,000 a year, according to Hyde 1966, 274. On the Lemici family's opposition to the Carrara, see Hyde 1966, 271.

[74] On the opinion of Paduan theologians on natural philosophy, see Marangon 1997, 429 n. 107 and 451–452.

[75] The origin of the dispute between Mussato and Fra Giovannino is recounted by an anonymous Paduan, whose account is recorded alongside the epistle. See Dazzi 1964, 110–111.

[76] On Paolo da Teolo, his connections with the Dominicans of the monastery of Sant'Agostino, and his role in the rise of the Carrara family to the *signoria*, see Hyde 1966, 135–136. (Guido) Billanovich 1976, 68 notes in passing that he was a friend of Mussato, presumably because da Teolo's sister had married Lovato's brother-in-law and because he had connections with the *cenacolo padovano*. See, however, Hyde 1966, 274, where he notes that Mussato lost many of his previous alliances with the notarial class of intellectuals once the controversy of Cangrande came to its turning point with the election of Giacomo da Carrara as capitain-general.

and that Virgil through poetry presaged the Christian faith (as one can see in the verses of Proba).[77]

Fra Giovannino counters Mussato's reasons by saying: (1) that poets treat the divine truthfully (*de vero*) but erroneously, according to fictions (*de falso, seu fictis diis*); (2) similarly, that poets treat divine things falsely; (3) that the name *Vatis*, according to Isidore of Seville, has different valences for poets, philosophers, priests, and prophets: for poets it comes from *vieo vies*, i.e., *ligare*, not *vas Dei*; (4) that poetry is not a gift from God but a human invention; (5) that poetry is marvelous because it tells of monstrous things that cause stupor and that it is delightful not because of the truth of its content but because of exterior beauty; (6) that even if Moses composed poetry, he did so for women; and just because theology was expressed in verses it does not mean that poetry is divine; (7) that poetry seems to resemble Scripture because both make use of metaphors, but a radical difference separates them: poetry uses metaphor for fiction and delight, while Scripture uses it to veil the holy word; (8) that poetry does not possess eternal beauty because it only goes back to the time of Moses (when the first poets Orpheus, Museus, and Linus lived), while theology goes back to the time of Adam; and that the laurel crown does not signify eternity but the power of the men whose actions poets sang; (9) that the *centones*, or patchwork poems made of the words of Virgil do not bear the intent of the pagan poets but of their Christian interpreters.[78] Fra Giovannino, however, concludes his letter with a conciliatory note, defining his objections as doubts that he invites Mussato to resolve: "These are my doubts, venerable poet, and if they will be completely resolved, I will be able to fulfill your mandate, and when it will be fit to speak about this, I will be able to commend poetry deservedly to divine wisdom" ("Haec sunt dubia, venerande poeta, quae si ad plenum fuerint enodata, potero vestrum complere mandatum, et cum fuerit sermo ad hoc conveniens, poeticam divinae sapientiae commendare merito").[79] The friar extends this *quaestio* further, offering to lend his public authority to that of the poet, if indeed there is an affinity between poetry and theology.

In response to this letter Mussato composed his final defense of poetry as a response to Giovannino's detractions. In it, Mussato continues to claim that poetry is another theology: "If since the first beginnings of the

---

[77] Mussato's reasons for the inclusion of poetry among the sciences are listed at the beginning of Fra Giovannino's letter of rebuttal in prose. Fra Giovannino's response is in Garin 1958, 3–19. For Mussato's reasons, see Garin 1958, 4–6.

[78] See Garin 1958, 6–13.   [79] Garin 1958, 13.

world this art was theological, it still remains so, always divine and a good subject" ("pur fuit a primis ars ista theologa mundi / principiis, manet ipsa tamen divinaque semper / subiectumque bonum").[80] His aim is to assert an origin for poetry in the deep past that equals or surpasses that of the Hebrew prophets. From its source, poetry maintains its nobility: "poetry comes from a holy spring; yes, it does, since it takes its beginnings from this source" ("a sacro iam fonte venit divina poesis; / quippe venit, siquidem hec exordia traxit ab illo").[81] His argument against the attacks of the Dominican, as has often been pointed out, parallels poetry and theology on multiple fronts. He highlights the similarities between the cults of Christian saints and pagan gods: "But our people did not allow such men to be called gods, and preferred to call them by another name, saints" ("Sed non passa deos tales gens nostra vocari / maluit hos alio dici prenomine sanctos").[82] The spirits of the water are linked to baptism: "You object that God could be in the liquid waves? What have you said, if by your law you have contradicted yourself? There, you yourself conclude that in the sacred water of baptism there is the God of our life and beneath that fount the faults of our forebears are left behind" ("quodque insit liquidis Deus obtestaris in undis? / Lege tua tibi quid si contradixeris ipsi / dixeris? Ecce, sacra tu tu concludis in unda / baptismi nostre numen consistere vite / et veterum culpas illo sub fonte relinqui").[83] And the laurel is equated with the olive:

> You strive to mix something tasteless with the leaves of the laurel. It would be easy to play with figurative words. Let no one joke about the leaves of the sacred olive! So don't you condemn with biting words, so undeserved, the ivy earned with study and the garlands with vigils. Let it be enough for you to praise the circle of your tonsure and let that which moves around your own centers suffice you.

> (Niteris et lauri foliis immittere quicquam / insipidum. Leve sit fictis alludere verbis; / absit quisque sacre foliis allusor olive! / Ne studiis emptas ederas vigilataque serta / tu nimis indignis mordacibus argue verbis; / sitque satis vestre ciclos laudare corone / sufficiant vestris circumque ferentia centris.)[84]

The friar, like Mussato, bears a crown (*corone*) in his tonsure that signals his authority, just as the laurel does for Mussato. The poet seems to be drawing a parallel between their respective positions, which are beholden

---

[80] Mussato 2000, 45 (*Epistola* 18.83–85).   [81] Mussato 2000, 46 (*Epistola* 18.100–101).
[82] Mussato 2000, 44 (*Epistola* 18.49–50).   [83] Mussato 2000, 44–45 (*Epistola* 18.69–72).
[84] Mussato 2000, 47 (*Epistola* 18.143–149).

to separate codes (*leges*) that are nevertheless parallel. Unlike in the other letters, however, here Mussato omits any direct reference to the local political structure. In response to the friar's concluding invitation, he even seems to offer poetry to the Dominican as a common theological ground between their opposing world-views.

He concludes the letter, in this light, by reminding his Dominican reader that poetry and Christian theology can work together:

> Oh good herald of the true God, you who are so severe, what more do you ask? Does not whoever seeks God, the One, the True, and the Just, does he not seek him in our gardens and does he not sing with our lyre in various poems? . . . And so you, *lector*, do not despise the humble maids [the Muses] who will support you and willingly obey you, if only you wish it. Envy has no effect on them: they come to follow your orders and to adore your tracks always, even if from afar.
>
> (O veri bone preco Dei, sic arduus ultra / Quid poscis? Nonne <ille> Deum scrutatus et unum / Et verum et iustum nostris quesivit in ortis / Concinuitque lira vario sub carmine nostra? // Tuque tibi famulas humiles ne despice, lector, / que faveant, tantum ipse velis, parere volentes. / Has non livor habet: veniunt ut iussa sequantur / de longe tantum et vestigia semper adorent.)[85]

Mussato is clearly trying to point out to the friar that the similarities between poetry and theology should not divide them but rather should bring them closer together, toward a similar purpose. The closing line seems to allude to the final lines of the *Thebaid*, in which Statius acknowledges his indebtedness to Virgil: "Live, I pray you: and do not put the divine *Aeneid* to the test, but follow it at a distance and always adore its traces. Soon, if some dark envy still stretches a cloud over you, it will perish, and deserved honors will be offered you after my time" ("vive, precor; nec tu divinam Aeneida tempta, / sed longe sequere et vestigia semper adora. / mox, tibi si quis adhuc praetendit nubila livor, / occidet, et meriti post me referentur honores").[86] With this allusion, his words to the friar intimate that poetry could follow theology as the *Thebaid* followed the *Aeneid*, both challenging and revering the predecessor, and work toward similar ends.

The divide between poetry and theology in Mussato's exchange with Fra Giovannino mirrors the political divide between Mussato's faction and that of the Carrara. The common theological ground that Mussato

---

[85] Mussato 2000, 48 (*Epistola* 18.164–167; 177–180).
[86] Statius 2004, 308 (*Thebaid* 12.816–819).

proposes to reconcile that divide also functions politically. By putting poetry on the same level as theology Mussato was not only claiming a new epistemological status for it, he was also and more importantly justifying its public status, which he hoped the friar would bolster in his sermons when the time was right. Mussato was trying to bridge the divisions that would bring ruin on his city by appealing to the universal, divine origins that make poetry the equal of theology. Although Fra Giovannino had questioned the epistemological validity of poetry as a science along with its moral standing, and his attack must have also been a devaluation of the political ideology associated with the *Ecerinis*, Mussato responded by placing the two forms of discourse in dialogue with one another, with poetry in the service of theology. The concluding lines of the defense seem to offer a way out of the ideological divisions that separated not only the major families from one another but also the major religious orders of the city from one another. Mussato wanted to recreate the political theater of the city by establishing a global similarity between their factional identities. Thus, when he invokes poetry as a divinely inspired theological discourse, he is calling the universal to his aid in service of the local.

The *De obsidione*: A Theological Poetry of the City

The result of Mussato's theorizations of the intersection of Christian theology and a poetry based on classical models is his local epic poem on the year-long siege of Padua by Cangrande between 1319 and 1320, *De obsidione Canis Grandis de Verona Ante Civitatem Paduanam*.[87] Probably written for the first anniversary of the Paduan victory over Verona in the summer of 1321, the poem was requested by the Paduan guild of notaries:

> You ask me repeatedly, and you insist more inconveniently than you should, Palatine Society of Notaries, to translate what I have already written in Latin about the destruction of our city, about the ruin that Cangrande brought against it recently with divine and human favors, the ruin that was later turned around when enough contrary successes were turned against him. You want me to translate it for your solace and that of the citizens, into a certain musical meter, agreeing to your petition that whatever the meter is, the language should not be high or tragic but sweet and close to the understanding of the common people. And just as much as our history, in a higher and more distinguished style, may serve the educated, this metrical work, cast beneath a gentler muse, can be a delight to notaries and schoolboys. For most times one takes pleasure in what one understands,

---

[87] On Mussato's *De obsidione*, see Dazzi 1964, 96–98; Gianola 1999; and Witt 2000, 131–134.

and one rejects and holds in disdain what one does not. Like the book by Cato, who judges about morals, which brought into the form of an exemplum that which is reckoned in the treatise of L. Annaeus Seneca. Because it taught very holy ideas with a plain grammar very similar to common speech, it incited sweet applauses when it was heard by the more popular classes. And you say that the greatest deeds of kings and generals are usually translated from various languages into the common speech with the rhythms of measured feet and syllables, so that they might be understood by the common people, and performed in the theaters and pulpits and sung as songs. Therefore, since I am unable to refuse, and since your request was posed in a friendly way, I agree with you, my brothers, to use the heroic meter as well as I can; and I will carry this out in a popular manner as far as the material will allow, myself a beginner with the beginners.

(Percontamini me frequens, importunius, quam opportunius instans, Notariorum Palatina Societas, jam seposita in literas exitia nostrae urbis, quae in illam divinis humanisque favoribus per haec tempora intulit Canis Grandis, quae et post versis satis versa sunt contrariis successibus in auctorem, ad vestrum civiumque solatium in quempiam metricum transferre concentum, hoc postulationi vestrae subjicientes, ut et illud quodcumque sit metrum, non altum, non tragoedum, sed molle et vulgi intellectioni propinquum sonet eloquium, quo altius edoctis nostra stilo eminentiore deserviret historia, essetque metricum hoc demissum sub camoena leniore notariis, et quibusque clericulis blandimentum. Plurimum enim unumquemque delectat, quod intelligit, respuitque fastidiens, quod non apprehendit. Illud quoque Catonis, qui de moribus censuit, in exemplum adductis, quod L. Annaeo Senecae imputatur opusculum. Quod quia plane grammate vulgari idiomati fere simillimum sanctiores sententias ediderit, suaves popularium auribus inculcavit applausus. Et solere etiam inquitis amplissima regum ducumque gesta, quo se vulgi intelligentiis conferant, pedum syllabarumque mensuris variis linguis in vulgares traduci sermones, et in theatris et pulpitis cantilenarum modulatione proferri. Nihil ergo recusandum disponens, quod vestra deposcat amica suasio, fratribus meis annuens, qua licet et sciero, heroico usus metro, exigente materia populariter morem geram rudis ego cum rudibus.)[88]

The notaries asked that he not write in the "high style of tragedy," but that he use a language that was comprehensible to the crowd and a source of pleasure to the lower notarial and clerical classes.[89] The notaries' demands for accessibility of language and style are perhaps to be connected to the difficulties they would have encountered in understanding the message of

---

[88] Mussato 1999, 3–5 (*De obsidione*, Prologue).
[89] On the characteristics of the language of the *De obsidione*, see Witt 2000, 131–134; Gianola 1999, xlvi–xlix.

the *Ecerinis*, written as it was in imitation of Seneca in a meter that was rare in the Middle Ages, but also the classicizing prose of his histories. He establishes a connection between his epic poem, written in the hexameters common to Latin grammar school texts, and his historical writings in terms of the relationship between the *Distycha Catonis* and the moral writings of Seneca. The parallel establishes Mussato as both the theological poet Seneca and the vernacularizing poet who translates a privileged vision of history into more easily accessible forms. As Witt notes, however, the language of his poem is far from easy and one may doubt how much of it was actually intelligible to his audience.[90] Nevertheless, its sense would likely have been understood by the audience of notaries and novices that Mussato describes and, as Giovanna Gianola suggests, may very well have been intended to become a grammar school text alongside the *Distycha* and other post-classical Latin poetic texts.[91] Other elements of the poem would have had a powerful effect even on an illiterate public, thanks to its employment of local saints' legends and elements of liturgy.

The poem narrates in three cantos the trials brought on Padua by the siege of Cangrande in a Latin language that is less erudite and complicated than that of the *Ecerinis*. Like the prose history of these events in the *De gestis Italicorum post Henricem VII Cesarem*, there is a heavily anti-Scaligera tone and a deep suspicion of the Carrara family.[92] Given the historical context of the poem and its composition, it is worthwhile to review some of the events that led up to the siege. Following the invasion of Cangrande into Paduan lands in the Euganean Hills in 1317–18, Giacomo da Carrara organized a peace with the Veronese tyrant according to which exiled Ghibelline families would be allowed to return. This led to his election to the *signoria* and to the subsequent exile of Guelph families, including Mussato himself. Giacomo da Carrara took on full powers as *capitaneus et dominus generalis* in July 1318 as a result of this peace. When, however, Cangrande returned in 1319 after a failed attempt to take Treviso, many of the Guelph families sided with him in revenge for their exile. To appease the traditionally Guelph *popolo*, Giacomo invited back those Guelph families who had not betrayed the city. For this reason, Mussato found himself in Padua during the siege, after a brief trip to Bologna, Florence, and Siena in which he futilely asked those Guelph cities for help against Verona.

[90] See Witt 2000, 134.
[91] See Gianola 1999, xlix. On the teaching of Latin in the Middle Ages and Renaissance, see Black 2001.
[92] On the relationship between the *De obsidione* and the *De gestis Italocorum*, see Gianola 1999, xl–liii.

There are two aspects of the poem that help elucidate the civic role that Mussato tried to construct for himself in his last defense of poetry. The first is the 200-line interruption of the narrative sequence by the speech of an unnamed man, who masks the voice of the poet as he addresses the reasons for the state of the city.[93] Considering the fact that this poem would have been read aloud publicly,[94] such a speech would have had the effect of a kind of secular sermon. Second, I would like to point out how Mussato inserts aspects of the Christian supernatural into the narrative action of the poem, enacting in verse the ideas that he had expressed in his metrical letter to Fra Giovannino.

The speech opens with words reminiscent of Lucan's *De bello civili*:[95] "And someone let forth laments with a great complaint, referring the present situation to the ancient ones with a great protest" ("Atque aliquis magna fudit lamenta querela, / antiquis magno referens presentia questu").[96] The juridical language of the notaries (*querela, questu*) is mixed with the humanist approach of reading the present through the past. Indeed, this speech reads the present in a typological relationship with the past, much like biblical history was read in relation to current events. This speech is fascinating for a number of reasons that do not fall within the purview of this book but what is directly relevant here is the sermon-like tone with which it reproaches the municipal and individual morality of the Paduan citizens. Mussato does not attribute the current state of affairs to the actions of an individual citizen, or even to Cangrande himself, but he focuses on the moral decadence of the political body. Poetry, through the *prosopopea* of the anonymous man who delivers this speech, allows Mussato to distance himself from the political role he carried out for the city at the time. In this way, the poem is not mere political propaganda for his own ideology but a space in which ideology is put into question. For example, after praising the character and wisdom of the Trojan founders of Padua, who lived off the land in a kind of golden-age bliss, founding the city "beneath the omen of peace" (*sub omine pacis*), the anonymous citizen recalls the relationship between cultural memory, political stability, and the practice of vice.[97]

---

[93] See Modonutti 2017 for Mussato's tendency to include his own speeches in his historical works, including moralizing invectives. Although Mussato names himself in the third person in the histories, here in the epic he masks himself behind the Lucanian anonymous citizen.

[94] See Gianola 1999, xliv–xlv, where Ferreto Ferreti's account of Mussato's habits of reading aloud are cited. See Ferreti 1908–20, 1.6–7.

[95] Lucan 1928, 60 (*De bello civili* 2.67). [96] Mussato 1999, 13 (*De obsidione* 1.23–24).

[97] Mussato 1999, 15 (*De obsidione* 1.35).

A simple age, unaware of fraud, lives from honestly obtained gains and from the wealth of the earth. It enjoys a balanced peace, and while it values the tranquility of peace, in complete security, it defends its territories without violence. Of course, the memories of ancestral ruin warn the citizens, who mindfully recount the abominable offences of the past, and curb their burning and daring spirits. As long as the elders live the Republic lives. When they die inimical pride begins to arise. Luxury crawls forth from it, along with usury and cruel desire, with far-reaching plans to unite the spacious fields of country, but also to erect in the city high buildings in the sky, and to color wood with copper and put gold on it, to scorn the food of our fathers, and say that the legume is for animals, and to accustom our bodies to turnip juice. They decide to renew fertile dishes with better bred suckling lamb and young veal. They praise capons, and game meat, and dishes seasoned with the spices of the Arabs. They begin to despise neighboring peoples and to wish to be feared; they break the pacts of the old fathers and hatefully rescind the old law. Then envy moves into place and spite rages in hearts inciting citizens to divide into contrary pursuits, infecting the ancestral tranquility with ever growing hatred. Then suddenly factions emerge and ascend within, treachery rules, sharp worries devour anxious hearts. They devise violent plots and perhaps launch new accusations against hated citizens, so that they are able to rouse the common people rapidly to a frenzy and force the impetuous plebs to enact punishment. Alas, the plebs is always too credulous of the victors. It follows the voices of those who call out the loudest and rushes where the loud voice calls out and asserts the crime of the guilty. No faith or order of law will prevail. Let the crime committed without examination be considered civil, but only if an order of truth dissolves it after the fact. Alas, too late, does so much rage cause regret after damages have been done! Then fury, madness, and inevitable destruction entirely expel them from their own land or make their homeland available to a nearby tyrant. But it is always surprising that the credulous plebs advances without rebellion along the paths of a simple horse naturally and according to holy precept. Still, tricked by the fraud of the nobles, which it trusted too much, it undeservedly suffers cruel destruction.

(Una etas simplex et fraudis nescia vivit / de bene quesitis lucris et munere glebe, / equa pace fruens, dum diligit otia pacis / defendit suos sine vi tutissima fines. / Quippe monent cives patrie monimenta ruine / preterite qui dum memores infanda renarrant / scandala, candentes animos aususque cohercent. / Dumque senes vivunt vivit respublica, cumque / deficiunt oriens inimica superbia surgit. / Serpit ab hac luxus fenusque et dira cupido, / intuitu longo spaciosos iungere campos / rure, sed urbe domos altas extollere celo / pingere et ere trabes aurumque apponere tignis, / aspernare epulas patrum pecudumque legumen / dicere seu liquidis assuescere corpora rapis. / Decernunt pingues patinas lactentibus edis / instaurare satis melius teneroque iuvenco. / Eunuchos laudant pullos carnesque ferinas /

ferculaque ex Arabum spicis condita sapore. / Spernare finitimas gentes et
malle timeri / incipiunt veterumque irrumpere federa patrum / atque vetus
nullo rescindere fedus amore. / Tunc locus invidie, furit in precordia livor /
divisos acuens studia in contraria cives / et patriam inficiens odio excres-
cente quietam. / Tum raptim exorte subeunt in viscera partes / invigilant-
que doli, mordentes anxia cure / corda vorant que seva struant molimina
queve / forsan in exosos iaciant nova crimina cives / quo valeant rapidum
vulgus concire furore / illaque precipiti plectenda impingere plebi. / Credula
ve nimium semper victoribus illa / exequitur voces clamantum atque irruit
illo / quo vox alta sonat scelus obtestata reorum / quos non ulla fides iurisve
evicerit ordo. / Fit civile nefas comissum examine nullo; / non nisi sed veri
series post acta liquescit. / Heu sero tantum post vulnera penitet ire! / Tum
furor et rabies et inevitabile prorsus / exitium propria se se depellere terra /
vel sibi vicino patriam prebere tiranno. / Deprensum tamen est semper
quod credula plebes / seditione carens graditur per simplicis equi, / natura
monstrante, vias dictamine sancto; / fraude tamen procerum que circum-
venta suorum / fisa nimis, patitur sevas indigna ruinas.)[98]

According to the speaker, the decline of the city was due not only to its
opulence but to the loss of historical memory. The juxtaposition of the
simple golden age with the new behavior of the Paduan people pivots
around the novelty of decadent modern habits, from the decoration of
buildings to the spicing of foods. These new habits correspond to the seven
capital vices. Pride, luxury, greed, envy, and wrath are named explicitly,
while gluttony and sloth can be inferred from the behaviors themselves.
These vices lead to the division of the city into factions of noble families,
which manipulate the common people. The closing remarks aim to warn the
populace against falling unaware into the factionalism of the nobles. From a
perspective that strongly reflects his own experience of exile and conflict
with the masses and magnates, Mussato calls on the people to follow nature
and simplicity and not to be dragged into ruination and tyranny.

The speaker follows up on this list of sins and their consequences by
beseeching the people to look to the past for an example: "If someone seeks
an example from the earliest origin." ("Si petat exemplum quivis ab origine
prima").[99] Mussato aims to teach them, so to say, how to read the events of
the past, from the Trojan war to the war with Ezzelino, in a morally and
politically fruitful way. He even refers to his own *Ecerinis* as an example of
how the present may remember the past: "One of the poets, with a weeping
tragic complaint, told of these things in small volumes with Archilochian
verses." ("Hec aliquis vatum tragica defleta querela / tradidit Archilocis in

---

[98] Mussato 1999, 15–18 (*De obsidione* 1.42–87).   [99] Mussato 1999, 18 (*De obsidione* 1.93).

parva volumina metris").[100] Before going on to exhort his fellow citizens to find the reasons for the tyranny of Ezzelino in themselves, not in fate or in the wrath of God, he turns his focus back to the sin of pride:

> but do not blame these errors on hostile fates or on the extreme inflamed wrath of God; O Paduans: blame them on yourselves. It is what you deserve. Indeed, afterwards many things grew in abundance, given by the fertile earth, the sea, and the air. Opulence quickly made your minds weak and ill-advising pride invaded your spirits, then you scorned neighboring peoples in your region and you imagined no one to be as powerful as yourself.

> (non tamen he fatis culpe impendantur iniquis / aut nimis accense divini numinis ire; / o Patavi, potius meritis impingite vestris. / Nam postquam excrevit tantarum copia rerum, / quas foecunda dabat tellus, et pontus, et aer: / continuo mentes inopes opulentia fecit / invasitque animos malesuada superbia vestros, / spernere finitimas vestro sub climate gentes / et nullas vestris equas presumere vires.)[101]

Mussato's stoic outlook finds at the origin of his city's prideful behavior the opulence that wealth brought with it. He goes on to list and interpret the events of the most recent past that led up to the current strife, including the election of Giacomo da Carrara as captain-general. As a preface to the events of a war that the Paduan citizenry had only won a year earlier, its public reading must have been particularly poignant as a warning of the political ramifications of moral corruption. Mussato was trying to speak to his public's Christian moral sensibility, not only their historical and cultural memory. In this sense, the *De obsidione* as a historical epic is marked as a work of poetic theology as well, primarily in regards to ethics and politics. It uses an authority based both on the local institutions of the city and the classical authors, not to mention a Christian moralizing rhetoric. The citizens' responsibility to act in the present moment is evoked publicly within the economy of the poem in a way that parallels religious rhetoric, but without recourse to a transcendental moral universe. The examples from the past, in lieu of Christian *exempla*, serve to guide the listeners in taking action for ethical and political change. The poem enacts the parallel between poetry and theology that Mussato asserted in his letter to Fra Giovannino.

The religious rhetoric of the initial speech is brought up again at key moments throughout the poem, when Mussato inserts Christian *divinae personae* who, as Gianola has noticed, act like the pagan gods in classical

---

[100] Mussato 1999, 22–23 (*De obsidione* 1.133–134).
[101] Mussato 1999, 23–24 (*De obsidione* 1.138–146).

epic.[102] More than just the duplication of a classical literary device, however, the employment of Christian figures in poetry places human agency and divine intervention in a tension that activates the religious imagination of Mussato's audience. Events that had been ascribed only human agency in his prose history (*De gestis italicorum*) are given a deeper meaning and evoke a far greater cultural pathos by bringing the saints and even Jesus Christ into the sequence of events. For example, toward the end of the first book, when the Paduan families who had sided with Cangrande try to sneak into the city from its southern border, near Prato della Valle, where the monastery of Santa Giustina sits, it is Saint Prosdocimo who intervenes, upon direct order of God:

> The bodies of the saints wailed in their hollow tombs. They put forth a low roar and their case was heard in heaven. The Omnipotent on high listened from the highest sphere, and from among the saints he called out Prosdocimus, the patron of the Paduan people. "Why, saint, are you so slow to act?" – he said – "You have heard the groans of those who suffer in the Paduan slaughter. You see the fierce battles waged on your people. You see how much bloodshed is threatened without any fighting. You see how much blood this people of Priam has reluctantly shed already. The opening before the city gate belongs to you. There beneath it lie hidden the first group of young knights threatening to bring death."

> (Ingemuere cavis sanctorum corpora bustis / auditum celo querulum fundentia murmur. / Audiit Omnipotens spera sublimis ab alta, / sevocat a sanctis Patava de gente patronum / Prosdocimum. "Quid, sancte, facis sic segnior?" - inquit - / "Audisti gemitus Patava de clade dolentum / seva parata tue genti certamina sentis, / sentis instantes ullo sine Marte cruores / quantos vix Priami gens hec sub tempore fudit. / Urbi porta patens locus est tuus, ecce sub ipsum / prima latet minitans mortes glomerata iuventus.")[103]

Saint Prosdocimo responds that he and the other saints were saddened by their city's fate, but that they were waiting on God to do something, since he had allowed Cangrande to become so powerful. God responds that Prosdocimo cannot fathom His reasons (*nostras causas*), which the saint would surely approve if he knew them, but that there is no time to waste:

> "Hurry, now is the time to oppose these many dangers. If we delay any more with small talk, the enemy will take the valley. Descend through the thin air, go quickly, bring help, push the traitors back from the city, but let a small number of them receive punishment; the walls, let it be just enough for now that your first line of men, incited by fury to face death first, keep

---

[102] See Gianola 1987.   [103] Mussato 1999, 55 (*De obsidione* 1.584–594).

the walls safe; and when much has been overcome, you will see greater things." As if he were a white robe in the windy air, our patron jumps down into Padua and he stirs the guards lying in sleep and he quickly canvasses the valleys, carried by a white horse. He stirs the people with an uproar and rouses the entire city to be on guard. Beware, mortals, and learn of the power of spirits against whom neither weapons nor crowds nor soldiers have any power. All courage abandons their heart and fear and confusion dissolves their efforts."

("Accelera, nec enim tantis obstare periclis / tempus adest. Paulo si plus sermone moremur / hostis habet vallum. Tenues descende per auras, / vade citus, fer opem, translatos urbe repelle, / cede tamen modica dent penas; menia, primi / quos furor incendit primas impendere mortes, / sufficiat iam nunc tantum si menia servent / tuta tui; subito multo maiora videbis." / Sicut erat cana ventosa per aera palla / desilit in Patavum presul somnoque iacentes / excitat excubias et valla citissimus ambit, / candenti convectus equo, gentesque tumultu / admovet et totam tutele suscitat urbem. / Discite mortale moniti quid numina possunt / que contra non arma valent numerusque virorum / bellantumve manus. Cadit omnis pectore virtus / et confusa suos demictit cura labores.)[104]

The purpose of combining Christian elements with the style of the Roman historical epic is less hortatory than it is consolatory. Mussato is trying to represent the recent historical events that shook the city in terms that make them meaningful within a more universal narrative of history. This is not pure political propaganda, however, as Ronald Witt and Michele Feo have suggested.[105] Rather, it is meant to speak to moderately educated people (notaries and novices), who along with Mussato himself believed that God could intervene in history.

In a passage that seems to parallel the chain of grace that descends to Dante when the pilgrim is lost in the dark wood, from the Virgin Mary and Saint Lucy to Virgil, Mussato concludes the final battle by allowing for the intervention of Christ Himself. During the final battle, Mussato juxtaposes Cangrande's bold plans with the eternal design in heaven: "but another plan was sent from heaven on high." ("altera sed summo lata est sententia celo").[106] He describes a heavenly counsel in Christian terms, in which Santa Giustina consults with Christ and beseeches him to save her people, who are his faithful:

"A witness is present, if the wise Prosdocimo, who was sent to [the city] and pronounced himself by decree a disciple of Peter, taught the truth. What

[104] Mussato 1999, 59–60 (*De obsidione* 1.645–661).
[105] See Witt 2000, 124 and Feo 1991, 49–50.　　　[106] Mussato 1999, 106 (*De obsidione* 3.94).

people in this world, then, is more faithful and has built greater temples for you and your saints through all the lands in order to glorify you with everlasting worship? And yet I am virtually widowed of my [burial] place now, in my wonderful basilica; with my guardian driven out I am unhappy and abandoned. I seek nothing inauspicious. Put your hand in your quiver and just pierce Can[grande] with an arrow and, wounded, make him leave my land." The divine Son smiled on the holy girl and with his robe he dried her eyes, wet from crying. And he placed his hand on her head and gently aproved her complaint with these words: "My graceful virgin, we do not thus ignore the old deeds of Padua of the race of your father and you; but it is our opinion to treat the city of Padua with free favors, and this is on account of you and out of the love of my saints those cloisters hold."

("Testis adest, si vera sacer transmissus ad illam / Prosdocimus docuit, Petri se dogmate fassus / discipulum. Populus quisnam orbe fidelior isto / templa tibi sanctisque tuis maiora per omnes / astruxit terras cultu celebranda perenni? / Et tamen ipsa meo vix iam viduata locello, / basilica gavisa nova, nunc preside pulso / deseror infelix. Non importuna requiro. / Pone manum pharetre et saltem quacumque sagicta / fige Canem victumque mea fac cedere terra." / Arrisit sanct proles divina puelle / et flentis madidos palla detersit ocellos / apposuitque manum capiti plausitque querenti / leniter his verbis: "Non sic mea virgo decora / res Padue veteres generis patrisque tuique / negligimus; nostre sed stat sententia menti / gratuitis Patavam tractare favoribus urbem / hocque tui causa sanctorum et amore meorum / quos ea claustra tenent.")[107]

Mussato's lines both capitalize on and reinforce popular belief systems connected with the cults of saints. Christ's presence in the poem reassures the audience of His presence in history. This must have been a pressing concern for Mussato's audience, as we may infer from the chorus of the *Ecerinis*, which, in the same vein as Job and key Psalms, questioned God's role in the chain of events that led to Ezzelino's mad tyranny. The tragedy of the *Ecerinis* is replaced by the divine intervention that marks the end of the *De obsidione*. At the end of his speech, Christ tells Saint Giustina not to worry: "Ask no more. Your Padua will go away happy" ("Nec plus quere. Tuus Patavus contentus abibit").[108] At the end of the battle, when Ulrich of Walsee saves the day and an arrow hits Cangrande, Mussato suggests to his audience that it may well have been Christ:

[Cangrande] saw the long road to Monselice, bent beneath the weight of his armor and weakened by the cruel blow of the arrow, still hanging from him.

---

[107] Mussato 1999, 107–108 (*De obsidione* 3.108–126).
[108] Mussato 1999, 110 (*De obsidione* 3.146).

It is not known by whose hand it was sent, but they thought perhaps it had
been sent from heaven as you had requested, Giustina.

(Longum iter ad Montem visum sub pondere fesso / armorum et pulsu
pendentis crure sagitte. / Huius nota manus non est, sed forte putarunt /
demissam celo quam tu Iustina petisti.)[109]

By mixing the historical epic with religious elements, Mussato is descend-
ing from the high status of his role as poet of the *Ecerinis* and historian of
grand events. His "sweeter song" in the *De obsidione* may not be any easier
to understand for a mixed audience of literate and illiterate, but the
underlying theme of Christian salvation and grace that can redeem the
city in its time of need certainly reaches out to people whose faith was a
central part of their experience of the world. If Mussato declares in his
metrical letter to Giovannino that the Muses will obey the theologian,
following his orders and adoring his tracks, it is with the *De obsidione* that
Mussato himself takes over the role of theologian as poet, not in order to
confirm the political realities of the present but in order to engage with
them. Unlike Dante in the *Commedia*, Mussato elides his own presence
from the economy of the poem. He remains a poet on the outside of his
poem, in the city, while Dante stages the assumption of authority within
the poem itself. Mussato's own individual narrative of exile bears no
importance on the narrative of civic salvation that underlies the *De
obsidione*. Whereas Dante will make himself central to the possibility of
the historical redemption of Florence and of Italy that the poem offers,
Mussato's stance in the midst of the city impels him to employ his own
voice as poet against the quotidian conflicts that make life a hell on earth.

*

In conclusion, I would like to turn to the inevitable comparison of Mussato
and Dante, whose political vision of the poet will be the focus of the next
chapter. Critics such as Giorgio Ronconi have devalued Mussato's thought
in favor of the universalizing, encyclopedic vision of the universe that Dante
represents. The center of this universe lies outside the bounds of the
history of a single civic locale, as Dante himself did as an exile. For Ronconi,
the value of Mussato's poetics is primarily in its aesthetic advancement,
as is evident when he praises Mussato for considering "art a *quid* that
only the inspired can express."[110] Yet by claiming divine inspiration for

---

[109] Mussato 1999, 119 (*De obsidione* 3.240–243).
[110] Ronconi 1976, 48: "l'arte un *quid* che sa esprimere solo chi è ispirato."

poetry – a claim of authority over both spiritual and temporal matters – Mussato was not merely deifying poetry as an art: he was establishing it as an ethical and political mode of representation that works together with other forms of ideology, including theology. If he sought to raise poetry to the level of the theological, he did so because it allowed him, as a poet of the city, to try to unite the politically divided intellectuals of Padua, laymen and clergy alike, under the aegis of a universal theological vision. Unlike Dante, Mussato always directed the universality of his vatic vision onto a living civic reality. For him the convergence of the divine city and the earthly city had to happen in Padua itself.

In another of his letters (*Epistola* 9, written after 1315), addressed to a Dominican friar named Benedetto active in the monastery of Sant'Agostino, about the significance of a comet that was seen to pass in the sky, Mussato defends his position vis-à-vis the transcendental.[111] It is Mussato's response to a letter from the friar answering Mussato's questions about the nature of the comet, which he had sent to the friar (*Epistola* 8). The poet responds, perhaps to the friar's suggestion that he write a poem about celestial matters, with an erudite declaration of humility:

> I do not raise myself on high or attempt excessive flights, lest I be destroyed by a deadly fall. Phaeton, killed by the gift of his father one day, and the bloody shores of the river Po, act as warning to me. I am mindful of Icarus' fall, beneath a great witness. I wish my name to be given to no sea. Nor do I descend into the earth in order to probe the depths of dark Avernus or the black waters of the accursed Styx. I do not take great joy in visiting the shades in Hell, from where I am not so quick that I think I could return. I am not the worthy child of Jove, that Tyrinthian Hercules, nor does my club destroy the vigilant dog. I do not think that I can return safely from the Elysian Fields, like Aeneas did, accompanied by a Sybil. It is always easy for us to descend into the depths, but it is hard to return. The Thracian Bard appeased the infernal gods, but he still lost his Eurydice. I will be happy enough if I may enjoy the air of the middle world and pass my time in the common manner together with the flock.

> (Non ego me sursum tollo, nimiosque volatus / experior, casu ne graviore ruam. / Me monet occiduus patrio pro munere quondam / Phaeton, et Eridani ripa cruenta vadi. / Sum memor Icariae magno sub teste ruinae, / Nulla velim pro me nomina dentur aquae. / Nec subeo terras, ut opaci

[111] On the dating of this letter to the period between the laurel crowning and 1319, see Lombardo 2018, 61–62. See also Chevalier 2000, cxxi–cxxiv, where he suggests it was written on the occasion of the passing of Halley's comet in 1301. Chevalier also notes that it may have also been written in 1315, after the passing of another comet, which Mussato records in his *De gestis Henrici VII Cesaris*. On the identity of the friar, see Gargan 1971, 8.

scruter Averni / intima, iuratae stagna vel atra Stygis. / Non nimis inferno delector visere manes, / unde citus non sic posse redire putem. / Digna Jovis proles nec sum Tyrinthius ille, / Mactaret vigilem nec mea clava canem, / Nec velut Aeneas ulla comitante Sybilla / Tutus ab Slysiis credo redire locis. / Stat nobis semper facilis descensus ad ima, / Inde pedem tamen est posse redire labor. / Infera Threicius placavit Numina Vates, / Perdidit Eurydicem nec minus ille suam. / Sat contentus ero, media si perfruar aura, / et modo communi cum grege mixtus eam.)[112]

Mussato situates his role as a poet within the body politic, here represented as a flock. Although his authority as a poet within that flock depends upon the theological and sometimes otherworldly poetry that describes the celestial flights and katabases referenced here (the mythical flights of Phaeton and Icarus, and the descents of Aeneas in the *Aeneid*, of Orpheus in the *Georgica*, and of Hercules in Seneca's *Hercules furens*), Mussato relegates himself to the historical world.[113] He imagines a role for the poet that connects his position in the here and now to poetry's history as a means of reflecting upon God and the cosmos.

Dante will go even further than Mussato in asserting de facto and in practice the nature of poetry as a theological discourse to his role as poet in the world. Always an exile, Dante lacks the civic context that gives Mussato the place to imagine a civic role for the poet in the city. Dante was also unwilling to yoke himself politically as poet to the many benefactors who sponsored him in his exile. Unlike Mussato, who created a poetic genealogy that led to himself, Dante will equate his authority as a poet with the universalism of a theological poetry, as represented in both the classical and the biblical traditions. He will not associate it with a specific role in the political realm, among the flock, but he will use it to situate himself outside and above the city, onto which he gazes from above with a critical eye.

[112] Mussato 1722, 57, col. 46 (*Epistola* 9.21–40). On this passage, see the erudite reading in Lombardo 2018, where the possibility of an intertextual relationship between Mussato and Dante is explored in detail. Lombardo concludes that the Mussato's possible engagement with Dante in the letter does not necessitate an intimate knowledge of Dante's writings, only a general knowledge of Dante. See also Dazzi 1967, 303, which presents Mussato's refusal to write about the other world as a possible allusion to Dante; and Raimondi 1970b, 145–146, where the critic notes a possible connection with Dante. More generally on the connections between Mussato and Dante, see Lombardo 2014 and Ronconi 2017. See also Albanese 2016 and 2017.

[113] Even though Mussato later goes on to write a brief narrative poem in Latin about the afterlife, in his *Somnium* (1319), he brings the here-and-now to the underworld, representing it as a city. On the *Somnium*, see Dazzi 1964, 71–80; Pastore Stocchi 1987; and Chevalier 2000, cxix–cxlviii.

CHAPTER 2

Dante Alighieri, Poet without a City

That Dante was a poet driven by political necessity and ideology is a commonplace in Dante studies. Whether we read his *Commedia* as defined by his exile from Florence, by his championing of the return of empire and his reaction to the *nuove genti* of Florence and the cities of the Italian peninsula, or by his turn toward the city of God, Dante's politics still undergird our understanding of his life and work.[1] There is a tendency, however, to play down the political groundedness of Dante's poem in favor of an apolitical aesthetic vision or suprapolitical theological paradigm that grants the work a surprisingly ahistorical universal scope.[2] This critical

---

[1] The critical tradition on Dante and politics and on his relationship with specific cities is vast. I limit myself to citing two recent specialized studies, Honess 2006 and Keen 2003, which represent the major approaches to the question. Both scholars see the city as functioning for Dante as the "normative human community" (Keen 2003, 15; Honess 2006, 5). Honess sees Dante's poetical and theological concerns as emerging from his sense of belonging and not belonging to various human communities, from historical earthly cities to Jerusalem and the heavenly city. Keen presents a global picture of Dante's politics from the perspective of his thoughts on cities, which had been eschewed in past studies in preference for viewing Dante's political vision in terms of empire (e.g., Davis 1957 and Ferrante 1984). My own view lies somewhere in between the two scholars, with whom I concur that Dante is a civic poet, but closer to Honess' view, inasmuch as Dante abstracted his relationship to specific cities. Although I do not think that Dante's political ideology was necessarily as pious as Honess makes it out to be, I do agree that he was obsessed with making himself relevant to diverse communities, especially Florence, throughout the poem. D'Entrevès 1952 also remains a fundamental point of reference. Other important studies on Dante's political and historical vision in relation to his poetics, especially in the *Commedia*, which I have found particularly relevant to the current chapter are Mazzotta 1979, 107–146; Schnapp 1986; Steinberg 2007; and Steinberg 2013. See also Woodhouse 1997. For a survey of Italian criticism about Dante as a political thinker, see Ciampi 2009.

[2] The aesthetic approach is exemplified by Benedetto Croce's analyses of Dante, against which both the philological-historical and theological-philosophical approaches to Dante, as exemplified by Gianfranco Contini and Charles Singleton, were aimed. We can further trace these genealogies into late twentieth-century Anglophone approaches to the poem: John Freccero's Augustinian approach to Dante; Mazzotta's text-based reflections on Dante's theology and poetry and their place in the history of thought; Barolini's historicist intertextual and narratological readings of the *Commedia*; Ascoli's historically and philologically informed reflection on Dante's formulation of authority; Barański's philological-historical approach to Dante's theological poetry; and Steinberg's approach to reading Dante's works in their material and historical context. The list could go on. In

63

tendency is accounted for by Dante's poetics – it is in fact built into the poem itself, which draws both the fictional pilgrim and his authorial persona away from the everyday toward the universal.

Whereas Albertino Mussato harnessed the history of poetry as a universalizing theological discourse for local political purposes within the bounds of the city, Dante gradually builds a universalizing poetic discourse in an extramoenial non-place that as an exile he came to inhabit. While local civic issues are surely at the center of Dante's concerns, the author of the *Commedia* uses poetry to connect individual experiences with a vision of eternal design, and ultimately to subsume and reflect all of history – in order to unveil its course for the future. Yet, there is a significant point of convergence in which the two poets' concerns meet. That is, in the importance of the individual will to change the present state of things. Dante's theological poetry acts in a similar way to establish a relationship between the individual and collective responsibility and the presence of God in the human experience of history.

One of the most striking characteristics of Dante's *Commedia*, however, is that he carefully avoids linking it to a single city so that it could be claimed by one of his patrons. The expectation in the period was surely that a poem of this caliber be dedicated to the poet's most powerful or intimate patron, as Mussato had done in dedicating his *Somnium* to Florentine Bishop Antonio d'Orso. Dante's ambitions to impact the political situation in Florence, however, determine how he imagines his role as a poet. As an exile, he must construct a place outside of Florence that puts him in relation to the city, without entirely compromising himself politically by openly ascribing his poem to another civic context. That is, Dante never allows himself to become the poet of Cangrande della Scala in Verona, even if he is certainly bound to the lord by necessity and by friendship, or of Guido Novello da Polenta in Ravenna, where he chooses to live at the end of his life.[3]

my view the difficulties in historicizing Dante are the product of two medieval humanistic phenomena: first, Dante situates himself as a poet in such a way as to remove himself and his poem effectively from the realm of history (cf. Ascoli 2008, 45); second, his reception from Boccaccio onward is marked by a concerted and self-conscious effort to depoliticize (or re-politicize) the poet by representing him as a theologian. On the history of Dante's reception between Boccaccio and the Renaissance, see Gilson 2005, esp. 97–131. See Steinberg 2014 for a discussion of the tendency to de-historicize Dante, which is framed in terms of the divide between philological-historical approaches to Dante and theological-philosophical ones. For a material approach to world literature that takes Dante's *Vita nova* as its testing ground, see Eisner 2011 and 2021. See also Lummus 2011b.

[3] For a cautious historical account of Dante's life, see Inglese 2015. According to the most recent accounts, Dante arrived in Ravenna between the second half of 1318 and the first half of 1319. See

In this chapter, I aim to show how Dante establishes a role for the poet from a location beyond the city. Unlike Mussato, Dante was never involved in a public debate on the nature of poetry, so in order to demonstrate Dante's theorization and assumption of a civic role for the poet, my reading will need to address different sorts of texts. My analysis will focus on his pastoral dialogue with Giovanni del Virgilio between 1319 and 1321, in which Dante refuses del Virgilio's offer to take up residence in Bologna and to write a civic poem in Latin. My reading of the *Egloghe* will be preceded by a summative account of Dante as a public intellectual manqué in Florence and of Dante's ideas on language and poetry as linked from the beginning to cultural politics and to exile. In conclusion, I will turn to the *Paradiso* to show how the role of the poet that Dante imagines in the *Egloghe* also emerges in the *Paradiso* in terms of the humanist *poeta theologus*. If Dante has been excluded from the pantheon of early humanists because of his universalizing theological poetry, this chapter will provide the basis for reinserting him among those civically engaged poet intellectuals.[4]

Politics and Poetics: From Florence to the *Commedia*

As a poet, Dante did not have the chance to become the poet of the city of Florence in the way that Mussato was for Padua in that brief period between 1314 and 1320. Yet there is every reason to believe that by the time of his exile he was on the path to becoming that poet. Of course, his brand of municipal poetry would have been distinct from that of Mussato inasmuch as it would have emerged from an altogether different cultural milieu. Instead of the Latin-writing notaries who formed the circle of humanists known as the *cenacolo padovano*, Dante's public poetry would have emerged from the philosophical vernacular poetics of the *dolce stil novo*.

Casadei 2019, 122. For a document-based account of Dante's circle in Ravenna, see Albanese and Pontari 2018. See also Albanese and Pontari 2017. For Ravenna's importance in the reception of Dante's works, see Petoletti 2015.

[4] On Dante as humanist, see esp. Barolini 2014 and Eisner 2014. For my understanding of Dante's humanism, I am indebted to Barolini's ideas of Dante's self-conscious "cultural commingling" (Barolini 2014, 171), which is distinct from the traditional and more reductive understanding of humanism as the mere recovery of the Classics or as the philological approach to reading and writing Latin. The idea of Dante as a layman intellectually engaged in temporal matters, that is as humanist, also seems to be at the foundation of Barański's recent work. See Barański 2017. See also Dell'Oso 2017. See Ascoli 2009 for a sophisticated account of Dante's role in the creation of Petrarch's humanistic ideas.

As Zygmunt Barański has recently observed, it seems that Dante chose to enter Florentine public life as a public intellectual just as Brunetto Latini was exiting it due to his exile.[5] It is likely that Dante's *Vita nova* was intended to secure Dante's status among a circle of poet-intellectuals in Florence. This status was broadly civic in nature, even if founded upon his standing as a poet. Already in the *Vita nova*, however, there is a distance between Dante's conception of himself as poet and that of someone like Brunetto Latini, who employed poetry as one of many rhetorical tools to reinforce his standing within the civic sphere. For Dante, who was highly aware of his social difference within a circle of poets intellectually headed by a magnate like Guido Cavalcanti, his civic standing emerged in tandem with his status as poet.

When Dante is exiled, however, he is forced to rethink the terms of his status as poet and intellectual within a larger sphere. His first attempt at doing so is the *De vulgari eloquentia*, where he establishes the theoretical and historical foundations for a poetic language in the vernacular, a rhetorically constructed language that is not derived from a singular civic context. If Dante had already demonstrated a tendency toward the universal in the *Vita nova*, it is in the *De vulgari* where that tendency manifests itself as an abhorrence for the municipal. In his search for an illustrious vernacular, Dante constructs a transhistorical narrative of the vernacular lyric from which he elides local municipal poets such as Brunetto Latini and Guittone d'Arezzo. As Justin Steinberg has shown, however, "Dante is [not] unconcerned in the *De vulgari* with the links between politics and culture, but rather ... he sets up a clear distinction between the verse of those poets whose output is determined by and only intelligible within the confines of municipal politics and the larger scope, both temporally and spatially, of the texts of the illustrious poets."[6] This elan toward the transhistorical and the universal is connected to Dante's experience of exile. It will emerge as a part of his poetics in the *Convivio*, where, as Laurence Hooper observed, "his novel literary practices are dependent on his broader experience after his exclusion."[7] This is all to say that Dante's literary career after his exile takes a turn whereby his poetic practices and thus his conception of himself as a poet mirror his lack of belonging to a specific civic context. If he is the poet of exile, then this partly means that his image of a civic role for himself as poet reacts against municipal politics.

[5] Barański 2017, 7–8. Cf. Steinberg 2007, 61–94.   [6] Steinberg 2007, 103.
[7] Hooper 2012, S87. See also Ascoli 2008, 238–239 on the political concerns of the *Convivio* and *De vulgari*.

In the *Commedia*, Dante continues in a movement away from the municipal toward the universality of his poetic voice. As Teodolinda Barolini has shown, Dante's concept of the poet within the *Commedia* is restricted to refer only to classical poets and himself.[8] He carefully builds his persona vis-à-vis his contemporaries and immediate predecessors. He is always represented as having surpassed them, whether in oppositional terms, such as in his encounter with Brunetto Latini in *Inferno* 15, or in generative terms, such as in his encounter with Guido Guinizzelli in *Purgatorio* 26. With regard to his classical forebears, Dante is both bold and deferent. He quickly inserts himself within the Parnassus of classical poets in Limbo in *Inferno* 4, a poetic community that will accompany him until the end of his life.[9] This boldness is attenuated by the poetic genealogy that he creates between himself, Statius, and Virgil in *Purgatorio* 21–22. Dante's novelty as a vernacular Christian poet is underwritten by the way he relates himself to classical examples.[10]

As he constructs his status as a poet in the *Commedia*, Dante's conception of the poet's civic role is not abandoned in the name of his individual standing as author of the text. Rather, as Justin Steinberg has shown, when Virgil crowns and miters the pilgrim as master of himself in *Purgatorio* 27, Dante is staging his achievement of the status of poet as bound by his role in the community.[11] This literary performance, based on a civic ceremony, shows how aware Dante is of the nature of poetic duty vis-à-vis society. In establishing himself as poet, he continually negotiates his identity within different communities, be they imaginary or real.[12] In his self-consciousness about his role as poet and in the historical perspective that he takes in constructing that role, we can glimpse Dante's humanism. He was no artist for art's sake, nor was he a contemplative just for the sake of ideas themselves. His turn away from the world in his exile forced him to rethink his relationship to the communities that constitute human society and to imagine a role for himself founded outside the scope of any local community. We can see this thematized across the *Commedia*, especially in the *Paradiso*, but Dante's *Egloghe* provide the most vivid representation of Dante's defense of his poetic program within the humanist world of which Albertino Mussato was the most prominent representative.

---

[8] See Barolini 1984, 269–270.
[9] On Dante and the "bella scola" in Limbo, see Barolini 1984, 263–270 and Iannucci 1993.
[10] See Barolini 1984, 256–269.   [11] See Steinberg 2007, 9–10; 53–60.
[12] See Honess 2006, 151–179.

The *Egloghe:* Establishing the Poet on the Margins

In the second half of 1319, Bolognese professor and poet Giovanni del Virgilio took it upon himself to contact Dante, exhorting him to write a poem in Latin so that he could receive the laurel crown in Bologna.[13] The exchange puts Dante into contact with the humanist milieu of Bologna, which was linked with Padua both politically and intellectually, and forces him to define and defend his vernacular poetics and to assert a different kind of political role than that assumed by Albertino Mussato. In my reading of the exchange between the two men, I will show how Dante takes it upon himself not only to defend himself as a vernacular poet against the expectations of an erudite Latinate readership but also to establish himself vis-à-vis the civic context of such a readership as a poet whose authority resides beyond the confines of any specific city.[14]

---

[13] The precise dating of the *Egloghe* is difficult to establish, but there is a general consensus: del Virgilio sent his first missive between the end of 1319 and the beginning of 1320; Dante's initial response and del Virgilio's rebuttal were written and sent before the end of 1320. Dante's response dates to the summer of 1321, just a few months before his death in September. See the synthetic discussion in Casadei 2019, 122–124.

[14] Dante's *Egloghe* are among his most neglected poetic works. Recently, however, they have piqued critical interest. On them, see the critical editions and extensive annotation in Albanese 2014; Pastore Stocchi 2012; and Alighieri 2016 (ed. Petoletti), as well as Reggio 1969. I have used Petoletti's edition for the text and as my main point of reference. The only scholarly edition with an English translation remains Wicksteed and Gardner 1902. Some important recent contributions are Raffa 1996; Allegretti 2004 and 2010; Pertile 2010; Villa 2010; Annett 2013; and Combs-Schilling 2015. For an exhaustive effort to contextualize the *Egloghe* historically through archival research in Bologna and Ravenna, see Albanese and Pontari 2016 and 2017; as well as the important observations in Casadei 2019, 120–132. My reading of this exchange coincides on important points with that of Raffa, who sees Dante as placing himself "above the sign of poetic glory – the laurel crown – that Del Virgilio would like to bestow upon Dante in Bologna" (Raffa 1996, 272). Furthermore, like Combs-Schilling, I see the Dante of the *Egloghe* as mediating between the historical poet and the representation of the Dante-pilgrim and -poet in the poem (Combs-Schilling 2015, 3–4). While I agree in spirit with Annett's perspective that the *Egloghe* allow us to appreciate better how Dante engaged with the "world beyond his texts" (Annett 2013, 38), I cannot follow his principal argument that the eleven cantos of *Paradiso* 15–25 were written as an addendum to Dante's exchange with del Virgilio. See Allegretti 2004 for a discussion of the narrative complexity of Dante's first eclogue, esp. 293, where the possibility of the eclogue's continuity with *Paradiso* 15 is discussed. Pertile argues for a continuity between *Paradiso* 23 and the first eclogue, suggesting that the ten pails of milk referred to at the end of the first eclogue could be the final ten cantos of the *Paradiso*. He also provides a review of the perplexities presented by Dante's second eclogue. While I agree that there is a significant continuity between Dante's eclogues and the final ten to twelve cantos of the *Paradiso*, I see no need to link them to the exchange in terms of cause and effect. They were written contemporaneously. On the authenticity of the second eclogue, see Allegretti 2010, in which she finds a general coherence between Dante's two eclogues. The authenticity of the eclogues has often been challenged based on the hypothesis that they were forged by Boccaccio. This challenge has by now been put to rest. See, e.g., Petoletti 2016, 503–504.

The First Exchange: The Promise of the Laurel Crown and Dante's Angry Response

Giovanni del Virgilio, in a Horatian metrical letter composed in dactylic hexameters, recognizes his addressee's poetic prowess and dedication to the Muses, creating a rapport of equality between the two. Yet, he opens with an attack on Dante's choice to write a poem in the vernacular and invites him to address the true audience of poetry, scholars who are pale from study. His attack is lightly veiled by a stance of bafflement at Dante's choice to address the masses:

> Nurturing voice of the Muses, who soothes the death-flowing world with new songs, as you desire to raise it up with the vital branch, disclosing the limits of the triple fate assigned to souls according to what they deserve – Hell to the criminals, the Lethe to those who seek the stars, and to the blessed the celestial kingdoms – why, alas, do you always throw such serious arguments down to the common folk, and we who are pale from study read nothing from you, a poet?

> (Pyeridum vox alma, novis qui cantibus orbem / mulces letifluum, vitali tollere ramo / dum cupis, evolvens triplicis confinia sortis / indita pro meritis animarum – sontibus Orcum, / astripetis Lethen, epyphebia regna beatis –, / tanta quid heu semper iactabis seria vulgo, / et nos pallentes nichil ex te vate legemus?)[15]

Del Virgilio goes on to question as impossible Dante's poetic operation of teaching the "ignorant people" (*gens ydiota*) with the secrets of Heaven and Hell.[16] The Bolognese professor boldly questions Dante's choice of having written in the vernacular for an erudite audience, inasmuch as men of letters despise vernacular works, which are written in a thousand idioms.[17] Referring to the famous episode in *Inferno* 4 of the five classical poets who accept Dante as their sixth, del Virgilio reminds Dante that no classical poet, not even Virgil, wrote in the "language of the city square" (*sermone forensi*).[18] Del Virgilio here may be seen to represent the perspective of the learned Latinate academic and notarial classes of northern Italy.

This bold beginning leads del Virgilio, who is already familiar with a part of Dante's poem, to the purpose of his letter: to invite Dante to write a poem in Latin for a crowd similar to that of Mussato, on a topic of direct political relevance. He writes:

---

[15] Alighieri 2016, 516 (*Egloge* 1.1–7).   [16] Alighieri 2016, 522 (*Egloge* 1.10).
[17] Alighieri 2016, 524 (*Egloge* 1.16).   [18] Alighieri 2016, 524 (*Egloge* 1.18).

But, I pray, summon voices that can distinguish you for a poem worthy of a
Latin poet, sharing yourself with both the literate and the illiterate. Already
there are many things that call for the light of your narratives: come, speak
about the flight of the arms bearer of Jove who sought the stars; come,
speak about those flowers, those lilies that the plowman has broken; speak
about the Phrygian deer, mangled by the bite of the Molossian hound;
speak about the mountains of Liguria and the Parthenopean fleets, with
which song you can touch the Pillars of Hercules, and for which the
Danube will marvel at you and flow backwards; and the lighthouse of
Alexandria will know of you, as will the kingdom once governed by Dido.
If fame delights you, you will not be content to be encircled by a small
boundary or to be raised by the judgment of the common people.

(At, precor, ora cie que te distinguere possint / carmine vatisono, sorti
comunis utrique. / Et iam multa tuis lucem narratibus orant: dic age quo
petit Iovis armiger astra volatu, / dic age quos flores, que lilia fregit arator, /
dic Frigios damas, lacerates dente molosso, / dic Ligurum montes et classes
Parthenopeas, / carmine quo possis Alcide tangere Gades / et quo te refluus
relegens mirabitur Hyster, / et Pharos et quondam regnum te noscet
Helysse. / Si te fama iuvat, parvo te limite septum / non contentus eris,
nec vulgo iudice tolli.)[19]

The subjects that del Virgilio suggests, veiled in classicizing double-speak,
are of particular relevance for understanding the expectations of Dante's
equals in a humanist context. These lines were decoded for the first time in
glosses copied by Giovanni Boccaccio.[20] The first suggestion uses the myth
of Ganymede to veil Henry VII's failed campaign to take over Italy, which
ended with his death in 1313. The second refers to Ghibelline Uguccione
della Faggiola's victory over the Florence-led Guelph coalition at
Montecatini in 1315. The third likely refers to Cangrande della Scala's
campaign against Vicenza and Padua in 1317–18. The final suggestion
singles out King Robert of Naples' successful naval campaign against the
Ghibelline siege of Genoa led by Marco Visconti in 1318–19.[21]

---

[19] Alighieri 2016, 528–532 (*Egloge* 1.23–34).
[20] The manuscript in question is Florence, Biblioteca Medicea Laurenziana, MS 29.8 (henceforth
referenced as BML 29.8). For the text of the glosses (henceforth referenced as *Glosse*) see the first
appendix to Alighieri 2016, 632–648.
[21] I have followed the critical tradition in identifying these referents, which are based on the glosses in
BML 29.8, with the exception of the dating of the attack on Padua by Cangrande. If del Virgilio
penned this letter in late 1319, as is the general consensus, then he would probably not be referring
to the attack on Padua that was currently underway, and which would end in failure in 1320, but
rather to Cangrande's generally successful campaign in 1317–18 to maintain Vicenza and various
castles in the territory that was contested with Padua. This conflict ended in a peace treaty that saw
the repatriation of Ghibellines to Padua and the election of Giacomo da Carrara as *capitano del
popolo*, or captain of the people. Cf. Casadei 2019, 123. On this campaign, see Hyde 1966,

Each theme suggested by del Virgilio is expressly political and military, in consonance with the request that the Paduan notaries made around the same time to Albertino Mussato, but in a higher style and with a much broader scope. The first three of the four military actions that del Virgilio notes as appropriate for Dante are in line with Dante's own political views. They would be poems that recount the actions of Ghibelline heroes, dead and alive. The final suggestion, however, aims to turn Dante's creative faculties toward a conflict won by a Guelph leader of whom Dante did not have a high opinion.[22] Each suggestion has been understood by scholars as a distinct subject for a Latin poem, but it is worth noting how all four themes flow into a conclusion that addresses a single Latin poem (*carmine*) that will guarantee Dante's fame across the Latin-reading world – from the pillars of Hercules in the west to the lighthouse of Alexandria in the east and from the Danube in the north to Carthage in the south. The topics, while distinct, move in chronological order following the death of Henry VII and recount the continued conflict between Guelphs and Ghibellines across the major territories of Northern Italy up until 1319, when the epistle must have been sent.[23]

Rather than suggesting four separate subjects for a poem, it seems that del Virgilio is requesting a single Latin poem that recounts the fate of the Italian territories after the death of the emperor. For del Virgilio, a poem that brings together these diverse epic battles will guarantee Dante's fame across the old Roman empire. Del Virgilio, then, not only requests that Dante write in Latin but suggests that the poet turn his eye back toward the historical world after recounting the afterworld in his vernacular poem. The Bolognese professor links this historical engagement with Dante's fame, which cannot be disengaged from a political vision for the humanist milieu. It is important to note that del Virgilio's comment about the judgment of the common people suggests that he saw Dante's choice of subject and language as a gambit for the acquisition of fame among the people, whom he doubted could understand Dante's poetry. Unlike the extremely local topics that Mussato had taken on in the name of a

---

266–267. On the historical references in this passage, see Petoletti's notes to these lines in Alighieri 2016, 528–532.

[22] On Dante's opinion of King Robert of Naples, see *Paradiso* 8.76–93 and 8.145–148, where the pilgrim converses with Robert's brother Charles Martel.

[23] The dating of this letter is linked to the final reference on King Robert's fleets attacking Genoa, depending on when this conflict is understood to have ended. Several dates are possible between 1318 and 1320. However, July 27, 1318, when Robert was given lordship over the city for ten years, and February 5, 1319, when Robert definitively won the naval battle, seem the most likely referents. See Petoletti's note to line 29 in Alighieri 2016, 530–531 for a discussion of the question.

universal poetic authority, del Virgilio's topics speak to Dante's universalizing vision of the role of the poet, which would confer fame in the present
and future.

Del Virgilio continues by offering himself as the guarantor of Dante
who will present the future Latin poet to the academy in Bologna, where
he will be crowned with the laurel. The description that del Virgilio gives
of the imaginary ceremony is expressly military and at odds with del
Virgilio's earlier evocation of an academic readership of Dante's poetry.
He seems to superimpose onto Dante, poet-laureate/author of a militaristic
Latin epic poem, the crowning ceremony due to an emperor returning
victorious from war:

> Here I am now, the first, if you will think me worthy, clerk of the Muses,
> slave of Virgil in my name, I will be delighted to bring you forth to the
> academies, perfuming your illustrious temples with the laurel crowns of the
> triumphant, just as the loud herald, who runs ahead of the horse, congrat-
> ulates himself on announcing to the happy people the joyous victories of
> the general.

> (En ego iam primus, si dignum duxeris esse, / clericus Aonidum, vocalis
> verna Maronis, / promere gignasiis te delectabor, ovantum / inclita Peneis
> redolentem tempora sertis, / ut prevectus equo sibi plaudit preco sonorus /
> festa trophea ducis populo pretendere leto.)[24]

By penning an epic poem in Latin, del Virgilio would like Dante to
understand, Dante will succeed in becoming recognized by a local community that will embrace him. The unspoken corollary to this declaration,
however, to which del Virgilio alludes in his opening lines, is that a
vernacular poem about the afterlife will not provide Dante with the
recognition necessary for the creation of a community in which he as a
poet can act as leader (*dux*) and "restrain the heavy struggles of men"
("tantos hominum compesce labores").[25] Before concluding with an invitation to Bologna, del Virgilio tells Dante that if he does not compose a
poem about these events, then they will remain in silence. Del Virgilio's
political concerns are not so different from those of Dante. He wishes these
events to be recorded in order to respond to the brokenness of Italy, which
he sees and hears all around him: "Already my ears shrink from the
clanging of the sounds of war: why does father Apennine stand with
mouth agape in astonishment? Why does Nereus disturb the smooth
Tyrrhenian Sea? Why does Mars gnash his teeth in both directions?"

---

[24] Alighieri 2016, 532–534 (*Egloge* 1.35–40).   [25] Alighieri 2016, 536 (*Egloge* 1.44).

("Iam michi bellisonis horrent clangoribus aures: / quid pater Appenninus hiat? Quid concitat equor / Tyrrenum Nereus? Quid Mars infrendet utroque?").[26]

This letter helps to shed light on the kinds of expectations humanists had of a poet like Dante, who had never openly associated himself with another city since being expelled from Florence. The humanist poet championed by del Virgilio, whose concerns were not far from those of Mussato and his milieu, needed an urban base of action and a defined public with whom to engage. For del Virgilio, the vernacular idiom that Dante had chosen as his poetic language in the *Commedia* and the associated imagined readership among the common people would never be able to give Dante the kind of fame and impact that he presumably desired. For him, the Latin language guaranteed a poem's impact in the present, longevity in time, and comprehensibility across the multiple idioms, Romance and non, of what remained of the Roman Empire. The ceremonial recognition as poet laureate would seal Dante's potential future impact by initiating it in a specific time and place, within a specific intellectual and civic milieu.

Del Virgilio's request of Dante to become the poet of the city, the poet of post-imperial conflict, is brilliantly refuted in Dante's response in the form of an eclogue, which coopts the space of the pastoral *locus amoenus* in order to establish the poet as necessarily inhabiting a space on the margins of the city.[27] In the very choice of responding with an eclogue, Dante makes a statement about his stance as a poet. If del Virgilio evokes the epic Virgil in the voice of Horace in his exhortation of Dante to write a high-style Latin poem on war, then Dante aligns himself with the low-style Virgil of the *Bucolica*.[28] Dante sets the scene with himself as Tityrus along with a companion Melibeus (Florentine Dino Perini) sitting beneath an oak tree speaking about the epistle of Mopsus (Giovanni del Virgilio) as the goats pass by.[29] Perini/Melibeus insists on knowing what del Virgilio/

---

[26] Alighieri 2016, 534 (*Egloge* 1.41–43).

[27] Cf. Combs-Schilling 2015, 3–4, where the critic astutely recognizes that Dante "capitalizes" on the fact that the pastoral places the poet "on the margins, far from the city."

[28] On the boldness of Dante's choice, see Barański 2005, 561–562. The history of the pastoral genre with which Dante would have been familiar and which defined Virgil's *Bucolica* as *humilis* is recounted in the proem to Servius' commentary on Virgil's *Bucolica*. See Servius Grammaticus 1887, 1–4. For a discussion of the humble style as it is debated in the *Egloghe*, see Villa 2010.

[29] The identification of Melibeus as Dino Perini is derived from BML 29.8. Perini/Melibeus is continually represented as an uninitiated onlooker into the world of poetry and will be the recipient of ridicule across the rest of the exchange. See Combs-Schilling 2015, 8–9 for a discussion of how ascribing a pastoral name for del Virgilio allows the poet to place the humanist

Mopsus has written, but Dante/Tityrus dismisses him as a novice in the questions of poetry, a discipline that is represented by the very *locus amoenus* which they inhabit. Its simplicity is juxtaposed to the locale inhabited by del Virgilio/Mopsus:

> "You do not know the meadows on which Maenalus, who conceals the descending sun, casts his shadow with his high peak – fields which are painted with the varied color of grasses and flowers. They are surrounded by a humble channel, covered by the foliage of a willow, which wets the shores, from their highest edge, with its perpetual waters. Where it is placid, it freely makes itself a path for the waters, which the mountain from above sends forth. Mopsus, in these fields, as the oxen play in the pliant grass, rejoices and contemplates the struggles of men and gods. Then, blowing on his reeds, he reveals his internal joys, such that the flocks follow the sweet melody, and the domesticated lions rush down from the mountain into the fields, and the waters flow backwards, and the Maenalus fluctuates in its foliage."

> ("Pascua sunt ignota tibi que Menalus alto / vertice declivi celator solis inumbrat, / herbarum vario florumque impicta colore. / Circuit hec humilis et tectus fronde saligna / perpetuis undis a summo margine ripas / rorans alveolus, qui quas mons desuper edit / sponte viam, qua mitis erat, se fecit aquarum. / Mopsus in his, dum lenta boves per gramina ludunt, / contemplatur ovans hominum superumque labores. / Inde per inflatos calamos interna recludit / gaudia, sic ut dulce melos armenta sequantur, / placatique ruant campis de monte leones, / et refluant unde, frondes et Menala nutent.")[30]

The pastoral landscape here represents the aesthetic space of classicizing poetry inhabited by poets like del Virgilio, wherein war can be contemplated with such beauty that wild beasts become domesticated and the natural flow of rivers is reversed.[31] The simple space inhabited by Dante/Tityrus, where the work of the shepherds (to be understood as the work of poetry) is interrupted with conversation, is in opposition to the magical *locus amoenus* of del Virgilio/Mopsus' world, where poetry's effects are marvelous. Dante/Tityrus' attitude toward Perini/Melibeus seems to mock del Virgilio/Mopsus' notions that poetry can be easily impactful. In this treatment, Dante seems to intimate that a notary like Perini, exemplary of

---

"under his discursive control." See also Albanese and Pontari 2017, 330–345 for a general discussion of Dante's friends in the *Egloghe*, including Perini.

[30] Alighieri 2016, 546–548 (*Egloge* 2.11–13).

[31] The subtext here is clearly the myth of Orpheus. See Annett 2013, 51. On the myth of Orpheus in Dante in the context of medieval thought, see Barański 1997.

Dante's audience in either language, would not possess the tools to understand such poetry.

Dante continues, recognizing del Virgilio's dedication to the Muses in opposition to the pursuits of others who "bustle about to be taught the laws of the courts" ("'satagunt ... causarum iura doceri'").[32] Yet his description of the Bolognese professor goes so far in its honeyed praise that it seems almost sarcastic. He notes that del Virgilio/Mopsus "made himself pale" ("perpalluit") from spending so much time in the "shade of the sacred forest" ("sacri nemoris ... umbra") and that he "bathed in the poet-making waters, filling up his bowels with the milk of song and becoming full up to his throat" ("vatificis prolutus aquis et lacte canoro / viscera plena ferens et plenus adusque palatum").[33] This follower of the Muses, bloated and almost choking on their milk, Dante/Tityrus informs his clueless companion, has invited Dante to receive the laurel crown. Dante's tactic in addressing del Virgilio overstates his addressee's status in order to ironize it vis-à-vis that of his pastoral companion, who is not an initiate in the exclusive world of poetry, but who could be part of an audience for the *Commedia*. By beginning his response in this way, Dante establishes himself as in between the worlds of del Virgilio/Mopsus and Perini/Melibeus, the Bolognese devotee of high Latin poetry and a man representative of a Florentine audience, unschooled in classicizing poetry.[34]

Perini/Melibeus goes on to ask Dante/Tityrus what he intends to do – if he will remain in the meadows without the laurel forever. Dante/Tityrus begins to answer that the prestige of poets has all but disappeared, but then he is overtaken by a familiar indignation (*indignatio*).[35] With this indignation, Dante exclaims: "How many bleats will the hills and fields sound out, if I, with my hair made green, raise a paean with my lyre" ("Quantos balatus colles et prata sonabunt, / si viridante coma fidibus paeana ciebo!").[36] His irony and anger are directed at the idea of an incoronation in Bologna, which he describes in pastoral terms as "crags and fields that do not know the gods" ("saltus et rura ignara deorum").[37] It remains unclear what exactly Dante intends with this description of Bologna,

---

[32] Alighieri 2016, 550 (*Egloge* 2.29).   [33] Alighieri 2016, 550 (*Egloge* 2.30–32).

[34] See Combs-Schilling 2015, 10, where the hierarchical relationship established between Tityrus and Melibeus is viewed in terms of Dante's relationship with the readers of the *Commedia*. As Combs-Schilling notes, following Pertile, poetry as nourishment is a theme throughout. See Pertile 2010, 153–156.

[35] Alighieri 2016, 552 (*Egloge* 2.36–38).   [36] Alighieri 2016, 552–554 (*Egloge* 2.39–40)

[37] Alighieri 2016, 554 (*Egloge* 2.41).

which he says that he fears (*timeam*). The glosses to Boccaccio's manuscript of the text indicate that the gods are the emperors, explaining the line in terms of political factions: "of the gods: that is of the emperors, because Bologna was then against the faction of Dante" ("deorum: idest imperatorum, quia contraria parti Dantis tunc Bononia erat").[38] While it is true that Bologna would not have been a safe city for Dante, given his political ideology and background, it seems rather that with the formulation "that do not know the gods" (*ignara deorum*) Dante intends to describe a lack of civilization more generally and, perhaps, with poetic civilization more specifically. The formulation was likely taken by Dante from the eighth book of the *Aeneid*, where Evander describes the ritual feasting in honor of Hercules as not being "an idle superstition, ignorant of the gods of old" ("vana superstitio veterumque ignara deorum").[39] In this light, I see Dante as backing away from the invitation because he questions the interests of the Bolognese academy in assigning him the laurel crown. He is, in effect, rejecting the local civic model of poetry that Albertino Mussato had embodied in Padua. Desiring something more meaningful than a politicized ceremony in a single city, he does not want to limit himself to a vain celebration that will not have reverberations beyond the city limits. Dante's fear here will return in a similar context in his second response.

That Dante's principal concern was not with political factions creating a danger for him in the city of Bologna, but rather the ceremony itself, should be evident from the alternative he suggests: Florence, where he would face far greater dangers than in Bologna. Yet, the poet's relationship with the city remains marginal, even imaginary, in the lines that follow. In asking Perini/Melibeus about the possible incoronation in Florence, Dante juxtaposes his past and future self: "Would it not be better that I style my triumphal hair and hide it, since it is gray, beneath a woven bough on the shores of my native Arno, I whose hair once shone with youth." ("Nonne triumphales melius pexare capillos / et patrio, redeam si quando, abscondere canos / fronde sub inserta solitum flavescere Sarno?").[40] The question is posed in a way that demands a positive response, but also so as to indicate its unreality and impossibility. We must not forget that these lines are pronounced by Dante/Tityrus in indignation. In the opposition of the young and old Dante, the poet highlights the passage of time between his youth on the Arno and his old age – time that he has passed in exile.

---

[38] Alighieri 2016, 639 (*Glosse* 2.41).   [39] Virgil 1916–18, 2.72–73 (*Aeneid* 8.187)
[40] Alighieri 2016, 554–556 (*Egloge* 2.42–44).

Florence would be better than Bologna, but it would not turn back time. We must read these lines as consecutive with those introduced by his indignation, which begin with the ironic exclamation about the ceremony in Bologna. In consideration of the indignation of the speaker, these lines about Florence express Dante's enthusiasm about receiving the laurel crown with a significant irony. Dante is highly aware of the true impossibility of returning to Florence at this point in his life and he does not hide his bitterness.

The response of Perini/Melibeus, who has not comprehended the source of Dante's anger, naively reminds Dante/Tityrus to pay attention to the swift passage of time, noting in coded pastoral language that the *Commedia* is not yet complete.[41] Dante/Tityrus' reaction signals the bitter irony of the entire passage: he will be willing to take on a crown of laurel only upon completion of the *Paradiso*, not for some Latin epic. He makes no mention, however, of a city or a ceremony, only that he would receive the honor only for his vernacular poem: "When the bodies that surround the world and the inhabitants of heaven will be manifest in my song, just as the under regions, I will be delighted to subdue my head with ivy and laurel" ("Cum mundi circumflua corpora cantu / astricoleque meo, velut infera regna, patebunt, / devincere caput hedera lauroque iuvabit!").[42] Although critics have taken this exclamation at its word, seeing in it Dante's desire to be crowned poet laureate in Florence for the *Commedia*,[43] the context in which it is expressed is still determined by Dante's indignation. It is spoken as a sign of Dante's resentment at del Virgilio's offer, especially since del Virgilio had attacked the very source of Dante's fame as the poet of the *Commedia*. In response to del Virgilio, not only does Dante reject being the poet of a city other than Florence, which, it is important to note, he situates temporally as the place of his youth away from which he has grown old, but he also claims the honor for his vernacular poem, which del Virgilio had deprecated.

[41] See Alighieri 2016, 558 (*Egloge* 2.45–47). On the possible references to the composition of the *Commedia* in these lines, see Pastore Stocchi 2012, 174.

[42] Alighieri 2016, 558 (*Egloge* 2.48–50).

[43] It is hard to believe that Dante would have permitted himself to hope even in private, much less publicly, for a return to Florence in 1320, to say nothing about being crowned poet laureate there. The strength of the post-Boccaccian association of Dante as poet of Florence has been such that critics have failed to see that the ironic enthusiasm of Dante's response about Bologna continues in the lines about Florence. Both statements are pronounced under the sign of his indignation, which comes to its apex when he explains to Perini/Melibeus that del Virgilio/Mopsus has insulted the *Commedia*.

He therefore indirectly invites del Virgilio/Mopsus to give up on turning him away from the *Commedia* (*concedat Mopsus*),[44] reminding Perini/Melibeus that del Virgilio/Mopsus had condemned the language of the poem (*comica verba*), because "it both resounds as common on the lips of women, / and it shames the Muses to accept it" ("tum quia femineo resonant ut trita labello, / tum quia Castalias pudet acceptare sorores").[45] Dante's angry response builds to its conclusion in these lines. Because del Virgilio does not recognize the value of Dante's *Commedia* in his cultural milieu and invites Dante to write a political epic in Latin in order to be crowned poet laureate in Bologna, Dante rejects his invitation with indignation and ironic enthusiasm on all accounts. The value of his vernacular poem must be that which allows him to achieve lasting fame, but it will not take place in a city like Florence or Bologna. Rather, Dante's public authority is located in a place outside the bounds of the city in an eternal non-place and in the poetic communities created by and represented within his poem.[46] The work-related pastoral setting returns at the end of the poem, when Dante/Tityrus prepares to milk a single milk-laden sheep for del Virgilio/Mopsus (i.e., the pastoral) and promises to send ten more pails of milk.[47] He concludes by reminding his companion Perini/Melibeus to tend to the goats and to "learn how to get his teeth around the hard pieces of bread" ("et duris crustis discas infigere dentes"), indicating the hard work of being a poet and of engaging with poetry. This again highlights the differences in the worlds inhabited by the two poets, which had been suggested at the beginning of the eclogue. Dante/Tityrus and his companion inhabit a world where the poet's profession is work and not magic, where empty civic ceremonies do not consign a lasting significance on his work. The pastoral setting of Dante's response separates him from the humanist civic poetics represented by del Virgilio and Mussato and reinforces his positioning of himself as the poet without a city.

---

[44] Alighieri 2016, 558 (*Egloge* 2.51).   [45] Alighieri 2016, 560 (*Egloge* 2.53–54).

[46] In regard to the discrepancy between Dante as poet of the *Egloghe* and Dante as poet of the *Commedia*, which is argued by Combs-Schilling, I see the poet of the *Egloghe* as carrying on the work of the *Commedia* and defending it in public, not as taking a different direction. The significant differences in his authorial persona are determined by the public nature of the debate, by his engagement with an alien poetics, and by the pastoral genre itself.

[47] I find with many others that this is not, as has been the traditional reading, ten cantos of the *Paradiso* nor Virgil's *Bucolica*. Rather, with Casadei and Lorenzini, it seems more likely that it is in reference to a continued pastoral correspondence with del Virgilio. See Casadei 2013, 56–60 and Lorenzini 2011, 4–7.

The Second Exchange: Polyphemus and the False Promise of the City

Giovanni del Virgilio's response takes up Dante's choice of genre and coopts the pastoral setting. His *naïveté* in addressing Dante in such an openly critical fashion, perhaps expecting to impress the Florentine poet with his Horatian Latinity, has been checked by Dante's indignation, sarcasm, and masterful manipulation of Virgil's most humble genre. Del Virgilio's eclogue opens by establishing the pastoral setting, with del Virgilio/Mopsus sitting alone in a "natural cave" (*nativo antro*), which likely stands in for his situation in Bologna, while no one tends to the herd.[48] He claims that he has long been the only inhabitant of the woodlands, abandoned by his usual companions, while "the others rushed to the city for pressing reasons" ("irruerant alii causis adigentibus urbem").[49] Del Virgilio's first move, then, is to reestablish his stance of equality with Dante as a dedicatee of the Muses, who shuns city life. Unlike Dante's first eclogue, however, del Virgilio's response is uneconomical in its imagery and engagement with the Virgilian model-text; it overstates the pastoral environment and paints it as a place not of simplicity but of abundance and sensory overstimulation.[50]

He addresses the choice of the pastoral genre by comparing himself to Dante and by drawing a parallel connection to Virgil. In the spirit of veiled competition proper to the bucolic genre, del Virgilio seems to say that if Dante can compose a pastoral poem, then so can he: "If Tityrus sings of sheep and goats or leads herds, why ever did you sing a civic song sitting in the city? Since the pipes once of Benacus, sounding in the pastoral fashion, wore down his lips, let him hear you too, rustically, sing in the forest." ("Si cantat oves et Tityrus hircos / aut armenta trahit, quianam civile canebas / urbe sedens carmen? Quando hoc Benacia quondam / pastorale sonans detrivit fistula labrum, / audiat in silvis et te cantare bubulcum").[51] Del Virgilio realizes that he has underestimated Dante's expertise in the classics, inasmuch as he sees that Dante has rejected becoming a Horatian *vates* by styling himself as a Virgilian *pastor*. That is, Dante has rejected the high style for the low by expertly employing a classicism that Del Virgilio could recognize. The Bolognese professor's approach in this letter, then, is

---

[48] Alighieri 2016, 572 (*Egloge* 3.3).   [49] Alighieri 2016, 574 (*Egloge* 3.7).
[50] See Alighieri 2016, 574–580 (*Egloge* 3.9–24), lines which are dedicated to setting the scene for the arrival of Dante's eclogue.
[51] Alighieri 2016, 580–582 (*Egloge* 3.26–30).

defensive in relation to Dante's rebuttal. He must reassert his position as a follower of the Muses.

Del Virgilio/Mopsus then turns to praising Dante/Tityrus by equating him with Virgil, so as to link himself with Dante/Tityrus not only as a follower but as the individual to whom it is allowed to recognize Dante as a new Virgil: "Ah, divine old man, ah so you will be the second after him: you are second, or you are him, if it is permitted to Mopsus to believe the Samian poet just as it is permitted to Melibeus" ("Ha, divine senex, ha sic eris alter ab illo: / alter es, aut idem, Samio si credere vati / sic liceat Mopso, sicut liceat Melibeo").[52] Del Virgilio/Mopsus misreads Dante/Tityrus' indignation as directed solely toward Florence, which he denotes as "ungrateful city" (ingrata urbs),[53] and invites Dante to accept his friendship in terms that echo a classical marriage topos, formulated as the closeness between elm and vine: "and do not cruelly torment yourself or he, whose love embraces you so much, I say, so much, gentle old man, as the vine surrounds the lofty elm with chains tied a hundred times" ("nec te crucia, crudelis, et illum, / cuius amor tantum, tantum complectitur, inquam, / tam te, blande senex, quanto circumligat ulmum / proceram vitis per centum vincula nexu").[54] Del Virgilio/Mopsus then expresses his hope, in the form of an optative subjunctive (si ... videas), that Dante/Tityrus could see himself crowned with laurel in Florence, but invites him again, in the meantime, to join him in his cave (antrum), where they could rest and sing together. He offers Dante what he sees as the next best thing to Florence, a place where del Virgilio passes his time in leisure (otior), as opposed to the work that underscored Dante's pastoral poem.[55]

Del Virgilio/Mopsus goes on provide a long description of his cave, which he says is calling out to Dante/Tityrus. Similarly to Dante/Tityrus' description of Mopsus' locus amoenus in the preceding eclogue, del Virgilio/Mopsus' representation of his cave shows it to be a place of leisure and beauty, where everything is provided:

> So that you will come, this place itself calls you. A spring of water irrigates the inside of the caves, which are covered by rocks and fanned by brushwood; around it oregano emits its scent, and there is also the poppy, the herb that causes sleep, as they say, creating a welcome oblivion. Alexis spread out a bed of wild thyme, and I could ask Corydon himself to call him. Nisa herself, ready and willing, will wash your feet and prepare your

---

[52] Alighieri 2016, 583–584 (Egloge 3.33–35).   [53] Alighieri 2016, 584 (Egloge 3.38).
[54] Alighieri 2016, 584–586 (Egloge 3.40–43). The topos of the elm and ivy is also Christian. See Demetz 1958.
[55] Alighieri 2016, 586–588 (Egloge 3.44–51).

dinner. Testilis, in the meantime, will dress the mushrooms with pepper, which will have been mixed with much garlic to tame them, in case perhaps Melibeus will have gathered them in the gardens without care. The buzzing of bees will remind you to eat honey. You will pick apples and you will eat those that equal the cheeks of Nisa, and you will save many more, which are defended by an excessive beauty. And the ivy vines crawl over the cave with their roots, already prepared as a wreath for you. No pleasure will be missing. Come here. Here the young and old Parrasians will come, who are burning to see you and who would happily desire to admire your new songs and to be taught the ancient ones. They will bring you woodland goats and the spotted hide of the lynx, just as your Melibeus loved.

(Ut venias, locus ipse vocat. Fons umidus intus / antra rigat, que saxa tegunt, virgulta flabellant; / circiter origanum redolet, quoque causa soporis / herba papaveris est, oblivia, qualiter aiunt, / grata creans. Serpilla tibi substernet Alexis, / quem Corydon vocet ipse rogem: tibi Nisa lavabit / ipsa pedes accincta libens cenamque parabit; / Testilis hec inter piperino pulvere fungos / condiet, et permixta doment multa allia, siquos / forsitan imprudens Melibeus legerit hortis. / Ut comedas apium memorabunt mella susurri. / Poma leges Niseque genas equantia mandes / pluraque servabis nimio defensa decore. / Iamque superserpunt hedere radicibus antrum, / serta parata tibi. Nulla est cessura voluptas. / Huc ades; huc venient, qui te pervisere gliscent, / Parrasii iuvensque senes, et carmina leti / qui nova mirari cupiantque antiqua doceri. / Hi tibi silvestres capreas, hi tergora lincum / orbiculata ferent, tuus ut Melibeus amabat.)[56]

The glossator whose marginalia Boccaccio transcribed finds in this overwrought description clear signs of the Bolognese academy, whereby the oregano signifies philosophy, the mushrooms are the sayings of the ancients, and the buzzing of the bees indicates the sentences of poetic fables.[57] This kind of one-for-one allegorical interpretation, while not entirely unfeasible, is unnecessary. It is enough to note the kind of life that is offered to Dante in these pastoral caves. Dante/Tityrus' status in the pastoral environment of labor that the poet had described in the previous eclogue causes del Virgilio to describe Dante/Tityrus, an exile, as a simple laborer: "covered in dust you are dressed in a coarse mantle" ("pulvereus . . . stes in tegmine scabro").[58] Del Virgilio offers him instead a place where every pleasure will be his and where he will be attended by his Arcadian admirers. It is somewhat unclear what precisely the new and ancient songs indicate in this passage. It seems likely, however, given the shift in verb from the deponent "admire" (*mirari*) to the passive "to be

[56] Alighieri 2016, 588–592 (*Egloge* 3.52–71).   [57] Alighieri 2016, 643 (*Glosse* 3.52–68).
[58] Alighieri 2016, 584 (*Egloge* 3.36).

taught" (*doceri*) that the new songs are Dante's poems, be they the
Commedia and the *Egloghe* or solely the latter, while the ancient songs
are classical Roman poetry.[59]

Turning toward his conclusion, del Virgilio has Mopsus beseech Dante/
Tityrus not to fear Bologna, where the abundant pastoral landscape will act
as guarantee. He interprets Dante/Tityrus' fear as political: "Here there are
not plots or injustices, as much as you believe them to be" ("Non hic
insidie, non hic inuria, quantas / esse putas").[60] He then offers himself as
guarantor of the poet's safety, assuming dominion over the city: "Do you
not believe me who loves you? Do you perhaps look down upon my
kingdoms?" ("Non ipse michi te fidis amanti? / Sunt forsan mea regna tibi
despecta?").[61] Del Virgilio confronts Dante's dismissal of his offer by
making it a question of friendship and trust, and by claiming a political
power over the city. He questions Dante's allegiances by insinuating that
Dante's political associations outweigh his friendship in poetry with del
Virgilio. This becomes clearer in the following lines, where del Virgilio/
Mopsus suggests that Dante/Tityrus is reticent to come to Bologna
because of Guido Novello da Polenta, who is represented with the pastoral
name Iollas: "Mopsus, why are you foolish? Because Iollas will not allow it;
he is courteous and sophisticated, while your gifts are rustic, and a cave is
not now safer than those huts, in which he may sing more opportunely."
("Mopse, quid es demens? Quia non permittet Iollas / comis et urbanus,
dum sunt tua rustica dona, / hisque tabernaculis non est modo tutius
antrum, / quis potius ludat").[62] Thus, del Virgilio suggests that Dante has
a political obligation to his lord in Ravenna, who is keeping him safe and
giving him a space to be a poet. He is challenging Dante's reticence to
become a poet of the city by describing him as a poet of the court.

In closing, del Virgilio reiterates his admiration and thence love of
Dante, but he warns the poet that he is not unreplaceable: "Scorn me;
I will alleviate my thirst with the Phrygian Muson, that is – don't you
know? – I will drink from my ancestral river" ("Me contempne; sitim
Frigio Musone levabo, / scilicet, hoc nescis?, fluvio potabor avito").[63] The
river Muson, to which these lines refer, is a river in Padua, which is
commonly denoted as Phrygian due to its mythological origins with the
Trojan Antenor.[64] The allusion here is clearly to Albertino Mussato,

---

[59] On the debate about this line, see Petoletti's note to line 69 in Alighieri 2016, 592.
[60] Alighieri 2016, 592 (*Egloge* 3.75).   [61] Alighieri 2016, 592 (*Egloge* 3.76–77).
[62] Alighieri 2016, 594 (*Egloge* 3.80–83).   [63] Alighieri 2016, 596 (*Egloge* 3.88–89).
[64] On the myth of Antenor in Padua, see Beneš 2011, 39–62.

whom del Virgilio met during that period and to whom he threatens to turn in the event of Dante's further refusal.[65] This final effort to convince Dante to take up a place within a civic and academic context will ultimately fall on deaf ears. It fails to address Dante's principal concerns about his *Commedia* and about its place in the world. In Dante's view, his authority as poet is achieved and recognized within the poem itself.[66] His exile from Florence determines that the civic context to which he is attached as a poet must always be constructed in *via negativa*. That is, the civic context must remain Florence, to which he is bound by the nomenclature of exile and absence, as "undeserved exile" and "Florentine by birth, not habit" ("exul inmeritus" and "Florentinus natione, non moribus").[67]

Dante's response to del Virgilio's appeal aims both to explain his reticence to take up residence as poet laureate in Bologna and to under- score the appeal of Ravenna, where he is free and autonomous. Dante's final eclogue opens with a grandiose description of his current locale that evokes astrological signs in a manner that has been recognized as recalling certain *loci* of the *Commedia*:[68]

> Swift Eoos, released from the fleeces of Colchis, and the other wing-footed steeds were bearing the beautiful Titan. The orbit, where it first began to be bent from its summit, held each chariot-bearing wheel in equilibrium, and the things that shine with light, which are usually overcome by the shadows, conquered the shadows and made the fields seethe with heat. On account of this, Tityrus and Alphesibeus fled to the forest and each felt pity for himself and for his sheep.

> (Velleribus Colchis prepes detectus Eous / alipedesque alii pulchrum Titana ferebant. / Orbita, qua primum flecti de culmine cepit, / currigerium cantum libratim quemque tenebat, / resque refulgentes, solite superiarier umbris, / vincebant umbras et fervere rura sinebant. / Tityrus hec propter confugit et Alphesibeus / ad silvam pecudumque suique misertus uterque, / fraxineam silvam, tiliis platanisque frequentem.)[69]

---

[65] In fact, the Bolognese professor will write to Mussato with an eclogue several years later, in 1327, shortly before the latter's death. See Lorenzini 2011, 175–195.

[66] I refer here generally to Ascoli 2008, on the poet's lifelong reflection on authority. This topic will be addressed more directly in the following section.

[67] These are the descriptors that Dante uses in his correspondence. He uses *exul inmeritus* in the opening lines of *Epistole* 3, 5, 6, and 7, where he also refers to himself as *Florentinus*. See Alighieri 2016, 80; 102; 132; 154. He employs *Florentinus natione, non moribus* in the opening lines of *Epistola* 13, his letter to Cangrande. See Alighieri 2016, 326.

[68] See Albanese 2014, 1756. On astrological incipits in the *Commedia*, see Cornish 2000.

[69] Alighieri 2016, 600–604 (*Egloge* 4.1–9).

These opening lines enact several operations that set the stage for the rest of the poem.[70] First of all, by describing the time of day in astrological terms,[71] the poet situates himself in the world as seen from a cosmological perspective. The researched mythological terms for the movement of the sun then shifts directly into a vivid description of the heat of the day, which causes the two shepherds Dante/Tityrus and Alphesibeus, perhaps the physician Fiduccio de' Milotti, to take refuge in the woodlands.[72] The moment of the poem, then, is circumscribed within a typical pastoral moment of forced leisure that is in opposition to the opulence described in del Virgilio's eclogue. Dante's place in the world is furthermore out in the open, beneath the movement of the sun and stars, not within a cave, such as that offered by del Virgilio/Mopsus. Finally, these lines complicate the bucolic genre inasmuch as they recount the pause in labor of the two shepherds in the third person, from without. The entire eclogue is recounted from this outside perspective, as if the author of the *Commedia* were looking down upon the pastoral environs in which the poem's action is staged.[73]

As Dante/Tityrus lies down on a bed of poppies beneath a maple tree and de' Milotti/Alphesibeus stands leaning against a pear-wood staff, the latter begins to speak in similarly grandiose, philosophical terms about human nature. Beginning with the nature of the human soul, he concludes by questioning del Virgilio/Mopsus' desire to live in Bologna:

> "I am not amazed," he was saying, "that the minds of men are carried to the stars, whence they came to be, when new they came into our bodies, because white birds like to fill the Caystros with sound, happy with the temperate weather and the marshy valley; because the fish of the sea come together and leave the sea, where the rivers first touch the borders of Nereus; because the Hyrcanian tigers taint the Caucasus with blood; and because in Libya the serpent sweeps the sands with its scales. For each likes things that are similar to its life, Tityrus. But I am amazed, and all the other shepherds with me that inhabit the fields of Sicily are amazed as well, that Mopsus likes the arid rocks of the Cyclopes beneath Aetna."

---

[70] See Raffa 1996, 276–277. He sees here in the reference to the myth of the Golden Fleece a part of an allegory about the dangers of prizes, which he connects to the later reference to Midas' golden touch.

[71] For a reading of the opening lines as indicating the time of day and not a season, see Casadei 2013, 57.

[72] On Fiduccio de' Milotti, see Albanese and Pontari 2017, 346–375.

[73] It is likely that Dante completed the *Paradiso* before penning this eclogue. See, e.g., Reggio 1969, 18–20; Bologna 2010, 150; and Casadei 2013, 196–200. See Combs-Schilling 2015, 22 n. 19 for a discussion of the question.

("Quod mentes hominum" fabatur "ad astra ferantur, / unde fuere, nove cum corpora nostra subirent, / quod libeat niveis avibus resonare Caistrum, / temperie celi letis et valle palustri, / quod pisces coeant pelagi pelagusque relinquant, / flumina qua primum Nerei confinia tangunt, / Caucason Hyrcane maculent quod sanguine tigres / et Libies coluber quod squama verrat harenas, / non miror: nam cuique placent conformia vite, / Tityre. Sed Mopso miror, mirantur et omnes / pastores alii mecum Sicula arva tenentes, / arida Ciclopum placeant quod saxa sub Ethna.")[74]

By setting the scene newly in Sicily and the question of del Virgilio's allegiance to Bologna within a philosophical *quaestio* about nature, Dante highlights the force of his celestial *incipit*. His privileged position there, which resembles that of the poet looking down on "the little threshing floor that makes us so ferocious" ("l'aiuola che ci rende tanto feroce") of *Paradiso* 22, is here represented in terms of the philosophical distance of the two shepherds' discussion.[75] The geographical locales mentioned by de' Milotti/Alphesibeus indicate positions to the east and south of Sicily, which are comprehensible despite their exoticism.[76] Without questioning del Virgilio as a poet, as he did in the first eclogue, Dante is nevertheless able to put into question the very identity of his interlocutor. Either del Virgilio is naturally attracted to the locale that perturbs Dante or he is there unnaturally. Dante reasserts his control over the representation of del Virgilio. The anger of the first poem has transformed here into a detached perplexity.

The awkwardness of Dante's tactics in this eclogue of both relocating the pastoral setting to Sicily and composing it from the perspective of a third person has caused some critics to postulate that he died before completing it or that he did not write it at all.[77] The shift of the pastoral landscape causes confusion in the references behind each symbolic locale. The caves of the Cyclopes beneath Aetna are early on identified with del Virgilio's Bolognese academy, while Dante's Ravenna remains hidden in the pastoral cipher, described in line 46 as the "dewy fields of Pelorus"

---

[74] Alighieri 2016, 606 (*Egloge* 4.16–27).

[75] Alighieri 2011, 444–445 (*Paradiso* 22.151). For the Italian text of the *Commedia* and the English translation, I have followed the three-volume edition by Durling and Martinez, which follows Petrocchi's text in the main.

[76] On the classical sources for these allusions, see the notes to these lines in Alighieri 2016, 606–607. The Caystro was a river in Lydia near current-day Izmir. Nereus, a god of the sea, was thought to inhabit the Aegean Sea. The Caucasus and Hyrcania indicate the area between the Black Sea and the Caspian Sea. Libya indicates the eponymous area in North Africa. On Dante's geographical imagination, see Cachey 2014.

[77] For a discussion of the question of authenticity, see Petoletti's note to line 70 in Alighieri 2016, 621.

("roscida rura Pelori"), in modern day Punta del Faro, near Messina. Later on, however, in line 66, Dante/Tityrus divulges to de' Milotti/Alphesibeus that del Virgilio/Mopsus

> thinks that I live on the right shore of the Po, to the left of the Rubicon, where the Adriatic Sea borders the land of Emilia, and recommends to us the meadows of the shores of Aetna, not knowing that the two of us live in the soft grass of the Sicilian mountain, than which no other Sicilian mountain more fertilely feeds its sheep and cattle.

> (litora dextra Pado ratus a Rubicone sinistra / me colere, Emilida qua terminat Adria terram, / litoris Ethnei commendat pascua nobis, / nescius in tenera quod nos duo degimus herba / Trinacride montis, quo non fecundius alter / montibus in Siculis pecudes armentaque pavit.)[78]

According to Dante/Tityrus' description, del Virgilio/Mopsus has mistakenly understood that Dante is in Ravenna, while he is actually in an imaginary pastoral version of Sicily. Later on, as well, the pastoral references rise to the surface, when de' Milotti/Alphesibeus expresses his hope that Dante/Tityrus never leave his pastures: "Ah, my life, I pray you, may the accursed pleasure never overcome you, such that the Reno and that Naiad close up that illustrious head of yours, for which the pruner already hurries to choose the perpetual leaves on the high virgin" ("Ha, mea vita, precor, nunquam tam dira voluptas / te premat, ut Rhenus et Nayas illa recludat / hoc illustre caput, cui iam frondator in alta / virgine perpetuas festinat cernere frondes").[79] That is, de' Milotti/Alphesibeus reveals the reality behind the pastoral cipher of del Virgilio/Mopsus' location. We must then contrast this to the fact that Dante/Tityrus denies the correspondence between the pastoral cipher of his location in Pelorus and his actual location in Ravenna. The effect of estrangement is undeniable. The readings of this estrangement as accidental or as the result of interpolation by another poet after Dante's death are unsatisfactory.[80] Rather, I suggest that Dante purposefully maintains the distance between his historical location and that of the imaginary pastoral cipher in order to reinforce the fact that he is not beholden to his patron in Ravenna.

Dante has good reason to maintain this ambiguity. In this eclogue, his goal is to respond to the insinuation that he is kept in Ravenna by Guido

---

[78] Alighieri 2016, 620–622 (*Egloge* 4.67–72).   [79] Alighieri 2016, 620–622 (*Egloge* 4.84–87).
[80] See Combs-Schilling 2015, 24 n. 32 for a discussion of the question. I generally agree with Combs-Schilling's assessment of the shift to Sicily as exemplary of Dante's effort to control the representation of del Virgilio within the pastoral space, though I think it is also connected to the eclogue's underlying operation of undermining del Virgilio and questioning his intentions.

Novello da Polenta and also to defend his rationale for not going to Bologna. Thus, he insinuates the lack of correspondence between his pastoral locale and Ravenna and explains his fear of visiting del Virgilio in Bologna. In regard to this latter question, Dante had declared in his previous eclogue that he feared "the fields that do not know the gods." I have suggested that we should understand Dante's fear here in general terms of civilization: in Dante's eyes, Bologna lacked a sincere cultivation of poetry that could truly appreciate his poem. It would subjugate his authority as poet to a local role in the city. In this final eclogue, Dante explains through the pastoral cipher the precise nature of this fear.

As the two shepherds are resting under the shade of the maple tree, Perini/Melibeus arrives out of breath with del Virgilio/Mopsus' eclogue. A group of older shepherds tease him about what could be so important to cause such a rush, but he lets his pipes speak for him and plays the first line of the eclogue.[81] Having understood immediately, de' Milotti/Alphesibeus expresses his concern that Dante/Titryus will leave Pelorus for the "cave of the Cyclops" ("antrum Ciclopis"), that is leave Ravenna for Bologna.[82] Dante/Tityrus responds with confusion, wondering why his friend would doubt him or put him to the test. De' Milotti/Alphesibeus then offers a summary of his worries veiled in a mythological cipher:

> "Do you not hear the flute make sounds by virtue of a spirit and similar to the reeds born from the murmur, the murmur that showed the most disgraceful temples of the king, who stained the sands of the Pactolus by order of Bromius? That it calls you to the shore of Aetna covered in pumice, blessed old man, do not believe the false acclamation, but have compassion for the Draiads of this place and of your sheep. The hills, the crags, the rivers will cry over you if you leave as will the nymphs with me, fearful of the worst, and the envy that Pachinus now feels will fall upon us. It will also grieve us shepherds to have met you. Blessed old man, do not wish to desert the springs and well-known fields, depriving them of your long-lived name."

> ("Tibia non sentis quod fit virtute canora / numninis et similis natis de murmure cannis, / murmure pandenti turpissima tempora regis / qui iussu Bromii Pactolida tinxit harenam? / Quod vocet ad litus Ethneo pumice tectum, / fortunate senex, falso ne crede favori, / et Driadum miserere loci pecorumque tuorum. / Te iuga, te saltus nostri, te flumina flebunt / absentem et nymphe mecum peiora timentes, / et cadet invidia quam nunc

---

[81] On the levity of this episode within the economy of the poem's mocking critique of del Virgilio, see Raffa 1996, 279.
[82] Alighieri 2016, 614 (*Egloge* 4.46–47).

habet ipse Pachinus. / Nos quoque pastores te cognovisse pigebit. / Fortunate senex, fontes et pabula nota / desertare tuo vivaci nomine nolis.")[83]

The first four lines of this passage allude to specific elements of the myth of Midas. First, Perini/Melibeus' pipes are compared to the reeds that divulge to the four winds the shame of Midas' donkey ears, which he had earned in punishment for opposing Apollo in his singing contest against Pan.[84] Second, the following lines refer to how Midas was able to undo his mistake of requesting that everything he touch turn to gold. Bacchus tells him to wash his head in the Pactolus river, whereby the river takes on the quality of bearing gold.[85] The first allusion evokes the consequences of his poor judgment of music, which are connected to unwanted fame that results in public shame. The second allusion points to the consequences of greed, which were already associated with the story of Midas in Dante's *Purgatorio*.[86] De' Milotti/Alphesibeus seems to be showing Dante/Tityrus that the correspondence with del Virgilio/Mopsus is affecting the poet's reputation, presumably because of the insinuation that he would be motivated by greed to take up residence in Bologna.

This interpretation of these allusions is reinforced by de' Milotti/Alphesibeus' exhortation of the poet not to believe in del Virgilio/Mopsus' false goodwill (*falsus favor*).[87] He goes on to exhort the poet to remain and not to deprive his companions (in Ravenna) of his name, lest they regret ever having met him. This would cause not only sadness but envy, which has already beset another city, referred to here as Pachinus – a mountain of Sicily that some have connected to Verona.[88] There are two important elements that emerge from these lines: (1) Dante represents his companions as worried that his reputation will be sullied by moving to Bologna, and (2) at least three cities are represented as desiring to link themselves to his fame. The representation of the poet's relationship to a civic context, which will have lasting effects on his posthumous fame, is his principal concern here. Thus, these lines harken back to Dante/Tityrus' rejection in the previous poem of the idea that a Latin epic poem would be that which can guarantee his fame. In Dante's eyes, such a poem would be potentially damaging. He is aware that the city in which he takes up residence will

---

[83] Alighieri 2016, 614–618 (*Egloge* 4.50–62).
[84] See Ovid 1926, 2.130–133 (*Metamorphoses* 11.146–193).
[85] See Ovid 1926, 2.130–133 (*Metamorphoses* 11.85–145).
[86] Alighieri 2003, 330–331 (*Purgatorio* 20.106–108).   [87] Alighieri 2016, 616 (*Egloge* 4.55).
[88] See Petoletti's note to line 59 in Alighieri 2016, 618 for a discussion of the question of the identity of Pachinus.

feed off of his reputation, just as much as he knows that his reputation itself will be affected by the nature of his relationship with that city.

In his response to de' Milotti/Alphesibeus, Dante/Tityrus seeks to assuage his companion's doubts and fears by describing his relationship with him and with del Virgilio/Mopsus in terms of friendship: "'Oh, you who are deservedly more than half of this breast,' said the long-lived Tityrus, and he touched his own breast, 'Mopsus, who is connected with me by an equal love on account of those women who fearfully fled Pyreneus, who burned wrongly for them'" ("'O plus quam media merito pars pectoris huius' (atque suum tetigit) longevus Tityrus inquit, 'Mopsus amore pari mecum connexus ob illas / que male gliscentem timide fugere Pyreneum'").[89] Thus, Dante/Tityrus aims to put at ease his companion's insinuations about the possible motives that could attract him to leave Ravenna. If he were to join del Virgilio/Mopsus, then it would be in the terms of a friendship defined by a genuine love of poetry. Dante is careful, however, to juxtapose del Virgilio's association with him through a shared love of the Muses with the mad desire of Pyreneus, who had trapped the Muses in his home in order to rape them.[90] If the equation of his friendship with the two men, which seems to define by extension his connection with each civic context, functions rather clearly to deflate the underlying suggestion that he would go to Bologna for financial gain, then the juxtaposition of del Virgilio/Mopsus and Pyreneus opens an ambiguous space that recalls the original doubts about del Virgilio/Mopsus' nature expressed at the beginning of the eclogue. On the one hand, del Virgilio/Mopsus is represented in a positive light, inasmuch as Dante/Tityrus is linked to him in an intellectual friendship founded upon a mutual admiration of the Muses. On the other hand, by defining the Muses in terms of their escape from rape at the hands of Pyreneus, Dante leaves open the possibility that del Virgilio's love of the Muses may be a kind of false veneration. This last perspective may, then, recall Dante's preoccupation with the "fields that do not know the gods" in his first eclogue, which I have linked to Dante's suspicion that the incoronation promised by del Virgilio would be an empty gesture. It may, thus, signal to del Virgilio Dante's persistent concern about the Bolognese professor's intentions in lavishing him with praise.

After explaining to de' Milotti/Alphesibeus that del Virgilio/Mopsus mistakenly thinks him to be located in Ravenna and not in Pelorus,

---

[89] Alighieri 2016, 618–620 (*Egloge* 4.63–66).
[90] See Ovid 1926, 1.256–259 (*Metamorphoses* 5.273–293).

Dante/Tityrus advances the notion that he would in fact visit his fellow devotee of the Muses, were it not for his fear of Polyphemus: "But, although the rocks of Aetna must be placed after the green land of Pelorus, I would leave this flock and go to see Mopsus, if I did not fear you, Polyphemus" ("Sed quanquam viridi sint postponenda Pelori / Ethnica saxa solo, Mopsum visurus adirem / hic grege dimisso, ni te, Poliphemo, timerem.").[91] The nature of Dante's fear here has been linked to his fear of persecution by the Guelphs of Bologna, as embodied by Polyphemus. The Cyclops has been linked to several historical figures, but most strongly to Fulcieri de' Calboli, who had been recently elected *capitano del popolo* in Bologna.[92] Yet, the glossator copied by Boccaccio, who is always ready to decipher the pastoral allegories of these poems, merely notes that "he was a Cyclops, about whom Virgil writes near the end of the third book of the *Aeneid*" ("Ciclops fuit, de quo Virgilius En(eydos) III° circa finem").[93] While it is possible that Dante had in mind possible persecution and it is not inconceivable that he had in mind specifically Fulcieri de' Calboli, I aim to explain the function of Polyphemus within the economy of the del Virgilio-Dante correspondence itself, keeping in mind especially the fact that Dante is in effect positioning himself as a poet in contrast to the designs of del Virgilio and his Bolognese academy. I would like to suggest, in this light, that Dante invokes Polyphemus here as a response to del Virgilio's invitation to visit him in his cave (*antrum*) in order to express with unfailing vividness his fears about the nature of the city that would celebrate him as poet laureate and of the individual who was leading the city's effort.

The operation of shifting the pastoral setting from a Virgilian Arcadia to the Sicily of Theocritus-via-Ovid has allowed Dante to respond to del Virgilio's insistent reference to his own pastoral location as a cave, as Pertile notes. Dante's response has also already brought up del Virgilio/Mopsus' cave in terms of the "arid rocks of the Cyclopes" in the opening conversation about why he has chosen them and in de' Milotti/Alphesibeus' worry that Dante/Tityrus would abandon Pelorus for the "cave of the

---

[91] Alighieri 2016, 622 (*Egloge* 4.73–75).

[92] For a review of the questions opened by this enigmatic figure, see Petoletti's note to line 75 in Alighieri 2016, 622–624. See also the new historical evidence presented in favor of Polyphemus as Calboli in Albanese and Pontari 2016, esp. 24–37. While the archival material the authors present in favor of this reading makes the identification verisimilar, it does not make it necessary. Importantly, however, the authors have confirmed that Calboli was already in Bologna as *capitano di guerra* before becoming *capitano del popolo*. On the verbal link between Polyphemus and del Virgilio's description of his abode as a cave, see Pertile 2010, 163.

[93] Alighieri 2016, 647 (*Glosse* 4.75).

Cyclops." The invocation of Polyphemus, which may be the very element that defines the new Sicilian setting, is consonant with the pastoral framing of the poem in Sicily. It also allows Dante to elaborate on his reservations about the "fields that do not know the gods," inasmuch as the Cyclopes were typically representative of the uncivilized and uncouth.[94] Furthermore, Polyphemus, who will be described in the verses that follow in relation to his role in the Ovidian tale of the nymph Galatea, is linked thematically with the mention of Pyreneus inasmuch as both were abusers of poetry and potential rapists. If Pyreneus had captured the Muses in order to take advantage of them with violence, Polyphemus – in Ovid's masterful parody of Theocritan rustic simplicity – took on the garb of a pastoral poet in order to woo Galatea away from her lover Acis, hiding his violence beneath a facile transformation. In exhibiting his fear of Polyphemus, Dante is identifying himself with Galatea and, by association, with the Muses. I will now turn to the Ovidian intertext in order to show how it responds to Dante's concerns with Bologna and Giovanni del Virgilio.

At the end of Book 13 of Ovid's *Metamorphoses*, Galatea tells to Scylla (near Pelorus) the story of her love for Acis and her struggle against Polyphemus, beginning with these lines, from which Dante takes the vocative address of the Cyclops (*Polipheme*):[95]

> Him [Acis] did I love, but the Cyclops loved me with endless wooing. Nor, if you should ask me, could I tell which was stronger in me, my hate of Cyclops or my love of Acis; for both were in equal measure. O mother Venus, how mighty is thy sway! Behold, that savage creature, whom the very woods shudder to look upon, whom no stranger has ever seen save to his own hurt, who despises great Olympus and its gods, he feels the power of love and burns with mighty desire, forgetful of his flocks and of his caves. And now, Polyphemus, you become careful of your appearance, now anxious to please; now with a rake you comb your shaggy locks, and now it is your pleasure to cut your rough beard with a reaping-hook, gazing at your rude features in some clear pool and composing their expression. Your love of slaughter falls away, your fierce nature and your quenchless thirst for blood; and ships come and go in safety.

> (hunc [Acidem] ego, me Cyclops nulla cum fine petebat. nec, si quaesieris, odium Cyclopis amorne / Acidis in nobis fuerit praesentior, edam: / par

---

[94] Cf. Ascoli 2009, 129. It is worth noting, in this regard, that Giovanni del Virgilio himself had interpreted Polyphemus in his *Allegorie librorum Ovidii Metamorphoseos* as a figure for corruption, especially moral corruption of the heart. See Del Virgilio 1933, 98 (*Allegorie* 13.6). Cf. Raffa 1996, 283–284.

[95] See Pertile 2010, 165 n. 29.

utrumque fuit. pro! quanta potentia regni / est, Venus alma, tui! nempe ille
inmitis et ipsis / horrendus silvis et visus ab hospite nullo / inpune et magni
cum dis contemptor Olympi, / quid sit amor, sentit validaque cupidine
captus / uritur oblitus pecorum antrorumque suorum. / iamque tibi formae,
iamque est tibi cura placendi, / iam rigidos pectis rastris, Polypheme,
capillos, / iam libet hirsutam tibi falce recidere barbam / et spectare feros
in aqua et conponere vultus. / caedis amor feritasque sitisque inmensa
cruoris / cessant, et tutae veniuntque abeuntque carinae.)[96]

In these lines, Galatea describes how, in the name of love, Polyphemus
changed his ways from someone who not only did not know the gods but
who despised them, into an exemplar of a narcissistic individual who cares
about his appearance and puts an end to his savage violence in order to
capture the object of his desire. The change will be short-lived, since the
ultimate expression of his love will be the murder of Acis, an episode that
de' Milotti/Alphesibeus will go on to recount in Dante's second eclogue.[97]

In Galatea's story, Polyphemus is represented as a grotesque version of a
pastoral poet, while he prepares to sing Galatea a love song:

Hither the fierce Cyclops climbed and sat down on the cliff's central point,
and his woolly sheep, all unheeded, followed him. Then, laying at his feet
the pine-trunk which served him for a staff, fit for a vessel's mast, he took
his pipe made of a hundred reeds. All the mountains felt the sound of his
rustic pipings; the waves felt it too.

(huc ferus adscendit Cyclops mediusque resedit; / lanigerae pecudes nullo
ducente secutae. / cui postquam pinus, baculi quae praebuit usum, / ante
pedes posita est antemnis apta ferendis / sumptaque harundinibus conpacta
est fistula centum, / senserunt toti pastoria sibila montes.)[98]

The Cyclops' pastoral tools are enlarged almost so as to become laughable.
His staff is not made of pine but is an actual pine tree, while his one
hundred-reed pipe is so loud as to make the mountains shake. He goes on
to sing for her a love song in which she is compared to every natural
element of the shepherd's surroundings, in a form of exaggerated blan-
dishment. His effort to attract her to him also includes a description of his
belongings:

---

[96] Ovid 1926, 2.281–283 (*Metamorphoses* 13.755–769).
[97] In his description, Alphesibeus confuses Polyphemus' threats to tear Acis to pieces with the
circumstances of his death, which is recounted by Ovid to have occurred by being crushed by a
piece of mountainside launched at him by the Cyclops.
[98] Ovid 1926, 2.282–283 (*Metamorphoses* 13.780–785).

I have a whole mountain-side for my possessions, deep caves in the living rock, where neither the sun is felt in his midsummer heat, nor the winter's cold. I have apples weighing down their branches, grapes yellow as gold on the trailing vines, and purple grapes as well. Both these and those I am keeping for your use. With your own hand you shall gather the luscious strawberries that grow within the woody shade, cherries in autumn-time and plums, both juicy and purple-black and the large yellow kind, yellow as new wax. Chestnuts also shall be yours and the fruit of the arbute-tree, if you will take me for your husband; and every tree shall yield to your desire. And all this flock is mine. Many besides are wandering in the valleys, many are in the woods, still others are safe within their cavern-folds. Nay, should you chance to ask, I could not tell you how many in all I have. 'Tis a poor man's business to count his flocks. And you need not believe my praises of them; here you can see for yourself how they can hardly walk for their distended udders. And I have, coming on, lambs in my warm folds and kids, too, of equal age, in other folds. There's always a plenty of snow-white milk. Some of it is kept for drinking, and some the rennet hardens into curds.

(sunt mihi, pars montis, vivo pendentia saxo / antra, quibus nec sol medio sentitur in aestu, / nec sentitur hiems; sunt poma gravantia ramos, / sunt auro similes longis in vitibus uvae, / sunt et purpureae: tibi et has servamus et illas. / ipsa tuis manibus silvestri nata sub umbra / mollia fraga leges, ipsa autumnalia corna / prunaque non solum nigro liventia suco, / verum etiam generosa novasque imitantia ceras. / nec tibi castaneae me coniuge, nec tibi deerunt / arbutei fetus: omnis tibi serviet arbor. / Hoc pecus omne meum est, multae quoque vallibus errant, / multas silva tegit, multae stabulantur in antris, / nec, si forte roges, possim tibi dicere, quot sint: / pauperis est numerare pecus; de laudibus harum / nil mihi credideris, praesens potes ipsa videre, / ut vix circumeant distentum cruribus uber. / sunt, fetura minor, tepidis in ovilibus agni. / sunt quoque, par aetas, aliis in ovilibus haedi. / lac mihi semper adest niveum: pars inde bibenda / servatur, partem liquefacta coagula durant.)[99]

Polyphemus' effort to represent himself to his unresponsive beloved establishes him as a shepherd-king of the mountain, whose control over the natural world has produced an astonishing abundance, which he offers for Galatea's enjoyment. He concludes this part of his entreaty by ordering her not to turn him down: "Now come, Galatea, and don't despise my gifts" ("iam, Galatea, veni, nec munera despice nostra!").[100] A few lines later, in conclusion, Polyphemus admits that his burning desire for her is the source of violent intentions toward Acis, whom he threatens to tear to

---

[99] Ovid 1926, 2.284–287 (*Metamorphoses* 13.810–830).
[100] Ovid 1926, 2.286–287 (*Metamorphoses* 13.839).

pieces: "I'll tear his vitals out alive, I'll rend him limb from limb and scatter the pieces over the fields and over your waves – so may he mate with you! For oh, I burn, and my hot passion, stirred to frenzy, rages more fiercely within me; I seem to carry Aetna let down into my breast with all his violence" ("viscera viva traham divulsaque membra per agros perque tuas spargam [sic se tibi misceat!] undas. uror enim, laesusque exaestuat acrius ignis, cumque suis videor translatam viribus Aetnen pectore ferre meo").[101] When Galatea is found by Polyphemus with Acis, Polyphemus' civilized manner falls away and he violently hurls a piece of the mountain-side at them, hitting and murdering Acis.[102] This story provides a powerful model for the false poet, especially within the context of the pastoral genre.

Ovid's story of Polyphemus' unfulfilled love for Galatea lies unspoken between the naming of Polyphemus and the description of Polyphemus' cruelty given in response by de' Milotti/Alphesibeus:

> "Who would not shudder at Polyphemus," Alphesibeus said, "who is accustomed to wetting his jaws with human blood, already from that time when Galatea saw him, alas, tear to pieces the bowels of poor Acis, whom she had left behind? She barely escaped herself; or would the power of love have prevailed, while his cruel wrath boiled over with such madness? What to say about the fact that Achaemenides, who only saw him from afar bloody from the slaughter of his companions and was barely able to save his life."

> ("Quis Poliphemon," ait "non horreat" Alphesibeus / "assuetum rictus humano sanguine tingui, / tempore iam ex illo quando Galathea relicti / Acidis heu miseri discerpere viscera vidit? / Vix illa evasit: an vis valuisset amoris, / effera dum rabies tanta perferbuit ira? / Quid, quod Achimenides sociorum cede cruentum / tantum prospiciens, animam vix claudere quivit?")[103]

Guy Raffa interprets this intrusion of violence into the peacefulness of the pastoral world as an example of how "Dante distinguishes himself" from the pedantic engagement with classical literature by the likes of Giovanni del Virgilio by "grounding his vision in politics and history."[104] While there is no doubt that Dante's literary practice "arises from a personal and historical urgency,"[105] we need not seek out a concrete historical referent for Polyphemus outside of the economy of the poem or in Dante's

---

[101] Ovid 1926, 2.288–289 (*Metamorphoses* 13.865–869).
[102] With help from Galatea, Acis is able to metamorphose into a stream and survive in a new form.
[103] Alighieri 2016, 624–626 (*Egloge* 4.76–83). See Ovid 1926, 2.312–317 (*Metamorphoses* 14.167–222) for the source of the description of Achaemenides.
[104] Raffa 1996, 283.   [105] Raffa 1996, 283.

persecution complex.[106] Boccaccio's glossator, again, offers no suggestion about the identities of Galatea, Acis, or Achaemenides, noting merely that each is a "proper name" ("nomen proprium").[107] The question of Polyphemus' identity within the poem can be answered by comparing the words of Polyphemus to Galatea with Giovanni del Virgilio's approach to flattering Dante. What I aim to suggest here is that Polyphemus is an alternative pastoral cipher for Giovanni del Virgilio himself, whose intentions had already been questioned in Dante's first eclogue and whose very nature as Mopsus was being discussed at the beginning of Dante's second eclogue.

The correspondences between Polyphemus' profession of love and del Virgilio/Mopsus' approach of Dante/Tityrus are several. Del Virgilio's lavish praise of Dante and the fawning love that he professes for him in his eclogue may be seen in the parodic light of Polyphemus' mad love for Galatea. He had, after all, said that his love surrounded the poet so much that it resembled ivy wrapping around the elm. Polyphemus' list of his belongings, which he offers to Galatea, can be seen to correspond with Giovanni del Virgilio's description of Mopsus' cave, in which he says that Dante will have access to the abundance of nature. Furthermore, del Virgilio/Mopsus lays claim to the caves that he describes as his dominion (*mea regna*), which he asks if Dante despises (*sunt tibi despecta*). Similarly, Polyphemus describes what nature offers as belonging to him (*sunt mihi* and *hoc pecus omne meum est*) and he beseeches Galatea not to despise it (*nec despice*). Furthermore, at the end of his eclogue, del Virgilio had asked, "But why does my heifer bellow around now? Do her four flowing udders weigh on her wet haunches?" ("Quid tamen interea mugit mea bucula circum? / quadrifluumne gravat coxis umentibus uber?").[108] Dante's Ovidian allusion asks the reader to reconsider this display of overabundance through the lens of Polyphemus' pathetic address of Galatea, when he says that his flock can barely walk because their udders stretch out to their legs (*ut vix circumeant distentum cruribus uber*). It is also important to note that this intertext brings about a correspondence between Dante and Galatea, who both speak about love to a companion in Pelorus, when their narrative is interrupted by a vocative (*Polypheme*) that refers to the Cyclops who lies outside of the immediate context of the interlocutors. Dante sees himself and his reputation as precarious and vulnerable.

---

[106] It is worth noting in this regard that Dante/Tityrus responds to the description of Polyphemus' violence by silently smiling in agreement. Alighieri 2016, 627 (*Egloge* 4.88–89).

[107] Alighieri 2016, 647–648 (*Glosse* 4.78–82).   [108] Alighieri 2016, 596 (*Egloge* 3.90–91).

Dante's Polyphemus may then refer to Giovanni del Virgilio specifically, as the alter ego of Mopsus, who claims to be Dante's friend in poetry.
Dante seems to respond mockingly to del Virgilio's overwrought praise
and lavish offerings by insinuating that they may very well be as empty as
those of Polyphemus for Galatea and potentially as violent. Such a reading
also corresponds to Dante's generic fear, expressed in his first eclogue, that
the Bolognese laureation ceremony might be offered as a kind of vain
superstition that did not recognize its true meaning. The violence of
Polyphemus could then correspond to the potential damage to Dante's
reputation, which we have seen to be one of the poet's concerns. As
Jonathan Combs-Schilling has argued, there is a clear engagement with
futurity across Dante's eclogues, an engagement which goes beyond the
poet's life into posterity.[109] Furthermore, Dante has shown in this eclogue
a self-consciousness about the slippage between reality and pastoral cipher.
The caves of the Cyclopes are clearly Bologna, but Pelorus maintains its
ambiguity between the historical reality of Dante's location in Ravenna
and the pastoral imaginary. Perhaps a similar ambiguity applies to the
figure of Mopsus himself. Dante may wish to believe that del Virgilio is a
Virgilian Mopsus, a friend in the Muses and not like Pyreneus, but the
eclogue begins with Alphesibeus questioning Mopsus' nature: Why would
he live with the Cyclopes? Dante's answer (and challenge) is that del
Virgilio may be Polyphemus himself, an uncouth man who pretends to
be a poet in order to achieve his desire.

Whether Polyphemus is in fact an alter ego of Mopsus or a personifi-
cation of Dante's more general concern about the praise coming from del
Virgilio's milieu in a politically dangerous Bologna, it is clear that Dante's
shift of the pastoral setting to Sicily is governed by the Ovidian story of
Galatea, which takes on the pastoral genre through parody. Through
Ovid's Polyphemus, Dante is able to deflate the pompous classicism of
del Virgilio's eclogue and to maintain his superiority beyond the realms of
civic poetry. It is the conclusion, though, that responds to del Virgilio's
insinuation that Dante remains in Ravenna because he is beholden to his
lord there, Guido Novello da Polenta. After the shepherds leave the forest
for the valley at the end of the day, we learn in the final lines of the poem
that the entire episode has been overheard by Iollas, the pastoral cipher

---

[109] See Combs-Schilling 2015, 10–11 and 16–17. It is also possible that Dante was aware that he was
near death as he wrote this poem and that it was not sent by Dante to del Virgilio before his death.
See Albanese and Pontari 2016, 77. In this regard, we might see the identification of Alphesibeus
as a physician friend and Dante's prone position on a bed of poppies at the beginning of the
eclogue as signs that he was on his deathbed.

that del Virgilio had employed for the lord of Ravenna. The poem concludes: "The astute Iollas in the meanwhile lay hidden. He heard everything and repeated it all to us. He composed for us and we for you, Mopsus" ("Callidus interea iuxta latitavit Iollas, / omnia qui didicit, qui retulit omnia nobis: / ille quidem nobis et nos tibi, Mopse, poymus").[110] Thus, we discover that the entire exchange between Dante/Tityrus and de' Milotti/Alphesibeus is recorded and referred by da Polenta/Iollas. The kind of relationship posited here between Iollas and Tityrus, as the pastoral ciphers of Dante and his patron, is one of laissez-faire and even of mutual collaboration. Da Polenta is in effect represented as Dante's scribe. In response to del Virgilio, then, Dante shows himself to be in perfect freedom and in control of the relationship with political power, which is at his service rather than vice versa. He exists in a Ravenna that is precisely Pelorus, a pastoral environment that never gives way to a civic reality that can control him or manifest itself in his poetry as such. His host remains attentive in the background and takes note; he collaborates but does not intervene.

In his brief correspondence with Giovanni del Virgilio, Dante succeeds at defending his vernacular poetics and at situating himself as a poet within a cultural milieu that guaranteed him freedom from the petty municipal concerns that he had always abhorred in his poetics. As Guy Raffa notes, "Dante shows once and for all the inadequacy of prizes and even public recognition for a project born out of exile and a rich theological imagination."[111] In contrast to the local honorifics offered him, Dante suggests that his place as poet was in relation to no real city but on the margins, in a pastoral universe defined by freedom and work. It is likely that Dante, at the end of his life, was thinking of his posterity, of the future that would receive his *Commedia* with only his authorial persona as guide. He was wary of associating himself with an academic like del Virgilio, who would have taken dominion over Dante's name as poet.[112] Combs-Schilling has noted how the departure of the shepherds from the forest toward the end of Dante's second eclogue seems to echo the approach of the pilgrim Dante and Virgilio in *Inferno* 4. The conclusion he draws is that Dante has found his ideal community among the shepherds of Pelorus, a community that resembles the *bella scola* of classical poets of whom he fashions

---

[110] Alighieri 2016, 630 (*Egloge* 4.95–97).   [111] Raffa 1996, 273.

[112] On the nature and importance of Dante's early reception in Bologna, especially as regards the *Egloghe*, see Albanese and Pontari 2016, esp. 86–89, where it is made clear that del Virgilio's appointment as a publicly salaried professor of poetry and versification was a result of his correspondence with Dante.

himself the sixth.[113] If this is the case, we can understand even further the extent to which Dante's bucolic representation of himself as a poet without a city coincides with his representation of himself as poet within the *Commedia*. In Ravenna, Dante can remain unchained from the duties of the civic poet and fully assume the role of author of the *Commedia*, a work of poetry that belongs to no city and to all.

If we compare Dante's defense of himself and his poetics against an overzealous humanist to Mussato's defenses of poetry, we see that both claim specific realms of human experience for themselves, one embracing the civic role of the poet, the other shunning it. Albertino Mussato, however, always links poetry to theology, in order to establish his authority in the world of history. In the *Egloghe*, Dante never once mentions theology. His authority derives from himself and from his poetic mastery; it is not imitable and it does not depend on anyone else present or past.[114] Yet he does rely on the connection between poetry and theology to construct his authority within the economy of the *Commedia*, in a way that we can connect to Mussato. As the link between poetry and theology was part of Mussato's authorization of his own role as poet of the city, so Dante's association of the two disciplines helps to authorize his role within the *Commedia* as a universal poet, a poet without a city.

Authorizing the Poet without a City in the *Paradiso*

In light of the way Dante situates himself as a poet without a city in the *Egloghe*, I would like to look back at his *Paradiso* to show how one of its functions is to establish the theological and political authority of the poet as universal. The specter of Florence is always present in the background of Dante's conception of himself and of his poem. He is very careful, however, never to link himself to the present Florence of "the most wicked Florentines within the city" ("scelestissimis Florentinis intrinsecis") as the source of his poetic authority.[115] Rather, he figures the mandate of his poem as if it emanated from the Florence of the past, be it the Florence of Cacciaguida or that of his birth and baptism. As he does this, across the *Paradiso* Dante figures the transformation not only of his fictional self, the

---

[113] Combs-Schilling 2015, 14–15.

[114] On the exceptionalism of Dante's poetics and concept of himself as author, see Barolini 1984, 285–286 and Ascoli 2008, 368.

[115] Alighieri 2016, 132 and Alighieri 2007, 59 (*Epistola* 6.1).

pilgrim Dante, into the poet, as Contini and Singleton pointed out long ago,[116] but also of the poet into the poem itself.[117] The *Commedia* as a work will be that which will bear Dante as poet in the world after his death. It will thenceforth belong to all cities and none, and will perhaps be that which will allow for Dante's repatriation as the poet of Florence.

The recognition that he hopes he and his poem will receive would not be based upon any civic ceremony like that which he rejects from Giovanni del Virgilio. Rather, it is performed within the poem itself after Dante undergoes an examination in the three theological virtues at the hands of Saints Peter (faith), James (hope), and John (charity). By Saint Peter he is given a poetic authority that renders him the theological equal of the Pope, the vicar of Christ on earth. In this way, Dante stages his authority as poet-theologian par excellence, not in order to bolster his authority within the limits of a single city but to make him, through poetry, the singular representative of all human citizens. Even if he remains a poet without a city, Dante sets the stage for his reception as the poet of any and every city, hoping especially that his poem will allow him to achieve an impact on Florence.

Paradiso 15–17: The Poet and the City, between Florence and Verona

At the center of the *Paradiso*, in Cantos 15–17, Dante places the encounter between the pilgrim and his ancestor Cacciaguida, who lived in Florence in 1061 and fought in the Crusades. This episode is a homecoming. If there is a place in the *Commedia* where Dante feels pride for his homeland it is here. For the pilgrim, it is a moment of self-discovery through an encounter with the past that locates him as Florentine within the greater movements of history and fortune. For the poet, it is a moment of self-authorization whereby he stages his poetic mandate to speak his truth as exile, from without.[118] As I will try to show, however much Dante the poet is attracted by his place of birth, he never fully commits himself to

---

[116] See Contini 1970 and Singleton 1956.
[117] We could see this along with Ascoli as the transformation of the pilgrim into the *auctor* of the *Commedia*. See Ascoli 2008, 301–405.
[118] These cantos are crucial for understanding the link between Dante's role as poet and his vision of history. They have thus been the focus of several critics. I have found particularly helpful the perspectives provided in Mazzotta 1979, 124–130; Barolini 1984, 282–283; Schnapp 1986; Barolini 1992, 137–140; Mazzotta 1993a, 215–217 and 239–240; Honess 2006, 160–167; Honess 2013; and Steinberg 2013, 119–126. See also the detailed readings of these cantos in Staüble 2002 and Ledda 2015 (15); Fachard 2002 and Marcozzi 2015 (16); and Ambrosini 2002 and Montuori 2015 (17).

representing the city as its poet. Rather, similarly to how he speaks of Florence in the *Egloghe*, he situates himself as belonging to a Florence that is other than that of the present.

In Canto 15, the pilgrim is greeted by his forebear as Aeneas is by Anchises in Elysium, after the light descends from the Cross inhabited by other holy warriors.[119] He quickly discovers that Cacciaguida is his "root" (*radice*), his link to his family origins in Florence.[120] Cacciaguida's introduction of himself to the pilgrim quickly turns into a description of the Florence of his day with that of the pilgrim's present. His ideal Florence, he says, "dwelt in peace, sober and modest" ("si stava in pace, sobria e pudica").[121] In contrast to current women, he says, in his Florence, "This one watched late in her care of the cradle, and, comforting, used the idiom that first delights fathers and mothers" ("L'una vegghiava a studio de la culla, / e, consolando, usava l'idïoma / che prima i padri e le madri trastulla").[122] Viewed in relation to Dante's poetics, this tercet connects the moral purity of the Florence of the past with the language in which Dante writes his poem: a Florentine idiom that precedes the corruption of the city. Before going on to recount at the end of the canto his death fighting in the Crusades on behalf of the Emperor Conrad, Cacciaguida concludes his odd paean to their shared native city by invoking the city as the place of his baptism: "To so peaceful, so comely a life of citizens, to so loyal a citizenry, to so sweet a dwelling, Mary gave me, invoked with loud cries, and in your ancient Baptistry I became at the same time a Christian and Cacciaguida" ("A così riposato, a così bello / viver di cittadini, a così fida / cittadinanza, a così dolce ostello, / Maria mi diè, chiamata in alte grida; / e ne l'antico vostro Batisteo / insieme fui cristiano e Cacciaguida").[123] This community into which Cacciaguida was born by extension acts as the origin of Dante's identity as a Florentine. The mother tongue that he so deftly defends in his eclogues originates in this perfect city, whose place is no longer on earth. It exists only within the nostalgic world of Dante's poetic creation.

That this episode is integral to Dante's performance of his Florentine identity becomes clearer in the following canto, which reinforces the differences between the present Florence and that of Cacciaguida. He addresses Cacciaguida and requests that he inform him about the history

---

[119] Alighieri 2011, 302–303 (*Paradiso* 15.25–27).   [120] Alighieri 2011, 306–307 (*Paradiso* 15.89).
[121] Alighieri 2011, 306–307 (*Paradiso* 15.99).
[122] Alighieri 2011, 308–309 (*Paradiso* 15.121–123). On the critique of Florence through its women inhabitants, see Honess 1997. See also Olson 2016.
[123] Alighieri 2011, 308–309 (*Paradiso* 15.130–135).

of his family and his city, beginning with the words: "You are my father, you give me all boldness to speak, you lift me up so high that I am more than myself" ("Voi siete il padre mio; / voi mi date a parlar tutta baldezza; / voi mi levate sì, ch'i' son più ch'io").[124] Already, the voice of the pilgrim who will become the poet is becoming bold. His identity is expanding, from the Florentine of now to the Florentine who is the link between the present and the past. In speech that follows, Cacciaguida recounts the fallen city that Florence has become, principally due to the external influences brought into the city by immigrants from surrounding communities.[125] Besides its scathing critique of the socio-economic and cultural changes that have occurred in Florence in the time between his life and that of Dante, Cacciaguida's speech is a striking example of the view of history under the sign of decadence.[126] In the four tercets that introduce a laundry list of Florentine families who have brought about their city's ruin, Cacciaguida warns Dante that cities, like all human constructs will die:

> If you look at Luni and Orbisaglia, how they have gone to ruin, and how Chiusi and Sinisgaglia are following in their wake, to hear that lineages perish will not seem a strange thing or difficult, since cities have their end. The things of your world all have their deaths, just as you do, but in some it is hidden, for they last a long time, and lives are short. And as the turning of the heaven of the moon covers and uncovers the shores without pause, so Fortune does with Florence.
>
> (Se tu riguardi Luni e Orbisaglia / come sono ite, e come se ne vanno / di retro ad esse Chiusi e Sinigaglia, / udir come le schiatte si disfanno / non ti parrà nova cosa né forte, / poscia che le cittadi termine hanno. / Le vostre cose tutte hanno lor morte, / sì come voi; ma celasi in alcuna / che dura molto, e le vite son corte. / E come 'l volger del ciel de la luna / cuopre e discuopre i liti sanza posa, / così fa di Fiorenza la Fortuna.)[127]

Cacciaguida's words rehearse Dante's relationship as a poet with the city. They help explain his stance in the *Egloghe*, where he shunned the municipal ceremony represented by the laurel crown. Cacciaguida is mouthpiece for Dante the poet's farsighted historical perspective, which

---

[124] Alighieri 2011, 322–323 (*Paradiso* 16.16–18).
[125] The view of socio-economic change expressed in Cacciaguida's speech has led intellectuals like Edoardo Sanguineti, among others, to understand it as the ideological foundation of Dante's reactionary historical thought in response to an emerging capitalist economy. See Sanguineti 1992, 282–284. On this view of Dante, see Lummus 2013b. For a reading of Cacciaguida's comments in terms of legal issues surrounding citizenship, see Steinberg 2013, 119–126.
[126] See Ferri 2015 for a reading of this vision of history as characteristic of Italian historical thinking in modernity.
[127] Alighieri 2011, 326–327 (*Paradiso* 16.73–84).

he hinted at in his second eclogue and which he will go on to rehearse in Cantos 22 and 27. If Dante as a poet would like to achieve a lasting fame that will ensure that his poetry has an impact, then he should not associate himself with a specific city. For although Dante thought, along with Aristotle, that humans were political animals, as a poet he had to reach beyond the bounds of a single city, even Florence.

If Canto 16 demonstrates Dante the poet's cooptation of Cacciaguida as a figure for his own historical perspective on the present through the past, then in Canto 17 the poet turns that perspective toward the future.[128] In the famous speech that occupies most of the canto, Cacciaguida describes the circumstances of Dante's exile and his friendship with Cangrande della Scala in Verona. Given the representation of Dante as the plaything of Fortune, as a victim of factionalism with his exile and after it, when he is mistreated by the White Guelphs, one might expect this canto to establish Dante's host as the guarantor of his poetic voice. Surprisingly, this is not the case. Although Cacciaguida represents Cangrande in a very positive light, as a paragon of courtliness and generosity, he does not link Dante's poem to his patron.[129] In fact, Cacciaguida tells the pilgrim to conceal what he will tell him about the lord, and the poet leaves it out of the poem: "'and you will carry written in your memory about him, and will not say' – and he said things that will be incredible to those who witness them" ("'e portera'ne scritto ne la mente / di lui, e nol dirai' – e disse cose / incredibili a quei che fier presente").[130] The purpose of the elision here is to distance Dante the poet from his patron while at the same time situating the poet as the recipient of his magnificence. Dante the poet goes to great lengths to represent his relationship with Cangrande carefully, avoiding any sense that he is beholden to him. Whatever Cangrande's true character might have been, it is important that his benefits and generosity be represented as deriving from his adherence to courtliness, the same value system of Cacciaguida.[131] Motivated by virtue, the courtly lord would never ask

---

[128] That the question of perspective is relevant here, see the opening of the pilgrim's request for Cacciaguida's prophecy, Alighieri 2011, 342–343 (*Paradiso* 17.13–18), where his point of view in eternity is compared to a geometrical operation, and compare with Cacciaguida's response, Alighieri 2011, 344–345 (*Paradiso* 17.37–39).

[129] For the portion of the speech on Cangrande, see *Paradiso* 17.70–93. On the historical figure of Cangrande, see Di Salvo 1996.

[130] Alighieri 2011, 346–347 (*Paradiso* 17.91–93).

[131] Mussato certainly would not have agreed with this representation of Cangrande. On the differences between Mussato's Cangrande and that of Dante, see Gianola 1988. Cangrande's reputation for generosity becomes thematized in Boccaccio's *Decameron* 1.7. See Olson 2014, 99–102 and 110.

anything in return. According to Cacciaguida, Dante will become a true friend to Cangrande: "who will have such kind regard for you that of doing and asking, between you two, that will be first which among others is last" ("ch'in te avrà sì benigno riguardo, / che del fare e del chieder, tra voi due, / fia primo quel che tra li altri è più tardo").[132] This representation of Dante's relationship with Cangrande coincides with the way in which the poet situates himself vis-à-vis Guido Novello da Polenta in the *Egloghe*.[133] Even under the protection of a lord, Dante will continue to be autonomous: "so that for you it will be well to have become a party unto yourself" ("sì ch'a te fia bello / averti fatta parte per te stesso").[134]

Cacciaguida goes on to promise that Dante will survive those who have done violence to him, "since your life enfutures itself far beyond the punishing of their treacheries" ("poscia che s'infutura la tua vita / vie più là che'l punir di lor perfidie").[135] The notion of futurity here promises more than Dante's mere physical longevity. It is a promise of his survival through his poem into future generations as a poet detached from his city, "if the dearest place is taken from me" ("se loco m'è tolto più caro").[136] In fact, the pilgrim's reaction to this prophecy is to ask about how to approach the poetic composition of his experiences in the afterlife. He is worried that a truthful account will alienate him from his present readers, but that an untruthful account will ensure his death in the future: "and if I am a timid friend to the truth, I fear I will lose life among those who will call this time ancient" ("e s'io al vero son timido amico, / temo di perder viver tra coloro / che questo tempo chiameranno antico").[137] In response, Cacciaguida gives the future poet of the *Commedia* license to speak his truth: "For if your voice will be painful at the first taste, it will leave vital nourishment later, when it is digested. This cry of yours will be like a wind that strikes hardest the highest peaks, and this is no small claim to honor"

---

[132] Alighieri 2011, 346–347 (*Paradiso* 17.73–75). Compare with the opening salutation of his letter to Cangrande, in which Dante refers to himself as his "greatest devotee and friend" ("devotissmus et amicus") and goes on to defend his use of the term even in a situation of social inequality. Alighieri 2016, 332 (*Epistola* 13.1.3). On the general authenticity of this section of the letter (the *nuncupatoria*), see Casadei 2014, 823, where it is dated to the period between 1315 and 1317 when Dante would have asked Cangrande for support and protection. See also the discussion and bibliography in Casadei 2013, 25–34, as well as Casadei 2019, 31–101. On the valences of friendship in Dante's works, see Barolini 2015, esp. 58 and 68 n. 31; Coggeshall 2012; and Modesto 2015.

[133] Cf. Albanese 2014, 1776–1777.   [134] Alighieri 2011, 344–345 (*Paradiso* 17.68–69).

[135] Alighieri 2011, 346–477 (*Paradiso* 17.98–99). On Dante's notion of futurity in its medieval context, see Boitani 2000.

[136] Alighieri 2011, 348–349 (*Paradiso* 17.110).

[137] Alighieri 2011, 348–349 (*Paradiso* 17.118–120).

("Ché se la voce tua sarà molesta / nel primo gusto, vital nodrimento / lascerà poi, quando sarà digesta. / Questo tuo grido farà come vento, / che le più alte cime più percuote; / e ciò non fa d'onor poco argomento").[138] As Jonathan Combs-Schilling has noted, these lines recall the emphasis on nourishment in the *Egloghe*, where Dante defends his vernacular readership.[139] It is important to note that this reflection on Dante's status as a famed poet who will be read after his death is founded upon his status as an exile, a man who is a party unto himself, as a poet without a city. Dante builds to this conclusion across the three cantos at the center of the final canticle. His spiritual homeland is the untainted city of Florence in which Cacciaguida became a Christian, while his own city's vices culminate in his own unjust exile. In that exile, he will be hosted by one of the last bastions of courtly virtue, but his patron's political authority is disjoined from Dante's poetic outcry. Here, then, as in the *Egloghe*, Dante maintains creative independence from any present city or court, while at the same time allowing himself to be a poet engaged with the civic contexts in which it is human nature to exist. By not restricting himself to one city or court, the poet opens himself up to communities of the future that he can access through his poem itself.

Paradiso 22–27: Dante Poet Laureate, Poet-Theologian

As much as Dante manipulates theological discourse throughout the *Commedia*, he never directly declares himself a *poeta theologus*.[140] Giovanni del Virgilio, in his epitaph for the poet, will be the first to ascribe him with that status.[141] In the second half of the *Paradiso*, however, Dante succeeds in achieving the status of a poet-theologian within the poem's narrative through a series of interactions that recalls an academic ceremony. His role as such both allows him to achieve a historical perspective that undergirds his moral authority as a poet of history and sanctions the authority of his poetic voice to pronounce judgment on God's creation. While this by far exceeds the scope of Mussato's operation in defending poetry, it is not categorically different. In the brief survey that follows, I will not be able to

---

[138] Alighieri 2011, 348–349 (*Paradiso* 17.130–135).

[139] See Combs-Schilling 2015, 10–11 and 24 n. 38. See also Pertile 2010, 153–156, who connects the theme of nourishment in the first eclogue to *Paradiso* 23.

[140] On Dante and the topos of the *poeta theologus*, see Hollander 1976 and Ascoli 2008, 393 n. 136.

[141] Del Virgilio's epitaph begins "Dante, the theologian" ("Theologus Dantes"). See Wicksteed and Gardner 1902, 174–175, for the text.

do justice to the complexity of the cantos in question.[142] My goal is to demonstrate how Dante builds his authority as a poet-theologian to sanction further his poetic voice, which is definitively detached from any specific civic reality.

Canto 22 of the *Paradiso* recounts the pilgrim's movement away from the active life of the just rulers toward the contemplative life of theologians.[143] After climbing the ladder of contemplation,[144] from the heaven of the fixed stars, in the quadrant of his birth sign, Gemini, the pilgrim is invited to look downward onto earth in order to hearten him for the intellectual difficulties that await him. His home below appears insignificant: "I saw this globe to be such that I smiled at its base appearance" ("vidi questo globo / tal, ch'io sorrisi del suo vil sembiante").[145] After scanning the path of his earthly and heavenly journey, the pilgrim turns his eyes back to Beatrice and away from the world of action.[146] This does not mean that Dante has given up on the active life or on the purpose of his poem as prescribed by Cacciaguida. Rather, in order to build for himself as poet and for his poem the theological authority necessary to achieve his worldly goals, he must first be confronted with poetic and intellectual challenges.

First, in Canto 23, the pilgrim is presented with a vision of Christ and Mary that defies the poet's abilities to represent, such that Dante's "consecrated poem" ("sacrato poema") must change its direction and "leap" ("saltar") in order to proceed.[147] This mystical lyric moment of the poem, which exemplifies and prefigures the difficulties that Dante will encounter when trying to represent the Empyrean, is where the poem is first called divine. In Cantos 24 through 26, Dante's examination on the three theological virtues is staged. As Peter Hawkins and Ascoli have noted, these cantos are essential to the process by which Dante authorizes himself.[148] In contrast to the mystic vision of Christ in Canto 23, the

---

[142] I have found particularly useful the critical readings of these cantos in Barolini 1992, 222–233; Mazzotta 1993a, 154–173; Ascoli 2008, 357–405. See also the detailed readings in Barański 2002 and Vecce 2015 (22); Perugi 2002 and Mocan 2015 (23); De Marchi 2002 and Ariani 2015 (24); Fumagalli 2002 and Prandi 2015 (25); Stierle 2002 and Pirovano 2015 (26); Antonelli 2002 and Frasso 2015 (27). For understanding the philosophical underpinnings of Dante's cosmology, I have learned from Moevs 2005 and Barsella 2010.

[143] On Dante's treatment of contemplation in *Paradiso* 21 and 22, see Mazzotta 1993a, 154–173. On Dante's concept of *contemplatio* and its importance for his formal, semantic, and ideological vision, see Barański 2002.

[144] Alighieri 2011, 440–441 (*Paradiso* 22.100–105).

[145] Alighieri 2011, 442–443 (*Paradiso* 22.134–135).

[146] Alighieri 2011, 444–445 (*Paradiso* 22.154).

[147] Alighieri 2011, 460–461 (*Paradiso* 23.62). See Barolini 1992, 223–229.

[148] See Hawkins 1992 and Ascoli 2008, 372–391.

examination on faith in Canto 24 establishes Dante as the equal of a scholastic philosopher, as he makes poetry of syllogistic speech. He exits this exam a full-on theologian, resting on the authority of his examiners above any school on earth below.

It is in Canto 25, before Dante's examination on hope, where the historical world intrudes, as the poet expresses what seems to be a hope to be crowned poet laureate one day in Florence:

> If it ever happen that the sacred poem, to which both heaven and earth have set their hand, so that for many years it has made me lean, vanquish the cruelty that locks me out of the lovely sheepfold where I slept as a lamb, an enemy of the wolves that make war on it, with other voice by then, with other fleece I shall return as poet, and at the fount of my baptism I shall accept the wreath: for there I entered the faith that makes souls known to God, and later Peter so circled my brow because of it.
>
> (Se mai continga che 'l poema sacro / al quale ha posto mano e cielo e terra, / sì che m'ha fatto per molti anni macro, / vinca la crudeltà che fuor mi serra / del bello ovile ov' io dormi' agnello, / nimico ai lupi che li danno guerra; / con altra voce omai, con altro vello / ritornerò poeta, e in sul fonte / del mio battesmo prenderò 'l cappello / però che ne la fede, che fa conte / l'anime a Dio, quivi intra' io, e poi / Pietro per lei sì mi girò la fronte.)[149]

It is a critical commonplace to associate these lines with Dante's correspondence with Giovanni del Virgilio. They are typically understood, in terms of Dante's first eclogue, as demonstrating that Dante did indeed entertain the fantasy of returning to Florence, or at least that he felt disappointed by the impossibility of such a return.[150] There is a certain triumphal tone here in the future indicative tense of *ritornerò*.[151] As Honess has noted, however, "it can only be in a metaphorical sense that Dante can receive the poet's *capello* [sic] ... it is the poet's wish that his text be read and accepted ... by its Florentine readers."[152] Dante here reiterates the reference to his poem as sacred from Canto 23, locating it in

---

[149] Alighieri 2011, 500–501 (*Paradiso* 25.1–12).

[150] For a discussion of these lines in relation to the *Egloghe*, see, e.g., Villa 2009, 183–200 and Bologna 2010. See Fumagalli 2002, 393–404 for a discussion of what is meant by *cappello*. See also Albanese and Pontari 2016, 51 for its possible relationship with the Florentine ceremony of oblation for those returning from exile. Cf. Casadei 2019, 121 n. 5. On Dante's conception of the laurel crown, see Picone 2005, 1–13. See Sturm-Maddox 2009, 290–294 for a discussion of the theme of coronation in relation to both Mussato and Dante. See also Brownlee 1984.

[151] Barolini 1984, 269.

[152] Honess 2013, 102. Honess sees Dante's hope here as a recantation of the persona assumed in his political letters. I am convinced by her reading, even if I do not see Dante's message as necessarily "filled with hope." Rather, I see Dante's political ideology here and in the political letters as continuous.

a place between heaven and earth. His hope is that the poem itself may be able to transform the bestiality of the Florentines, which was referenced in the Caccaguida cantos. Florence oscillates between past and future: it is first the fold wherein he was a lamb, but it is then transformed into the fount where he was baptized. It does not exist in the present tense of the poet, writing in Ravenna at the end of his life. Rather, by projecting himself into the future Dante insinuates that this return will be in the form of the *auctor* who is as much a part of his poem as God is of creation.[153] There are also verbal signs that lead us to understand that Dante will return in the form of a book. The "other voice" that he has acquired may be understood as the voice of a reader, while the "other fleece" (as *vello* is translated and interpreted) might be understood as a double entendre, indicating both a garb and the *vellum*, or parchment, through which Dante's voice will be available to future readers.[154] After all, the agent of the first half of the conditional is the sacred poem itself. The reference to his baptismal fount may refer more generally to the structure of the baptistery itself, and thus to the public square in which it stood and where the poem might have been read. Thus, if Dante will return triumphantly to Florence, it will be as born by the poem itself, in which he has already been crowned. As Robert Hollander has noted, Dante's mention of Saint Peter in the last tercet refers to his incoronation at the end of Canto 24:[155] "so, blessing me in his song when I fell silent, three times the apostolic light encircled me" ("così, benedicendomi cantando, / tre volte

---

[153] Ascoli notes regarding these lines that "there is no longer any substantive distinction" between pilgrim and poet in terms of the authority that is being asserted. Ascoli 2008, 363–364.

[154] It is worth noting that this kind of transformation into book may be connected to the metamorphosis of Marsyas, who is evoked in *Paradiso* 1.20 as a figure for the poet, just after a reference to the laurel crown: "O good Apollo, for this last labor make me such a vessel of your power as you require to bestow the beloved laurel. Until now one peak of Parnassus has been enough for me, but now with both of them I must enter upon what of the field remains: come into my breast and breath there, as when you drew Marsyas forth from the sheath of his members" ("O buono Appollo, a l'ultimo lavoro / fammi del tuo valor sì fatto vaso / come dimandi a dar l'amato alloro. / Infino a qui l'un giogo di Parnaso / assai mi fu, ma or con amendue / m'è uopo intrar ne l'aringo rimaso: / entra nel petto mio, e spira tue / sì come quando Marsïa traesti / de la vagina de le membra sue"). Alighieri 2011, 22–23 (*Paradiso* 1.13–21). Perhaps Dante is hoping for a poetic inspiration that will figuratively excoriate him, making of his skin the parchment of his book. That is, he is calling on Apollo (God) to help him transform into the poet who will live on in his poem. This is the transformation that takes place in *Paradiso* 22–27. For a discussion of the scholarly debate on these lines, see Hollander 2010. See also Brownlee 1991. On medieval writers' meta-poetic self-consciousness about writing on skin, see Kay 2006 and 2017.

[155] See Hollander 2007 on *Paradiso* 25.1–9, which includes a discussion of the interpretations of Dante's expression of hope for the laurel as either optative (Scott 2004, 98) or resigned (Sarolli 1971, 384–389; Chiarenza 1983, 147–148; Chiavacci Leonardi 1988, 268).

cinse me, sì com' io tacqui, / l'appostolico lume").[156] What I wish to get across here is that Dante is not expressing some far-fetched hope to be crowned poet laureate in Florence, nor a resignation to oblivion. Rather, in his identification with the text of the poem as its author, his hope is to be recognized by future readers in his native city.[157]

After a brief examination on charity by Saint John in Canto 26, Dante seals his authority as a vernacular theological poet in the pilgrim's consultation of the source of the human community. His address of Adam recalls the filial relationship he felt with Cacciaguida, though the epic mode gives way to the language of devotion. Dante feminizes his relationship with the first man by addressing Adam as "O ancient father to whom each bride is daughter and daughter-in-law" ("O padre antico / a cui ciascuna sposa è figlia e nuro).[158] From Adam, Dante learns the origins of human language and its connection with God. Adam gives the poet license to speak his mother tongue, which is a sign of love: "for no rational effect, because of human preference, which changes following the heavens, has ever been enduring. It is a natural operation that man speaks, but whether in this way or that, Nature allows you to do as it may please you" ("ché nullo effetto mai razïonabile, / per lo piacere uman che rinovella / seguendo il cielo, sempre fu durabile. / Opera naturale è ch'uom favella; / ma così o così, natura lascia / poi fare a voi secondo che v'abbella").[159] Like Cacciaguida, Adam speaks of exile, language, and the fallenness of human creations. Yet, this time the historical perspective is biblical and universal. Dante has gained the theological poet's ultimate authority over history.[160]

The result of Dante's turn to contemplation, of the examination on the theological virtues, and of the colloquy with Adam can be seen in the following canto, which precedes his ascent into the Empyrean. Here, in Canto 27, the heavens celebrate Dante's success and Saint Peter assigns Dante his authority as voice of the Church militant. Saint Peter offers a scathing critique of the current state of the institution of the Church on earth, which he claims has been made a "sewer of the blood and stench that placate the perverted one down there, who fell from up here" ("cloaca

---

[156] Alighieri 2011, 486–487 (*Paradiso* 24.151–153).

[157] During his examination on hope (*Paradiso* 25.73–75), Dante quotes the Psalms, suggesting that we see his poem also as a "divine song" ("tëodia") and associating himself with the poet-prophet of the Old Testament. Alighieri 2011, 504–505. See Barolini 1984, 275–279.

[158] Alighieri 2011, 522–523 (*Paradiso* 26.92–93).   [159] Alighieri 2011, 524–525 (26.127–132).

[160] On the significance of Dante's colloquy with Adam for his construction of authority, see Ascoli 2008, 391–399.

/ del sangue e de la puzza onde 'l perverso / che cadde di qua sù, là giù si placa").[161] The Church has been made a living hell. Saint Peter addresses Dante as the true mouthpiece of the vicar of Christ on earth: "and you, my son, who because of your mortal weight will go back down again, open your mouth and hide not what I do not hide" ("e tu, figliuol, che per lo mortal pondo / ancor giù tornerai, apri la bocca, / e non asconder quel ch'io non ascondo").[162] Saint Peter's mandate echoes that of Cacciaguida, but adds to it a more than temporal authority. Here Dante has become poet laureate of a community that is beyond the earthly just as much as it is directed toward earthly affairs. Dante's return, furthermore, is not limited to a single city; rather, it is directed to the entirety of the earth. It is with this new-found theological authority that the pilgrim looks down again, at the invitation of Beatrice, to see "how you have turned" ("come tu se' vòlto").[163] Before his view is blocked by the passage of the sun, the pilgrim sees once more the same "little threshing-floor" ("aiuola") that he had viewed in Canto 22.[164] It is from this privileged perspective of the *poeta theologus* achieved by the pilgrim that the poet provides (in the words of Beatrice) his final polemical diatribe against the current fall of humanity below before ascending to the Empyrean, where he will become a *scriba Dei* and *autore*.[165]

These cantos represent Dante's final vision of the temporal world within the poem and the final performance of his authority not only as poet laureate but as poet-theologian. We need not imagine that Dante wrote these canticles in response to Giovanni del Virgilio's bold attack and belittling invitation to Bologna. Yet it is clear that, as he was finishing the *Commedia* and defending himself to del Virgilio, Dante was of a single mind. In his view of himself as poet and of the sacred function of his poem, no specific civic allegiance could contain his ambitions. Nevertheless, he engages with prevailing humanist ideas about the civic role of the poet and he transforms them into a universalizing vision for all human communities.

*

[161] Alighieri 2011, 538–539 (*Paradiso* 27.25–26).
[162] Alighieri 2011, 540–541 (*Paradiso* 27.64–66).   [163] Alighieri 2011, 542–543 (*Paradiso* 27.78).
[164] Alighieri 2011 (*Paradiso* 27.86), but see 27.79–87 for the description of what he sees. Cf. Ascoli 2008, 390–391.
[165] On Dante as *scriba Dei*, see, e.g., Sarolli 1971, 189–336; Hollander 1976; Mazzotta 1979 ; Barański 2000; and Ascoli 2008, 121 n. 88. Ascoli notes that the word *poeta* is subordinated to that of *autore* by the end of the poem. See Ascoli 2008, 400–405. As I see it, Dante as pilgrim, poet, and author converge at the end of the poem in the closure of a circle that binds them to the textuality of the work itself.

In view of the consideration of Mussato in the previous chapter, I hope to have shown how Dante's poetics engage with a similar vision of the poetic office as conceived in relation to the city. While it would not be not unwarranted to see Dante's Christian theological stance in the *Commedia* as categorically different from that of Mussato in his defenses of poetry, it is necessary to recognize that Dante is creating himself as poet within a cultural context that was beginning to have certain expectations of poets. He must engage with the expectation that a poet would be a civic leader, a moral guide, and a public intellectual who wields the authority of poetry's origins as theological discourse. This is precisely what he does in the *Egloghe*, as he refutes Giovanni del Virgilio's offer of the laurel crown in Bologna, where he figures his relationship with the city in terms of pastoral marginality. He categorically rejects the offer not only because del Virgilio fails to understand Dante's renewal of the classical tradition in the *Commedia* but because the association with and engagement in any civic context would make his posterity as poet just as vulnerable to violence as he had been in his life.

Dante, as poet of the *Commedia*, is entirely committed to engaging with the world from within the poem. He thus transfers the role of the civic poet to a city that is both beyond the bounds of historical reality and linked to that reality. If it is true that Dante "acts on the world by being outside of it," as Giuseppe Mazzotta has written,[166] then we must see Dante's removal of himself from the world of human affairs at the end of the *Commedia* as the assumption of the ultimate vantage point from which to view the human through the image of God.[167] Even as a historical poet toward the end of his life, Dante maintains this removal from the world of violence to which he must speak in the form of his poem. He figures his poetic authority in the *Paradiso* as belonging to a utopian Florence of the past, which places its seal on his vernacular poem through Caccaguida's mandate, and as emanating from the theological authority that he gains as a contemplative near the end of the pilgrim's journey. These cantos of the *Commedia* must not be seen as undermining Dante's humanist values, as an engaged man of letters who participated in renewing the classical tradition. Rather, they fully authorize those values within a Christian context, much in the same way as Mussato's claims to be a theological poet reinforce his moral voice and historical perspective within the city. Mussato, it must be admitted, did not aspire to the nature of poetic authority that Dante creates for himself in the *Commedia*. And Dante

---

[166] Mazzotta 1979, 138.   [167] See Alighieri 2011, 666–667 (*Paradiso* 33.130–132).

did not coopt theological discourse by applying it to pagan poets – this is Mussato's radicalism. He kept the Christian and classical separate, but combined them in himself.[168] Yet it is clear that the two poets' efforts to authorize themselves as poet-theologians emerge from a similar dissatisfaction with the direction their civilization was taking and from a similar impulse to make their voices heard. Here the question of Latin versus vernacular, the product of the pedantic perspective of Giovanni del Virgilio, falls away into irrelevance. Both Mussato and Dante turned to a new kind of poetry whose language and form of engagement emerged from the cultural contexts in which they found themselves: one a Paduan civic leader and public intellectual, the poet of the city; the other a Florentine and undeserved exile, the poet without a city. It is between these two poles that representations of the civic role of the poet will oscillate in the works of Petrarch and Boccaccio.

---

[168] Dante's method of separation and combination of the Christian and the classical can be seen in the character of Statius, whom Dante portrays as a secret convert to Christianity (as a result of his reading of Virgil). Statius stands between Virgil and Dante as the imaginary historical link between the two worlds and as a reminder that Dante is the first poet of his kind.

CHAPTER 3

Francesco Petrarch, Poet beyond the City

Petrarch's career as a poet is intricately interwoven with his many other activities as a historian, diplomat, and humanist. Of the figures examined in the current study, he is the individual most associated with the defense of poetry as it is inherited by Boccaccio and Salutati.[1] As we have seen, however, in the previous two chapters, the idea of poetry as theology and of the public crowning of the man of letters as poet was already embedded in the civic and poetic culture of the early fourteenth century. The two models represented by Mussato and Dante will be negotiated by Petrarch in his own public representation of himself as a poet.

It is important to keep in mind, however, that the poet known in the fourteenth century as Petrarch is not the poet as we know him today. His *Africa* was never made public in its entirety during his lifetime, nor were his *Trionfi*. Even the *Rerum vulgarium fragmenta*, or the *canzoniere* with which he is most often associated, were known only by a select few of his friends and patrons.[2] In his lifetime, Petrarch was a Latin poet and historian, famous for his Roman laurel crown, which he was awarded for his promise as a poet and historian, and revered for his works of ethical philosophy and his learning.

In this chapter, I examine four moments between 1341 and 1353 that shed light on the path that Petrarch pursued in his representation of himself as a poet, with the aim of showing how he figures for himself a public role that was both inside and outside of the city. Like Dante, he will reject the association between himself as poet and a specific civic context. He refuses to be the poet of the city that Mussato had been. Yet with both

---

[1] See, e.g., Ronconi 1976, 96–114 and Witt 1977. See also Greenfield 1981, 95–109.
[2] It is clear from Boccaccio's *Epistola* 24 that not even Petrarch's closest friends had copies of the *Africa* or *Trionfi*. On this letter in the context of Petrarch's death and on the status of Petrarch's fame at the time of his death, see Lummus 2017. On the history of the diffusion of the *Rerum vulgarium fragmenta*, see Santagata 1996. See also Eisner 2013, 74–94.

poets he shares the conviction that poetry's meanings can have an impact on human communities. Therefore, the position he imagines for himself is not entirely removed from a civic context or from human affairs. Rather, Petrarch carefully creates an imaginary historical space that secures his place as poet in society. If in the *Paradiso* and *Egloghe* Dante created for himself an ideal space, which was outside the limits of any real civic reality, Petrarch imagines such a space in the ideal of memory and in a modified version of Dante's pastoral non-place. His laureation ceremony in 1341 makes him an honorary citizen of Rome, a city that becomes in Petrarch's imagination a phantasm of the ancient place and is detached from the historical reality of the fourteenth century. His authority as poet derives from the historical imaginary of the eternal city. It is with this authority that Petrarch will increasingly intervene in political affairs, such as the brief uprising in Rome led by Cola di Rienzo.

Following his crowning in Rome, Petrarch will defend poetry three times, in three separate contexts that recalibrate his relationship with the active life of the city. As with much of Petrarch's epistolary production, even if these compositions can be traced to a specific point in his life, they are also revised and represented in book form years later. The removal of these discourses from their historical context by Petrarch serves the purpose both of signaling their value outside of it and of giving them a new value as a book, so that the historical circumstances of their original composition become marginalized. The documents in question are: *Epystola metrica* 2.10 (1344); *Familiares* 10.4 (1349); and the *Invective contra medicum* (1352–53; 1355). In the period between 1341 and 1353, Petrarch moves from his first public assertion of himself as a poet to the almost complete rejection of poetry as a profession. In my analyses of these works, I endeavor to show how Petrarch constructed for himself the persona of a poet of solitude, whose authority in human affairs derives from his location beyond the realm of the city, in the landscape of pastoral tranquility that Petrarch will describe in the *De vita solitaria*. There is a fundamental irony in this, of course, which plays a part in Petrarch's own self-representation and in its reception among his contemporaries, since during and after this period Petrarch became increasingly embroiled in political affairs on an international level. It is in this way, as the poet of the city who figures himself as outside of the urban context, that Petrarch combines the attitudes of Dante and Mussato. As with both these poets, Petrarch's goal in defending poetry goes beyond asserting its truth value in a Christian context. Defending poetry also gives him the opportunity to imagine a role of authority for the poet in relation to society.

Becoming the Poet of Rome: The *Collatio laureationis* and the *Privilegium laureationis*

In a letter dated September 1, 1340, Petrarch notified his friend and patron Cardinal Giovanni Colonna that in a single day he had received invitations from both Paris and Rome to be recognized for his learning.[3] Upon the advice of Colonna, Petrarch chooses Rome in order to receive the laurel crown as poet and historian, but there is every indication that there was no choice to be made. The entire situation seems to have been organized by Petrarch himself with the help of his patrons in Avignon and Rome, the Colonna family.[4] Besides his vernacular verse compositions, which had not yet been compiled into a song book or rendered public, Petrarch had not exactly been productive as a poet or historian. The assignment of the laurel crown, for the 36-year-old Petrarch, was a gambit to achieve social status and to assert the validity of the profession of poet. In order to receive the laurel crown, Petrarch would need to undergo an examination by King Robert of Naples and give a speech on the Capitoline in front of the Senate of Rome. The ceremony that took place had the symbolic cultural value of renewing an ancient tradition, but also gave to Petrarch specific privileges, making him a *magister* of the arts and a citizen of ancient and modern Rome. With his coronation in Rome, Petrarch inaugurates above all, however, his entrance into society as a poet, with a real and symbolic civic status that was recognizable across what had been the Roman Empire.

Petrarch records the ceremony and its meaning in several documents, but the most revealing of the new status that he creates for himself are the *Collatio laureationis*, his coronation oration, and the *Privilegium laureationis*, the laurel diploma.[5] E. H. Wilkins divides the *Collatio*, a tour-de-force in medieval oratory, into three parts. The first is an explication of a line from Virgil's *Georgica*: "But a sweet longing urges me upward

---

[3] See Petrarch 1938–42, 1.167–168; Petrarch 1975–85, 1.188–189 (*Familiares* 4.4).

[4] The circumstances of Petrarch's invitation to Rome can be read between the lines of his correspondence in Books 4 and 5 of the *Familiares*. In *Familiares* 5.2, Petrarch thanks Giovanni Colonna. See Usher 2009, 161 and 180.

[5] Other descriptions of the ceremony can be found in *Epystola metrica* 2.1, addressed to Giovanni Barrili; *Familiares* 4.7 to Robert of Naples; and *Familiares* 4.8 to Barbato da Sulmona. On the *Collatio Laureationis*, see Smarr 1982; Looney 2006; and Mazzotta 2006b. On the laurel crown as a connection between Dante and Petrarch, especially for Boccaccio, see Sturm-Maddox 2009. On the *Privilegium*, see Mertens 1988 and Usher 2009. The former includes a critical edition of the document. For a reading of Petrarch's literary profession in these texts as a romance-quest, see Biow 2002, 27–44.

over the lonely slopes of Parnassus" ("Sed me Parnasi deserta per ardua dulcis / raptat amor").[6] In it, Petrarch seeks to define the nature of the accomplishment of the laurel crown in terms of its extrinsic difficulties (the difficulty of poetry itself; the difficulties presented by fortune; and the difficulties due to the state of human affairs) and in terms of what enabled him to overcome these difficulties (love of country; personal glory; and the desire to be a leader for other men of letters). The second part of the oration is focused on what Petrarch calls the "profession of poetry" ("poetice professionis"),[7] while the third is a long description of the meaning of the laurel crown itself, as reward for the poet. In his interpretation, Petrarch links the characteristics of the laurel leaves back to his earlier description of the task of the poet.

Here I would like to focus on two elements of the oration: Petrarch's definition of the poetic profession and the way in which he links the current state of affairs to the past. My aim is to show how Petrarch is able to become the ultimate civic poet through the ceremony without effectively becoming the poet of the city of Rome. Petrarch opens the oration by differentiating the "ways of poetry" ("more poetico") from the "minute distinctions that are usually to be found in theological declamations" ("distinctionibus illis minutissimis quibus in theologicis declamationibus uti solent").[8] Here, Petrarch is interested in distinguishing the task of the poet from others and he will not claim that poetry is similar to theology until eight years later. Petrarch's discussion of the poet's task focuses on claiming a specific kind of civic value for poetry that gives the poet authority. This role is founded upon both the poet's exceptionality and the effective work of the poet, in terms of his studies and of the difficulties that present themselves from without. Petrarch's idea of the exceptional nature of the poet comes from Cicero's *Pro Archia*, in which the Roman orator defended the claim to citizenship of a foreign poet.[9] The poet, according to Cicero and Petrarch, possesses "a certain inner and divinely given energy [that] is infused in the poet's spirit" ("interna quadam et divinitus in animum vatis infusa vi").[10] In Petrarch's oration this divine gift, in the spirit of Cicero's legal discourse, does not give a sense of poetry

---

[6] Petrarch 1953, 1242; Petrarch 1988a, 29 (*Collatio laureationis* 1.1). The quotation is from *Georgica* 3.291–292.

[7] Petrarch 1953, 1246; Petrarch 1988a, 42 (*Collatio laureationis* 9.9).

[8] Petrarch 1953, 1242; Petrarch 1988a, 29 (*Collatio laureationis* 1.4–8).

[9] See Cicero 1923, 26–27 (*Pro Archia* 8.18). On Petrarch's discovery of Cicero's *Pro Archia* and the importance of his manuscript, see De Keyser 2013.

[10] Petrarch 1953, 1242–1243; Petrarch 1988a, 31 (*Collatio laureationis* 1.28–29).

as theology, rather it distinguishes the work of the poet as civically relevant. In this portion of the oration, Petrarch insists on work of the poet as *labor*, citing as authorities Virgil, Juvenal, and Lucan.

Later on, this *labor* will be presented as the foundation of "the office and the profession of the poet" ("poete officium atque professionem").[11] This office is described in terms of a specific form of historical poetry, in a quotation taken from Lactantius: "For the office of the poet consists in this, that he should take things that have really come to pass and transform them by means of subtle figures into things of a different sort. To make up all that one writes is to be a fool and a liar rather than a poet" ("cum officium poete in eo sit ut ea, que vere gesta sunt, in alia specie, obliquis figurationibus, cum decore aliquo conversa traducat. Totum autem quod referas fingere, id est ineptum esse et mendacem potius quam poetam").[12] This is the epic poetry of Ennius, Virgil, and Homer, which Petrarch was seeking to revive in his *Africa*.[13] In this kind of poetry, Petrarch claims, "poets have included, beneath the veil of fictions, physical, moral, and historical matters" ("poetas, sub velamine figmentorum, nunc fisica, nunc moralia, nunc hystorias comprehendisse"),[14] just as in philosophy and history: "the difference between a poet on the one hand and a historian or a moral or physical philosopher on the other is the same as the difference between a clouded sky and a clear sky, since in each case the same light exists in the object of vision, but is perceived in different degrees according to the capacity of the observers" ("inter poete et ystorici et philosophi, seu moralis seu naturalis, officium hoc interesse, quod inter nubilosum et serenum celum interest, cum utrobique eadem sit claritas in subiecto, sed pro captu spectantium, diversa").[15] The function of the poet is not then in pure service to the truth but itself emerges from the poet's representation of that truth.

The nature of the poet's relationship to society is addressed in the final section of the oration, where Petrarch speaks of fame, which is the reward of the poet as symbolized by his laurel crown. According to Petrarch, the poet is given an immortality, which "is itself twofold, for it includes both the immortality of the poet's own name and the immortality of the names of those whom he celebrates" ("eaque duplex: prima in se ipsis, secunda in

---

[11] Petrarch 1953, 1246; Petrarch 1988a, 42 (*Collatio laureationis* 9.11–12).
[12] Petrarch 1953, 1246; Petrarch 1988a, 42 (*Collatio laureationis* 9.15–18). Cf. Lactantius (*Divinae Institutiones*, 1.11.24–25).
[13] On the *Africa*, see, e.g., Schnapp 2003 and Marchesi 2006.
[14] Petrarch 1953, 1246; Petrarch 1988a, 43 (*Collatio laureationis* 9.30–31).
[15] Petrarch 1953, 1246; Petrarch 1988a, 43 (*Collatio laureationis* 9.32–35).

his, quos tali honore dignati sunt").[16] The poet's work, then, which consists in the figurative recording of historical events, results in the ability to give immortality to grand historical figures. He writes, "Many mighty men and warriors, and others who have deserved eternal memory, have passed into oblivion simply because they had not the good fortune to be recorded by capable authors" ("Fortes autem et bellicosi, vel alias etherni-tatem nominis promeriti, in oblivionem abierunt quia non contigit eis scriptor idoneus").[17] Petrarch hereby offers himself as poet in fulfillment of this lack, which is connected to the current age, in which poetry is held in disregard. A new Horace,[18] he goes on to say that "Certain illustrious men, foreseeing such a possibility, have kept poets with them and held them in high honor, so that there might be someone who would hand down their praises to posterity" ("Quod providentes quidam ex illustribus viris secum in magno honore habuere poetas ut esset aliquis qui eorum laudes trans-mittere posset ad posteros").[19] Although Petrarch refers to Cicero's oration throughout, he elides Cicero's main point, which is that poets are good citizens because they incite others to virtue. Instead, Petrarch insists that the poet's principal function is to immortalize illustrious men. He seems here to be offering himself up to his audience in this capacity, as the civic poet of the prince – a courtly version of the office that Mussato had defended – but there is some ambiguity about the nature of Petrarch's relationship with his current time and place.

Petrarch is highly aware of the gap between ancient and modern Rome. Early on in his oration, he claims in contrast to his own time that "there was an age that was happier for poets, an age when they were held in the highest honor ... especially when Caesar Augustus held imperial sway, under whom there flourished excellent poets: Virgil, Varus, Ovid, Horace, and many others" ("Fuit enim quoddam tempus, fuit etas quedam felicior poetis, quando in honore maximo habebantur ... presertim sub imperio Cesaris Augusti, sub quo vates egregii floruerunt: Virgilius, Varus, Ovi-dius, Flaccus multique alii").[20] The time of Rome's greatness, which coincided with the apex of poetry, has passed during the great hiatus in which no one was awarded the laurel crown in that city. A part of what Petrarch says led him to receive the laurel crown in Rome instead of in

---

[16] Petrarch 1953, 1247; Petrarch 1988a, 44 (*Collatio laureationis* 10.4–5).
[17] Petrarch 1953, 1247; Petrarch 1988a, 46 (*Collatio laureationis* 10.33–35).
[18] There are several classical analogues for the idea that poets prevent rulers' names from being forgotten. See, e.g., Horace *Odes* 4.8 in Horace 2004, 240–243.
[19] Petrarch 1953, 1247; Petrarch 1988a, 46 (*Collatio laureationis* 10.40–42).
[20] Petrarch 1953, 1244; Petrarch 1988a, 34 (*Collatio laureationis* 4.2–6).

Paris was the desire to return the practice of poetry to its past greatness – a desire he describes as *amor patriae*. It is through his persona that this gap will be elided.

The memory of the ancient city is evoked for the purposes of political and cultural justification. The key moment of Petrarch's reappropriation of Roman antiquity in the oration falls in his commemoration of the honor of the Republic, in which he recalls the past poets who had received the laurel prize and explains his decision to receive the crown in Rome and not at the Parisian *Studium*. He cites Cicero in an effort to justify his choice of Rome over the university in Paris, whose fame is consigned to the present:

> I was much moved also toward this decision by a certain affection and reverence for those ancient poets of excellent genius who flourished in this very city, who lived here, who are buried here – even as Cicero well says in the second book of his *Laws*: "I regard this as a sound reason for your coming here by preference and for your loving this place," and continuing: "Our emotions are somehow stirred in those places in which the feet of those whom we love and admire have trodden. Thence even Athens delights us not so much through its magnificent buildings and its exquisite works of ancient art as through the memory of its great men: it was here they dwelt, here they sat, here they engaged in their philosophical discussions. And with zeal I contemplate their tombs." This, I confess, was not the least of the causes for my coming to Rome. But, whatever the cause, I trust that my coming, because of the novelty of the occasion if for no other reason, may serve to bring some glory to this city, to the city whence I come, and to all Italy.

> (nec negaverim plurimum me in hanc sententiam impulisse affectum quemdam et reverentiam veterum poetarum qui excellentibus ingeniis in hac eadem urbe floruerunt, hic vixerunt, hic denique sepulti sunt; ut enim prelcare Marcus Tullius, secundo De legibus, ait: "Ego tibi istam iustam causam puto cur huc libentius venias atque hunc locum diligas"; et sequitur: "Movemur enim, nescio quo pacto, locis ipsis, in quibus eorum, quos diligimus aut admiramur, assunt vestigia. Inde quidem ipse ille nostre Athene non tam operibus magnificis exquisitisque antiquorum artibus delectant quam recordatione summorum virorum, ubi quisque habitare, ubi sedere, ubi disputare sit solitus, studioseque eorum sepulcra contemplor"; hec ille. Michi autem-fateor-hec non ultima causa fuit Romam veniendi. Ceterum, quecunque sit causa, adventum ipsum et huic urbi et illi de qua et universe Ytalie, ipsa saltem rei novitate, non inglorium futurum esse confido.)[21]

---

[21] Petrarch 1953, 1245; Petrarch 1988a, 38, modified (*Collatio laureationis* 6.22–36).

Petrarch replaces more than resuscitates the dead whose memory he evokes here, in an accentuation of his own *novitas* (novelty or modernity).[22] The Rome that he recreates anew does not occupy a true geographical place but a place in his own memory, a *locus memoriae.* The Rome of the present day is replaced by the phantasm of memory of the ancient city in the mind of the poet. The laureation ceremony publicly authorizes him to monumentalize that ancient city in his works. Petrarch, the poet, becomes the mediator between the ancient and modern city, creating a new political theater that brings the ancient city's glory to the modern city and to all of Italy. It is important to notice that the result of this rhetorical maneuver is not to assert his belonging to present-day Rome or to the Rome of the Caesars but to create an ideal city of which the poet is citizen that resides outside of time. Petrarch's veiled offer to commemorate the deeds of great men and warriors in the concluding portion of the oration is given further ambiguity by the very vision that Petrarch has in mind for cultural renewal. He is offering himself as poet to the great men of Italy, just as he distances himself as poet from the current state of affairs. As a potential civic poet, he is maintaining an aloofness toward real political engagement. He is both a poet of the city and a poet in historical exile from that city. Like Dante before him, he seems reticent to locate himself irrevocably within a single civic context.

If the oration provides an ambiguous representation of Petrarch's real privilege as poet laureate and his relation to a civic context, then the diploma that he receives and takes away with him is far more practical in its scope. Jonathan Usher notes that the differences between the two documents "derive from an acute awareness of documentary status, mode of delivery and intended recipients."[23] He describes the diploma, which it seems Petrarch must have written himself,[24] as "an instrument: its function is normative and declarative, not expository and hortatory ... The *Privilegium* is an opportunistic passport to institutional recognition in the world Petrarch actually inhabited, not a manifesto (like the *Collatio*) for the one he hoped would be reborn through his efforts."[25] The diploma, then, translates into reality the ambiguities of the idealizing oration. The diploma is divided into two parts, the first of which is a "justificatory preamble (*arenga*)" and the second a "bureaucratic declaration

---

[22] Cf. Petrarch 1938–42, 1.171–174; Petrarch 1975–85, 1.193–195; Petrarch's letter to King Robert of Naples, *Familiares* 4.7.
[23] Usher 2009, 162.   [24] Usher 2009, 185 n. 3.   [25] Usher 2009, 162.

(*dispositio*)."[26] The declaration officially recognizes Petrarch as a poet and historian, as a *magister* in poetry, who has the authority to read and comment on poetry in public and private and to publish his own works. It even gives him the right to dress like a poet and to wear laurel, myrtle, or ivy crowns. He is essentially given the public recognition due to a professor of the arts. Each of these privileges is linked to Petrarch's public enactment of the poet's profession. Finally, he is granted Roman citizenship with both ancient and modern rights, a benefit that will give him license not only to speak in Roman affairs but also to practice the profession of poetry across the old Roman empire.

What in the oration was a general defense of the poet's labor and profession, linked to the poet's ability to immortalize history, is here translated into an official recognition that Petrarch can transfer to other realms beyond the city of which he is poet. Usher notes that "Petrarch's own assumption of the title of poet is meant to give him a place within the public scheme of things, and specifically to make him visible to rulers."[27] This observation links back to Petrarch's insinuation that the poet has the ability to make great men famous. His diploma gives him the bureaucratic recognition necessary to practice his profession. Petrarch is clearly interested in creating some civic role for himself as poet. The specification that Petrarch was granted Roman citizenship "with the old and new privileges" indicates Petrarch's awareness that he needed to locate the bureaucratic authority of his new professional role within a real civic context. Yet it also leaves room for the symbolic meaning associated with ancient Rome that he will carry with him in his perennial absence from the city. The document itself gives no explanation of what this dual citizenship would mean. According to Usher and Dieter Mertens, the claim to Roman citizenship is "a piece of political propaganda [that] cannot afford to be precise."[28] The diploma, then, does its best to translate into practical use the ambiguities of the oration. What we can take away from their juxtaposition is that Petrarch was not only torn between old and new, ideal and practical, but that his idea of the civic role of the poet in its initial formation was itself ambiguous. He wanted the practical professional rights that came along with official civic recognition, but he also wanted to maintain his distance from actual engagement. He was no Mussato. Rather, as we can see in his choice of subject for the *Africa*, his vision was centered on the past, on using the examples of the ancient Roman heritage to incite virtuous behavior in the present.

---

[26] Usher 2009, 163.   [27] Usher 2009, 165.   [28] Usher 2009, 180.

The Poet of Rome's Polemic against the City: *Epystola metrica* 2.10

A few years after his recognition in Rome, in 1344, Petrarch received a letter that attacked him as poet laureate and the art of poetry itself. In it, Wilkins observes, "Petrarch's coronation was said to be undeserved and premature, and his poetry was said to be generally unknown; and poets were called mendacious and mad, and their writings puerile."[29] The letter, it seems, was sent to Petrarch by Lancellotto Anguissola, a nobleman associated with the Visconti, at the behest of Brizio Visconti, an illegitimate son of Luchino Visconti, the lord of Milan.[30] Petrarch records his response to Brizio in *Epystola metrica* 2.10, a 290-line metrical letter in hexameters, in which he refers to his assailant as Zoilus.[31] In his self-defense in this metrical letter, Petrarch recalibrates his relationship to city life by separating himself as poet from the city as the place of the masses.

Petrarch responds vehemently to the suggestion that he did not deserve the laurel crown because he was not famous enough. His response to this attack on his fame indicates the elitist perspective on society that Petrarch takes as poet:

> Say, would it have become me to parade through every city with my temples decked with fronds renewed? Or to have summoned throngs of witnesses? To seek by shameful means for popular approval? At that time my aim was to win praise from but a few. What profit were there in the ignorant applause of all the thousands that compose the herd, or in the vapid murmurings of idle theatre-goers? Is it then for me less glorious to have pleased the King of Sicily with my song than to have won the favor of the raving multitude throughout the land? Did it avail me less to mount the steps of the Capitoline in the Queen City than to make my way with plodding purpose over empty swamps or lonely forest trails or through bleak fields inhabited by loutish yokels, dwelling in scattered squalid huts? Your town knows naught of what I've written; why do your crude walls impede my progress? Let them not complain. To me it seemed sufficient to seek out the world's great capital.

---

[29] Wilkins 1961, 46.

[30] For a discussion of the identity of Petrarch's addressee, see Ricci 1947; Wilkins 1961, 47; and Bergin 1983, 184–185.

[31] As Bergin 1983 remarks, "Zoilus was a Greek grammarian of the fourth century B.C., notorious for his acerbic criticism of Homer; a sketch of him may be found in Vitruvius, *De Architectura* (7 *Praef.* 8), a book known to Petrarch" (186). This letter has been for the most part neglected in studies of Petrarch's theory of poetry. See, however, Ronconi 1976, 65–82. On the *Epystole metrice* in general, see Wilkins 1956; Schönberger and Schönberger 2004; Velli 2006; and Martinez 2015.

(Nunquid / non satis est meminisse semel? Decuitne per urbes / circumferre nova viridantia tempora fronde? / Testarique greges hominum populique favorem / infami captare via? Laudarier olim / a paucis michi propositum. Quid inertia vulgi / millia contulerint, quid murmura vana theatri? / Ergo ne Trinacrio minor est mihi carmine Regi / gloria quam turbe passim placuisse furenti? / regineque minus Capitolia profuit urbis / scandere quam vacuas studio lustrasse paludes / avia quam nemorum, rudibus quam rura colonis, atque inopes sparsasque casas? Incognita vestro / carmina nostra foro. Quid rustica menia nobis / obiiciunt? Quo jure fremunt? satis esse putavi / terrarum petiisse caput.)[32]

The juxtaposition of the city of Rome and the towns of Italy could not be clearer. If Petrarch is a poet of the city – specifically of Rome – it is in the figurative sense of the city as the capital of the world. Being the poet of Rome allows him to exist beyond the "crude walls" of the towns and villages of the world. He also sees his fame as deriving from an elite few, not from the popular classes of the city, which he will later associate with Dante's vernacular. He goes on to list how cities become famous thanks to their poets – a list which lacks Milan.[33]

The language of vituperation of the lower classes of the urban environment is scattered across the rest of the letter. At a later point, he writes that he would even give up the laurel crown if the approval of the people should be necessary: "And as for me, my verses must upraise me; without them I shall be nothing. But must they win the vulgar herd's approval? Nay, I'd rather forego the name of bard and tear the wreath of laurel from my brow and, head uncrowned, languish for long years, inglorious and unknown" ("Scriptis ego sum tollendus in altum; / his sine nullus ero. Nunquid tamen illa probari / est opus et vulgo? Titulo caruisse poete, / abiecisse graves spoliator vertice ramos / maluerim, et longis latuisse inglorious annis").[34] With these words, Petrarch asserts that he would relinquish the *titulus poete*, or the sign of public rank that he had gained with the laurel diploma. The status of his title, while civic, is seen as separate from the standard ranks of humanity. As he goes on to say: "Vulgar concerns are left most properly beneath one's feet" ("Vulgaria oportet / linguere sub

---

[32] Petrarch 1983, 190–193 (*Epystola metrica* 2.10.41–56).

[33] It is interesting to note that Petrarch here recognizes that Padua has become famous because of the efforts of Mussato, whose laureation he describes (*Epystola metrica* 2.10.70–74). In this letter, at least, Petrarch associated Mussato with the classical revival and not with the kind of petty civic poetics that Zoilus demanded. It is particularly ironic that Petrarch should be attacking Milan, the place where he would later move and spend ten years at the service of the Visconti. It is likely that Petrarch anonymized the name of his attacker because of his later association with his family.

[34] Petrarch 1983, 198–199 (*Epystola metrica* 2.10.132–136).

pedibus").[35] Much of Petrarch's posturing about the city in this letter
seems to emerge from an anxiety about the nature of his privileges in the
diploma. His attacker asked him to specify "by what name I'd be known"
("quo nomine signer"), as a challenge to his new title. In response, Petrarch
distances himself from the public privileges that the laurel diploma had
given him, questioning the bureaucracy that his attacker participated in:
"Has our case then come to a court of justice; does the law require my
presence and my documents? Nay, who I am and on what path I tread my
pen makes clear, needing no words from me" ("Anne ad pretoria ventum
est? / Iure agitur mecum consignatisque tabellis? Qui sim, quemve sequar
callem, stilus ipse, tacente / me loquitur").[36] Thus he denies the interest in
public documentation that his diploma belies, and he reasserts the exceptionality of the poet as described in the oration. Here again the question of
his language lies just below the surface, since *stilus* can indicate both the
instrument of writing and the language. Petrarch's noble Latin language
speaks for him.

The anxiety about public recognition leads Petrarch to distance the
role of the poet from the city proper. His attacker evidently brought up
that Plato had banished poets from the city. In his response to this
claim, Petrarch asserts that the poet properly exists beyond the walls of
the city-state:

> From the city's heart you fain would banish us? Nay, wait a little; we are
> already leaving by our choice. We love the streams and hidden woodland
> groves and scorn the madding crowd and are content to stroll through
> pleasant meadows. He who first concerned himself with matters of the
> state, knowing we poets would be alien to habits of the masses, and the folk
> intolerant of our manners and our zeal for study, ruled the masses should
> possess the clamorous town, while the calm countryside should be the
> home of solitary bards. The good man granted them as well the peace of
> woods unpeopled and a wide space of land.

> (Media nos pellis ab urbe? / Sed paulum expecta: iam sponte recedimus;
> amnes / et nemorum secreta placent, turbamque nocentem / odimus, ac leti
> campis spatiamur amenis. / Hinc quia prospexit, cui primum publica cure /
> res fuit, adversos populi nos moribus, illum / moribus infestum nostris
> studioque futurum, / discrevit populo strepitum, rus vatibus almum /
> solivagis, vacueque bonus dedit otia silve / liberiusque solum.)[37]

---

[35] Petrarch 1983, 200–201 (*Epystola metrica* 2.10.168–169).
[36] Petrarch 1983, 208–209 (*Epystola metrica* 2.10.263–267).
[37] Petrarch 1983, 202–203 (*Epystola metrica* 2.10.174–183).

The pastoral landscape that Dante had juxtaposed to the city-space of Giovanni del Virgilio is here represented as the proper place of the poet. Yet, the terms that Petrarch uses in his defense are also easily transposed onto Petrarch's public disdain for vernacular poetry, especially that of Dante, which he famously criticizes in *Familiares* 21.15 for its low style that spoke to the urban non-elite, much in the same way as del Virgilio had. Petrarch here unveils that the civic ritual that he had undergone in Rome did not make him a poet of the people. His aspirations were higher: like Virgil and Homer he would write a historical poem that would "move the minds of men through myriad toils along the road to virtue" ("animos ageret per mille labores / perque altum virtutis iter").[38] The city to which he belonged was beyond the questions of legality and fame that define the local urban environment.

The Poet of Rome in Action: Petrarch and Cola di Rienzo

Despite Petrarch's distancing of himself from the populated city in preference for the phantasmatic Rome that existed only in his imagination, he did end up trying to take advantage of his Roman citizenship and of his status as poet in political affairs.[39] In three of his letters connected with the popular uprising led by Cola di Rienzo in Rome, Petrarch authorizes himself to opine about the situation there as a *civis romanus*.[40] In May of 1347, di Rienzo, "a young visionary with a gift for oratory," took control over Rome from the nobility and the pope.[41] After a misguided attempt to restore the Roman Republic, he eventually became a tyrant who bore the name of Tribune. After seven months, he ended up in exile and then in Prague, at the court of Emperor Charles IV. He was tried for heresy in 1352 in Avignon but was eventually freed and sent to Rome as a

---

[38] Petrarch 1983, 204–205 (*Epystola metrica* 2.10.197–198).

[39] On the revolution of Cola di Rienzo and Petrarch's involvement in it, see Musto 1996; Mazzotta 2006b; Crouzet-Pavan 2010; and Fenzi 2011. On Cola di Rienzo, see Porta 1979. On the *Liber sine nomine*, see Martinez 2006. On Petrarch's uncollected letters, see Westwater 2006.

[40] The first letter is *Epistola varia* 48 (now *Lettera dispersa* 8) of June 1347, in which he encourages di Rienzo to free the Romans from slavery. The second is *Familiares* 11.6 of August 1351, in which he advises the Cardinals appointed to reform the government in Rome. The other is the letter from the *Liber sine nomine* 4, of 1352, addressed to di Rienzo in prison. As Usher 2009, 191 n. 30, notes, Petrarch also mentions his Roman citizenship in *Familiares* 4.12, a consolatory letter to Giovanni Colonna on the death of his brother Giacomo, of September 1341, and in the *Apologia contra cuiusdam Galli calumnias*, a polemic written in 1373 against Jean de Hesdin concerning the necessity of returning the pope to Rome.

[41] Musto 1996, xiii.

papal emissary to restore order. He met his end in Rome in 1354, when he was killed by a mob at the Capitoline.

With the revolution of Cola di Rienzo in Rome, Petrarch sees the possibility of creating a real place for a new ancient Rome in the modern world, in which the Curia would be returned to the seat of Saint Peter. The role he takes in his rapport with the Tribune of the plebs is authorized by Petrarch's Roman citizenship: "Hastily I seized my pen that, in the midst of such great and such remarkable harmony of a delivered people, my voice might also be heard, though from a distance, that I too might perform my duty as a Roman citizen" ("Itaque calamum festinabundus arripui, ut in tanto tam celebri libertatis populi consensus vox mea de longinquo saltem audiretur et vel sic Romani civis officio fungerer").[42] In June 1347, Petrarch sees in the deliverance of the Roman people the possible foundation for the Rome he had imagined in the *Collatio* – a Rome for which he would be able to write the true imperial epic (beyond the unfinished *Africa*): "Crowned with Apollo's wreath, I shall ascend lofty and inspiring Helicon. There at the brim of the Castalian font, I shall recall the Muses from their exile and sing resounding words in abiding memory of your glory, words that will ring throughout the ages" ("Appollinea fronde redimitus desertum atque altum Helicona penetrabo: illic Castalium ad fontem Musis ab exilio revocatis ad mansuram glorie vestre memoriam sonantius aliquid canam quod longius audietur").[43] The recall of the Muses is associated with the renovation of ancient Roman freedom, which his poetry will spread to the world. Across the correspondence connected with the event, Petrarch relies on his privilege as poet-citizen of Rome in order to pronounce himself.

A part of the correspondence is the fifth eclogue of his *Bucolicum carmen*, sent to di Rienzo in July 1347 along with an explanatory letter that decoded the pastoral cipher for him. Even when Petrarch resides in his poetic solitude, in the forest, removed from history, nevertheless his mind is in the city. His poetry only lightly veils the political concerns that vex him: a general lack of ethics, political factionalism, and lack of historical perspective. Even if he does not mention his Roman citizenship, he enacts his citizen's privilege in his function as a civic poet. In a letter to di Rienzo from a month later, Petrarch quotes lines from his *Africa*, as he is authorized to do in his official diploma:

---

[42] Petrarch 1994, 76; Petrarch 1996, 23 (*Lettera dispersa* 8.476–479).
[43] Petrarch 1994, 76; Petrarch 1996, 24 (*Lettera dispersa* 8.483–486).

An illustrious name is not to be gained cheaply, nor is it kept cheaply. "Guarding a great name is itself a great task." Pardon me for quoting you a slight verse of my own, which pleased me so much that I was not ashamed to transfer it bodily from my daily letters to my epic *Africa*. Please release me from this most bitter necessity: do not let the lyric verses that I began to compose in your praise and over which – as my pen can testify – I have spent much toil, end in satire.

(Non queritur gratis clarum nomen nec servatur quidem, "Magnus enim labor est magne custodia fame." Permitte michi meo versiculo tecum uti, qui adeo michi placuit ut eum ex quotidianis epystolis non puduerit ad *Africam* transferre; et hanc michi quoque durissimam necessitatem exime, ne lyricus apparatus taurum laudum, in quo – teste quidem hoc calamo – multus eram, desinere cogatur in satyram.)[44]

Here Petrarch is not only worried about di Rienzo's name but also his own. Their destinies are connected in the enterprise of founding a new Rome.

In a letter to the Cardinals appointed to reform the government of Rome, sent on October 25, 1351, Petrarch stages his authority to advise the cardinals again in terms of his laurel crown:

The safety of our common country and mother was at stake; and he who is not moved by the woes of his dear mother is not a true son. In addition to this debt that humanity in general owes, there is added a certain special claim that the city of Rome has on my services for its former favors: by extraordinary privilege she elected me her citizen.

(Comunis patrie et parentis publice salus in ambiguo vertitur; non est filius quem pie matris non tangit inuria. Accedit ad humani generis universale debitum singulare quoddam erga me meritum urbis Rome, que et suum me insigni privilegio civem vocat.)[45]

Here, at the end of the political debacle, Petrarch seeks to reapply his Roman citizenship for the Roman nobles, from whom he alienated himself. By the end of the brief revolution, Petrarch had to distance himself as poet from the failed endeavor. If the *Collatio* had staged a theatrical overcoming of the past greatness of Rome, giving it fleeting presence in the present, then di Rienzo similarly offers a brief possibility of overcoming Rome's present barbarity and founding it anew. The poet experiences the same sense of lack for the recent past as he does for the ancient past. The potential of both turn out to be an empty ghost.

[44] Petrarch 1938–42, 2.110; Petrarch 1996, 100 (*Familiares* 7.7.31–39).
[45] Petrarch 1938–42, 2.357; Petrarch 1996, 107 (*Familiares* 11.16.5–11).

In the aftermath of the event, when Petrarch addresses the Roman people in a letter from October 1352, he takes on a hortatory role once again as a citizen of Rome and as poet laureate. In this letter, he wishes to assert that di Rienzo's efforts confirm the greatness of Rome as the rightful place of Empire. He affirms di Rienzo's innocence for the crime of heresy. He does not sign his name to the letter but only defines himself as a citizen of Rome: "Yet I too remain silent, nor do I affix my name to this letter, supposing that the style will be sufficient to reveal the writer. I add only this: that it is a Roman citizen who addresses you" ("nunc taceo, neque his ipsis ad vos scriptis meum nomen adicio, stilum ipsum sufficere arbitratus, hoc adiecto, civem romanum esse qui loquitur").[46] The Petrarch who is a citizen of Rome and the people of Rome whom he addresses, however, belong to two separate categories of citizenship. Petrarch is citizen of the Rome of memory and of the potential new Rome, while the people belong to the modern city. He is exhorting them to become more than they are. He, in fact, is more Roman than they are, because he belongs to the idea of a new Rome that does not yet exist, the Rome first staged in the *Collatio*. This becomes clear in the concluding exhortation:

> Dare something, I earnestly ask you, in memory of your past history, for the ashes and the glory of your ancestors, in the name of the empire, out of mercy for Jesus Christ, who commands us to love our neighbors and to aid the afflicted. . . . You who once with an insignificant embassy freed a king of Egypt from the siege of the Syrians, now liberate your fellow citizen from undeserved imprisonment.

> (Audete aliquid, adiuro vos, per memoriam rerum romanarum, per maiorum cineres ac gloriam, per nomen imperii, per misericordiam Ihesu Christi, qui diligi proximum et succurri iubet afflictis! . . . Et qui parva quondam legatione regem Egyptium ab obsidione syriaca liberastis, civem nunc vestrum ab indignis carceribus liberate!)[47]

Petrarch's exhortation functions as a call to be Roman and Christian at once. The superimposition of biblical and classical imagery echoes the passage he quoted from Cicero's description of Athens in the *Collatio*. This is a call for moral and cultural renewal that is based on ideals his audience could not have comprehended. As a public intellectual bent on realizing a political ideal, Petrarch's efforts were an utter failure. For the poet at the

---

[46] Petrarch 1974b, 54; Petrarch 1996, 156 (*Sine nomine* 4).
[47] Petrarch 1974b, 60 and 64; Petrarch 1996, 159 and 160 (*Sine nomine* 4).

end of 1352, this letter signaled both his final act as citizen-poet of Rome and his imminent move back to Italy, to Milan, where he thought he might have an impact on the condition of Italy and Europe more broadly. He will hereafter fashion himself as an intellectual in exile from the future Rome that he failed to create.

Petrarch's letters to di Rienzo seek to provide his correspondent with an awareness of his position in history, so that he may learn how to comport himself in power without becoming a tyrant. Petrarch's role as the ethical conscience of political power is enabled by the privileges he receives as poet laureate. His involvement in the disastrous events that befell di Rienzo, however, contributed to Petrarch losing favor among the Papacy in Avignon and among the nobles of Rome, who had been integral to arranging his laurel coronation.[48] This event had lasting consequences for Petrarch's vision of the role of the poet. He would never again commit himself to a political enterprise as a poet. Although he would continue to associate with political power in Milan, in Padua, and elsewhere, and his public fame was in large part due to his title of poet, he would not employ poetry in an explicitly political and hortatory way. In reimagining the role of the poet, he would fall back on the idea of the poet as outside of the city that was already a part of the tension of the *Collatio* and of the metrical letter to Zoilus. With this came an increasing vitriol toward the city itself as the place of discord caused by the people.[49] The document that testifies most clearly to this crisis of place in Petrarch's conception of the poet's relationship with the city is *Familiares* 10.4.

Finding a Place for Poetry: *Familiares* 10.4 and *Bucolicum Carmen* 1

By far the best known of Petrarch's discourses on poetry is his 1349 letter to his brother Gherardo, who had become a Carthusian monk at Montreux in 1343.[50] It is here, for the first time, that Petrarch engages with the

---

[48] See Usher 2009, 180.

[49] Baron 1968, 7–50 argues that Petrarch entered a period of pessimism and retreat after the di Rienzo affair. As I understand it, however, Petrarch's cultural ideology remained much the same – he sought to engage in political affairs. His move to Italy, however, did signal an abandonment of his fashioning of himself as poet, which he no longer needed to secure patronage for his intellectual and political pursuits.

[50] Petrarch dates his letter December 2, 1349. On *Familiares* 10.4 and *Bucolicum Carmen* 1, see Greene 1982; Mazzotta 1993b, 147–166; and Ascoli 2009. On Petrarch's ideas about the place of poetry in spiritual life, see also Barsella 2006, 207. See also Yocum 2013 on Petrarch's engagement with Carthusian monasticism. On the place of this letter in the history of the topos of the *poeta theologus*, see (Giuseppe) Billanovich 1947, 121–125 and Witt 1977, 542–544. On Petrarch's

question of poetry's vicinity to theology. The relationship between poetry and theology is presented as a fraternal connection, inasmuch as they both derive from the same source. The letter is meant as a companion piece to Petrarch's *Parthenias*, the first eclogue of the *Bucolicum carmen*, which he composed in 1346 and whose allegory the letter explicates. The eclogue recounts a dialogue between two shepherds, Monicus (Gherardo) and Silvius (Petrarch), who as brothers have pursued different paths. The former, a life of removal from society, the latter a life of wandering and exertion through study guided by Parthenias (Virgil). Silvius recounts his love of the Muses and his calling to write poetry, while Monicus counters with a call to enter his cave where he can hear the Psalms of David. Their conversation is interrupted by Silvius' desire to return to the drafting of the *Africa*. The eclogue, like the famous letter on the ascent of Mont Ventoux,[51] stages an internal conflict in Petrarch about his secular profession, which is often described as a spiritual crisis that began in 1343 and that was exacerbated by his visit to his brother's monastery in 1347.[52] As much as this may be true, it is also indicative of Petrarch's very real struggles in the realm of politics, which had ended in failure around the same time.

The rhetorical division of the letter requires the reader to reconcile the discourse on theology and poetry in terms of the dialogic indeterminacy of the eclogue. Thomas M. Greene noticed that there exists an underlying struggle between the two brothers and what they represent: the religious path to salvation through a rejection of society (theology) and the secular path to fame through the active life of the humanist (poetry).[53] This struggle is not only external but internal. Both brothers could be seen as representing a general tension in the Petrarchan self between the Christian and the classical. As Ascoli convincingly shows, however, Dante "is hiding in plain sight" in both the letter and the eclogue that it seeks to explain.[54] Ascoli further claims that beneath the figure of Monicus in the eclogue (who represents Gherardo) lurks the specter of Dante for Petrarch.[55] Starting from this key observation, I would like to show how the letter's representation of the relationship between theology and poetry is thematized in terms of the location of both in relation to the social world. I see Petrarch as entertaining the idea of a retreat from society at the same time

---

probable knowledge of Mussato's defenses of poetry, see (Giuseppe) Billanovich 1947, 121–122 and Ronconi 1976, 131–132. For a general discussion of the *Bucolicum Carmen*, see Carrai 2006.
[51] Petrarch 1938–42, 1.153–161; Petrarch 1975–85, 1.172–180 (*Familiares* 4.1).
[52] On Petrarch's representation of this period of his life, see Ascoli 1991.
[53] See Greene 1982, 38–39.   [54] Ascoli 2009, 135.   [55] Ascoli 2009, 135.

as he reasserts his engagement with society from the distance of his Christian classicizing epic.

Petrarch opens his letter by asking his brother not to judge his poem harshly, just because it is "inharmonious with your profession and contrary to your goals" ("professioni tue dissonum adversumque proposito").[56] Before explaining the poem, he promises to show how "poetry is not in the least contrary to theology . . . I might almost say that theology is the poetry of God" ("theologie quidem minime adversa poetica est... parum abest quin dicam theologiam poeticam esse de Deo").[57] The perspective that Petrarch takes on the relationship between theology and poetry is the opposite of that taken by Mussato. The Paduan had claimed that poetry was like theology – indeed, that poetry was a second theology – placing the two forms of discourse on the same level from the perspective of the poetic. Here Petrarch takes the point of view of his brother, claiming that theology itself has poetic elements. This, of course, was a part of Mussato's argument as well, but with the purpose of augmenting the power of poetry to bear his moral and political ideology.

Poetry and theology share, according to Petrarch, the expression of truth through figurative speech, especially allegory. Like Mussato, he cites the idea taken from Aristotle's *Metaphysics* that the first theologians were poets, and he traces a brief history of poetry as the beginning of religious thought. Poets, Petrarch offers, were once the elite leaders of a religious cult:

> men, once ignorant but desirous of the truth and especially knowledge of God – a desire natural to men – began believing in a certain superior power that governs mortal affairs. They considered it proper that this power be venerated with a submission more than human and a worship more than venerable. Thus, they chose to build magnificent buildings called temples and to have consecrated ministers whom they named priests, as well as splendid statues and golden vases, marble altars and beautiful vestments. Furthermore, lest their praise remain mute, they determined to appease the divinity with high-sounding words and to bestow sacred flattery on the divinity in a style far removed from common and public speech. In addition, they employed rhythmical measures in order to provide pleasure and banish tediousness. Indeed, it had to be an uncommon form of speech and possess a certain artfulness, exquisiteness, and novelty. Since such language was called *poetes* in Greek, those who used it were called *poets*.
>
> (olim rudes homines, sed noscendi veri precipueque vestigande divinitatis studio – quod naturaliter inest homini – flagrantes, cogitare cepissent esse

---

[56] Petrarch 1938–42, 2.301; Petrarch 1975–85, 2.69 (*Familiares* 10.4.1).
[57] Petrarch 1938–42, 2.301; Petrarch 1975–85, 2.69 (*Familiares* 10.4.1).

superiorem aliquam potestatem per quam mortalia regerentur, dignum rati sunt illam omni plusquam humano obsequio et cultu augustiore venerari. Itaque et edes amplissimas meditati sunt, que temple dixerunt, et ministros sacros, quos sacerdotes dici placuit, et magnificas statuas et vasa aurea et marmoreas mensas et purpureos amictus; ac ne mutus honos fieret, visum est et verbis altisonis divinitatem placare et procul ab omni plebeio ac publico loquendi stilo sacras superis inferre blanditias, numeris insuper adhibitis quibus et amenitas inesset et tedia pellerentur. Id sane non vulgari forma sed artificiosa quadam et exquisita et nova fieri oportuit, que quoniam greco sermone "poetes" dicta est, eos quoque qui hac utebantur, poetas dixerunt.)[58]

This passage seems like a strange way of trying to defend poetry as a kind of theology that his brother – a Carthusian monk – could embrace. This kind of worship seems to speak to the idolatry, wealth, and civic engagement that the monk's simple life was meant to reject. Petrarch is painting a picture of poetry as theology that is oriented toward the manifestation of the divine in society and not of the inner quest for knowledge of God. Already, then, there is something of a tension in Petrarch's explanation. This tension can be explained in terms of the inner meaning and the outer appearance of poetry, which is the topic to which Petrarch turns before concluding.

Petrarch goes on to cite classical and biblical sources in defense of his understanding. He offers up the Psalms as the prime example of theological poetry that his brother could embrace. The Psalms of David, he says, maintain their poetic qualities even in Jerome's Latin translation. He closes this portion of the letter, which he terms a "defense of style" ("pro stili excusatione"),[59] by telling his brother:

> Concentrate on the meaning; if it is true and wholesome, embrace it regardless of the style. To praise food served in an earthen vessel while feeling disgust at the same meal served on a golden platter is a sign either of madness or hypocrisy. To thirst for gold is a sign of greed; to be unable to tolerate it is a sign of the petty mind. A meal surely becomes neither better nor worse because of gold. I most certainly do not deny that, as with gold, poetry is more noble in its own class, just as lines drawn with a ruler are straighter than those drawn freehand.

> (sensibus intende, qui si veri salubresque sunt, quolibet stilo illos amplectere. Laudare dapem fictilibus appositam, eandem in auro fastidire, aut dementis aut ypocrite est. Avari est aurum sitire, non posse pati pusilli

---

[58] Petrarch 1938–42, 2.301–302; Petrarch 1975–85, 2.69 (*Familiares* 10.4.3–5).
[59] Petrarch 1938–42, 2.303; Petrarch 1975–85, 2.71 (*Familiares* 10.4.9).

animi est; non fit auro melior cibus certe, nec deterior. Profecto autem sicut
aurum sic carmen in suo genere nobilius non nego, quanto scilicet rectiora
sunt que ad regulam fiunt, quam que temere.)[60]

The inner nature of poetry and theology, Petrarch offers, is what makes
them alike. Yet, the outer appearance of poetic language (gold) is opposed
to the simple words (earthenware) of his brother, just as the outward
opulence of the first poet-theologians is implicitly juxtaposed to a simplicity of faith. What is at stake here are appearances. Under what conditions
can poetry and theology be considered unopposed? Petrarch suggests that
it is a question of style, or of language. Poetry and theology are merely
different styles of doing the same thing. Embedded in this "defense of
style" is a reflection on the relationship between the places of theology/
Gherardo and those of poetry/Petrarch. Petrarch's theological poetry is
represented as a foundation of human society. It is associated with civic life
and religious practice, but as the initiator of that life and practice it also
resides above and beyond the framework of what it builds. By being
beyond "common and public speech," the poet resides beyond the city.
Although the question of Latin versus vernacular composition here is not
under discussion, the ideology expressed here could easily be coopted in
favor of the Latin language over more common forms of expression.

In the letter's summary and explication of the eclogue, Petrarch inter-
rogates the question of style in the spatialized terms of the pastoral cipher,
claiming as his space both the removed locales of the monk's repose and
the peopled locations of the world. The initial description of the two
characters, Monicus and Silvius, are indicative of what they represent:
"Seeing Monicus alone and enjoying an enviable repose in a certain cavern,
Silvius speaks admiringly of his good fortune. He laments his own misfortune because Monicus had found peace after deserting the countryside
and his flock, while he himself still roamed the barren hills in great
discomfort" ("Silvius ergo Monicum solum et invidioso otio felicem videns
sub antro quodam quiscentem, alloquitur quasi fortunam illius admirans
et suam deflens, quod ille grege ac rure posthabito requiem invenerit, ipse
vero asperos colles multo cum labore circumeat").[61] Already, there is an
association between the simplicity of Gherardo/Monicus and the environment that he inhabits, as there is between the golden style of poetry and
the environment assigned to Petrarch/Silvius. In the explication proper,
this association continues, but it is also complicated. Petrarch writes:

[60] Petrarch 1938–42, 2.303; Petrarch 1975–85, 2.70 (*Familiares* 10.4.8–9).
[61] Petrarch 1938–42, 2.304; Petrarch 1975–85, 2.71 (*Familiares* 10.4.13).

This is my explanation of the names. The first is called Silvius because he had spent his life in the woods, and because from an early age there had been planted in him a hatred of the city and a love of the forest. This is why many of our friends generally call me Silvanus rather than Franciscus. For the second shepherd, on the other hand, the name is appropriate since one of the Cyclops is named Monicus, as if he were one-eyed. Such a name seemed in a certain respect fitting for you since of the two eyes that we mortals usually use, one to gaze upon heavenly things and the other upon earthly ones, you renounced the one that beholds earthly things, being content with the better eye.

(Nominum ratio hec est: primi quidem tum quod in silvis res acta est, tum propere insitum ab ineunte etate urbis odium amoremque silvarum, prop-tere quem multi ex nostris in omni sermone sepius me Silvanum quam Franciscum vocant; secundi autem quida cum unum ex Cyclopibus Mon-icum dicant quasi monoculum, id quodam respectu proprie tibi convenire visum est, qui e duobus oculis, quibus omnes comuniter utimur mortales, quorum altero scilicet celestia altero terrena respicimus, tu terrena cernen-tem abiecisti oculo meliore contentus.)[62]

What the two characters represent spatially is posited in terms of their relationship with the world. Monicus is a one-eyed Cylcops because he no longer looks upon worldly affairs. Silvanus, too, wanders the woodlands, because he hates the city. The two seem to share something in the way they relate to the rest of humanity.

This relationship is further explained in spatial terms by the eclogue, as Petrarch's explanation goes on to specify. "The cavern where Monicus dwells in solitude," he writes, "is Montreux where you now lead a monastic life amidst grottoes and groves ... Interpret the countryside and the flocks – for which it is said you did not care – as the city and mankind that you relinquished in fleeing into solitude" ("Antrum ubi solitarie degit Monicus, Mons Rivi est, ubi tu nunc monasticam vitam agis inter spe-luncas et nemora ... Rus ac gregem, quorum sprevisse curam dicitur, pro civitate et hominibus intellige, quos in solitudinem fugiens reliquisti").[63] Monicus inhabits a space of solitude that is not unlike the one claimed for poets in Petrarch's *Epystola metrica*. Yet, he has succeeded in finally rejecting the city which Silvius hates and in accepting his ultimate solitude. The explanations of the pastoral locales inhabited by Silvius similarly show that his woodlands are far from unpopulated. The mountain peak that he ascends is the Capitoline and the deserts are his studies, while "the mossy

[62] Petrarch 1938–42, 2.305–306; Petrarch 1975–85, 2.72–73 (*Familiares* 10.4.20).
[63] Petrarch 1938–42, 2.306; Petrarch 1975–85, 2.73 (*Familiares* 10.4.21).

cliffs are the powerful and the wealthy covered with their patrimony as though it were moss. The resounding springs can be called men of letters and men of eloquence" ("muscosi scopuli sunt potentes ac divites, patrimonio velut musco obsiti; fontes sonantes literati et eloquentes homines dici possunt").[64] Just as Monicus, having given up on society, inhabits the caves of monasticism, Silvius wanders beyond his native woodlands into the valleys of the social world, populated by men of letters and the powerful and wealthy – by his colleagues and his patrons. Monicus inhabits a "secure abode" ("certa sedes"), while for Silvius "there is nothing thus far but extensive wandering and an uncertainty about all things" ("michi autem adhuc vagus error et incerta omnia").[65]

The spaces inhabited by the pastoral characters not only represent a specific relation to society – a style of being in the world with others – but also a specific style of poetry. We are told early on in the description that it was Silvius' love of the Muses which pushed him to wander the world and that Monicus offers him instead the sound of a "sweeter song" ("dulciorem cantum") in his cavern.[66] Silvius traces his origins to Virgil and thence to Homer in a pastoral description of their places of origin. Petrarch explains the landscape of the pastoral cipher: "The savage forests and lofty mountains that to Silvius' astonishment were not interested in the sweetness of poetry signify the uncultivated public and prominent rulers" ("Silva horrida et aerii montes quos miratur Silvius non sequi dulcedinem canentium, vulgus incultum est et principes eminentes").[67] The landscape inhabited by Silvius, then, is not only populated by learned men and patrons but also by those who ignore the value of poetry. It is a veiled cityscape in need of a new Virgil. Later in the explication, the sweet music of which Monicus speaks is identified with the Psalms of David. Although Petrarch had earlier offered up the Psalms as an example of theological poetry, Silvius "disparages his voice and style of song while exalting his own shepherds" ("vocem modumque canendi deprimit attollens suos").[68] The pastoral valleys, woodlands, and mountains come to represent the classical style of poetry that Petrarch practices, while the caverns of the monks in turn are associated with the uncultivated "hoarseness" of David in his Psalms.

The story of the eclogue, with its typical Petrarchan juxtaposition of the worldly and the spiritual, takes a violent turn the end when Petrarch

[64] Petrarch 1938–42, 2.306; Petrarch 1975–85, 2.73 (*Familiares* 10.4.23).
[65] Petrarch 1938–42, 2.306; Petrarch 1975–85, 2.73 (*Familiares* 10.4.22).
[66] Petrarch 1938–42, 2.305; Petrarch 1975–85, 2.72 (*Familiares* 10.4.16).
[67] Petrarch 1938–42, 2.307–308; Petrarch 1975–85, 2.74 (*Familiares* 10.4.27).
[68] Petrarch 1938–42, 2.305; Petrarch 1975–85, 2.72 (*Familiares* 10.4.18).

describes the overtaking of Hannibal by Scipio Africanus. Ascoli notes that the expression Petrarch employs in the eclogue is taken directly from Dante's citation of Ovid's episode of Galatea and Polyphemus in the second eclogue: "Say, has he not, Polyphemus, by force thrust into your caverns?" ("Te, Polipheme, tuis iam vi stravisse sub antris?").[69] In the letter, this line is explained: "The young man concerning whom Silvius has begun to weave a song is Scipio Africanus, who overthrew on the African shore Polyphemus, namely Hannibal, commander of the Carthaginians. Just as Polyphemus had one eye, so did Hannibal after losing an eye in Italy" ("Iuvenis de quo cantilenam texere Silvius cepit, Africanus Scipio est, qui in litore afro Poliphemum stravit, hoc est Hanibalem Penorum ducem; sicut enim Poliphemus, sic et Hannibal monoculus fuit post oculum in Italia amissum").[70] Greene noticed that the one-eyed Polyphemus evokes for the reader the one-eyed Cyclops Monicus, whose name was explained earlier. This superimposition seems to denote a struggle between the humanist Petrarch and his spiritually oriented brother. Noticing the Dantean citation here and an implicit critique of Dantean geography earlier in the letter, Ascoli has interpreted this struggle as a performance of Petrarch's overcoming of Dante, as the classical poet who challenges Dante as a *scriba Dei*.[71] Without addressing Petrarch's possible anxiety about his own poetic novelty vis-à-vis Dante, I would like to suggest a slightly different reading of the function of Petrarch's reemployment of Dante's Polyphemus.

For Dante, as I have suggested, Polyphemus' cave, in which Dante had been invited, indicated the potential violence to which the poet would be subjected in an urban environment. Dante opposed to the caves of the Cyclopes the pastoral *locus amoenus* that he was provided in Ravenna, supposedly free of civic responsibilities as poet. Petrarch here reverses the meaning of the Cyclopes' caves, making of them not the city and its university but the place of individual solitude and of theological reflection beyond the bounds of human community. Ascoli's argument that Petrarch associates Dante with Monicus and his Davidic poetics is convincing. By suggesting an act of violence by a classical hero on the Cyclops, however, Petrarch is not necessarily asserting the novelty of his classicizing project. Rather, I would suggest, he is staging the heroic takeover of the place of theological Davidic poetry that Dante and Monicus inhabit. In this way,

---

[69] Petrarch 1974a, 15 (*Bucolicum carmen* 1.115). See Ascoli 2009, 127–128.
[70] Petrarch 1938–42, 2.309; Petrarch 1975–85, 2.75 (*Familiares* 10.4.32).
[71] Ascoli 2009, 130–134.

Petrarch's Christian classicizing epic can inhabit both spaces, poetic and theological, Davidic and Virgilian. The violence of this takeover is striking. Petrarch is intimating that Dante's removed prophetic voice as poet has abandoned society and, with the violent superimposition of the historical epic, he is demanding its replacement by a poetic voice that is more directly engaged with the historical world. Unable to reconcile spiritual removal with an engaged historical vision, he violently inscribes the latter onto the former.[72]

What this suggests, then, is that Petrarch's crisis as a political poet needed to be resolved by forcefully combining the active world of the city with the removed, contemplative world of the theologian. He is asserting implicitly that Dante's mode of removal from the city – likened to a monastic rejection of society – would not be enough to incite humanity to virtue. His struggle with Dante takes the form of penetrating the remove of the Florentine poet and bringing history there so that it can be celebrated in a sufficiently cultivated manner and not in Dante's hoarse prophetic voice. This forced combination of solitary removal and civic engagement will define the rest of Petrarch's career as a public intellectual. As he assumes more authority in his public voice, and is no longer in need of his professional diploma, he will direct verbal violence against the professional classes of the city, especially physicians. The respect given to their technical knowledge and to their mundane service to the community will come to stand in for the intellectual ills of modern society. From the purely figurative realms of solitary isolation, then, he will angrily assert his position against the "ignoramuses" of the city.

The Angry Voice of the Poet beyond the City:
Invective contra medicum

Petrarch's final assertion about the status of the poet dates to the years 1352–53, when he found himself in an altercation with a group of papal physicians about the health of Pope Clement VI. In a letter to Clement, Petrarch advised the pope to avoid the "mob of doctors" ("medicorum turbam") and to employ a single, trustworthy physician who was "outstanding not because of his eloquence but because of his knowledge and trustworthiness" ("non eloquentia sed scientia et fide conspicuum").[73]

---

[72] Cf. Mazzotta 1993b, 153.

[73] Petrarch 1938–42, 2.44; Petrarch 1975–85, 1.278–279 (*Familiares* 5.19.5). The letter was written on March 13, 1352. Petrarch cites the second phrase at *Invective* 1.3 [20] and repeats the first almost

When one of Clement's physicians, possibly the famous surgeon Guy de Chauliac,[74] learned about Petrarch's letter, he responded with a personal attack on Petrarch and on the profession of poetry. In response, Petrarch penned four letters, which he collected into the *Invective contra medicum*, his first of four collections of invectives. Petrarch's attack on the physician will be the first of many assertions of his intellectual superiority against the profession. For him, physicians were not only on the lower end of the intellectual ladder, they were also rivals for positions of power in political circles, like the Curia in Avignon.

The reason behind Petrarch's desire for control can be found in the original subject of his letter to Clement, in which he counsels the pope to abandon the train of doctors who surround him and to choose a single doctor in order to avoid the discord that the group brings. The power wielded by these doctors over the pope was in direct competition with Petrarch's own power in the papal court, which he was in the process of abandoning for Italy. It is impossible to detach the claims that Petrarch makes in his defense of poetry in the *Invective* from the political subtext of his arguments; they are embedded in a failed power-play for influence over the pope and over the political fate of Italy in general. When Petrarch initially began the exchange of insults with the physician in 1352, he was planning his departure from Avignon for Viscontian Milan.[75] His return to Italy was instigated by multiple factors, though most of them were political in nature.[76] Petrarch's involvement with Cola di Rienzo had been disastrous. It had likely prohibited him from advancing in the Curia in Avignon, and, in any case, it had alienated him from his Roman patrons, the Colonna family.[77] Although he was made several offers for minor

---

verbatim at 1.11 [53], "crowd of quarreling physicians" ("turbam dissidentium medicorum"). Petrarch 2003, 4–5, 10–11. On the origins and manuscript tradition of the *Invective*, see Ricci 1955 and Bausi 2005. For a reading of the *Invective* that focuses on the theme of sight, see Singer 2011, 62–76. On Petrarch's invectives in general, see Marsh 2015. When citing the text of the *Invective*, I place Marsh's paragraph numbers first, with Bausi's paragraph numbers in brackets.

[74] Guy de Chauliac (1300–1368) was the Archiater of the Curia for Clement VI, Innocent VI, and Urban V, and was the author of the *Chirugia magna*, a treatise on surgery that had an immense influence on late medieval medical culture. Although Petrarch's adversary in the *Invective* has traditionally been identified with de Chauliac, Bortolo Martinelli has argued against this identification. See Ricci 1978, 211. Singer, however, makes the case that de Chauliac is linked to Petrarch's physician, even if it is impossible to make the identification. See Singer 2011, 75–76.

[75] See Wilkins 1958, 3–7.   [76] See Wilkins 1958, 12.

[77] In 1347, Petrarch resigned from his position as chaplain for the Colonna family, which he had held for 17 years, because of Giovanni Colonna's opposition to Cola di Rienzo. Although he remained involved in Avignon politics, he had lost his protectors and would soon leave. The period between 1347 and 1353 was marked for Petrarch by significant travel in Italy, where he was actively searching for a new patron, between Parma, Padua, and Milan. It is a matter of some debate

ecclesiastical posts, he desired more.[78] Finally, with the death of Clement in December 1352, Petrarch no longer saw a possibility of exerting influence in Avignon or of returning the papacy to Rome, which had been a major motivating factor behind his backing of Cola di Rienzo. Combined with the devastation wrought by the plague and the continual failure of his influence in civic and ecclesiastical matters, Petrarch sought the patronage of a powerful lord who could secure his well-being, allow him to pursue his intellectual activities, and give him a stronger position from which to engage in international political affairs.[79] After the experience in Rome, his intolerance of the multitude grew considerably in this period and he sought out the single most powerful man in Italy, Giovanni Visconti of Milan.

In the *Invective*, Petrarch's representation of the poet's relation to the city capitalizes on and repeats the ideas he had expressed in the *Collatio* and in his letter to his brother in an angry tone similar to the one he had used in his *Epystola metrica* to Zoilus. His use of the angry voice of the invective violently asserts his authority in the public sphere, just as it expresses a disgust about the public sphere itself. This voice is the dark underbelly of Petrarch's insecure and self-inquiring voice in search of peace, with which we are so familiar today as readers of the *Rerum vulgarium fragmenta* and *Secretum*.[80] The invective, as a genre, pits one man's virtues against another's vices, placing all debate on an individual level, and its purpose is to drown out the voice of the other with one's own authority.[81] In the *Invective contra medicum*, Petrarch takes on the role of the intellectual warrior who attacks the physician for the centrality of his political role in the papal court. The intellectual authority of the physician among people of power threatens Petrarch's own authority so much that the poet must

whether or not Petrarch's ideas about ancient Rome changed after the failure of his effort to support Cola di Rienzo. I find that Petrarch's ideas in the *Invective* are consistent with those of the *Collatio*, even if they are more pronouncedly anti-popular.

[78] See Wilkins 1955, 63–80 and 82–83. Wilkins argues that the refusal of Petrarch's desire for a higher position in the papal Curia was behind his move to Vaucluse in 1351 and to Milan in 1353.

[79] For an account of Petrarch's political activities during and after this period that presents them as generally coherent with Petrarch's ideology and system of values, see Dotti 2001. Although Dotti does not mention it, it is possible that Petrarch saw his role in Milan (and possibly even earlier as poet-citizen of Rome) in terms of Marsilio da Padova's role for Louis IV of Bavaria. Petrarch had been in the business of representing the interests of the lords of northern Italy since the summer of 1335, when he advocated for Mastino della Scala, who had seized Parma. His friendship with Azzo da Correggio, who took back Parma in 1340, was central to his laurel crowning. Moving to Italy, Petrarch was not changing his ideological commitment to these patrons. Rather, he was abandoning the Curia as the place of his political influence.

[80] On Petrarch's voice in another of his invectives, see Barański 2007.

[81] On the invective as a literary and philosophical genre, see Arena 2007 and Eisenhauer 2007.

reassert his individual worth by destroying that of his attacker. The invective leaves no room for dialogue.

The strategy of Petrarch's *Invective contra medicum* is one of unilateral attack. David Marsh has explained that Petrarch responds to his attacker's vices by praising his own virtue, opposing the "liberal art of rhetoric" to "the mechanical science of medicine," the "edifying allegory of poetry" to the "sterile dialectic of scholastic Aristotelianism," and "his idyllic life in the country" to the "sordid practices of physicians."[82] The self-oriented strain of his defense of the poet's worth becomes clearer here than in his earlier attempts to self-authorize. Petrarch's main models for his invectives were (according to Marsh) Cicero and Jerome, both of whom criticized their opponents from a high moral pulpit. Petrarch cannot imagine a role for poetry that does not allow him to impose his voice upon others. Addressed to his primary competitor for power in the papal court, the main purpose of the *Invective* is to drown the voice of the other so that it might be replaced by his own.

Petrarch modifies one of the main generic traits of the invective – the public naming the addressee – in order to destroy even further the subjectivity of the physician.[83] Throughout the four invectives he refuses to name his attacker, not allowing that the physician gain fame through his attack on Petrarch. By not naming him Petrarch takes control of the subjectivity of the physician and subjugates it to his own. The first two words of the first invective demonstrate the control that Petrarch will begin to wield over his attacker throughout:

> Whoever you are, your relentless barking has roused an idle pen and a sleeping lion, as it were. You shall soon learn that it is one thing to carp up at another's fame with a prurient tongue and another to defend your own fame with reason.

> (Quisquis es qui iacentem calamum et sopitum – ut ita dixerim – leonem importunis latratibus excitasti, iam senties aliud esse alienam famam prurienti lingua carpere, aliud propriam ratione defendere.)[84]

We can understand from this opening line that what is at stake for Petrarch is his reputation in the present. By denigrating poetry, the physician had called into question the source of Petrarch's authority in the Curia.

---

[82] Marsh 2003, ix.   [83] On the naming of the recipient of invectives, see Arena 2007, 149.
[84] Petrarch 2003, 2–3 (*Invective contra medicum* 1.1 [1]). When citing the text of the *Invective*, I place Marsh's paragraph numbers first, with Bausi's paragraph numbers in brackets.

Anonymizing his attacker's identity, Petrarch can proceed to link it neg-
atively to his own and assume power over it. Petrarch's didactic persona
can teach by subsuming power over the self of the other, effectively
denying any form of dialogue. Petrarch figures his vituperation as defensive
and goes on to say that he is being forced into a response because silence
might be understood as complacency: "and I must therefore speak. If
I remained silent in my contempt for your affairs . . . you might take
pleasure in my silence" ("et loqui aliquid necesse est, ne, si . . . propter
contemptum rerum tuarum tacuero, tu tibi forsan ex mea taciturnitate
complaceas").[85] Petrarch cannot bear that his attacker might hold any
power over him and so, through vituperation, he takes control not only of
the discussion but also of his attacker's identity.

Petrarch had advised Clement to disband the cadre of doctors that
surrounded him and to choose a single, worthier doctor whose knowledge
did not have need of rhetorical flourishes. In the first invective, Petrarch
tells the physician that "you are clearly not that one. If you were, you
would never have written such a windy letter to answer my criticisms of
factious and ignorant physicians. You must have been cut to the quick to
have cried out so loudly" ("tu tamen ille unus proculdubio non es, quod, si
esses, nunquam discordes ac nescios medicos increpanti tam ventosa
respondisses epystola. Profundissime tangebaris, tam graviter excla-
masti").[86] Petrarch's purpose, then, is to show that the physician cannot
be the singular adviser to the pope. If he were, then he would not have
responded with a letter attacking Petrarch but would have subjected
himself to Petrarch's authority. The physician represents a threat to the
power that Petrarch imagines for himself in the court, not because he is
ignorant but because he disagrees, or is discordant. To interpret the
mentality behind Petrarch's response, one could apply to Petrarch's rebut-
tals the same reasoning that Petrarch himself applies to the physician's
letter. As the physician responded with hostility to Petrarch's letter and was
"cut to the quick," so when Petrarch responds with such vituperation to
the physician's insinuation that he had ingratiated himself with the pope[87]
we must ask why he is so enraged. It seems that the physician has cut to the
heart of the matter, since he has elicited such a passionate reply from the
poet. Petrarch is threatened by the power that others hold over the pope,

---

[85] Petrarch 2003, 2–3 (*Invective contra medicum* 1.1 [5]).
[86] Petrarch 2003, 6–7, modified (*Invective contra medicum* 1.5 [22]).
[87] Petrarch 2003, 6–7 (*Invective contra medicum* 1.6 [24]): "In your confused babbling, you did not
scruple to insinuate that I fawn on the pope" ("Nec puduit illud etiam inter confusum murmur
inserere, me pontifici adulatum").

especially discordant groups that do not accept unilaterally his own intellectual authority.

While the source of the debate revolves around the kind of learning that each man represents, what is at stake are their respective positions of political influence. The physician had criticized the art of poetry in his original attack on Petrarch:

> If you were sane, you should have replied to the pope, not to me, since I didn't write to you. Perhaps with your herbal and medicinal eloquence, you might have persuaded him to entrust his life and his affairs to you, and to place his hopes for life and health in your hands alone. In turn, he might have shunned me and my fellow scholars as a harmful and useless breed, whether you chose to call me a poet or something else. I think you will go to any lengths, ignoramus. In your hatred of me, or rather your hatred of the truth, you unjustly inveighed against poets.

> (Debuisti, si sanus esse, non michi rescribere, qui tibi nil scripseram, sed eidem illi scribere, si sibi forsan aromatico illo tuo ac medicinali suadere posses eloquio, ut tibi se ipsum et res suas crederet, vitam ac salutem suam nisi tuis e manibus non speraret, contra autem me studiisque meis deditos, nocivum atque inutile genus hominum, declinaret, seu me poetam seu quodlibet aliud dicere libuisset. Omnia enim tibi licere arbitror, ydiota, qui propter mei, quin potius veri odium, in poetas immeritos es invectus.)[88]

Here Petrarch brings to the forefront of his argument the common origin of medicine and poetry in the arts of rhetoric. Both arts (*facultates*) vie for power through words and eloquence, but the Scholasticism of the physicians sought to subsume rhetoric and poetry in the study of logic.[89] Poetry's power, however, resides in its ability to immortalize its subjects and Petrarch asserts such a power by denying it to the physician, as he goes on to state: "Perhaps your impudence should compel me to write about you in my poetry, exposing you to be torn apart by future generations. But you seemed unworthy of a place in my little works that would make you known to posterity" ("Cogeret me forte procacitas tua poetice aliquid de te loqui teque omnibus seculis lacerandum tradere, nisi quia indignus visus es qui per me posteris notus esse aut locum in meis opusculis invenires").[90] By refusing to name his attacker Petrarch is withholding the power of poetry from him. He is taking control of his attacker's selfhood in order to deny him the ability to dissent. The attacker's place in Avignon is denied

[88] Petrarch 2003, 12–13 (*Invective contra medicum* 1.12 [55]).
[89] On the relationship between rhetoric and logic in Scholasticism, see Ong 1958, 138–139.
[90] Petrarch 2003, 12–13 (*Invective contra medicum* 1.12 [58]).

along with his search for worldly fame, both of which represent threats to Petrarch's own desire for fame and power through his connection with political power. In the conclusion to the first invective Petrarch reiterates that he will not tolerate that anyone question his power. He threatens to be the "cause of great danger" ("magni periculi causa"), specifying that "for myself, I shall consider all your attacks as adding to my glory" ("ego michi quicquid attentaveris ad cumulum glorie ascribam").[91] He turns the terms of the physician's attack against him and uses them for his own rise to fame. The defense of poetry that follows is embedded in Petrarch's frustrated and angry assertion of his own power as an intellectual.[92]

Petrarch first defends poetry cursorily in the first invective in response to the physician's attack on poetry. He immediately cites the portion of Cicero's *Pro Archia* that he employed in the *Collatio*, where the Roman orator claims that poets excel by natural ability, not by learning, and that a poet "is inspired by the strength of his mind, and is filled with a sort of divine spirit" ("mentis viribus excitari, et quasi divino quodam spiritu inflari").[93] Unlike in the *Collatio*, where Petrarch first establishes poetry as a profession, here Petrarch does not aim to "ennoble the name of poets in your ears ... If I play the lyre to an ass, I may become more ridiculous than you" ("in auribus tuis nobilitare velle poetarum nomen ... Nescio an te ridiculosior sim, si asino lyram tangam").[94] Rather, the assertion serves to silence the physician's critique.

After criticizing the physician for taking up subjects about which he is ignorant, Petrarch proceeds to refute the physician's typical invocation of Boethius in his attack on poetry. In the *De consolatione philosophiae* Boethius hears Lady Philosophy say: "Who let these theatrical tarts in with this sick man? Not only have they no cures for his pain, but with their sweet potion they make it worse" ("Quis has scenicas meretriculas ad hunc aegrum permisit accede quae dolores eius non modo nullis remediis foverent, verum dulcibus insuper alerent venenis?"). She commands soon after: "Get out, you Sirens, beguiling men straight to their destruction! Leave him to *my* Muses to care for and restore to health" ("Sed abite potius Sirenes usque in exitium dulces meisque eum Musis curandum sanandumque relinquite").[95] These "theatrical tarts" are, Petrarch says, the muses of comic theater, which "enjoy no esteem even among poets" ("inter

---

[91] Petrarch 2003, 32–33 (*Invective contra medicum* 1.41 [177–178]).   [92] Cf. Marsh 2003.

[93] Petrarch 2003, 22–23 (*Invective contra medicum* 1.27 [120]).

[94] Petrarch 2003, 22–23 (*Invective contra medicum* 1.28 [124–126]).

[95] Boethius 1973, 134–135 (*Philosophiae consolatio* 1.1p.28–32, 39–41). Cf. Petrarch 2003, 26–27 (*Invective contra medicum* 1.33 [142–148]).

poetas in precio non haberi").[96] The reference to comic theater has civic resonances, inasmuch as this form of poetic representation is critiqued by Augustine in the *De civitate Dei* as a part of a pagan civil theology that he abhorred.[97] The real muses are those invested with a philosophical and allegorical meaning. He goes on to cite the same passage from Lactantius' *Divinae Institutiones* that he used to define the office of the poet in the *Collatio* as artificially representing history, not as representing falsehoods. Petrarch claims again that poets do not lie but merely hide the truth beneath a veil of imagery. This time, however, he positions the poet's task in a hierarchy of value that establishes its superiority to the medical profession. In introducing the physician's objection, he indicates that the physician spoke with the "temerity of a lowly craftsman" ("mira plebei artificis temeritate").[98] He furthermore claims that he "strive[s] to adorn the truths of the world with beautiful veils" ("studium est veritatem rerum pulcris velaminibus adornare"), not for delight but because "in this way, the truth eludes the ignorant masses, of which you are 'the very dregs'" ("ut vulgus insulsum, cuius pars ultima es, lateat").[99] As in his metrical letter to Zoilus, Petrarch dissociates poetry from the masses in language that will eventually coincide with his view on vernacular poetry.

He concludes the first invective with a claim that will be central to the conclusion of his defense of the solitary life of poets in the fourth invective – that poets are famous and precious because they procure fame for others:

> You will see the poets resplendent with glory and immortal fame, which they win not only for themselves but for others as well. It is their task above all else to preserve names that would perish; and even virtue itself needs their aid, not for its own sake but in its struggle against time and oblivion.

> (Videbis eos gloria et nominis immortaliate fulgentes, quam non sibi tantum, sed et aliis peperere, ut quibus ante alios perituris consulere nominibus datum est, et quorum adminiculo ipsa etiam virtus eget, non equidem in se ipsa, sed in eo quod habet cum tempore et cum oblivione certamen.)[100]

---

[96] Petrarch 2003, 26–27 (1.33 [147]).

[97] See Augustine 1965, 5.344–347 (*De civitate Dei* 6.9), where he critiques Varro's distinctions between different kinds of pagan theology, connecting the "mythical theology" ("fabulosa theologia") of the theaters to "civil theology" ("theologia civilis").

[98] Petrarch 2003, 28–29 (*Invective contra medicum* 1.35 [153]).

[99] Petrarch 2003, 30–31 (*Invective contra medicum* 1.37 [164]).

[100] Petrarch 2003, 30–31 (*Invective contra medicum* 1.39 [168]).

Petrarch claimed something similar in the *Collatio*, in his metrical letter to Zoilus, and in his letter to Gherardo. The socio-political context of the *Invective*, however, gives this assertion a new scope. The poet's ability to immortalize his subjects, which was implicitly promised in his coronation oration, is here presented as a tool for the acquisition not only of status but of power. The generic others here will become the great rulers of the present in the fourth invective. Like Cicero before him Petrarch ties the fortunes of poets to those of the princes whom they immortalize. Petrarch asserts a poetics that is intricately connected to legitimizing political power. Although Petrarch was highly aware of the delicate position he acquired in Milan as the subject of the Visconti, it is nevertheless undeniable that his conception of the work of the poet was intimately linked with the powerful assertion of a civic voice.

Before addressing the political role of poets that is asserted in the fourth invective, I would like to turn briefly to Petrarch's comments about poetry and the common people in the third invective, which are of direct relevance to his location of the poet within society. In the third invective Petrarch expands his rebuttal of the physician's attack on poetry as an institution. He addresses in specific terms the pagan religion of poets, the utility of poetry, the nobility of poetry, whether poetry is a liberal art, poetry's dependence on the mutability of language, the rarity of poets, the obscurity of poetic language, and the ethics of poets and their poetry. Petrarch's claims in response to the physician's attacks are both classical and patristic in origin, including citations of figures as diverse as Boethius, Isidore of Seville, Lactantius, Augustine, Jerome on the Christian side and Horace, Virgil, Cicero, Varro, and Juvenal on the Roman side. He asserts first that the pagan poets were monotheistic not through revelation but through reason and that they knew the Christian God through the materiality of creation. He goes on to say that poetry is useful for its nobility but not necessary, citing Horace's *Ars poetica*, that poetry is a liberal art while medicine is a mechanical art, and that the physician's claim about the mutability (and lack of authority) of poetic language is unfounded. He returns to the issue that Boethius seems to insinuate that poetry is inferior to philosophy, which he had addressed in the first invective. Finally, he claims that the rarity of poets is due to the fact that they are naturally precious, then that the obscurity of poetry is to protect it from the ignorant.

In response to the criticism that poetry is obscure, Petrarch parallels ancient poetry to Scripture and cites Augustine and Gregory on the advantages of the difficulty of exegesis. His point is that the difficulty of interpreting Scripture makes one appreciate its meaning all the more because of the effort one invests in it. This assertion is consonant with what he had claimed in earlier texts. There is, however, a significant difference in the respective roles of Scripture and poetry:

> If what they say is true of the Scriptures, which are offered to all people, is it not even truer of works destined for a very few? This is why, O great ignoramus, poets maintain the majesty and dignity of their style. Rather than begrudging those who can grasp our work, we offer them this pleasant labor in order to promote their enjoyment and recollection of it.

> (Que si de Scripturus illis recte dicuntur, que sunt ominibus proposite, quanto rectius de illis que paucissimis? Apud poetas, igitur, o nimium rudis, stili maiestas retinetur ac dignitas, nec capere valentibus invidetur, sed, dulci labore proposito, delectationi simul memorieque consulitur.)[101]

According to Petrarch, poetry is for the few who can afford the time and who are learned enough to interpret it, a select few who control the distribution of poetic wisdom. He specifically claims this a few lines later, saying that "not everyone can pursue such studies, but only those who have suitable intelligence and disposition, and who have received an abundance of life's necessities from fortune, or a contempt for them from virtue" ("non est enim omnium studia ista sectari, sed eorum tantum quibus et ingenium natura, et rerum vite necessariarum vel fortuna sufficientiam dederit, vel contemptum virtus").[102] Here Petrarch is proposing that poets belong to an elite caste that is both natural and social. They either have those necessities of life by fortune, or they lack the desire for them out of virtue. He does not mention by which path he arrived at the summit. If we look back at the *Collatio*, we can see here a connection to his claim to have achieved the summit of poetry by a labor against fortune. Yet, the realities of his life were perhaps closer to those who achieve what is necessary by good fortune. Poets, for Petrarch, "seek to please only a few" ("paucis placere propositum est") because "people of learning are few" ("pauci autem docti").[103] The poet's task is further restricted and closed off from society. Poets engage only with a very limited public.

The select few to whom the poet speaks prefer historical *exempla*, allegories from history along the lines of what Lactantius described as the office of the poet. As has been clear from the very beginning of Petrarch's descriptions of the duties of the poet, epic and history are essential. The

---

[101] Petrarch 2003, 110–111 (*Invective contra medicum*, 3.134 [178–179]).
[102] Petrarch 2003, 112–113 (*Invective contra medicum* 3.135 [182]).
[103] Petrarch 2003, 112–113 (*Invective contra medicum* 3.136 [186–187]).

social hierarchy onto which Petrarch grafts the civic role of the poet is also related to genre and, in fact, to language. As he is defending the exceptionality of poetry outside of the Scholastic conception of the liberal arts, he offers such a historical example to the physician, with the caveat, "I shall give you a notable example from the histories. I suppose you'd rather hear fables about Hell and witches, such as you usually hear by the fire after dinner, but now that you are no longer a boy in years, accustom yourself to higher things, if you can" ("Dabo tibi illustre exemplum ex historiis. Audires, credo, libentius fabellas, quas post cenam ante focum de orco et lamiis audire soles, sed annis certe iam non puer, si potes, adsuesce melioribus").[104] Here, in a moment of sarcastic levity, Petrarch differentiates the generic qualities of his poetry from the discourses enjoyed by the physician, who is connected with the multitude. If poets treat history, then the physician participates in storytelling in a domestic space defined by childhood. This is the space of the mother-tongue, the vernacular. The incompatibility of the vernacular with Petrarch's cultural politics will become clear in his correspondence with Boccaccio about Dante, but it is already active here. What is especially interesting here is that Petrarch's exclusion of the vernacular has nothing to do with an anxiety of influence about Dante. Rather it is a question of cultural politics that has everything to do with establishing his role in society as exceptional.

When Petrarch finally brings up the issue of the poet as theologian, he has already clearly established the parameters of the poet as a member of an elite class that engages only with the upper echelons of society. The underlying connection between the poet and political power emerges in the claims that Petrarch makes about the origins and uses of poetry in the third invective. He begins his explanation by rewording what he already wrote to his brother, Gherardo:

> Among the pagan nations, the first theologians were poets. This is attested by the greatest philosophers, confirmed by the authority of the saints, and indicated by the very name of poet, if you don't know. The most renowned of these poets was Orpheus, whom Augustine mentions in Book Eighteen of his *City of God*. "But they did not attain the goal they sought," someone will object. I admit it. For the perfect knowledge of the true God is not the result of human study, but of heavenly grace. Still, we must praise the spirit of these zealous people. For they clearly yearned to attain the coveted heights of truth by the paths available to them. In fact, in this great and necessary inquiry they even surpassed the philosophers.

[104] Petrarch 2003, 90–91, modified (*Invective contra medicum* 3.111 [56–57]).

(Primos nempe theologos apud gentes fuisse poetas et philosophorum maximi testantur, et sanctorum confirmat autoritas, et ipsum, si nescis, poete nomen indicat. In quibus maxime nobilitatus Orpheus, cuius decimoctavo *Civitatis eterne* libro Augustinus meminit. "At nequiverunt quo destinaverant pervenire," dicet aliquis. Laudandus tamen animus studiossimorum hominum, qui certe quibus poterant viis ad optatam veri celsitudinem anhelabant, adeo ut ipsos quoque philosophos in hac tanta et tam necessaria inquisitione precederent.)[105]

This kind of argument seems to give the privilege of divine knowledge to pagan poets through nature and reason. For Petrarch, however, the topos becomes a question of cultural politics. The ancients not only tried to reach knowledge of the divine through reason, they even arrived at "some kind of knowledge of the first cause and of the one God" ("prime cause et unius Dei qualemcunque notitiam") and "then they tried in every possible way to persuade others secretly that the gods worshipped by the deluded masses were false gods. But they dared not do this in public, since the living truth had not yet illuminated the world" ("ita deinceps omnibus modis id egisse, ut – quod publice non audebant, eo quod nondum viva veritas terries illuxerat – clam suaderent falsos deos esse, quos illusa plebs coleret").[106] Petrarch's re-writing of the history of religion here ascribes proto-Judeo-Christian monotheism to early poets just as it relegates pagan polytheism to the masses. He is effectively politicizing the commonplace of the *poeta theologus* by narrating the poets' attempt to convert the wise against popular belief.

When Petrarch goes on to defend the multiplicity of the gods in ancient poetry, he again separates the popular from the elite, and gives a unique privilege to poets:

Homer and Virgil portrayed the gods as warring with each other, and Cornelius Nepos tells us that for this very reason the Athenians thought Homer was mad. I believe of course that the common people thought so. But learned men understand that, if many gods exist, there may be discord and warring among them. It follows that when one party is victorious, the other must be vanquished. Such a deity cannot be either immortal or omnipotent, and consequently not even a God. Therefore, there is one God, rather than many; and the masses are deceived.

(Belligerantes deos invicem Homerus et Virgilius fecerunt; propter quod Athenis Homerum pro insano habitum Cornelius Nepos refert. Credo

[105] Petrarch 2003, 114–115 (*Invective contra medicum* 3.137 [196–200]).
[106] Petrarch 2003, 114–115 (*Invective contra medicum* 3.137 [201]).

nimirum apud vulgus; docti autem intelligunt, si plures sunt dii, et dis-
cordare illos et bella inter ipsos esse posse, et necesse esse ut, altero victore,
alter victus, atque ita nec sit immortalis nec omnipotens, consequenterque
ne deus quidem, unum esse igitur Deum et non plures, vulgus autem
falli.)[107]

The foundation of allegorical readings of classical poets is for Petrarch a
question of social class. By speaking only to the learned who understand
that the plurality of gods is false, and is representative of something else,
because of their own singularity, there is no danger of misunderstanding.
The people err because, in ignorance, its members see their own plurality
and discord reflected in the multiplicity of the gods. Petrarch speaks of the
plurality of gods as he would of a human plurality: the gods are discordant
and at war. He implicitly connects discord and plurality to the masses, and
the learned to the One.

The physician had brought up that the pagan gods fought among
themselves out of envy, claiming that poets propagated such erroneous
belief. As authority he had evidently brought up an argument in Aristotle's
Metaphysics, to which Petrarch responds:[108]

> At any rate, I don't see how it makes sense to reprove poets for their verbal
> license and then to excuse the envy of the gods, especially in a book that
> condemns any plurality of ruling powers and asserts the supremacy of a
> single ruler over all. But I am led to believe that you understand this passage
> no better than the others.

> (Quomodo autem consentaneum sit vel poetas in hac lingue libertate
> reprehendere, vel deorum invidiam excusare – in eo libro [metaphisico]
> presertim in quo, principatum pluralitate damnata, unus omnium princeps
> asseritur – non video; sed adducor ut credam te locum illum non melius
> intellexisse quam reliqua.)[109]

The language with which Petrarch speaks of Aristotle's metaphysical
principles is paralleled by his stance toward society. With what resembles
a nascent Platonism, Petrarch condemns the plurality of princes/powers
and asserts that there should be a single prince/power over all. The
metaphysical, or theological, question of the singularity of God is placed
in the context of the political value of the one over the many. The
physicians, Petrarch mentioned earlier, pander to the crowd and surround
the pope – representative of the convergence of political and theological

---

[107] Petrarch 2003, 114–117 (*Invective contra medicum* 3.138 [206–207]).
[108] See Petrarch 2003, 116–117 (*Invective contra medicum* 3.139 [117]).
[109] Petrarch 2003, 116–117 (*Invective contra medicum* 3.139 [215]).

power – with multiple discordant opinions, as a mob. Poets, Petrarch claims, have always served the One and have been in accord about the singularity of power on a theological and a political plane. If, he says, poets wrote of many gods in order to preserve their theology, it is an "offense which ... was extenuated by their fear of public opinion, which has often shaken even the most steadfast spirits" ("crimen ... quod ... publici iudicii metus levat, qui firmissima etiam interdum corda concussit").[110] Thus, the plurality of discordant gods that Petrarch tries to explain is traceable directly to the errors of the multitude, who are incapable of penetrating poetic meaning.

Finally, Petrarch arrives at what he calls the central point of his disagreement with the doctor: that the physician tries to subject all of the arts to medicine, making both poetry and rhetoric servants of that discipline. Petrarch rebuts the claim that rhetoric is a servant of the physician by saying that doctors use rhetoric only to hide defects and to console the survivors of the dead. While the poet uses the artifices of rhetoric to conceal the truth from the *vulgus* and preserve it, the physician uses these as tools to hide his lack of learning. By studying eloquence, Petrarch says, the physician has ceased to fulfill his duty, and has become an orator and a poet: "As I have often said: Rhetoric, whom you wish to make your servant, is your enemy. When you all chose to be rhetoricians and poets, you ceased to be physicians" ("Sepe tibi dixi, medice: rethorica, quam tibi servam vis efficere, hostis tua est; postquam rethores ac poete esse voluistis, medici esse desiistis").[111] In terms of the struggle among emerging professional disciplines, Petrarch sees the physician not only as trying to absorb the disciplines of poetry and rhetoric on the level of study but as trying to take over their role in society as well. The power that a physician could wield once he had subsumed the study of rhetoric threatens the poet's civic role.

The connections between poetry, medicine, and power become even more explicit in the final of the four invectives, in which Petrarch defends his solitary life and gives examples of the true power of poets, even if they do not inhabit the city. Contrasting the mechanical science of medicine with his own meditative vocation of scholar and poet, Petrarch criticizes

---

[110] Petrarch 2003, 116–117 (*Invective contra medicum* 3.140 [217]).
[111] Petrarch 2003, 132–133 (*Invective contra medicum* 3.159–160 [332]). I have slightly modified the Latin text and translation to reflect the different reading of the Latin by Bausi in his 2005 critical edition of the text. See Petrarch 2005, 130.

the physician's lack of care for the pope, who died during the course of the epistolary debate:

> When I saw that the pontiff was beset by disease on one side and by fraud and ignorance on the other, I warned him in good faith but to no avail, as the event proved. Although he recovered then, he soon fell into the old snares. Ignoring or disdaining my useful advice, he placed himself completely in your hands. As often happens, the better faction was defeated by the larger one. Your opinion, shared by other ignorant physicians, prevailed. Your ill-timed medications and your blood-letting (which people say were excessive) delivered this old man from his papal cares, although he might still be alive if he had been left alone.

> (Cum enim pontificem maximum hinc morbo, hinc quorundam fraude vel ignorantia cicumventum cernerem, eum certe fideliter sed – ut res docuit – frustra premonui. Licet enim tunc evaderet, in eosdem tamen laqueos mox reversus, utilisque consilii vel immemor vel contemptor, totum se vobis tradidit. Ubi – quod sepe accidit – melior pars numero victa est, tuaque et ceterorum ignorantium prevalente sententia, intempestivis remediis et immodica [ut fertur] senilis sanguinis rapina, illum, si sineretur adhuc forte victurum, pontificali solicitudine liberastis.)[112]

The exchange between the physician and Petrarch originated with the latter's move to oust the physician from Clement's circle of trust. He depicts himself as acting faithfully whereas his competitor for the pope's attention acted with fraud and ignorance. Petrarch's entire tirade in the fourth invective centers around the influence that a virtuous man can have on important men even if he lives outside the bounds of the city. For him the location of influence is not as important as the quality of influence. He accuses the physician of taking advantage of his position within the city for the sale of his faculties: "Where but amid crowds of credulous fools could you display the wares of your small talent?" ("Ubi enim, nisi inter turbas credulas fatuorum, ingenioli tui mercimonium ostentares?").[113] In the history of religion, the masses had continued in ignorance while the poet-theologians had discovered the truth. In Petrarch's world, these same masses have found their intellectual leaders in physicians, who take advantage of their ignorance for financial gain. The city is the doctor's proper place because, as Petrarch points out,

> In cities, there dwell kings, local governors, judges, and those who oversee the repression of the behavior of the common people. Their presence is

---

[112] Petrarch 2003, 152–155 (*Invective contra medicum* 4.180 [107–109]).
[113] Petrarch 2003, 150–151 (*Invective contra medicum* 4.177 [85–87]).

excused by the needs of the commonwealth which requires it. In cities, there dwell people occupied with important work. The power of necessity absolves them. In cities, there dwell voluptuaries and epicures – people who love "a brothel and a greasy tavern," as Horace says. In cities, there dwell swindlers, mimes, thieves, and all their breed. And finally there dwell the practitioners of the mechanical arts, who share a single goal: to deceive or make a profit.

(Habitant reges in urbibus, presidesque terrarum et iudices quique coercendis vulgi moribus presunt: quos reipublice necessitas excusat horum presentiam requirentis. Habitant ibi aliquo gravi negotio detenti: hos proprie vis necessitatis absolvit. Habitant ibi voluptuosi atque cupidinarii, quibus placet "fornix et uncta popina," ut ait Flaccus. Habitant ibi et circumscriptores, mimi, fures, totumque id genus. Ibi postremo habitant mechanici, quibus omnibus propositum unum: vel fallere, vel lucrari.)[114]

Petrarch views the city from without as a series of hierarchical concentric circles, listing the inhabitants of the city from the inside out, according to an ideal order of power that leads to the subjugation of the people. The physician, who belongs to the practitioners of the mechanical arts at the end of the list, should ideally take up a position on the periphery of urban power. Petrarch's criticism of the physician is based on his intolerance of the influence wielded by that man's profession over the men of power in the center. He seeks to correct the situation by relegating doctors to a position of minimal influence.

The institution which should hold influence over those men, however, does not belong to the city. This group – the poets and dwellers in solitude – should have the most influence over the men of power. Petrarch contrasts the active life of the doctor, lived among the dregs of the city, with the contemplative life of the poet, which takes place in tranquility on the margins of society, where virtuous men can still have access to him. He writes:

See how you race through lanes and squares, and you think me inhuman for sitting in solitude, as though we were born to run around. Please believe me. Every day many people pressure you, but many better people hold me dear. Unless you think I am boasting too relentlessly, I shall tell you what many already know. Such men have come to see me in my solitude, eager to be here for me alone, and have even sent from afar to encourage me and to find out what I am doing. If you approached these same men, they would be loath to see you, saying nothing, and scarcely replying to you. . . . But you should know that many lovers of the country are esteemed in the cities,

---

[114] Petrarch 2003, 152–153, modified (*Invective contra medicum* 4.179 [97–101]).

whereas many city-dwellers are hateful to the very cities in which they dwell. So you should recognize that solitude is not the enemy of the polity and that, even if I am solitary, I love virtuous people, and am loved by them no less.

(Ecce nunc tu per vicos ruis ac plateas, et quasi ad correndum nati simus, me in solitudine sedentem inhumanum putas. Crede michi, si placet: plures te quotidie impellunt, plures melioresque me diligunt; et nisi gloriari tibi importune et nimium videar, dicam quod multis est notum, tales ad me visendum viros in hanc solitudinem venisse, et propter me unum hic cupide fuisse, tales etiam misisse de longinquo ad cohortandum me noscendumque quid agerem, qui te, si ultro illos adeas, egre visuri sint, nichil dicturi, modicum responsuri. ... sed ut scias multos ruris amatores etiam in urbibus caros esse, multos habitatores urbium ipsis in quibus habitant urbibus odiosos. Ita non adversam solitudinem politie, meque, licet solitarium, et amare bonos noveris, et ab illis non minus amari.)[115]

The poet himself escapes the morally ambiguous distractions of city life by creating for himself a place outside of it – beyond the pressures of money, vice, and power to which human bodies are subject. The detachment of the poet reaffirms the freedom and virtue on which his public authority is based, because it removes him from the moral ambiguities of history itself, as David Wallace has suggested.[116] The contrast of his position with that of the doctor is indicative of how Petrarch sees his solitary life as authorizing his civic role. While the doctor assumes a passive role in the impositions on his daily life, Petrarch's relationship with virtuous men of power is one of mutual admiration. Beyond the city, he is their equal or superior. By drawing the attention of these men to him alone, the center of power in the city shifts to the periphery, where the poet's residence creates a new axis around which a circle of power can form. Petrarch's location beyond the city allows him to construct a new civic sphere that we can glimpse in his *Familiares*, letters in which he is the center of an intellectual and political republic of letters.

The superiority of Petrarch's marginality is marked by the effectiveness of his political influence, which is seen in the quality of the men who seek out his advice. He also receives the emissaries of important men, who are sent to take care of him and to keep him under watch. Petrarch's almost utopian solitude is maintained and guaranteed by these important men whom he advises and by whom he is frequented. The issue that is at stake

---

[115] Petrarch 2003, 142–145, modified (*Invective contra medicum* 4.170 [34–35, 37–38]).

[116] See Wallace 1997, 261–270 (esp. 267–268). The question of Petrarch's association with tyranny, first raised by Wallace, is discussed in more detail in relation to Boccaccio in the following chapter.

with the physician here and in the rest of the invectives is the very political power that sustains Petrarch's poetic and humanistic endeavors. His famous recourse to the *poeta theologus* commonplace, which only occupies a small part of the third invective, establishes a natural connection between the poetic vocation and the political power which is preserved by that vocation and which in turn preserves poets. By understanding the poet's relation to power as natural Petrarch implicitly gives the political power he serves a natural right that is guaranteed by a supernatural gift (the divine spirit of the *Pro Archia*) and by an inimitable access to the truth (the tradition of the poet-theologian).

When Petrarch compiles the *Invective* in Milan in 1355 and distributes them as treatises, they act as a textual performance of his public authority and as a reminder that he occupied a position of power. They reflect Petrarch's bitterness toward the Avignon papacy and toward the people who did not respect his status as poet or understand his cultural endeavors. For example, in one of his many hyperbolic criticisms of the physician, he enumerates the ills of the city in terms of the reprehensible people who inhabit it:

> "What then?" you will ask. "Is there no one good in the city?" I don't say that, but there are countless bad people. When possible, it is safer for both the beginner and the advanced student of virtue to avoid them. What's more, I have not been banished to the country so rigorously that my friends' entreaties don't summon me back to the city more often than I would like. And I often wander of my own accord, changing places to avoid boredom. You have heard the reasons for my behavior. If I now asked you in turn why you do not stop canvasing all the latrines, what reason will you produce? You will say you are healing the commonwealth, which I admit is sick. But I deny that it can be healed by you, except insofar as I hope that you rid it each day of many madmen, like a body infected with noxious humors.
>
> ("Quid ergo? Nemo" inquies "bonus in urbibus?" Non dico id quidem; sed innumerabiles mali, a quibus non modo proficientem sed profectum quoque, si possit, securius sit abesse. Accedit quod nec ita rure relegatus sum, quin sepius quam vellem amicorum precibus ad urbem retrahar, sepe etiam sponte mea vager, vitans locorum alternatione fastidium. Facti mei causam audisti. O, si te nunc scisciter, vice versa, quid tu latrinas omnes ambire nunquam desinas, qualem michi expedias rationem? Dices te sanare rempublicam, quam egram fateor, a te sanari posse nego, nisi quantum te spero quotidie multis illam dementibus, veluti corpus infectum damnosis humoribus, exhaurire.)[117]

---

[117] Petrarch 2003, 158–161, modified (*Invective contra medicum* 4.187–88 [152–57]).

Petrarch's vitriol against the physician is hardly able to veil his spite for the multitude and for the city in general. In the years following the plague, Petrarch seeks a scapegoat in the figure of the physician. He blames the discord of doctors and the fallibility of their science for the havoc of the times. The illness and death of Clement happened despite their efforts – or, as Petrarch would have it, because of their efforts. This figuratively reflects their failure to advise Clement effectively in his political efforts. Petrarch's angry defense of his profession and of his place in society at times transforms into a violent assertion of his superiority far beyond the one veiled in the allegorical interpretation of Scipio and Hannibal in his letter to Gherardo. His most strikingly anti-populist statement in the fourth invective parallels spiritual and political health, just as it seems to abandon all ties with human affairs: "For me, it is far more desirable to be saved alone than to perish with many" ("Apud me multo quidem optabilius solum salvari, quam perire cum multis").[118] This declaration is made following a list of the advantages of solitude for spiritual health, which could be compared to the solitude of Gherardo, who had also abandoned human affairs. In Petrarch's eyes, in order to have an impact on the sick body politic, he had to stand beyond it. Yet, if it is read in the context of the political choices that Petrarch had made in the years of its composition, it takes on a more ominous connotation. The use of this kind of rhetoric just a few years after the plague had wreaked havoc on Avignon, while Petrarch was in Parma, cannot be fully neutralized as a hyperbole of invective or as a figurative stance toward the city. With his retreat to Milan, where the plague had been controlled by a severe policy of ostracizing the sick,[119] Petrarch was indeed immunizing himself. When Petrarch praises in his letters to friends the spiritual advantages of solitude, which he gains with the protection of the Visconti, he is also praising the political and physical advantages of surviving and thriving in a time of both figurative and literal illness. He is praising the benefits of his patronage, which would cause an uproar among his Florentine admirers, including Boccaccio.

*

Between 1341 and 1353 Petrarch tests the limits of the status of the poet, from the heroic oration on the Capitoline when he first asserted himself as poet to the aftermath of Cola di Rienzo's failed attempt to take over Rome.

[118] Petrarch 2003, 146–147 (*Invective contra medicum* 4.172 [52]).   [119] See Benedictow 2004, 95.

The ambiguity of his position as a civic poet is present from the very beginning. He is both poet of the city and a poet whose interests place him beyond a local perspective on human affairs. In the various challenges he faced from political men like Brizio Visconti and urban professionals or advisers like the anonymous physician, Petrarch asserts a kind of removed engagement similar to what Dante embraced and figured in terms of a pastoral non-place. Yet he maintains a firm position that the poet's task is to engage in a historical poetry founded upon a sophisticated rhetorical style, in Latin. From the figurative distance of the solitary life, Petrarch the poet reaches into the city from beyond it.

By the end of this part of his life, Petrarch seems to have moved on from the limitations of the public office of the poet. At one point in the third invective against the physician, he claims: "I do not presume to call myself a poet. (I know that despite their intense efforts certain great men could not win this title. If it fell to me, I would not reject it; and in fact, I don't deny that in my youth I aspired to it)" ("Nam nec michi poete nomen arrogo – quod scio quibusdam magnis viris multo studio non potuisse contingere, quamvis, si michi forsan ultro contigerit, non respuam, et ad id me olim iuveniliter aspirasse non negam").[120] With these invectives, Petrarch the poet goes underground, even if he increases his political engagement through his association with the lords of northern Italy. His notoriety and political value would be authorized with a title more powerful than that of poet. In 1356, he will be named a Count Palatine in Prague by Holy Roman Emperor Charles IV. With the exception of the *Bucolicum carmen*, most of his poetic works would remain relatively unknown until after his death.[121] His cultural politics called him to other things, at least publicly, even if he would continue to profit from his fame as a poet. As a public intellectual and ethical philosopher, he nevertheless maintains the myth of his distance from the life of the city. On this will be based his well-known disdain for Dante, when Boccaccio attempts to bring Petrarch to Florence and to insert Dante into his canon of authors. In 1357, when the work had already been circulated, Petrarch sent the *Invective contra medicum* to Boccaccio, seven years after their first meeting and four years after their falling out over Petrarch's rejection of Florence and move to Milan. It is in response to this text that Boccaccio constructs an alternative poetics that brings together Latin and vernacular and that integrates with urban life the Petrarchan poet beyond the city.

[120] Petrarch 2003, 118–119 (*Invective contra medicum* 3.142 [230]).
[121] See Billanovich 1947, 297–419 for the history of the early fortune of Petrarch's works.

CHAPTER 4

Giovanni Boccaccio, Poet for the City

Boccaccio's approach to the civic role of the poet is conciliatory. In a spirit of inclusion, he brings together the diverse perspectives on the office of poetry that Mussato, Dante, and Petrarch represent. From the time of his return to Florence in 1341, Boccaccio increasingly engaged in the political life of the city, often to his personal detriment,[1] and produced poetry (broadly conceived) in the Florentine vernacular that brought together the classical and Romance traditions.[2] His political activities in Florence are indicative of a dedication to the life of the city that also manifests itself in a cultural vision that places the poet at the center of the city's intellectual life.[3] Boccaccio's efforts as a poet and intellectual have long been overshadowed by his illustrious predecessors. As critics have preferred Dante's vision of poetry over that of Mussato, Boccaccio's ideas on poetry have consistently been viewed as derivative of those of Petrarch.[4] Until very recently, it has been commonplace to view the second half of Boccaccio's career entirely through a Petrarchan lens. Before Petrarch, he was a vernacular poet and storyteller obsessed with love; after Petrarch, he became an admirer of classical culture who turned away from the vernacular and embraced Latin as the language of culture. As recent scholarship

---

[1] On the political activities of Boccaccio in Florence, see Ginsberg 2002, 105–147 and Filosa 2014. On the way his politics is manifested in the *Decameron*, see Olson 2014 and Milner 2015. See also the important revisions to common accounts of Boccaccio's public service between 1351 and 1353 in Caferro 2018b. For significant documentary evidence on how Boccaccio lived his civic duty, see Regnicoli 2013.

[2] See Lummus 2015 and Kriesel 2018.

[3] It is important to realize that Boccaccio's view of the poet's role was not exactly inclusive of the lowest classes of society, of the subaltern. See Wallace 2002. Cf. Armstrong, Daniels, and Milner, 2015b. He was, however, inclusive of the rising mercantile classes, which he tried to integrate with a more conservative aristocratic heritage. See Olson 2014.

[4] This is especially the case for Boccaccio's defense of poetry. See, e.g., Osgood 1930, xlii; Witt 1977; Greenfield 1981, 110–128; Zaccaria 1998a, 30–31; Pastore Stocchi 2004. For a reading of Boccaccio's approach to ancient culture in the treatise that differentiates it from that of Petrarch, see Mazzotta 2000.

has shown, however, Boccaccio maintained a cultural outlook distinct from that of Petrarch, which was mainly coherent over the course of his career.[5]

The extent of his difference from and engagement with Petrarch's humanist project has yet to be explored in all of its aspects. It is all too often described in terms of Boccaccio's championing of Dante and of vernacular poetic culture, a stance that Petrarch was unable to accept. While the reception of Dante was essential to his cultural politics, his vision of poetry was not determined by Dante either. Rather, Boccaccio tries to imagine the conditions in which Florence could become a cultural capital on a par with ancient Rome – a place where the life of citizens could be guided and enriched by poetry.[6] The most representative example of this would be his public readings and explications of Dante's *Commedia* at the end of his life.[7] In contrast with Petrarch's vision of a poetic elite, embodied singularly by himself as poet laureate, Boccaccio views poetry's function as a cultural container that includes all forms of knowledge. Boccaccio did not situate himself individually as the representative of this poetic culture. He elides himself from the project in moves of typical irony and false modesty. Instead, by authorizing the project through the example of others like Petrarch and Dante, as Martin Eisner has argued, Boccaccio authorizes himself as the standard-bearer of a new poetic culture.[8]

In this chapter, I will examine how Boccaccio reacts to and repurposes Petrarch's conception of the poet and his relationship to the city. Essential

---

[5] For the traditional narrative of Boccaccio's turn to Latin upon meeting Petrarch, see (Giuseppe) Billanovich 1947, 59–294, esp. 104–106. See also Branca 1975, 91 and Bruni 1990, 414–420. The complexity of the shift in Boccaccio's motivations as scholar and poet have been addressed by many of the essays in Kirkham, Sherberg, and Smarr 2013 and in Armstrong, Daniels, and Milner 2015a. The question of Petrarch's influence on Boccaccio and the nature of their friendship is still a matter of some debate. For a view that reverses the friendship model proposed in Billanovich and Branca, see Rico 2012. Cf. Lummus 2014. See also Usher 2007; Lummus 2012a; Veglia 2014; Zak 2015; and Lummus 2017.

[6] On Boccaccio's idea of cultural renewal in Florence, see Houston 2010, 128–133; Lummus 2012a; Eisner 2013, 1–73; and Lummus 2017. See also Gittes 2008.

[7] On Boccaccio's reading of and commentary on the *Commedia*, see Padoan 1978; Baldan 1996; Gilson 2005, 42–50; Papio 2009; Houston 2010, 133–155; Gilson 2013; and Hollander 2013. On Boccaccio's manuscripts of Dante's works and their cultural significance, see Bologna 1993, 1.157–181 and Eisner 2013, esp. 1–29. For a more general survey of Boccaccio's copying practices, including of Dante's works, see Arduini 2015. On the history and legacy of Boccaccio's copy of the *Vita nova*, see Banella 2017. More generally on Boccaccio and Dante, see Hollander 1997 and Armstrong 2015. See also the recent essays in Sandal 2006; De Robertis, Monti, Petoletti, et al. 2013; Azzetta and Mazzucchi 2014; and Bertelli and Cappi 2014. On the study of Dante's poem in *Trecento* culture, see Barański 2001.

[8] See Eisner 2013, esp. 1–29. Cf. Armstrong, Daniels, Milner 2015b.

to my analysis is the interaction between the two friends during the 1350s, when Boccaccio seeks to bring Petrarch to Florence. To this period we owe his biographies of Petrarch and Dante. The *De vita et moribus Francisci Petracchi* was written in an effort first to fashion Petrarch as a new Dante for the people of Florence, while the first version of the *Vita di Dante* seems to have been written for the Florentines after Boccaccio's failed attempt to bring Petrarch to Florence and later revised in an effort to fashion Dante as acceptable for Petrarch's canon of classical authors.[9] Petrarch's choice to move to Milan in 1353 led Boccaccio to rethink the relationship between his project of making classics of vernacular poetry and Petrarch's Latin poetry. Embittered by Petrarch's political choices, his intellectual affiliation with his friend is defined by the creation of an ideal Petrarch whose character is based on the poet laureate of the pre-Milan era.

It is on the tail of this failure of mediatory cultural politics that Boccaccio composes the *Genealogie deorum gentilium libri*, a work that occupied him from as early as the 1350s until 1372, three years before his death.[10] In it, Boccaccio rereads human history from the perspective of poetic creation, painting a picture of the poet-intellectual as a civilizing force.[11] His history of classical myth not only puts classical and vernacular authors on a par amongst themselves but also links them with the popular imagination. Indeed, in the *Genealogie*, the popular imagination is that which ensures the diffusion of the mythic figures and the meanings associated with them that will later be taken up by poets.[12] In the penultimate book of the *Genealogie*, Boccaccio defends poetry against its detractors, modifying the relationship between the poet and the city. For Boccaccio, as for Petrarch, the poet belongs outside the city, in the peace of solitude. Unlike Petrarch, however, Boccaccio sees the work that is pursued there as in service to a community. He recalibrates Petrarch's attitude toward the multitude and, at least in theory, imagines the task of the poet as a form of intellectual action for the city.

---

[9] On the Dante/Petrarch question in Boccaccio's cultural program, including Boccaccio's biographies of these poets, see Ginsberg 2002, esp. 105–147 and 190–239; Gilson 2005, 21–53; Houston 2010, esp. 64–73, 93–98, 124–156; Eisner 2013, esp. 1–29 and Filosa 2013.

[10] On the composition of the *Genealogie*, see Zaccaria 1998b.

[11] On myth and civilization in the *Genealogie*, see Mazzotta 2000. On cultural heroism as a theme in the *Genealogie*, see Marino 1980; Gittes 2002; Barsella 2004; Gittes 2008, 64–65; and Cherchi, 2018.

[12] See Lummus 2011a and 2012b.

Politics and Poetry between Petrarch and Boccaccio (and Dante)

For Petrarch, the authority of the poet and the utility of poetry depended upon the privilege of solitude. He figures his role in the world in terms of his separation from worldly affairs, even if he remains politically engaged. He claims on several occasions that the only place where he could find such freedom was in the service of a prince.[13] Upon leaving Avignon, his period in Milan was in fact the longest he ever spent in a single residence and one of the most productive of his life. Yet in his choice to live there, implicitly legitimating the Viscontian regime, he consciously refused other options. He twice refused a bishopric and the position of apostolic secretary, perhaps wishing instead to be appointed Cardinal but more likely recognizing that his influence in Avignon had been compromised.[14] He was appalled by the conditions of the Curia in Avignon and frustrated by his lack of success in returning political and ecclesiastical power to Rome. As early as 1352, when he first wrote in answer to the physician's attack, Petrarch was considering leaving Avignon for Italy. Although he was uncertain about where in Italy he would find patronage, he had narrowed his choices down to Parma, Padua, and Milan. Parma was probably ruled out because he feared that the duties of his archdeaconate there would detract from time spent in meditation, whereas Padua was in turmoil because of the recent assassination of Giacomo II da Carrara; the political situation was too unstable. Petrarch had also considered taking refuge in Rome, but never received acceptable conditions, refusing an offer from the Grand Seneschal of the Kingdom of Naples, Niccolò Acciaiuoli. In fact, the situation in these possible places of refuge was such that Petrarch left Avignon in early 1353 already knowing that he would take up residence in Milan if he were to receive an acceptable offer. In accepting this offer, he may have only been looking for an intellectual harbor from which he could have an impact on European politics beyond Avignon. He was seen by many of his contemporaries, however, as abandoning the ethical principles that undergirded his cultural project. For his Florentine friends especially,

---

[13] On the critical debate surrounding Petrarch's rationale for moving to Milan, see Bruni 1990, 414–422; Wallace 1997, 54–62 and 261–298; Dotti 2001; Fenzi 2005; and Ascoli 2011. On the historical circumstances preceding his move, see Wilkins 1958, 3–15.

[14] See Wilkins 1955, 63–80 and 82–83.

the choice of Milan – a major adversary of Florence – was especially difficult to fathom.[15]

On March 19, 1351, two years prior to his departure for Milan, Petrarch had been invited to return to Florence with the assurance of the restitution of his patrimony and a revocation of the charges that caused the exile of his father in 1302.[16] In a letter attributed to Boccaccio, Petrarch is called home as the city's Virgil or Homer and is offered a place of honor in the Florentine republic:

> Among your contemporaries and fellow citizens and compatriots you will find signs of a certain deep affection, you who always and rightly vindicated for yourself the grace of your father's persecution and benignity. To you, then, whom we have always honored with the affection due to a subject and a son, so that you should not have to bear anything perhaps with less equanimity, we concede you the fields of your ancestral land, and we give them to you unconditionally and willfully paid for from the public treasury by private citizens, out of the simple generosity of paternal love: a small gift, no doubt, if you consider the thing itself, but if you consider the laws and customs of our city – by which citizens have never been able to achieve this – it will balance out with a not small gratification of your glory.

> (Apud tibi coetaneos dominos ac cives et compatriotas tuos signa quedam interne dilectionis inveneris, qui tibi maioris persecutionis ac benignitatis semper gratiam rationabiliter vendicabas. Tibi igitur quem dominico ac paterno semper afectu prosequimur, ne quid in urbe tua fortasse minus equanimiter ferendum sit, ruris aviti pascua concedimus, ac de publico quidem erario a privatis civibus redempta sponte ac sine alicuius exemptionis titulo de mera paterne dilectionis liberalitate donamus: minus quidem parvum si ad rem respicias, si ad civitatis nostre leges ac mores, quique hoc cives assequi nequivissent, non modica laudum tuarum gratificatione pensandum.)[17]

---

[15] The Visconti regime in Milan had been expanding southward into Tuscany and had already taken a good part of northern Tuscany and was openly at war with Florence up until 1353, when a peace accord was signed at Sarzana. The conflict between Milan and Florence would pick back up again toward the end of the century. Bruni 1990, 414–422 argues that Boccaccio and Petrarch's other Florentine friends were provincial and did not understand Petrarch's cosmopolitan (European) political vision. His analysis mirrors Petrarch's own defense of himself but overlooks Petrarch's representation of his departure from Avignon in *Bucolicum carmen* 8. This discrepancy was precisely what the Florentines noticed in their critique of Petrarch. Rather than provincialism, Boccaccio especially would have had Petrarch enact his cosmopolitan vision from Florence rather than from Milan. On Boccaccio's cosmopolitanism, see Lummus 2012a and 2017.

[16] For the dating of the correspondence between Boccaccio and Petrarch, I have followed the table in Albanese 2003, 85–92.

[17] Boccaccio 1992, 550 (*Epistola* 7.2–3).

Boccaccio points out the exceptional nature of Florence's generosity toward Petrarch – a generosity that it had not shown toward its other great poet.[18] Boccaccio tries to insert Petrarch among the coetaneous citizens of Florence, calling upon his natal allegiance to the city. Petrarch, however, preferred to see himself as an individual without comparison, as detached from the discord of the multitude. Perhaps he worried that he could not function in a city in which he would find himself among equals. Boccaccio, in fact, advises him that Florence cannot compete with the Emperors and wealthy patrons of the world: "But we, since we are neither Caesars nor Maecenases nor as famous as the titles of such men . . . we will be proud professors of your study, as we will be extremely liberal and avid promoters of your honor" ("Nos vero tibi, quem nostra presens etas nobis accomodat, et si Cesares non sumus aut Mecenates aut talium illustres titulis, quos hactenus . . . incoluerunt, libentissime tui studii professores erimus, tantum tui honoris avidi ac promotores liberalissimi").[19] Here Boccaccio seems to be aware that Florence is competing with other patrons for the fame of Petrarch's name. He calls on Petrarch's sense of patriotism for his native land, hoping that it will win out over his desire for the security and stability that a monarch could offer. In conclusion to the letter Boccaccio's rhetoric of return reaches its high point:

> You have wandered enough and the customs and cities of foreign peoples are clear enough to you. Now, magistrates and private men, nobles and peasants, your ancestral *lares*, your regained land call on you. Come then, we await you. Come, give favor with your eloquent words to our under-takings. With a clear voice the fatherland does not just call you back but summons and consoles you who have been so long absent: there is hardly any memory that such a thing has ever happened to anyone.

> (Satis nempe pervagatus es et mores urbesque tibi exterarum gentium clare sunt. Te magistratus quilibet et privatus, te proceres et plebei, te lares aviti, te recuperatus ager exposcunt. Venias, igitur, expectate, venias, et eloquen-tie tue facundia ceptis fave, quem clara voce non revocat, sed absentem diu diuque advocat patria: quod vix unquam hoc pacto alteri contigisse meminimus.)[20]

---

[18] The mention of Florence's *leges ac mores* may be taken to be an oblique reference to the city's treatment of Dante, which Boccaccio brings up explicitly in the diatribe against Florence's ingratitude in *Vita di Dante*, 1.92–101. See Boccaccio 1974, 460–462.

[19] Boccaccio 1992, 552 (*Epistola* 7.7). The bracketed ellipsis here represents a corruption in the manuscript between "hactenus" and "incoluerunt."

[20] Boccaccio 1992, 554 (*Epistola* 7.18–19).

The environment that Florence offers is one in which the voices of public and private men, nobles and peasants can intermingle. Boccaccio asks Petrarch to add his distinguished voice to this group and to support it with his words.

In Boccaccio's exhortation of Petrarch to come to Florence there is a reverent tone, more modest than that which Giovanni del Virgilio maintained in his invitation to Dante to come to Bologna. Dante was, in fact, on Boccaccio's mind in his invitation to Petrarch. Shortly after his visit with Petrarch in Padua in March and April 1351, he sent Petrarch a copy of Dante's *Commedia* accompanied by a Latin *carmen* in hexameters, *Ytalie iam certus honos*, in which he asks Petrarch "to join him in praising Dante by offering him a kind of posthumous coronation."[21] In this poem, Boccaccio makes the case that even if Dante was never crowned poet laureate his vernacular poetry still deserves to be considered by Petrarch. It is effectively an invitation to Petrarch to assume his place as Dante's ideal successor in Florence, where he will fulfill Dante's promise as poet laureate in the city.[22] Petrarch's presence in the city as poet would also create the conditions necessary for Dante's hopes in *Paradiso* 25 to come true. He would return as author of his poem.

When Boccaccio and the other philo-Florentine men of letters came to know of Petrarch's decision to live in Milan they reacted with shock and abhorrence. Among the reproaches of Petrarch's friends, Boccaccio's allegorical letter to Petrarch stands out. The letter, sent on July 18, 1353, reprimands the poet's choice and uses his past words on the Visconti against him. Written in a subtly allegorical vein, the letter refers to Petrarch by his pastoral name *Silvanus* and divides the poet into two parts – before and after the move to Milan – suggesting that the move to Milan marked a substantial break in Petrarch's ideology. In their meeting in Padua two years earlier, the first Petrarch had told Boccaccio:

> How is it – leaving aside the rest – that we see the rustic man Aegon, who has abandoned the country rituals which Pan had once put in his charge – and has taken up arms and gathered together petty thieves, has occupied the

---

[21] Eisner 2013, 13. On the poem and its context, see also Velli 1992, 386–391; Sturm-Maddox 2009, 302–303; and Houston 2010, 97–99. On the circumstances of Boccaccio's gift to Petrarch, see the thorough discussion in Eisner 2013, 128–130 n. 72. On the Dantean subtext and its connection to the political circumstances surrounding the first meeting of Boccaccio and Petrarch and of Boccaccio's invitation of Petrarch to teach in Florence, see Caferro 2018a, 22–48.

[22] It has been suggested that Petrarch's laurel privilege would give him the right to crown other poets and therefore that Boccaccio wanted Petrarch to crown Dante post-mortem. See Eisner 2013, 130 n. 73. As Usher notes following Mertens 1988, however, this idea is based on a misreading of the text of the *Privilegium*. See Usher 2009, 166–168 and 188 n. 22.

forests of the Ligurians and almost all the fields washed by the Po and has stolen fraudulently the mountains and valleys of the Insubrians, and sharpened his teeth and nails in Emilia, Piceno, and the Etruscan hills of the Apennines?

(Quid est, ut omiserim cetera, cernere Egonem rusticanum hominem, omissis ruralibus sacris quibus illum dudum Pan prefecerat, sumptisque spiculis congregatisque latrunculis, Ligurum occupasse silvas, et omnia fere pascua que Eridanus abluit et montes vallesque Insubrum fraude suripuisse, et in Emiliam Picenum ac Appennini colles Etruscosque acuisse dentes et ungues?)[23]

This other Petrarch – the one of Boccaccio's memory of 1351 – saw the Visconti regime for what it was: a city-state under the protection of the Pope that went beyond its ethical and natural bounds to begin conquering surrounding states. This exclamation about the Visconti comes at the end of a long tirade on the poor state of the Italian peninsula that includes words against both the Pope and the Emperor. The Petrarch of 1351, Boccaccio reminds the Milanese Petrarch, was in agreement with himself:

Then you could see him, with his indignation growing, raise his eyes to the heavens and say many things and invoke every misfortune against Aegon. I remember that you too gave your assent to these words with a long discourse, and adding that out of hate for Aegon you had called on Daphni – with a long series of words and with all your power – to depose such an evil man and to restore the ancient decorum. I remember that I approved with words and committed to memory all of these things as worthy of praise.

(Inde, indignatione crescente, vidisse potuisti eum, ellevatis oculis in superos, multa dicentem atque in Egonem infausta omina imprecantem. Quibus et te multo sermone assensum prestitisse memini, atque superaddentem, ob odium in Egonem, longa verborum serie Daphnim pro viribus provocasse in deiectionem tam scelestium hominum et prisci decoris restaurationem; que omina tanquam laude digna, et aprobasse verbis memini et commendasse memorie.)[24]

Boccaccio represents Petrarch's move to Milan not only as contradictory to his words of a few years before but also to the entire cultural project that saw ancient Rome as a model to be recreated. Somehow, Petrarch's choice to live with tyrants was incongruent with his call for the restoration of "the

---

[23] Boccaccio 1992, 576 (*Epistola* 10.8). The pastoral names in the letter have the following referents: Aegon = Giovanni Visconti; Pan = Pope Clement VI; Daphni = Charles IV. On this letter, see also Houston 2012.

[24] Boccaccio 1992, 576 (*Epistola* 10.9–10).

ancient decorum." For Boccaccio, the ethical consequences of Petrarch's choice shook the very foundations of his cultural politics as poet laureate. At the very beginning of their friendship, Boccaccio and Petrarch find themselves utterly divided over a political question that becomes intertwined in their works over the next 20 years.

Petrarch never responded directly to Boccaccio's accusations and protests, but he did try to explain to a few others the reasons behind his choice. In a letter to Zanobi da Strada, in Naples, composed in June 1353, he explains his reasoning:

> Great is the name of the freedom and the leisure which are promised me under his command and which everyone knows I am so craving that anyone who should decide to capture me should not use pleasures, riches, or honors but only these two things as the sweetest bait for his traps.

> (Tanti est libertatis et ocii nomen, quae sub illius imperio promittuntur, quorum me ita cupidum norunt omnes, ut quisquis me capere decreverit, non voluptates, non divitias, non honores, sed haec duo tantum velut escam laqueis adhibeat dulciorem.)[25]

The authority of Giovanni Visconti is what promises Petrarch the freedom and leisure that he requires to sustain his life as a poet and scholar. The derivatives of such a career – the pleasures, riches, and honors – are not so important to him as the free time and solitude guaranteed by the tyrannical regime. In a letter written to his friend Francesco Nelli later the same summer, Petrarch tried to stage his decision to remain in Milan as a fortunate happenstance that had not been premeditated.[26] His excuses for remaining there, however, echo his desire for freedom and leisure:

> As excuses I could have used my preoccupations and my hatred of crowds, as well as my natural desire for peace, except that he had anticipated all I might say and promised me above all the most perfect solitude and leisure in his teeming city – so far, he has kept his promise to the best of his ability. I therefore yielded with the understanding that there was to be no change in my life, scarcely any in my dwelling, and no more infringement upon my freedom and leisure than was absolutely necessary.

> (Excusassem occupationes turbeque odium et quietis avidam naturam, nisi parantem loqui velut cuncta presagiens prevenisset, et in maxima frequentisimaque urbe solitudinem ille michi in primis et otium promisisset atque hactenus, quantum in eo est, promissa prestaret. Cessi igitur hac lege ut de

---

[25] Petrarch 1994, 130–132 (*Lettera dispersa* 19.12–16 [*Varia* 7]).
[26] Wilkins 1958, 13–15 has shown that Petrarch had been orchestrating the move to Milan as early as a year before and even went out of his way to stop there.

vita nichil, de habitaculo aliquid immutatum sit idque non amplius quam quantum fieri potest illesa libertate salvo otio.)[27]

Petrarch's refusal of the Florentine offer of repatriation seems to be explained in this defense to Nelli. Although Boccaccio had promised essentially the same thing for him in Florence, Petrarch felt that the Viscontian government could hold off the people of the busy city better than Republican Florence. In Milan, his reputed solitude would be secure. In a second letter to Nelli, written a few days later, Petrarch explains that he will have to give up nothing in order to remain there, because Visconti desired nothing but his presence:

> When I asked exactly what he wished of me, since I was ill-suited or ill-disposed for anything he might need, he replied that he wished nothing but my presence, in the belief that I would do honor to himself and his state. I must confess that, overcome by such kindness, I blushed and remained silent; and by so doing I consented or seemed to have consented.

> (Dum enim scrupulosius quererem quid ex me vellet, cum ad nichil eorum quibus egere videretur aptus essem aut dispositus, nichil ex me velle respondit nisi presentiam meam solam, qua se suumque dominum crederet honestari. Hic, fateor, humanitate tanta victus erubui; tacui et tacendo consensi seu consensisse visus sum.)[28]

His presence alone, however, legitimated the Viscontian regime, for, as Petrarch himself says, by remaining silent he consented to the tyrant's wishes.

This tacit consent is precisely what Boccaccio criticizes when he writes in conclusion to his pastoral reproach:

> But he cannot deny that he does this: that is, that together with Aegon he delights when he hears of the ruins, the fires, the imprisonings, the thefts, and the devastations and ignominies of his only fatherland; and this is a huge crime. But let us leave aside the matters of war. This egregious commander and cultivator of solitude, what is he to do surrounded by the multitude? He who regularly extols with sublime praise the free life and honest poverty, what will he do, subjected to a foreign yoke and adorned with dishonest riches? Furthermore, what will he celebrate, the most famous exhorter of virtue, once he has become a follower of vices? I know that nothing is left for me to do except blush and condemn his work, and sing that Virgilian song either in a chorus or alone: "What can you not

---

[27] Petrarch 1938–42, 3.205; Petrarch 1975–85, 2.318 (*Familiares* 16.11.9–10).

[28] Petrarch 1938–42, 3.208; Petrarch 1975–85, 2.321 (*Familiares* 16.12.9–10). On Petrarch's political activities as a courtier, see Kirkham 2006.

compel mortal hearts to do / accursed hunger for gold?" Now, eminent teacher, although many things remain that I could say against him, unless it is shown otherwise, what do you say, whose indignation and eloquence is greater? ... Since you know how much faith I put in you above all, I ask that you take him back and with your customs pull him back from such a reproachable crime and remove from that savage man so much splendid decorum.

(hoc quin factitet negare non potest: scilicet quin una cum Egone letetur dum audit ruinas incendia captivitates mortes rapinas et soli patrii desolationes et ignominias, quod pregrande piaculum est. Sed sinamus bellica. Hic solitudinem commendator egregius atque cultor, quid multitudine circumspectus aget? quid tam sublimi preconio liberam vitam atque paupertatem honestam extollere consuetus, iugo alieno subditus et inhonestis ornatus divitiis faciet? quid virtutum exortator clarissimus, vitiorum sectator effectus, decantabit ulterius? Ego nil aliud nosco quam erubescere et opus suum dampnare, et virgilianum illud aut coram aut secus cantare carmen: "Quid non mortalia pectora cogis / auri sacra fames?" Nunc, preceptor egregie, cum multa supersint que in eum, nisi aliud ostendatur, dicere possim, tu quid dices, cui indignatio maior et facundia amplior est? ... Cum igitur ratum habeam quoniam tibi pre ceteris fidem prestaturus sit, queso ut illum redarguas tuisque moribus a tam infausto scelere retrahas et ab immanissimo homine tam splendidum decus ... amoveas.)[29]

There is a contradiction between the Petrarch who had extolled the virtues of Rome and of the Church Fathers and the one who has bound himself to a tyrant who delights in destruction. There is no explanation that Boccaccio can find except that Petrarch must be there out of greed (*auri sacra fames*).[30] The irony of the concluding address (*preceptor egregie*) is biting and must be seen to condition the literary friendship for the rest of their lives. Their correspondence recommences within a few years and continues over the years, and they discuss and share manuscripts, but their cultural ideologies are never reciprocal. Besides the well-known differences between them on the cultural importance to be given to Dante and vernacular poetry, a political choice and a choice of place were at the bottom of their divergence. Their distinct view of the poet's relationship with the body politic conditioned the scopes of their poetics. The Petrarch who occupies such an important part of Boccaccio's cultural ideology will remain, after 1353, *Silvanus*, the poet laureate of Rome prior to his move to Milan.

---

[29] Boccaccio 1992, 580–582 (*Epistola* 10.26–30).
[30] The quotation of Virgil is from *Aeneid* 3.56–57, which was famously mistranslated by Dante in *Purgatorio* 22.40–41. On the intertext here, see Houston 2010, 99–100 and 190 n. 5. See also Caferro 2018a, 45, in which the intertext is shown to be also Petrarchan.

Soon after his failed attempt to bring Petrarch to Florence, Boccaccio wrote a biography of Dante, the *Vita di Dante*, in the tradition of the *accessus ad auctores*.[31] This biography of Dante is directed toward a Florentine audience that Boccaccio saw as rejecting its greatest poets. They had not done enough to bring Petrarch there and in anger had revoked the invitation along with its benefits.[32] By not bringing Petrarch to Florence, they were repeating the conditions of Dante's exile. But it is also a response to Petrarch's ideas about poetry and his behavior in rejecting Florence. In the biography, Boccaccio seems to represent Dante in Petrarchan terms. Dante is boldly described as the heir to Virgil and Homer and as a master of theology and poetry. Boccaccio attenuates the prophetic strain in Dante's representation of himself as poet-theologian by presenting him as a lay devotee of humanistic study and claiming that he studied theology in Paris.[33] Boccaccio also claims that Dante would have wanted to be crowned poet laureate, but was prohibited by Fortune – an element that Petrarch had described overcoming in his *Collatio*. There is a general superimposition of the figures of Dante and Petrarch that coincides with Boccaccio's original rationale for bringing Petrarch to Florence. By linking the two figures in the aftermath of Petrarch's refusal, however, Boccaccio is also suggesting that Dante can act in Petrarch's place. There are three main elements of the letter that scholars have linked to Boccaccio's engagement with Petrarch. The first is the opening sentence with a proverb attributed to Solon about the health of the republic.[34] The second is a diatribe against

---

[31] Boccaccio refers to the tract in his *Esposizioni* as a "trattatello in laude di Dante." The first redaction's full title is in Latin (*De origine, vita, studiis et moribus viri clarissimi Dantis Aligerii florentini poete illustris, et de operibus compositis ab eodem*), whereas the second redaction's title is almost identical, but in vernacular. I cite primarily from the first redaction, but I have indicated the redaction number before the paragraph number in the parenthetical citations. On the three redactions of the *Vita di Dante*, see Ricci 1974 and Paolazzi 1983. For a general overview, see Filosa 2013. For a succinct discussion of the differences between the two versions that convincingly argues that the first was directed to a Florentine audience, see Eisner 2013, 35–36. On the first redaction's implicit Petrarchization of Dante, see Boli 1988; Gilson 2005, 25–32; and Caferro 2018a, 39–40. See also Ginsberg 2002, 105–147, who reads the first two redactions in terms of Boccaccio's political life. On Boccaccio's sources, see (Giuseppe) Billanovich 1949; Larner 1990; Kirkham 1992; and Gross 2009. Boccaccio's first biography of Dante has been interpreted variously as being aimed at Petrarch or as being directed to a general Florentine readership. All agree, however, that it is a generally hagiographic and aggrandizing representation of the poet.

[32] In his bucolic letter to Petrarch, Boccaccio acknowledges the possibility that Petrarch felt indignation at the Florentine's revocation of their offer. See Boccaccio 1992, 580 (*Epistola* 10.22–25).

[33] See Dell'Oso 2017.

[34] See Boccaccio 1974, 438 (*Vita di Dante* 1.1). For an analysis of this passage in terms of Boccaccio's ideas of cultural renewal in Florence and his Dantism, see Eisner 2013, 31–35.

Florence for not rewarding those who deserve it. Both derive from Petrarch's letter in critique of the Florentines in *Familiares* 8.10 for not preventing the death of his friend, Mainardo Accorsi, at the hands of the Ubaldini.[35] The third is a history of poetry that derives partially from Petrarch's letter to his brother Gherardo (*Familiares* 10.4).[36] It is this third element on which I will focus.

Boccaccio begins his history of poetry with the material from Petrarch's letter that describes the origins of poetry in the exquisite speech of priest-poets about the one God. He adds to it a description of the process by which great men were made into gods by poets in service to a theocratic power. One passage has led some scholars to argue that this euhemeristic history of myth is a critique of Petrarch's political vision of the poet's role:

> Besides this, [the princes] went about deifying their fathers, their grandfathers, and their ancestors, so that they would be both more feared and revered by the multitude. These things couldn't easily be done without the office of poets, who – in order to increase their own fame, to please the princes, to delight their subjects, and to persuade everyone to act virtuously – which would have been against the intention [of the multitude] if expressed openly – with various and magisterial fictions, poorly understood by the stupid both today and at that time, they made [the multitude] believe what the princes wanted them to believe. For the new gods and for the men who pretended to be born from the gods, they took advantage of that same style that the first [poets] had used for the true God alone and for praising Him.
>
> (E oltre a questo diedono opera a deificare li loro padri, li loro avoli e li loro maggiori, acciò che più fossero e temuti e avuti in reverenzia dal vulgo. Le quali cose non si poterono commodamente fare senza l'oficio de' poeti, li quali, sì per ampliare la loro fama, sì per compiacere a' prencipi, sì per dilettare i sudditi, e sì per persuadere il virtuosamente operare a ciascuno – quello che con aperto parlare saria suto della loro intenzione contrario – con fizioni varie e maestrevoli, male da' grossi oggi non che a quel tempo intese, facevano credere quello che li prencipi volevan che si credesse; servando negli nuovi iddii e negli uomini, gli quali degl'iddii nati fingevano, quello medesimo stile che nel vero Iddio solamente e nel suo lusingarlo avevan gli primi usato.)[37]

---

[35] On the circumstances surrounding the death of Accorsi and Petrarch's letter, see Caferro 2013 and 2018a, 22–48.

[36] Boccaccio transcribed several of Petrarch's *Familiares* during his visit to Padua in 1351. On Boccaccio's close attention to Petrarch's *Familiares* 10.4 in the *Vita di Dante*, see Marcozzi 2002, 26–27.

[37] Boccaccio 1974, 471 (*Vita di Dante* 1.135–136).

David Wallace and Warren Ginsberg see in this passage a scathing critique of Petrarch's service of princes, which Boccaccio had expressed to Petrarch in no uncertain terms during the same period.[38] According to them, Boccaccio is saying that poets composed poetry in the service of the prince in order to persuade ignorant subjects, who did not understand what was going on. My translation follows this reading. Martin Eisner has recently suggested instead that the passage, in the spirit of Boccaccio's intent with his defense of pagan poetry, asserts that poets composed this kind of political poetry against their will and that the ignorant mistook the surface level of their fictions for the truth. In this reading, the "intention" mentioned in the passage would be that of the poets: that the poets did not believe in their own fictions. Eisner goes on to claim that, either way, "Boccaccio's discussion of the political pressures that produced pagan poetry ... can be understood not only as a justification of those potentially polytheist poets but also of Dante, who dedicated the three sections of the *Commedia* to major Ghibelline figures."[39] This is a perfectly reasonable reading as far as Dante is concerned. In the treatise, after all, Boccaccio was interested in recuperating Dante's posthumous reputation in Florence, which may have been sullied even further by an inevitable association with Petrarch. Both poets had taken up residence in enemy territories in the north of Italy, ruled by men that the Florentines considered tyrants.

Given the superimposition of Dante and Petrarch across the treatise and Boccaccio's anger at Petrarch's move to Milan, the reading of the passage as a critique of Petrarch is not unreasonable either. Eisner is right, however, to question what such a sentiment would be doing in a biography of Dante addressed to a Florentine audience, much less in a defense of pagan poetry.[40] I would like to suggest that Boccaccio's narrative about the political role of poets in principates is meant also to contextualize for the Florentines what had happened with Petrarch's refusal. The list of motives for the poets' association with political power – to gain fame, please princes, delight subjects, or to move people to act virtuously – contains possible rationales for interpreting Petrarch's decision, but also leaves open the question of why poets would collude with political power. The point is that poets participate in politics for various reasons and that one should not assume automatically that it is for the wrong one.[41]

---

[38] See Wallace 1997, 271 and Ginsberg 2002, 123–124. The interpolations I have made in the translated passage are based on this interpretation. See also Baldan 1996 and Stone 1998, 170.

[39] Eisner 2013, 44.   [40] Eisner 2013, 44.

[41] Eisner 2013, 42, following Garin 1954, 63–75, suggests that this history of myth in the *Vita di Dante* will be the foundation of his enterprise in the *Genealogie*. The critique of poets who are

Furthermore, the ignorant who do not understand poetry, misunderstand it whether it is written with positive intentions or not. It is relatively clear from his letters what Boccaccio thought about Petrarch's motivations as a poet in this period, but he could not publicly acknowledge this without compromising Dante's place in his project of Florentine cultural renewal. At that moment he was focused on using Dante to advance the study of poetry and the liberal arts in Florence. He had to divest the two poets and their intentions from one another in order to save his project from the negative consequences of Petrarch's refusal.[42]

The implicit parallels between Dante and Petrarch across the treatise have the effect of differentiating the vernacular poet from the Latin one. I will address two examples. According to Boccaccio, Dante had abandoned his poem in Florence after his unexpected exile, but when a friend brought it to him, he started it again. Boccaccio notes, perhaps with Petrarch's unfinished *Africa* in mind, that Dante was barely able to finish the *Commedia* by the time of his death, because of the interruptions caused by his exile.[43] Nevertheless, he was able to finish his poem, unlike Petrarch. Second, and more importantly, Boccaccio responds to the reasons of Dante's choice of the vernacular over Latin:

> Many men, including some wise men, advance a general question that goes like this: If Dante was such a distinguished man in learning, why did he decide to compose such a great and notable work, with such a lofty subject, like his *Comedy*, in the Florentine idiom? Why didn't he write it in Latin verse, like previous poets had done? To such a question, two major reasons, among many others, occur to me in reply. The first of them is to be more useful to his citizens and to other Italians. He knew that if he had written it in a Latin meter like past poets, he would have been useful only to the Latin literate. By writing in the vernacular he created a work that had never been made before, and he did not prevent himself from being understood by the literate, but, showing the beauty of our idiom and his excellent skill in it, he

---

compromised by political power in Bocaccio's history of poetry, however, is much more complex in the *Genealogie*, where he describes figures such as Jove as being created first by poet-theologians and only adopted generations later by politically compromised poets. These mythic figures are in turn sometimes recuperated by even later poets in a virtuous or at least scientific way. See Lummus 2012b, esp. 755–765. Boccaccio's critical perspective on compromised poets is the reason why he does not include Scipio Africanus or Alexander the Great among the gods. See Boccaccio 1998, 8.1350–1352 (*Genealogie* 13.71).

[42] Boccaccio will try again to bring Petrarch to Florence in 1365, offering him a canonry, after a failed attempt by Roberto Guidi di Battifolle to bring him to the Casentino in 1363–64. After Petrarch's death, Boccaccio tries to repatriate Petrarch through his works, as he had done with Dante. See Lummus 2017.

[43] Boccaccio 1974, 484 (*Vita di Dante* 1.183). Boccaccio finds that the first line of *Inferno* 8 indicates the moment of recommencement.

offered delight and understanding of himself to the unlearned, who had been abandoned by everyone in the past. The second reason, which moved him, was the following. He saw that the liberal arts had been completely abandoned, especially by princes and other powerful men, to whom poets were accustomed to dedicate their works. For this reason, the divine works both of Virgil and of other solemn poets were not only held in low esteem but were almost hated by most people. Since the loftiness of the material demanded it, he had started it like this in Latin: "I sing of the farthest realms adjacent to the world river, which lie wide open to spirits and which reward everyone according to their merits." He stopped there, imagining that he was in vain putting crusts of bread in the mouths of those who were still sucking milk, and he began his work again in a style suited to modern understanding and he continued it in the vernacular.

(Muovono molti, e intra essi alcuni savi uomini generalmente una quistione così fatta: che con ciò fosse cosa che Dante fosse in iscienza solennissimo uomo, perché a comporre così grande, di sì alta materia e sì notabile libro, come è questa sua *Comedia*, nel fiorentino idioma si disponesse; perché non più tosto in versi latini, come gli altri poeti precedenti hanno fatto. A così fatta domanda rispondere, tra molte ragioni, due a l'altre principali me ne occorrono. Delle quali la prima è per fare utilità più comune a' suoi cittadini e agli altri Italiani: conoscendo che, se metricamente in latino, come gli altri poeti passati, avesse scritto, solamente a' letterati avrebbe fatto utile; scrivendo in volgare fece opera mai più non fatta, e non tolse il non potere essere inteso da' letterati, e mostrando la bellezza del nostro idioma e la sua eccellente arte in quello, e diletto e intendimento di sé diede agl'idioti, abandonati per addietro da ciascheduno. La seconda ragione, che a questo il mosse, fu questa. Vedendo egli li liberali studii del tutto abandonati, e massimamente de' prencipi e dagli altri grandi uomini, a' quali si soleano le poetiche fatiche intitolare, e per questo e le divine opere di Virgilio e degli altri solenni poeti non solamente essere in poco pregio divenute, ma quasi da' più disprezzate; avendo egli incominciato, secondo che l'altezza della materia richiedea, in questa guisa: "Ultima regna canam, fluvido contermina mundo, / spiritibus quae lata patent, quae premia solvent / pro meritis cuicunque suis," etc. i lasciò stare; e, immaginando invano le croste del pane porsi alla bocca di coloro che ancora il latte suggano, in istile atto a' moderni sensi ricominciò la sua opera e perseguilla in volgare.)[44]

---

[44] Boccaccio 1974, 486–487 (*Vita di Dante* 1.191–192). It is interesting to note that this passage is slightly changed in the second redaction of the *Vita di Dante*. It is reorganized so that the Latin quotation appears at the beginning and not at the end, which is indicative of a shift in audience. The first prefaces Dante's intentions, while the second prefaces that he had begun the poem in Latin. Furthermore, the second shifts the order of the two reasons so that Dante's concern for the liberal arts is primary. There is also no mention of the Florentine citizens in the later text. Instead, it

Boccaccio represents Dante as a poet who had his city's interests at heart. Unlike those poets who had deceived the masses on behalf of the prince, Dante wrote so that the people could enjoy his work and come to know him, while the learned could still gain a full understanding. This passage further serves to differentiate Dante from Petrarch, detaching him from the common rhetoric that Boccaccio likely employed to argue for the invitation of Petrarch. Furthermore, this passage indicates that Boccaccio's project of education, which Eisner has connected to the anecdote about Solon that opens the treatise,[45] is linked solely to Dante's vernacular project with its populist outlook. Boccaccio seems to be responding to objections about Dante that may have emerged in Florence after Petrarch's move to Milan.

Boccaccio's efforts to convince Petrarch of Dante's cultural relevance continue several years later. The epistolary debate between the two poets shows the question of the vernacular to be both a political and a cultural question. In a letter to Boccaccio dated to May 1359 (*Familiares* 21.15), Petrarch responded to what is likely the second redaction of Boccaccio's biography of Dante. This version of the biography is much shorter and lacks the overstated praise of Dante and the diatribe against Florence. The history of poetry is also much shorter. While some of the changes are certainly due to shifts in Boccaccio's political situation in Florence at the time, the document's change in tone is indicative of the change in context and in audience. Boccaccio no longer needed to differentiate between Petarch and Dante for a Florentine audience. He received the *Invective contra medicum* in 1357 and so was entirely aware of Petrarch's view on poetry and on the office of the poet.[46] The new version of the biography is an attempt to attenuate the differences of opinion on the vernacular and on Dante between Boccaccio and Petrarch.[47]

---

attributes Dante's change of language to his desire to be understood by princes. The final statement on nourishment is also omitted, and in its place, Boccaccio writes that Dante aimed to exercise the intellects of the Latin literate and to give the non-Latin literate a reason to study. These changes further indicate the Florentine public of the first version and the Petrarchan audience of the second. See Boccaccio 1974, 528–529 (*Vita di Dante* 2.128–131).

[45] See Eisner 2013, 36–38. On the origins of the Solon anecdote in Petrarch's *Familiares* 8.10, see Filosa 2013, 218 and Caferro 2018a, 39–40.

[46] For the letter to Boccaccio that accompanied Petrarch's *Invective*, see Petrarch 1994, 314–321 (*Lettera dispersa* 40 [*Miscellanea* 1]).

[47] Cf. Gilson 2005, 40–41. For the relationship between the codicological context of the second version's placement in the Chigi codex and literary history, see Eisner 2013, 29–49. For different interpretations of Boccaccio's changing relationship with Petrarch as seen in the second version of the biography, see McLaughlin 1995, 54–59 and Ginsberg 2002, 139–140. See also Bruni 1990,

Although Petrarch writes in *Familiares* 21.15 that he is ready to give Dante the "palm of vernacular eloquence" ("vulgaris eloquentie palmam"), he says that he dislikes the vernacular because it can please listeners "without penetrating their minds" ("in animum non descendit") and he wonders "what can you expect to happen to our poet among the illiterates in the taverns and squares?" ("quid in hoc nostro inter ydiotas in tabernis et in foro posse putas accidere?").[48] To Boccaccio, who represented Dante as the descendant of Homer and Virgil, Petrarch continues: "How can someone who does not envy Virgil envy anyone else, unless perhaps I envied him the applause and raucous acclaim of the fullers or tavern keepers or woolworkers who offend the ones whom they wish to praise, whom I, like Virgil and Homer, delight in doing without?" ("Aut cui tandem invideat qui Virgilio non invidet, nisi forte sibi fullonum et cauponum et lanistarum ceterorum ve, qui quos volunt laudare vituperant, plausum et raucum murmur invideam, quibus cum ipso Virgilio cumque Homero carere me gratulor?").[49] In the rest of the letter, Petrarch does not distance himself from the subject of Dante's poem, which he recognizes as sublime (*nobilis*). Rather, it is Dante's style, which is popular (*popularis*), that opens up the possibility of misunderstanding and misrepresentation of the poet's words and thought among the people. What is at stake here is the civic role of the poet, and whether he should engage with all, some, or just a few, and therefore in what language. Petrarch, for whom vernacular poetry would remain a documentation of the shifting forms of the inner self, destined for posterity, denies Boccaccio the employment of Dante's poetry in a political context.

This difference of opinion on the nature of the poet's civic role, which is fundamental to their debate on Dante and vernacular poetry, continues throughout their correspondence, even after Petrarch leaves Milan. In a letter dated to 1367, Petrarch addresses Boccaccio's concerns for his freedom during Petrarch's period in Venice, Pavia, and Milan by contrasting the service of tyrants to another kind of service that he finds unbearable:

> I shall try, successfully I hope, not to learn servility as an old man, and to be free in spirit wherever I am, although it may be necessary to be subject in body and in other things to superiors, whether to one man in my case or to

---

421–422 n. 19 and Filosa 2013. On the terms of Petrarch's engagement with Dante, see Barański 2009; Cachey 2009, esp. 75–82; Mazzotta 2009; and Moevs 2009.

[48] Petrarch 1938–42, 4.96–97; Petrarch 1975–85, 3.204 (*Familiares* 21.15.13–15).

[49] Petrarch 1938–42, 4.99; Petrarch 1975–85, 4.205–206 (*Familiares* 21.15.22).

many as in yours. I know not whether to call your kind of yoke heavier and more troublesome. I believe it easier to bear one man's tyranny than a people's.

(Nitar tamen, et spero fore ne discam servire senex utque ubilibet animo liber sim, etsi corpore rebusque aliis subesse maioribus sit necesse, sive uni ut ego, sive multis ut tu. Quod nescio an gravius molestiusque iugi genus dixerim. Pati hominem credo facilius quam tyrannum populum.)[50]

The "one man" to whom Petrarch refers here is Galeazzo II Visconti, whom he served during his residence in Venice, Pavia, and Milan during the mid-1360s. The political visions of Boccaccio and Petrarch could not be more different, even fifteen years after Petrarch's first departure for the Milanese court.

Despite these significant differences, Boccaccio's approach to poetry is still often attributed to his supposed reverence for Petrarch. Boccaccio, in fact, does not hide that Petrarch is a source.[51] The correspondence just examined, however, points toward a significant difference in their outlooks on culture and politics. This difference manifests itself most clearly in terms of poetic theory in the defense of poetry in the *Genealogie*. While it is true that Boccaccio takes many of his assertions on poetry from Petrarch, sometimes verbatim, I shall show that he does so in order to adapt Petrarch's poetics to a new view of the civic role of the poet, which includes vernacular production and which is founded on an ethical engagement with the body politic.

The Poet and the Republic: *Genealogie* 14.1–5

Although Boccaccio's defense of poetry has long been known to descend from Petrarch's *Invective contra medicum* and *Familiares* 10.4, the tone and frame of his argument gives poetry a completely different role in relation to political power. Whereas in the fourth invective Petrarch approaches the hierarchy of power in the city from the inside out – from the monarch to the doctors – Boccaccio reverses this approach, instead moving to the center of power from the outside. The perspective of the outsider is a familiar one for Boccaccio, whose self-defenses in the *Decameron* present a

---

[50] Petrarch 1992, 2.191 (*Seniles* 6.2.1); Petrarch 2004–10, 1.682. For Petrarch's activities during this period, see Wilkins 1959, 39–138.

[51] Boccaccio openly cites the *Invective contra medicum* as a source during his defense. See Boccaccio 1998, 8.1436 (*Genealogie* 14.12.15).

detached and ironic form of authority based on Ovid and Horace.[52] In the defense of poetry in the *Genealogie*, Boccaccio continues to draw on the language of satire and exile, establishing a moral authority that is both a part of the world of the city like the satirist and beyond it like the exile. Assuming no recognition, he approaches power from without, in opposition to Petrarch's tone in the *Invective*. Whereas Petrarch assumes an aggressive position in his own defense, in an effort to de-authorize the physician's role in the court by disparaging his character, Boccaccio's preemptive attacks against the detractors of poetry in the first five chapters of Book 14 of the *Genealogie* seek to make room for poetic discourse in a polyphony of other forms of speech and knowledge.

Throughout the *Genealogie*, Boccaccio stages his enterprise as a sea-voyage in dangerous waters. Although he would like to descend from his little boat and garland it with laurel wreaths, he is threatened by his own contingency. In the Proem to Book 14, Boccaccio figures his precarious situation in terms of a sea-storm. Whereas the principal enemy force that threatens Boccaccio's enterprise throughout was the biting tooth of time (*tempus mordax*), in Book 14 it is the biting envy of his contemporaries (*livor edax*), as he explains to his patron King Hugh IV a few lines later:[53] "Besides there is a sort of gnawing malice, a disease, a death-in-life, which has so usurped men's hearts since the beginning of the world that, when this fever rages, almost no one can get fair judgment" ("Preterea livor edax, letalis viventium pestis, adeo occupavit a primevo hominum pectora, ut rarissima, eo exurente, equa in quem mavis prestentur iudicia").[54] Boccaccio's peculiar description of *livor* as a "lethal pestilence of the living" is indicative of the role that envy plays in his defense and of the audience that he is addressing. The formulation *livor edax* is an Ovidian turn of phrase, which that poet used in a similar fashion in the opening line of the last poem of Book 1 of the *Amores*.[55] This elegy is a meditation on Ovid's poetic practice and a claim to poetic immortality. For Ovid, *livor* is the principal enemy of the poet, since his work seems to be socially useless compared to that of soldier or the lawyer. But, Ovid says, it can only affect him while he is alive, since his poetry will make his name live on into posterity after his death.[56]

---

[52] See Hollander 1977, 112–116; Smarr 1987; and Marchesi 2001.

[53] On Boccaccio's dedication of the work to Hugh, see Zaccaria's note to the first proem in Boccaccio 1998, 8.1611 n. 1. Cf. Hortis 1879, 158–161.

[54] Boccaccio 1930, 17 Boccaccio 1998, 8.1360 (*Genealogie* 14.1.4).

[55] See Ovid 1914, 376–379 (*Amores* 15.1–6, 39–42).

[56] Ovid's battle against *livor* comes up throughout his works, always in an autobiographical context, such as in *Remedia Amoris* 365, 369, and 389 and in *Tristia* 4.10.123.

Boccaccio's use of *livor*, however, is not entirely concerned with how envy relates to poetic fame but also with how envy affects the judgment of the present on contemporaries and predecessors. In this light, Boccaccio may have in mind Tacitus, who employs the term at the opening of his history of Rome to explain how people read and understand history:[57]

> Many historians have treated of the earlier period of eight hundred and twenty years from the founding of Rome, and while dealing with the Republic they have written with equal eloquence and freedom. But after the battle of Actium, when the interests of peace required that all power should be concentrated in the hands of one man, writers of like ability disappeared; and at the same time historical truth was impaired in many ways: first, because men were ignorant of politics as being not any concern of theirs; later, because of their passionate desire to flatter; or again, because of their hatred of their masters. So between the hostility of the one class and the servility of the other, posterity was disregarded. But while men quickly turn from a historian who curries favor, they listen with ready ears to calumny and spite; for flattery is subject to the shameful charge of servility, but malignity makes a false show of independence.

> (nam post conditam urbem octingentos et viginti prioris aevi annos multi auctores rettulerunt, dum res populi Romani memorabantur pari eloquentia ac libertate: postquam bellatum apud Actium atque omnem potentiam ad unum conferri pacis interfuit, magna illa ingenia cessere; simul veritas pluribus modis infracta, primum inscitia rei publicae ut alienae, mox libidine adsentandi aut rursus odio adversus dominantis: ita neutris cura posteritatis inter infensos vel obnoxios. sed ambitionem scriptoris facile averseris, obtrectatio et livor pronis auribus accipiuntur; quippe adulationi foedum crimen servitutis, malignitati falsa species libertatis inest.)[58]

For Tacitus, once power had been conferred to one man alone, truth began to be violated primarily because of general ignorance of the republic and secondarily because of either flattery or dissension. Overcome by the preoccupations of the present, there was no longer any concern for posterity. But since flattery is easily opposed, it is *livor*, together with disparagement, that pushes people to misread history. The false kind of freedom that *livor* causes is what Boccaccio is worried about when he writes that it is impossible to receive fair judgment. He has combined the uses of *livor* by Ovid and Tacitus in order to establish the nature of his

---

[57] Boccaccio received a copy of books 11–16 of the *Annales* and of books 1–5 of the *Historiae* from Zanobi da Strada between 1360 and 1361. For a discussion of the extent of Boccaccio's knowledge of Tacitus, see Zaccaria 2001, 197–213.

[58] Tacitus 1925, 2–3 (*Historiae* 1.1).

attackers' charges. Envy not only affects the fate of poets when they are alive but also the fate of their works once they have been handed over to posterity, since it causes a distorted reading both of the present and of the past. The purpose of Boccaccio's defense is ostensibly to correct the place of both contemporary poets and ancient poets in the modern world.

Boccaccio is not only writing to those who disparage poetry *tout court* but also to those "erudite men" ("eruditi ... homines") who might not agree with Boccaccio's open approach to the study of antiquity in his work.[59] He invokes the imaginary authority of his patron, who died during the composition of the work, in an effort to convince these erudite men: "Of course, I am not wholly sure what your estimate of the work as a whole will be after a careful review; yet, it is my private opinion that, in pure justice, you will render a fair and unbiased judgment of both body and members" ("Verum, collectis omnibus, qualis de opere toto tua existimatio futura sit non satis certum habeo; hoc tamen mecum cogito te de corpore et membris, sola agente iustitia, sanam et integram laturum sententiam").[60] He intends to use the external opinion of the king to persuade those men who "follow the footsteps" ("sequentes vestigia") of the king.[61] He protects himself from the possible criticisms of erudite men by framing his defense with the authority of a monarch who is external to the social structure within which Boccaccio is writing. Given the fact that the King of Cyprus had no real authority in Italy or in the West and that Hugh IV himself was long dead by the time Boccaccio disseminated his work, Boccaccio's use of him as an authority is purely rhetorical in nature. These erudite men are those who commit "the shameful offense of servility" that Tacitus describes. Between the models of Ovid and of Tacitus, Boccaccio is taking on the role of poet and historian, just as Petrarch had in receiving his laurel crown.

There are those, however, who Boccaccio says do not respect the authority of the king, a "far more numerous crowd gathered about in a ring" ("longe numerosior multitudo, corona in circuitu facta") who will continue to attack his work.[62] This multitude is made of men from various walks of life, from the tavern-goer to the lawyer to the philosopher, and Boccaccio divides it into its constituent parts according to the level of influence that each group holds over the whole, and he approaches it from

---

[59] Boccaccio 1930, 17, modified Boccaccio 1998, 8.1360 (*Genealogie* 14.2.1).
[60] Boccaccio 1930, 17 Boccaccio 1998, 8.1358 (*Genealogie* 14.1.3).
[61] Boccaccio 1930, 17, modified Boccaccio 1998, 8.1360 (*Genealogie* 14.1.3).
[62] Boccaccio 1930, 18, modifiedBoccaccio 1998, 8.1360 (*Genealogie* 14.2.1).

the outside. These men are the inhabitants of the city, with whom Boccaccio must come to terms if he is to establish a place for the poet and for poetry within the city. In the second chapter of Book 14, Boccaccio begins his defense by inveighing against the ignorant (*ignari*), who are "certain madmen so garrulous and detestably arrogant that they presume to shout abroad their condemnation of everything that even the best men can do. It is their aim to cheapen and vilify, and, if possible, utterly damn them with their foul calumny" ("homines quidam insani, quibus tanta loquacitas est et detestabilis arrogantia, ut adversus omnia quorumcunque probatissimorum hominum presumant clamoribus ferre sententiam, eos flocci facere, vilipendere et, si queant, turpi damnare sermone").[63] These attackers are at the lowest rung of society. Their opinions are influenced by others and they criticize the poet for wasting his time on study while he could "have loved, drank, slept and spent so much time in pleasure." ("amasse, potasse, dormisse et tam grande tempus voluptatibus trivisse").[64] Their hedonistic reasoning is based on the imminence of death: "'For with all their time spent in study and disapproval of what is profitable, ere they know a single happy day of their lives, they meet death who spares none'" ("'nam, perdito lucubrationibus tempore, antequam diem unam letam sentiant, damnando probanda, in mortem concidunt equam cunctis'").[65] Since death is common to all and is always threatening, there is no reason to act in any sphere of life. Boccaccio continues, noting that "long before the miserable hour of their death, [they] have made the body the grave of an unhappy soul" ("ante quidem diem miserum atque caducum mortalitatis sue corpus, infelicis anime fecere sepulcrum").[66] Although there are no specific examples of the individuals who make up this group, Boccaccio does locate it within the economic sphere of the city by naming their haunts: "Let such men go, therefore, and gabble their applause to innkeepers, trainers, fishmongers, and prostitutes; and, sodden with wine and sleep, bestow their praises upon such as these" ("Vadant ergo tales et cauponibus, lanistis, cetariis atque meretriculis gannientes applaudant, et sommo vinoque marcentes suas illis laudes ingerant").[67] Boccaccio attacks these men, not because they are a multitude, as Petrarch had, nor because they threaten him in any direct way, but because they represent a social element that contributes

---

[63] Boccaccio 1930, 18 Boccaccio 1998, 8.1362 (*Genealogie* 14.2.2).
[64] Boccaccio 1930, 18, modifed Boccaccio 1998, 8.1362 (*Genealogie* 14.2.4).
[65] Boccaccio 1930, 19 Boccaccio 1998, 8.1362 (*Genealogie* 14.2.4).
[66] Boccaccio 1930, 19, modified Boccaccio 1998, 8.1362 (*Genealogie* 14.2.5).
[67] Boccaccio 1930, 19, modified Boccaccio 1998, 8.1362 (*Genealogie* 14.2.5).

nothing to the well-being of the community. Boccaccio was no more a lover of the multitude than was Petrarch but his engagement with this element of society is notably different. For one, he does not question their right to live. Rather he claims that what they call life is merely a hedonistic reaction to the imminence of death. They have reduced themselves to a state in which they cannot participate "in an assembly of men" ("in conventu hominum").[68] In contrast to Petrarch, Boccaccio's political context is concerned with the health of a plurality, not with the health of a single ruler who is representative of the state.

The second group of people that Boccaccio addresses is the group of the false wise, who, "before they have even seen the doorway of a school ... fake a certain gravity and thoughtful bearing, only having seen a lot of vernacular treatises, and only speak about superficial things." ("ante visum scolarum limen ... quadam ficta gravitate verborum et morum ponderositate visis aliquando non nullis libellis vulgarium, non nisi de apicibus rerum verba faciunt").[69] Boccaccio sees these fake scholars as little better than the ignorant because they spend time among the wise and listen to their discussions about sublime matters in order to repeat what they heard later to the crowd and to be considered wise men:

> And, finally, they memorize that which their weak and tired intellect has taken from the mouth of the most learned and, after a long sigh, they babble about and spit it out at the textile shops of women, or, rather, if they have the chance, at the crossroads as the ignorant rabble listen as if these men had consulted God himself. And they do this – not without great labor – hoping that it seem that what they have been saying was torn by their imagination and speculation from the depths of the divine mind.

> (Et tandem, quod ex ore probatissimorum hominum intellectus eorum tenuis et remissus excepit, servavitque memoria, apud muliercularum textrinas, seu potius, si prestetur, in triviis, ignaro ascultante popello, uti ipsum Deum consuluerint, post longum suspirium blaterantes emictunt, volentes ex hoc percipi quod non absque labore plurimo, quod dixerint ingenio et speculatione sua ex penetralibus divine mentis evulsum sit.)[70]

Boccaccio's tone in this passage is satirical and much of his vocabulary is taken from the Roman satirists. The term "rabble" (*popellus*), for example, emerges in the context of social commentary by Horace and

---

[68] Boccaccio 1930, 19, modified Boccaccio 1998, 8.1364 (*Genealogie* 14.2.6).
[69] Boccaccio 1930, 19, modified Boccaccio 1998, 8.1364 (*Genealogie* 14.3.1).
[70] Boccaccio 1930, 20, modified Boccaccio 1998, 8.1364–1366 (*Genealogie* 14.3.3).

Persius.[71] Boccaccio uses the term in a manner similar to the later satirist, in whose fourth satire Socrates criticizes Alcibiades "for his superficiality, lack of knowledge and expertise, and unfitness to hold political power."[72] Like Boccaccio's criticism of the demented false wise, Persius has Socrates attack Alcibiades for his own falsity: "So why then, since your pretty looks on the skin's surface are useless, why don't you stop wagging your tail for the flattering rabble before your time, when you'd be better off gulping down undiluted Anticyras?" ("quin tu igitur summa nequiquam pelle decorus / ante diem blando caudam iactare popello / desinis, Anticyras melior sorbere meracas?").[73]

The context of Boccaccio's use of the formulation "at the crossroads" (*in triviis*) also derives from satire.[74] But this specific use by Boccaccio seems to echo the caustic, satirical comment about street-singers by the shepherd Menalcas in Virgil's third eclogue: "You beat him at singing? Since when did you have a wax-jointed pipe? Didn't you, in the crossroads – you unlearned man! – use to spoil some miserable song with a screeching reed?" ("Cantando tu illum? aut umquam tibi fistula cera / iuncta fuit? Non tu, in triviis, indocte, solebas / stridenti miserum stipula disperdere carmen?").[75] The structure of Boccaccio's sentence (*in triviis, ignaro*) mirrors the Virgilian source (*in triviis, indocte*). The two uses are connected by the accusation of falsity that both writers make against opponents. Such allusions and word choice help establish Boccaccio's morally corrective tone in the context of the city. The position of the satirist – and of the satirical shepherd, in the case of Virgil – outside of the urban environment allows him a distance and detachment from which he can reconstitute the codes that govern it. In contrast with Petrarch, it is significant that Boccaccio models himself on the reconstructive social engagement of Roman satirists and not on the angry disparagement of the Ciceronian

---

[71] Horace uses the term "popellus" in *Epistulae* 1.7, in which he responds strongly to Maecenas' request to return to the city and fulfill his obligations to his patron. In this context, Horace is praising a man for being a humble hard worker and is comparing this man's detachment from great men to his own detachment from Maecenas. See Horace 1926, 298–299 (*Epistulae* 1.7.66): "selling cheap odds and ends to the common folk in tunics" ("vilia vendentem tunicato scruta popello"). On the classical meaning of *popellus*, see Strodach 1933, 13, 50, and 52.

[72] Braund 2004, 87.

[73] Persius and Juvenal 2004, 88–89 (*Satura* 4.14–16). Braund 2004, 89 n. 4 notes that Anticyras denotes the herb *hellebore*, which was "a classic cure for madness."

[74] Similar uses can be found in Horace's *Ars poetica*, 245; *Sermones* 1.9.59; and *Epistulae* 1.16.64 and 1.17.58.

[75] Virgil 1916–18, 38–39 (*Bucolica* 3.25–27). On this phrase in Virgil and its afterlife and on parallels among the satirists, see Booth 1980.

invective. His purpose is to reconstitute the community by engaging with it, not to purify it by destroying its most discordant members.

Boccaccio sees the fraudulent behavior of these false philosophers as having a direct effect on the functioning of the city. With superficial knowledge they control the amazement of the ignorant crowd (which is composed of the *ignari* of the previous section), claiming to have left behind the liberal arts for the higher calling of theology. They also engage other subjects of direct civic relevance: "In this manner they also treat the customs of men, the acts of heroes, the sacred laws and institutions and the legislators" ("Sic et de moribus hominum et gestis heroum ac de sacris legibus et institutis legumque latoribus").[76] This superficial neglect extends to poetry, which they condemn and vilify (*damnant, vituperant, floccifaciunt*) with the result that "the uneducated too can hardly tolerate [it]" ("vix tolerare possint etiam imprudentes").[77] Boccaccio sees their ignorance as not only harmful to themselves – and to poets – but also and especially as harmful to the city and its laws and institutions.

Still, Boccaccio does not entirely condemn this group, as Petrarch had done with the physician. Citing his sense of charity (*caritate mea*), he gives them a chance to redeem themselves to the community by dedicating themselves to true study:

> and if they are agitated by this desire for glory, to be esteemed wise, they should enter the schools, listen to teachers, turn the pages of books, stay awake and learn, and visit the fora of debaters … Once they have done this honorably and have reached the well-earned title, then if they wish they should come forward, lecture, debate, reprehend and correct, and with a harsh spirit oppose their opponents.

> (et si hac glorie cupiditate agitantur, ut sapientes existimentur, scolas intrent, audiant preceptores, libros evolvant, vigilent atque discant, et palestras disputantium visitent … Quod cum laudabiliter fecerint, et in bene meritum titulum venerint, si libet, in medium prodeant, predicent, disputent, redarguant et castigent, atque acri spiritu suis redargutoribus instent.)[78]

Boccaccio proposes a corrective for their ill civic behavior, suggesting that a poet's learning will enrich the community. He shows respect for the human capacity to care for one another and himself is guided by *caritas*

---

[76] Boccaccio 1930, 20, modified Boccaccio 1998, 8.1366 (*Genealogie* 14.3.5).
[77] Boccaccio 1930, 21, modified Boccaccio 1998, 8.1366 (*Genealogie* 14.3.5).
[78] Boccaccio 1930, 21, modified Boccaccio 1998, 8:1366–1368 (*Genealogie* 14.3.7–8).

toward his fellow citizens.[79] The tone of these passages, although it is didactic, is far removed from that of Petrarch's invective. Boccaccio represents himself as engaged in a political community which he seeks to change.

Gradually approaching the center of intellectual power, Boccaccio takes on the caste of lawyers. He first recognizes the importance of the civic function of practicing law: "the dishonest customs of men are held in check, innocence is extolled, and what is one's own is conceded upon request, and through them not only is the vigor of the republic served, but it grows better with perennial justice" ("frenantur hominum illecebres mores, extollitur innocentia, et quod suum est unicuique poscenti conceditur, quibus reipublice nervus non solum suis in viribus servatur, sed perenni iustitia augetur in melius").[80] But he quickly qualifies their intentions by specifying that they all "work out of greed for gold" ("auri cupiditate laborant").[81] This desire for money taints their judgment such that they would disapprove of poetry, not officially but in informal semi-private reunions:

> It is in their practice, especially during a lull in their duties, to leave bench and court, and join an informal gathering of friends; if, in the course of the conversation, anyone happens to mention poets, they always praise them highly of course, as men of great learning and eloquence. But at length with honey they mix poison – not deadly, to be sure. They say that poets can hardly be called wise to have spent their whole time following a profession that, after years of labor, yields never a cent. This explains, they add, why poets are always stark poor; they never make a brilliant showing with dress, money, nor servants; from this they argue that, because poets are not rich, their profession is good for nothing.
>
> (Consuevere quidem, relictis rostris et pretoria exeuntes, et potissime dum curis paululum soluti in conventum amicorum veniunt, si contingat inter loquendum fieri mentionem poetarum, illos extollere laudibus, quoniam eruditissimi atque eloquentissimi fuere viri; tandem post multa absconditum sub melle venenum, non letale tamen, emictunt dicuntque eos parum fuisse prudentes, in quantum, tempus omne terentes, facultatem secuti

---

[79] Boccaccio's religiosity and the Christian origins of his ethics have not been adequately explored. See, however, the important new work by Kriesel 2018. The *caritas* often invoked by the author of the *Genealogie* is mirrored in one of Boccaccio's most important eclogues, *Olympia*, in which Boccaccio stages an encounter between himself (Silvius) and his deceased daughter (Olympia as Violante). She implores him to care for others, blending the cares of the pastor with the acts of mercy and superimposing Christian ethics on the rules of hospitality from Virgil's Arcadia (*Buccolicum Carmen* 14.275–277). See Lummus 2013a.

[80] Boccaccio 1930, 22, modified Boccaccio 1998, 8.1368 (*Genealogie* 14.4.1).

[81] Boccaccio 1930, 22, modified Boccaccio 1998, 8.1368 (*Genealogie* 14.4.2).

sunt, ex qua post longos labores nulle consequuntur opes, super addentes
ob hoc pauperrimos homines fuisse poetas, nullo splendore spectabiles,
nullis divitiis, nullo famulatu insignes, volentes ex his intelligi, quia non
divites fuere, nullius pretii eorum extimanda facultas sit.)[82]

Their opinions become socially harmful once they become disseminated
among the people: "Such reasoning along with its unexpressed conclusion,
finds easy access to the ears and minds of others, since we are all somewhat
given to love of money, and foolishly take wealth to be the greatest thing in
the world" ("Que quidem verba una cum abscondita conclusione facile
audientium animos intrant, cum omnes in avaritiam proni simus, et stulta
credulitate arbitremur summum bonum possidere divitias").[83] While this
opinion, he goes on to say, might be respectable if it entered into public
opinion "from a charitable source" ("ex fonte caritatis"), since it comes
"from the obfuscated judgment of foolish men" ("ex offuscato appetitus
inepti iudicio") it should be refuted.[84] Again, Boccaccio's criticism of this
group is based on the foundations of their social engagement. They do not
act out of charity or care for the community but out of greed. Boccaccio,
however, claims to feel compassion for them, perhaps because he had been
trained as a lawyer in his youth or perhaps because he too would have liked
a certain affluence.[85] He shows, once again, that his purpose is to correct
public opinion in the different levels of society, so that poetry might take
its rightful place in guiding public affairs at all levels.

In his response to this group, Boccaccio contrasts the lawyer's cultivation of power through money with the poet's cultivation of virtue through
poverty. The contrast between lawyers and poets is a commonplace in the
Western tradition, and both Petrarch and Boccaccio often argue this
position.[86] Boccaccio's refutation of the lawyer's charges is quite simple:
he separates poetry and law by placing the former among the speculative
sciences and the latter among the mechanical sciences and usury, much in
the same way that Petrarch had characterized medicine.[87] Poetry concerns
itself with higher matters, while the "court lawyers . . . rear offices wherein
they fairly coin money with the stamp of a venal tongue, and make gold
out of the tears of the wretched by the transmuting power of their own

---

[82] Boccaccio 1930, 22 Boccaccio 1998, 8.1368–1370 (*Genealogie* 14.4.3).
[83] Boccaccio 1930, 22 Boccaccio 1998, 8.1370 (*Genealogie* 14.4.4).
[84] Boccaccio 1930, 23, modified Boccaccio 1998, 8.1370 (*Genealogie* 14.4.5).
[85] See Boccaccio 1930, 23 Boccaccio 1998, 8.1370 (*Genealogie* 14.4.5).
[86] See, e.g., *Familiares* 1.1, 14.2, 22.4, 24.1 and *Seniles* 14.1. Boccaccio repeats the accusation in *De
casibus* 3.10 and in his letter to Pietro Piccolo, *Epistola* 20.
[87] See Boccaccio 1930, 23 Boccaccio 1998, 8.1372 (*Genealogie* 14.4.7).

verbosity" ("causidici ... sibi officinas construunt, in quibus venalis lingue malleo numismata cudunt, et aurum ex miserorum lacrimis verbositate conficiunt").[88] For Boccaccio, lawyers cannot truly serve society because they feed off the misery of others in the sole service of money and power – they are even placed alongside usurers – whereas poetry

> descends to earth accompanied by the sacred Muses, and she never seeks a habitation in the towering palaces of kings or the easy abodes of the luxurious; rather she enters caves on the steep mountainside, or shady groves, or argent springs, and the retreats of the studious, however incredibly poor, empty, and dark they are; and there she dwells.

> (descendit in terras, sacris comitata Musis, non celsa regum palatia, non molles deliciosorum domos exquirit habitatura, verum antra atque prerupta montium, umbras nemorum, fontes argenteos secessusque studentium, quantumcunque pauperrimos et luce peritura vacuos, intrat et incolit.)[89]

This description of poetry defines it by establishing its dwelling on earth. The palaces of kings and luxurious homes are not proper to poets, but this does not affect the centrality of the poetic office to human life. Poetry, Boccaccio explains, violates the economic system of evaluation of worth since it originates in a higher authority than such a scale can measure. Lawyers have chosen a subject that is valued in "splendors made with hands" ("splendores manu factos"), which poets consider "useless and empty" ("futiles et inanes").[90]

All wise men, Boccaccio says, are faced with a choice about what to write. Poets have chosen to write of things themselves, whereas lawyers have chosen to treat only other men's writings:

> The poets have chosen a science or pursuit of knowledge, which by constant meditation draws them away into the region of the stars, among the divinely adorned dwellings of the gods and their heavenly splendors. Whether this be true testimony let the poems of the bards bear witness in their own words, written down as they are in excellent style by the pen of poets under direct impulse of this divine knowledge. Lawyers, in their practice of law, are skilled in mere memory of what is written, and dispense the decisions and rulings of legislators literally, but without intelligence.

> (Elegere poete scientiam, inter sydera, inter deorum sedes ornatusque celetes suos continua meditatione trahentem; nunquid hoc verum sit, testimonium reddant ipsa vatum poemata, impulsu trahentis eleganti stilo

---

[88] Boccaccio 1930, 23–24 Boccaccio 1998, 8.1372 (*Genealogie* 14.4.8).
[89] Boccaccio 1930, 24, modified Boccaccio 1998, 8.1372 (*Genealogie* 14.4.9).
[90] Boccaccio 1930, 24 Boccaccio 1998, 8.1372–1374 (*Genealogie* 14.4.10).

poetarum descripta calamo. Causidici vero, legum facultatem secuti, sola scriptorum valent memoria, non ex ingenio, sed ex licteris legum latorum iura reddentes.)[91]

For Boccaccio, lawyers exert their role in society by interpreting the law, a second-level discourse that – although essential to a healthy society – is nevertheless secondary to natural or ethical truth. Poets, however, contemplate the nature of things and describe it in their poems, which are meant both to preserve and to communicate it to society. Although this might seem to relegate poets to a minimal social role, it is their duty to form the words with which humans contemplate the divine, the same words used by the legislators and lawyers who then write and interpret the law. Boccaccio argues that law itself cannot be considered a first-level discourse by citing historical examples that demonstrate the changes of laws over geographical space and historical time.

Boccaccio continues his contrast of poets and lawyers by claiming that poets themselves also escape the economic evaluation with which lawyers measure their success, since they choose to be poor in order to write works that will ensure their everlasting fame and that of the community in which they live. Lawyers act as foils to Boccaccio's ideal poets, who rest somewhere in between complete detachment from and complete immersion within the morally precarious life of the city. He cites such examples as Homer, Plautus, Ennius, and Virgil, all of whom were poor in substance but rich in posthumous fame. Unlike Petrarch's examples of poetic greatness in solitude, all of which coincide with the interest of political power in poetic fame, Boccaccio cites examples of poets whose fame was usurped by princes either posthumously or against their will. Homer, for example, was revered by Alexander the Great centuries after he flourished, while during his lifetime he was so poor "that, when he lost his eyesight, he had not enough to pay a boy to lead him" ("ut non esset illi, luminibus capto, unde sumptus puero duci posset inpendere").[92] Plautus was the poorest poet who ever lived: "He, to feed himself honestly in his destitution, used all day to wear himself out working at the hand-mills for a pittance, then sit up all night writing his comedies" ("ut honeste ventrem pasceret, ad molas manuarias pretio fatigabatur die; noctes in componendis comediis ducebat insomnes").[93] Ennius lived with only a single servant despite his friendship with the Scipio family and was made a member of that family only after his

---

[91] Boccaccio 1930, 25, modified Boccaccio 1998, 8.1374 (*Genealogie* 14.4.11).
[92] Boccaccio 1930, 27 Boccaccio 1998, 8.1376 (*Genealogie* 14.4.15).
[93] Boccaccio 1930, 27 Boccaccio 1998, 8.1378 (*Genealogie* 14.4.16).

death. Virgil – the most imperial of poets – ordered that his poem be burned, even though Augustus "trampled all the authority of the laws under foot" ("omnis legum autoritas pedibus calcata est") and decided to save the poem for his own interests.[94] Boccaccio's point in naming all of these examples, which were also used by Petrarch to different ends, is not that poets and political power are inseparable, or that poets must always be in service of a powerful patron, but that the fame of poets is such that men of power cannot keep from associating it with themselves.

The centrality of the relationship between poetry and power for Boccaccio's defense of poetry becomes evident in a long aside on the value of poverty at the end of the fourth chapter. Although it most directly refers to lawyers, Boccaccio is speaking to all those who make decisions based on the promise of material gain. Understood in the context of his political quarrels with Petrarch before and during the composition of the *Genealogie* – when Boccaccio suggested that Petrarch took refuge among the Visconti because of *auri sacra fames* – this defense of poverty can be seen as an indirect response to Petrarch's service to tyrants. Boccaccio explains that poverty can be understood in two ways: as a paucity of perishable goods and as an illness of the mind. The first, he says, may be applied to poets, in that they seek only to subsist materially, because "with poverty as our leader, we by choice attain freedom and peace of mind, and with these honorable leisure; whereby, as we live in the midst of the lands, we taste heavenly things" ("[paupertate] duce libertatem volentes consequimur, animi tranquillitatem et cum his laudabile ocium, quibus mediis viventes in terris gustamus celestia").[95] It is only through poverty that a poet can truly dwell on the earth and meditate upon philosophical matters.

The kind of freedom and "honorable leisure" that Boccaccio addresses here is in direct contrast to the freedom and leisure that Petrarch said he had found among the Visconti in Milan. A true poet, Boccaccio says, can only find liberty, tranquility, and leisure by dwelling in independence from worldly goods. It is also thanks to poverty that poets can avoid – as much as is humanly possible – their own historicity and contingency in a world experienced through Fortune:

> Such poverty is founded upon a rock, fearing neither threat nor thrust of Fortune, who confounds this world. Let thunders fall and mad winds smite the earth; incessant rains submerge the fields, rivers wash them away; let

---

[94] Boccaccio 1930, 28 Boccaccio 1998, 8.1378 (*Genealogie* 14.4.17).
[95] Boccaccio 1930, 29, modified Boccaccio 1998, 8.1380 (*Genealogie* 14.4.21).

trumpets sound to battle and tumultuous wars arise, and plunder rage on every hand. Amid all, Poverty smiles at fire and ruin, and rejoices in sweet security.

(Hec in solido sita est, nec Fortune, mundana versantis, minas aut iacula timet: fulminet ether desuper, concutiat ventorum impetuosa rabies orbem, inundent campos ymbres assidui, diluant flumina, sonet classicum, tumultuosa oriantur bella, discurrant predones undique; hec, ruinas ridens et incendia, dulci securitate letatur.)[96]

The imagery of catastrophe with which Boccaccio describes the world in this passage echoes the imagery of the proems throughout the *Genealogie* and especially the Proem to Book 14. It is also evocative of Petrarch's use of sea metaphors and the image of wandering as representative of his subjugation to Fortune. Poverty, Boccaccio suggests, offers a security from the vicissitudes of history. It sets poets apart both from the masses and from the elite, who are all subject to the desire for wealth.

Boccaccio cites as examples a group of philosophers and common men, who lived lives independent and disdainful of the wealth offered by the political power of princes. The first major example is Diogenes the Cynic, whose reaction to power and wealth directly contradicts the historical example set by Petrarch:

> Lured by [poverty], Diogenes, most illustrious prince of the Cynics in his time, was able to and did spend all his wealth, which was very substantial, upon those who wanted it. He also preferred to dwell in a tub – a sort of movable house – instead of in a palace. He preferred to eat wild lettuce, washed by his own hands, rather than pay court to Dionysius for the sake of enjoying the sausages of kings. His voluntary rejection of wealth and his fame for learning were able to bring a proud young man, who already had in mind to rule the world, to come to see him. This Alexander of Macedon sought his friendship and offered him immoderate gifts, but in vain.

> ([Paupertate] delectatus. Dyogenes, sui evi splendidissimus Cynicorum princeps, divitias, quarum abundantissimus erat, omnes potuit largiri volentibus atque largitus est, doliumque, quasi versatilem domum, quam palatia habitare maluit et lactucas silvestres, suis lotas manibus, manducare, quam Dyonisio adulari, ut tuccetis uteretur regiis. Nec voluntaria rerum abiectio et claritas studiorum ad se visendum evocasse potuere superbum iuvenem atque iam animo orbis tenentem imperium, Alexandrum Macedonem, eius amicitiam exquirentem et frustra munera ingentia offerentem.)[97]

---

[96] Boccaccio 1930, 29 Boccaccio 1998, 8.1380 (*Genealogie* 14.4.21).
[97] Boccaccio 1930, 29 Boccaccio 1998, 8.1380–1382 (*Genealogie* 14.4.22).

For Boccaccio, Diogenes is to be praised both for his moral superiority and for his generosity to the people – both of which are questions of ethics that manifest themselves politically. His rejection of the wealth provided by political power is the consequence of an ethical code. In the story of Democritus, which follows, Boccaccio writes that "[Poverty] lured Democritus of his own accord to give his paternal lands and untold wealth to the republic of Athens, since he would rather enjoy the freedom to study in poverty than be harassed with the slavish care for money" ("Hac delectatus, Democritus patrios agros et innumerabiles opes rei publice Atheniensium ultro concessit, satius ducens cum paurpertate studiorum libertate letari, quam opum servili cura vexari").[98] The association of poverty and freedom here, while it is not necessarily directed at Petrarch alone, nevertheless challenges the conditions of Petrarch's achievement of leisure by association with power and money. Furthermore, this story seems like an ironic reversal of Petrarch's own history of not accepting the restitution of his ancestral lands from his own city and of choosing a foreign enemy. The "paternal lands" (*patrios agros*) that Democritus gives back to his city for love of liberty echo Petrarch's own ancestral lands (*ruris aviti pascua*), which Boccaccio insinuated that Petrarch had refused out of love of money.

Both of these examples, along with those of Xenocrates and Anaxagoras, are also employed in Petrarch's discussion of the lives of poets and philosophers in Book 2, Chapter 12 of the *De vita solitaria*, which Boccaccio kept bound in a volume alongside the *Invective contra medicum*.[99] Both writers retrieved them from Valerius Maximus, Macrobius, and others, but employed them in different ways. For example, Petrarch had written that he could hardly believe that the famous tub of Diogenes the Cynic was located in a city square, even if Jerome himself asserted as much:

> I would not be so easily persuaded, even if I should have nothing other than conjectures, that the house of any of them, whether that of Chrysippus or the tub of Diogenes, was in the squares of the cities, since the greetings of men offended the first, and the shadow of the high king offended the latter, if Jerome ... didn't say that Diogenes had lived "in the entrances of the gates and in the porticoes of the cities."

---

[98] Boccaccio 1930, 30 Boccaccio 1998, 8.1382 (*Genealogie* 14.4.23).

[99] Petrarch began the *De vita solitaria* and finished the first version of its two books at Vaucluse in 1346. He later edited and added to the manuscript, a copy of which he gave to Filippo di Cabassole in 1366. In 1371, he added a chapter on Romualdo. See Martellotti 1977, x. On Boccaccio's copy of the work, see Mazza 1966, 45–46.

(Michi quidem haud facile persuaeretur, etsi preter coniecturas nichil habeam, aut horum cuiusquam aut Crisippi domum aut dolium Dyogenis in plateis urbium fuisse, cum et illum salutatio hominum, et hunc umbra summi etiam regis offenderet, nisi Ieronimus ... habitasse Dyogenem diceret "in portarum vesibulis et porticibus civitatum.")[100]

Boccaccio inverts the significance of the example of Diogenes as it appears in Petrarch's text, so that not only did Diogenes live in the city but he also refused the gifts of kings.[101] The subtext of these individuals' behavior is the kind of ethics they represent in their political engagement.

In another example, Petrarch projects his own distrust of the crowd onto Democritus, writing, "Ask Democritus: he will confess that he ripped out his own eyes so that he would see the truth and not the people, who are the enemy of the truth" ("Quere a Democrito: fatebitur se sibi oculos eruisse, ut et videret verum et veri hostem populum non videret").[102] These examples from the *De vita solitaria* are less polemical than the *Invective* in their condemnation of the city, but are fully compatible with Petrarch's attack on the physician. Instead of trying to heal the body

---

[100] Petrarch 1999, 336–338 (*De vita solitaria* 2.12.20).

[101] It is important to note that the question of the tyrant of Syracuse had been brought up by Boccaccio in a lost letter to Petrarch, in which he may have criticized Petrarch for his association with tyrants and perhaps lamented the fact that he himself had not achieved the status of poet laureate. In a letter written from Milan in December 1355, Petrarch responded to Boccaccio: "I have read and understood the meaning of your allusions to Syracuse and Dionysus. But what of it?" ("Legi Syracusas tuas et Dionysium intellexi. Sed quid ideo"). Petrarch 1938–42, 3.301; Petrarch 1975–85, 3.68 (*Familiares* 18.15.1). Also at stake for Boccaccio in founding the poet's ethical engagement with society on a principle of poverty is what he saw as a possible proliferation of laurel crownings that nevertheless left him poor and unrewarded. In 1355, much to his, Petrarch's, and their friends' chagrin, the provincial Florentine grammar teacher, Zanobi da Strada, was crowned poet laureate in Pisa by German Emperor Charles IV. Boccaccio mentions it in his letter to Iacopo Pizzinga in 1371. See Boccaccio 1992, 668 (*Epistola* 19.30): "If I so wished, I could add to these men [Dante and Petrarch] my co-citizen Zanobi whose last name comes from his ancestral village 'de Strada,' who put down the rod he used to compel little boys who were trying to reach the first level of grammar out of their cradles. Desirous for glory, he aimed high for honors that I don't know if he deserved. He gave little weight to the ancient ritual and put on his head not the Roman but the Pisan laurel by the hand of the German Caesar, content to please only a single man with a few poems. As if he were sorry for the honor received, he was attracted by love of gold and went to the western Babylon where he fell silent. For this reason, since he brought little wealth and no glory at all to the sacred name [of the laurel], I decided to leave him out" ("His ego tertium concivem meum addere, si velim, possem, Zenobium scilicet ab avito rure cognominatum 'de Strata,' qui posita ferula qua ab incunabilis puellulos primum gramatice gradum temptantes cogere consuerat, avidulus glorie, nescio utrum in satis meritos evolavit honores, et veteri omni parvipenso ritu, boemi Cesaris manu non romanam lauream sed pisanam capiti impressit suo, et unico tantum homini paucis carminibus placuisse contentus, quasi eum decoris assumpti peniteret tractus auri cupidine in Babilonem occiduam abiit et obmutuit; quam ob rem, cum laboris modicum et fere nil glorie sacro nomini attulerit, omittendum censui"). For a full account of Zanobi, see Baglio 2013.

[102] Petrarch 1999, 318 (*De vita solitaria* 2.12.3).

politic, Petrarch had written that he would rather save himself. It seems clear that Boccaccio did not share this opinion of the city or the people. Even if he did, he nevertheless thought that the poet should bring them the truth in the streets anyway, not unlike the physician.[103] Yet Boccaccio does not entirely abandon the Petrarchan ideal of solitude. He absorbs it and adapts it to his own cultural model that demands an ethical, unremunerated engagement in civic life from intellectuals – poets, philosophers, or orators as they may be. Boccaccio does reject, however, the example set by the questionable ethics behind the historical Petrarch's political practices – practices that Petrarch himself knew to be in tension with his own ideals. Boccaccio's reiteration of these examples from Petrarch's works is an effort to manipulate the Petrarchan ideal to his own politico-cultural vision. More than a sign of adherence to his friend's model, it is a sign of how he was subverting it.

Boccaccio's reiteration of these stories used in the *De vita solitaria* seems to be out of place unless they are seen in relation to Petrarch. Perhaps even more out of place in a defense of poetry, one of the other major examples is a minor character from Lucan's *De bello civili*. Neither a philosopher nor a poet, the fisherman Amyclas could face the bellicose Caesar fearlessly because of his poverty: "She [Poverty] enabled Amyclas, a poor sailor, alone on the shore by night, to hear unperturbed the voice of Caesar, of which the proud kings stood in fear, as the great man called and knocked at the door of his hut" ("Huius opere Amiclas, pauper nauta, nocte in litore solus clamantem Cesarem, cuius vocem superbi timebant reges, ad hostium gurgustioli pulsantem audivit intrepidus").[104] However out of place a fisherman is in a defense of poetry, his story may be seen to be relevant if we recognize the Petrarchan subtext of this defense. In his eighth eclogue, *Divortium*, written in late 1347, Petrarch staged his relationship with Cardinal Giovanni Colonna using the pastoral name of Amyclas for himself. In the poem, Amyclas associates his freedom from the powerful Ganymede (Colonna) in terms of his poverty: he is leaving the Cardinal's service in order to find freedom in a pastoral paradise.[105]

[103] Among the figures that Boccaccio uses to represent himself as author of the *Genealogie* is that of Asclepius in service of Hippolytus. See Boccaccio 1930, 13 Boccaccio 1998, 7.62 (*Genealogie* 1. proem 1.41). On the crossover between Boccaccio's poetics and medicine, see Veglia 2006. See also Lummus 2015.

[104] Boccaccio 1930, 30 Boccaccio 1998, 8:1382 (*Genealogie* 14.4.23). The episode is recounted in Lucan 1928, 276–279 (*De bello civili* 5.515–539).

[105] See Petrarch 1974a, 114–127 (*Bucolicum Carmen* 8). On Petrarch's *Divortium*, see Wojciehowski 1995, 68–72. Petrarch also refers to Amyclas in *Familiares* 19.5, where he makes an effort to contextualize his move to Milan. See Ascoli 2011, 142–144. In *Convivio* 4.13.11–13, Dante refers

With the references to examples that he shared with Petrarch, Boccaccio is not only offering a critique of his friend but he is also appropriating the ideal Petrarch, *Silvanus*, who pre-dates the move to Milan.

Boccaccio concludes his digression on poverty by reminding his readers that the endless search for wealth causes constant anxiety: "If we may trust experience, so-called rich men suffer from a constant fever of anxiety. . . . The envy of friends, the stealth or violence of thieves, the intriguing of relatives, civil disorders – one or more of these keeps him in constant and foolish terror" ("Si experientie credimus, assidua ardentique semper premuntur sollicitudine, qui divites nuncupantur. . . . Amicorum invidiam, latronum astutiam, tumultus civicos, socordia vexatus assidua, expavescit").[106] Besides the fact that these anxieties are often a part of Petrarch's representation of his inner turmoil, this assertion also creates a system of value through which Boccaccio, who often lamented his own poverty and lack of recognition, authorizes his own position as poet for the city. In a sense, by devaluing the relationship between power and the poet, Boccaccio creates the conditions for his own recognition.

In the final prefatory section Boccaccio addresses the last of his attackers – the philosophers. Here again Boccaccio seeks to establish poetry's dwelling in relation to the city. He opens with a long, pseudo-allegorical description of the house of philosophy:

> There is also, O most serene of rulers, as you know far better than I, a kind of house established in this world by God's gift, in the image of a celestial council, and devoted only to sacred studies. Within, on a lofty throne, sits Philosophy, messenger from the very bosom of God, mistress of all knowledge. There she sits arrayed in royal robes and adorned with a golden crown, like the Empress of all the World. In her left hand she holds several books, with her right hand she wields a royal sceptre, and in clear and fluent discourse she shows forth to such as will listen the truly praiseworthy ideals of human character, the forces of our Mother Nature, the true good, and the secrets of heaven.
>
> (Est preterea, serenissime regum, ut tu longe melius nosti, divino munere domus in terris, composita ad instar celestis concilii, sacris tantum studiis dicata. In hac sublimi in solio ex Dei missa gremio phylosophia, rerum magistra, presidet augusta facie et divino splendore conspicua, regiis induta vestibus et aurea insignita corona, nec aliter quam mortalium imperatrix,

---

to Lucan's Amyclas in an argument relating material wealth and evil. It is also worth noting that Dante mentions Amyclas' fearlessness before Caesar in the allegory of Saint Francis' marriage to Lady Poverty in *Paradiso* 11.70–72. See Facchini 2020, 14–15.

[106] Boccaccio 1930, 31–32; Boccaccio 1998, 8.1384 (*Genealogie* 14.4.27).

cum premat sinistra libellos, dextra regale baiulat sceptrum, et diserto
sermone audire volentes qui sint laudabiles hominum mores, que nature
parentis vires, quid verum bonum et celestia docet arcana.)[107]

According to Osgood, this house is an allegorization of lady philosophy
and her house that contains the seven liberal arts.[108] The description of
philosophy has undeniable allegorical qualities, such as her robe and
crown, but the fact that it is grounded in this world belies a more concrete,
literal interpretation of the house. The apostrophe in which he addresses
the king can be taken to indicate, too, a historical connection to a
real place.

What is this literal house on the earth and why would the king know
any better about it than Boccaccio? I would like to suggest that in addition
to being an allegorical representation of philosophy it is also a figural
representation of the new university that stood at the center of Florentine
intellectual life during this period. The king, in fact, knew about the
university because he had been in communication with Pope Clement
VI during the years when it had received official status.[109] Boccaccio
complicates the abstraction of the allegory further by inserting human
beings into the picture. He writes:

> there, behind the mistress of the household, are certain men seated in high
> places, few in number, of gentile aspect and utterance, who are so distin-
> guished by their seriousness, honesty, and true humility, that you take them
> for gods not mortals. These men abound in the faith and doctrine of their
> mistress, and give freely to others of the fullness of their knowledge.

> (sunt ibi post dominam celsiori in sede locati homines, non multi tamen,
> mites aspectu atque eloquio et morum etiam gravitate, tanta honestate
> atque vera humilitate spectabiles, ut credas does potius quam mortales.
> Hi iam presidentis dogmatibus pleni, abunde aliis ingerunt que
> noverunt.)[110]

These men who seem to be gods are no doubt allegorical ideals of the
philosopher, such as the poets and philosophers in Dante's Limbo.[111]
They are archetypical or stereotypical in Boccaccio's presentation, but do
not manifest any of the numerological or symbolic qualities that one
would expect from an allegory. For example, they are few, but have no

---

[107] Boccaccio 1930, 32–33 Boccaccio 1998, 8.1386 (*Genealogie* 14.5.1).
[108] See Osgood 1930, 153 n. 1.
[109] On Hugh's connection with Avignon in the late 1340s and 1350s, see Setton 1976, 1.220–224.
[110] Boccaccio 1930, 33 Boccaccio 1998, 8.1386–1388 (*Genealogie* 14.5.3).
[111] Cf. Osgood 1930, 153 n. 1.

specific number that would link them to the liberal arts or cardinal virtues, and so on.

The problem for Boccaccio is that most of the philosophers who inhabit the Florentine house of philosophy belong to another kind of group, which does not entirely correspond to this ideal. This "noisy crowd" ("multitudo perstrepens") is composed of two kinds of philosophers: those who "have resigned all pride, and live in watchful obedience to the injunctions of their superiors" ("omni abiecta superbia, vigiles mandatis insistunt") and those who "grow so elated with what is virtually elementary knowledge, that they fall upon their great mistress' robes as it were with their talons, and in violent haste tear away a few shreds as samples; then don various titles which they often pick up for a price; and, as puffed up as if they knew the whole subject of divinity, they rush forth from the sacred house" ("fere rerum principiis auditis, elato animo in vestes imperatricis uncas iniciunt manus et, acri violentia quibusdam surreptis particulis, variis insigniti titulis, quos non nunquam extra domum venales comperiunt, non aliter quam si mentem omnem divinitatis perceperint, fastu quodam inflati, ex sacra se proripiunt ede").[112] These philosophers too lack the purely symbolic quality of merely allegorical figures, even if they too are generalized to the point that they have no personality beyond the stereotype that Boccaccio has created. They are men of learning who inhabit a place in time that is an imperfect reflection of the ideal, allegorical house of philosophy. The correspondence is imperfect and thus the objections to poetry that these men have do not correspond with its true nature. It is to their objections that the rest of Boccaccio's defense is addressed.

Boccaccio divides the city where he would bring poetry according to spheres of influence. The ignorant are in reality powerless (even if their wealth may give them political power) because they are influenced by those who can sway their opinion with the perception of wisdom. The false wise are similarly lacking in power because they establish the appearance of wisdom by repeating the words of others. Lawyers create influence from their practical control over the law, whereas philosophers can sway public opinion through the forum of instruction in the university. When Boccaccio organizes his counter-attack, he approaches them from without, as an exile with an ungrounded voice. The actual structure of Florence in the fourteenth century did not divide power or class so evenly, but Boccaccio organizes the effective strata of society as he found them mixed in the city

---

[112] Boccaccio 1930, 33–34 Boccaccio 1998, 8.1388 (*Genealogie* 14.5.4).

squares.[113] When he would give his lectures on Dante at the church of Santo Stefano della Badia, he was truly in the midst of things. The pastoral solitude of the poet was ceded to the urban heterocosm of the city square. The recently formed Florentine *Studium*, with its public lecturers, could exert an influence on the opinions of the members of various classes.[114]

Although there had been an unofficial *Studium generale* since 1321, which was recognized by the Florentine government in 1348, Florence's *Studium* was officially formed in 1349 by mandate of Pope Clement VI. The Florentine university offered degrees in canon and civil law, medicine, and the arts and was the first university in Italy that was allowed to offer degrees in theology. During the period in which Boccaccio turned to humanist scholarship the Florentine *Studium* expanded rapidly. Jonathan Davies notes that in the period "between 1357 and 1367 the number of teachers grew from 11 to 21" and surpassed the size of the older *Studium* in Bologna.[115] Katharine Park also notes that "despite its small size and precarious funding, the University of Florence played an important part in the intellectual life of the city."[116] In Park's and Davies' studies it is clear that the university exerted a great influence on the civic authorities of Florence and on intellectual and civic life more generally.[117] Boccaccio was dedicated to bringing poetry to the university. He had invited Petrarch to act as a professor of poetry, as he was entitled to do by his laurel privilege and, late in his life, Boccaccio himself was finally appointed to lecture on the *Commedia* in the city. Like Mussato, Boccaccio is interested in acquiring for poetry and for the poet a social recognition within a local civic context.

With the historical referent of the allegorical house of philosophy, we can sense the social responsibility that Boccaccio fears the professors of philosophy and theology do not embrace. He depicts them as impostors who improperly guide their students. They insinuate themselves among the impressionable, who believe them to be wise. He sees their behavior as nothing less than fraud: "They dress unpretentiously, not because they are really modest but only to mask themselves with sanctity" ("honesto

---

[113] On the make-up of the population of Florence and the relationship between profession and location in the city, see Fanelli 1980, 58.

[114] On the structure of Florentine society within the walls of the city, see Fanelli 1980, 39–68. See Park 1985, 189 on the locations where philosophy and theology were taught in the city. On the location of the university, see Davies 1998, 20–21.

[115] Davies 1998, 2.   [116] Park 1985, 200.

[117] Park also shows that the study of medicine was central to the influence of the university. On the early history of *Studium* and its importance to Florentine civic life, see also Brucker 1969 and 1977 and Denley 1983, 1988, and 1991. See also Coppi 1886.

vestimentorum utuntur habitu, non quia mens honesta sit, sed ut ficta sanctitate decipiant").[118] For Boccaccio, this kind of behavior was detrimental not only to poetry and rhetoric, which was being superseded by logic, but also to society in general. Boccaccio explains the effects they bring to bear on the city: "they proceed boldly to range about town, dabble in business, give advice, arrange marriages, appear at big dinners, dictate wills, act as executors of estates, and otherwise display arrogance unbecoming to a philosopher" ("civitates ambire, secularibus se miscere negociis, consilia prestare, connubia tractare, comestionibus interesse, testantium dictare tabulas, testamentorum executiones assumere, et multa minus phylosophos decentia agere presumptuose incipiunt atque prosequuntur").[119] Using their notoriety among the people of the city, they begin to exert power in matters that should not concern a philosopher. The result is that when they speak of poetry – which they do not understand – they rage against it: "like conspirators against a deadly enemy, in schools, in public squares, in pulpits, with a lazy crowd, as a rule, for an audience, they break out into such mad denunciation of poets that the bystanders are afraid of the speakers themselves, let alone the harmless objects of attack" ("quasi adversos eos [poetas], non aliter quam in letales hostes coniuratum sit, nunc in scolis, nunc in plateis, nunc in pulpitis, auscultante non nunquam vulgo inerti, in eos insano clamore prorumpunt, ut non de innocuis tantum, sed et de se timeant circumstantes").[120] Boccaccio goes on to enumerate the claims of these professors of philosophy, which will become the subject headings at the start of each of the remaining chapters of Book 14. He has established and progressed through the layers of influence within Florence in order to arrive at the most powerful group of intellectuals who seek to prevent the participation of the poet in civic life.

In responding to the philosophers' attacks on poetry, Boccaccio employs essentially the same arguments that Petrarch had mentioned in the first and third of his *Invective contra medicum*: that poetry is a useless art; that poets tell untrue stories; that poets are rustics; that they are too obscure and make absurd references to the gods; that they are seducers; that they are secondary to philosophers; that it is a crime to read poetry; that Plato banished poets from the state; and that Boethius referred to the Muses as

---

[118] Boccaccio 1930, 34 Boccaccio 1998, 8.1388 (*Genealogie* 14.5.5).
[119] Boccaccio 1930, 34 Boccaccio 1998, 8.1390 (*Genealogie* 14.5.7).
[120] Boccaccio 1930, 35 Boccaccio 1998, 8.1390 (*Genealogie* 14.5.9).

harlots.[121] The preface to the defense proper, however, sets up these claims in a larger civic frame that opposes Petrarch's frame in the *Invective*. Petrarch's defense of poetry is made within a battle for influence between two men. The larger community that Boccaccio describes in these first five chapters is explicitly rejected in the *Invective*. Boccaccio is not necessarily working against what has been called Petrarchan humanism, but he sees a different kind of forum in which it might flourish.[122] Boccaccio seeks to reinsert poetry into a different kind of civic space. The embeddedness of poetry within a community is the thread that connects the defense of poetry with the previous 13 books on myth, in which Boccaccio tells the story of myth as cultural memory as it develops over time.[123] In the history of the human imagination traced in the *Genealogie*, poetry is seen to have had a primary role in shaping human relations both among themselves (*ethologia*) and human relations to nature (*physiologia*).[124] The defense of poetry seeks to continue this story in Boccaccio's time by reclaiming the original dwelling of poetry among a "fellowship of men." In the final section of this chapter, I will analyze Boccaccio's claims about poetry in order to demonstrate his project of reestablishing an ethical civic role for both poetry and the poet.

Boccaccio's Poetics of Inclusion: *Genealogie* 14.6–22

In the last fourteen chapters of Book 14, Boccaccio defends poetry primarily against the attacks of the philosophers. Whereas his opponents are in name the same philosophical caste that Petrarch had in mind in his response to the physician, which had reduced the study of philosophy to logical syllogisms, Boccaccio is also revising Petrarch's own ideas about the role of the poet and of poetry in the city. His defense has two potential audiences: Scholastic philosophers and humanists. For Boccaccio, the most pressing of the arguments against poetry, both pagan and Christian, was that it had nothing useful to offer society. He will go on to translate and repeat the terms of his defense of poetry in his literal exposition of *Inferno* 1.73 (*poeta fui*) in an effort to bring poetry to the city square in practice, not only in theory.[125] It is significant that he frames the explanation of the word *poeta* in terms of the poet's *uficio*, or duty. Boccaccio's arguments are

---

[121] On the organization of Boccaccio's defense and its relation to Petrarch's *Invective*, see Hortis 1879, 208; Osgood 1930, 154 n. 6; and Zaccaria 2001, 165–190.
[122] Cf. Gullace 1989, 232–235 and Stone 1998, 147.   [123] See Lummus 2012b.
[124] See Boccaccio 1930, 123; Boccaccio 1998, 8.1548 (*Genealogie* 15.8.4).
[125] See Boccaccio 1965, 33–43 (*Esposizioni*, esp. litt.1.1. 69–112).

centered around the utility of poetry within the society to which he belonged: "Poetry is not only something real, but it is a venerable science; and – as was seen in the preceding pages and will appear in the following – it is not a futile art but full of vigor for those who wish to squeeze out the meanings from the fictions" ("Est non solum aliquid, sed scientia veneranda poesis, et, ut sepius in precedentibus visum est et in sequentibus apparebit, non futilis, sed succiplena facultas est, sensus volentibus ex fictionibus ingenio premere").[126] He argues that poetry is useful both because of its origins and history and because of its manner of meaning. In the defense, Boccaccio seeks to show that poetry is the original language of philosophy and that the discipline of philosophy as practiced in the modern age is separate from it. Petrarch had criticized the physician for subjecting the study of rhetoric to logic. His defense reversed this mindset by asserting that logic was a useless and mechanical science. Petrarch's philosophical views mirror his political stance in that he was uninterested in entertaining any other approach to knowledge. For him unity came through the sacrifice of the plurality, not through inclusion.

Boccaccio's method of defense takes a different, more inclusive approach. He does not seek to replace philosophy with poetry but by allowing for a poetry that is autonomous from philosophy as a discipline he seeks a reconciliation of the two by which both can coinhabit the same civic space. The dwelling of poetry, Boccaccio argues, while it is central to human society, is peripheral in location. It moves between the uninhabited solitude outside the city, where the poet may meditate and contemplate the divine, and the inhabited space of the city, where teaching and communication may take place. Poetry, then, does not replace philosophy in the community but is shown to be the original mode of contemplating the relationship between the human and the divine. Like Petrarch, Boccaccio's philosophical views mirror his political outlook, but for Boccaccio multiplicity is encouraged and allowed.

In order to substantiate his claim that poetry is useful, Boccaccio proposes a definition of poetry that traces its function to its origin. He opens his definition with a reference to Cicero's *Pro Archia*, which Petrarch had used to define and defend poetry since his coronation in 1341.[127] A divine inspiration incites poets to express with marvelous inventions that contain a notion of the truth beneath an allegorical veil. All of the effects of poetry originate in the desire of the poet to communicate in open discourse what

[126] Boccaccio 1930, 39, modified Boccaccio 1998, 8.1396–1398 (*Genealogie* 14.6.9).
[127] See Boccaccio 1930, 39 Boccaccio 1998, 8.1398 (*Genealogie* 14.7.1).

his mind is capable of conceiving. From this desire for communication derives other less sublime effects, such as arming kings, inciting to war, describing nature and the acts of humanity, and praising the deeds of the virtuous.[128] Boccaccio goes on to repeat Petrarch's etymology of the word *poeta* from the Greek word for quality, noting that it means "exquisite speech" (*exquisita locutio*), not "to make" (*poio, pois*), and thereby distinguishing poetry from fiction. With such speech poets may prove themselves useful to others. The usefulness he describes here is not restricted to the service of princes, as it had been in the history of myth that Boccaccio had employed in his biography of Dante. Rather, it spans human experience. Although the origin of poetry is in divine inspiration, its effects take place in the terrestrial realm. As with Petrarch, the poet and his language are the threads that connect the divine and the human. Yet Boccaccio expands the influence of the elite class of poets away from merely being the safe guards to a truth that they must keep from the masses.

In the following section, Boccaccio continues to support his claim for the utility of poetry by tracing the historical origins of poetry in human society, which he had done in the biography of Dante and which he treated in Book 1 of the *Genealogie*. He first wades through the opinions of authorities on the origin of poetry. Some, he says, find that poetry was born first among the Hebrews, with Noah's sacrifice to God after the flood. Others find that it was Abraham or Moses who was the first poet. Still others find that poetry began first among the Babylonians, at the time of Nemrod. He is drawn to believe, however, those who assert that poetry started among the Greeks, which he claims to have heard from Petrarch.[129] In the subsequent description of the birth of poetry among the Greeks, he accentuates the civilizing nature of poetic discourse. In the history of poetry that he tells, there is no hint of the political insinuations about poets and princes from the biography of Dante. Rather, the priesthood that emerged to care for a monotheistic worship of Nature was made "from among the wisest and gentlest of the people, whom they afterward called priests" ("ex prudentioribus atque nobilioribus populi homines, quos dixere postea sacerdotes").[130] Finally, Boccaccio writes, it seemed right to hold the rites with words in a style (*loquendi modus*) that was more elevated than common speech; poetry was invented for the first time. In the history

---

[128] See Boccaccio 1930, 39–40 Boccaccio 1998, 8.1398 (*Genealogie* 4.7.1).
[129] Boccaccio cites as authorities here Leontius Pilatus and Petrarch (*Familiares* 10.4.3–5). For the significance of combining Petrarch's Latinity with a modern Greek authority, see Lummus 2012a.
[130] Boccaccio 1930, 44 Boccaccio 1998, 8.1406 (*Genealogie* 14.8.5).

of humankind, sacrality and poetry converge at the beginning of civilization. The divine inspiration that causes poetry is also the motivating factor
behind the construction of civilization around religious rites. After this
description of the beginnings of poetry among the Greeks, Boccaccio tries
to give a name and date to the first poet. But without any certain
authorities he ends up conceding the invention of poetry to Moses. He
asserts, however, that it developed independently among the Greeks,
whose poets wrote inspired by the power of the mind (*vis mentis*). The
significance of Boccaccio's history of poetry as a civilizing institution lies in
the fact that he traces its origins back to two separate peoples, whose
descendants are the poets of the modern era, especially Dante. Christian
poets have as their ancestors both the pagan poets of Greece and the poet-
prophets of the Old Testament.

In the next two chapters, Boccaccio proceeds to claim a public utility for
poetry by arguing for the nobility of its meaning. Chapter 9 aims to show
that the fable is useful because its meaning helps to teach the reader.
Boccaccio concedes to his critics that poets are "tale-tellers" ("fabulosos
homines").[131] He goes on to define poetry as not only exquisite discourse
but as the composition of stories, or *fabulae*, which is also the word he uses
for myths. He traces the etymology of the term *fabula* back to the verb
"*for, faris*, hence 'conversation,' which means only 'talking together'" ("*for
faris* . . . et ab ea *confabulatio*, que nil aliud quam *collocutio* sonat").[132] The
exquisite speech of poets is based on simple dialogic speech. Key to the
moral function of these tales was allegorical discourse, which prized the
internal philosophical meaning of texts over the fictional outer covering.[133]
Following Macrobius,[134] Boccaccio goes on to describe four kinds of tale
within this system of meaning: the animal tale of Aesop, whose outer layer
is entirely fantastic but whose inner layer contains moral truths; the mythic
tale, whose outer layer mixes the fantastic with the true and whose inner
truth is both human and divine; the verisimilar tale, used by epic poets like
Virgil and comic poets like Plautus and Terrence, which is more similar to
history (*historia*) than to fiction (*fabula*), since the story's meaning is found
in the letter; and finally the kind of old wives' tale that contains no truth at

---

[131] Boccaccio 1930, 47, modified Boccaccio 1998, 8.1410 (*Genealogie* 14.9.1).
[132] Boccaccio 1930, 47 Boccaccio 1998, 8.1412 (*Genealogie* 14.9.3).
[133] For a discussion of Boccaccio's theory of allegory and its relation to vernacular poetry, specifically
Boccaccio's *Decameron*, see Kriesel 2009 and Lummus 2015. For a more in-depth study of the link
between vernacularity and allegory across Boccaccio's works, see Kriesel 2018, esp. 1–24.
[134] Boccaccio's list of genres reflects Macrobius' *Commentarium in somnium Scipionis* 1.2.7–11. For a
discussion of Boccaccio's engagement with Macrobius, see Kriesel 2009, 208–209.

all. With the exception of this last brand of tale, Boccaccio writes, each
kind of fiction can be found not only in the poetry of Greco-Roman
authors but also in the Bible itself, especially in the words of the prophets,
of Solomon, and of Christ. Citing a Horatian principle, he goes on to
claim poetry's social value: "such is the value of fables that the unlearned
may enjoy the fictional covering while the talents of the learned may work
on the hidden truths; and thus in one reading the latter are edified and the
former delighted" ("tanti quidem sunt fabule, ut earum primo contextu
oblectentur indocti, et circa abscondita doctorum exerceantur ingenia, et
sic una et eadem lectione proficiunt et delectant").[135] Similar to his
representation of Dante's poetics, here Boccaccio divides the effects of
poetry according to the capabilities of readers, assigning the delightful to
the unlearned and the useful to the learned.

Of the many examples that Boccaccio gives of poetry's utility, I will cite
only the first, which is especially indicative of his claim:[136]

> Truly, by means of fables ... we read often that minds incited with mad
> rage have been calmed and restored to their pristine mildness; such as when
> the Roman plebs was in dissention with the patricians and was called back
> to the city from the Sacred Mount by means of a fable [recounted] by
> Menenius Agrippa, a man of much gravity.

> (Fabulis quippe ... non nunquam legimus incitatos insano fervore animos
> fuisse sedatos et in mansuetudinem redactos pristinam; ut-puta-dum a
> Memnio Agrippa gravissimo viro, romana plebs a patribus dissidens, e
> Sacro monte in patriam per fabulam revocata est.)[137]

Thanks to poetic fictions, the factions of the city of ancient Rome were
able to reconcile their differences. This reference to Livy's *Ab urbe condita*
brings up the role that fables have in representing and changing the course
of history in the context of the city.[138] According to Livy's account, a

---

[135] Boccaccio 1930, 51, modified Boccaccio 1998, 8.1418 (*Genealogie* 14.9.15). For the source, see
Horace 1926, 478–479 (*Ars poetica* 333–334).

[136] The other examples are: great men are restored to their full energy when tired by the grave
occupations, comfort is given to those stricken by misfortune (for which he cites Apuleius' tale of
Cupid and Psyche), the spirit is called back from inertia (he cites that King Robert was considered
slow until he learned from poetry the wonders of philosophy).

[137] Boccaccio 1930, 50, modified; Boccaccio 1998, 8.1416 (*Genealogie* 14.9.12). It is worth noting
that Petrarch had referenced the episode of Menenius Agrippa in his 1351 letter to the four
Cardinals charged with reforming the Roman government after Cola di Rienzo (*Familiares*
11.16.22)

[138] The reference is the Livy, *Ab urbe condita* 2.32. The story was popular in the Middle Ages for
thinking about the body politic and it is at the basis of Dante's allegory of the body politic in the
figure of Ciacco in *Inferno* 6.

group of common soldiers violated their oath to the Roman consuls because they had not been relieved of their military service. In order to bring the plebs back into dialogue with the patricians, Menenius Agrippa told the soldiers a fable of how the parts of the body once revolted against the stomach because they did not feel like serving a single, idle unity. The body parts soon realized that in serving the stomach they were permitting the body to flourish, and thus they ended their revolt. Not only was the rage of the commoners placated but an agreement was made so that they would have their own political representatives through the Tribune of the plebs. Boccaccio's reference to Livy at this moment shows how he imagines the social role of poetry within a plural governing body. Poetry and fables can engage everyone from the common crowd to the ruling class to the intellectual elite.

The subject of the next chapter asserts that poetic fables can teach because the poets create meaning beneath the veil of their stories (*sensisse sub cortice fabularum*). After giving examples from Virgil's three works of poetry, he follows up by mentioning Dante's *Commedia*, Petrarch's *Bucolicum Carmen*, *De vita solitaria*, and *De remediis utriusque fortune*, and then his own Latin pastoral as examples of poetry with intended meaning. The genealogical connection that Boccaccio makes between Virgil, Dante, and Petrarch is consistent with what he expressed in his biography of Dante and in *Iam certus honos*. His conclusion to this chapter, however, further opens up the formative qualities of poetry for unlearned readers:

> Let the ignorant babblers be silent, and let the arrogant be mute, if they can, since it must be believed that not only great men – who were brought up on the milk of the Muses, frequented the homes of philosophy, and have been hardened by sacred studies – have always placed the most profound meanings in their poems, but also that there is nowhere such a delirious old woman who, around the household fire among the wakeful on winter nights, makes up and recites stories of Hell, or fairies, or witches, and the like (from which these inventions are often made), and does not intend beneath the pretext of the stories, in accordance with the powers of her modest intellect, some meaning, sometimes not at all ridiculous; a meaning through which she would like to cause terror in children, delight girls, or tease the old, or at least show the powers of Fortune.

> (Taceant ergo blateratores inscii, et omutescant superbi, si possunt, cum, ne dum insignes viros, lacte Musarum educatos et in laribus phylosophie versatos atque sacris duratos studiis, profundissimos in suis poematibus sensus apposuisse semper credendum sit, sed etiam nullam esse usquam tam delirantem aniculam, circa foculum domestici laris una cum vigilantibus hibernis noctibus fabellas orci, seu fatarum, vel Lammiarum, et

huismodi, ex quibus sepissime inventa conficiunt, fingentem atque recitantem, que sub pretextu relatorum non sentiat aliquem iuxta vires sui modici intellectus sensum minime quandoque ridendum, per quem velit aut terrorem incutere parvulis, aut oblectare puellas, aut senes ludere, aut saltem Fortune vires ostendere.)[139]

Boccaccio's animus here indicates that the question is of particular importance to him. He addresses not only the chattering ignorant but also the arrogant. These amount to his two audiences: those who deny poetry's value and those humanist poets like Petrarch who claimed that the production of meaning was the office of an elite class of poets alone. It also revises Boccaccio's earlier breakdown of poetry into genres from the previous chapter. Such stories, even if he had described them as entirely untruthful, are useful because of the meaningful intent of their inventor. Boccaccio's expansion of poetry to include popular fabulous discourse not only subverts the ethos of Petrarch's treatment of poetry in the *Invective*, it also directly takes up Petrarch's words to the physician and reverses their intent. In the third invective, Petrarch accused the physician of preferring precisely this type of story (*fabella*) over history (*historia*). As scholars have noticed, with increasing precision, Boccaccio seems to be making space for the kind of stories that make up the *Decameron*.[140] The *brigata* itself will take pleasure from the storytelling experience, while more learned readers will be able to make or find a higher form of understanding. As he claimed for Dante's *Commedia*, Boccaccio is here implying that even the most mundane form of poetic imagination can produce meaning through language.

    This self-authorizing reference to the kind of storytelling on which the *Decameron* is modeled, linking popular speech to philosophical discourse, functions in the text inasmuch as there are different levels of intent involved in the production of the story. The feigned oral storytelling of the *brigata*, which produces the literal–historical level of the fiction, is meant for pleasure. Boccaccio's intent as author is separated by the various diegetic levels from this intent and could include more sublime meanings. In the previous chapter of the defense, Boccaccio cited the story of Cupid and Psyche as an example of how stories can give solace to those who are burdened by Fortune. He refers to the story as he knew it through Apuleius' *Metamorphoses*: "He tells how the highborn maiden Charis, while bewailing her unhappy condition as captive among thieves, is in

[139] Boccaccio 1930, 54 Boccaccio 1998, 8.1422 (*Genealogie* 14.10.7).
[140] See Marcus 1979, 4–5 and Kriesel 2009, 222–223.

some degree restored through hearing from an old woman the charming story of Psyche" ("Quem penes Carithes, generosa virgo, infortunio suo apud predones captiva, captivitatem suam depolorans, ab anicula fabule Psycis lepiditate paululum refocillata est").[141] The same kind of *anicula*, who is also a drunk in Apuleius' novel,[142] is just as capable of recounting a useful and edificatory fable as are men like Menenius Agrippa. Each has an effect that depends on social station and intellectual capacity. But the political and social role of poetry is confirmed across the classes of society through the polysemous nature of poetic fictions. The tale of Cupid and Psyche is also an example of how a philosophically minded storyteller – a poet such as Apuleius or Boccaccio – can turn an old wives' tale into a philosophical allegory.[143] In this chapter, Boccaccio establishes himself, author of the *Decameron* and heir to Dante, as a poet whose engagement with the city is defined by the ability to produce meaning for the learned and pleasure for the unlearned, if not a desire to increase their knowledge.

The next stage of Boccaccio's defense concerns the specific nature of the poet's value to the city, in response to the philosophers' claims that "poets, for lack of urbanity and manners, prefer the open country, the mountains and woods, as habitation" ("poetas rura, montes et silvas incolere, eo quod urbanitate et moribus non valerent").[144] He addresses the relationship of the physical habitation of poets in relation to the city, much in the same way he did in his praise of poverty in the fourth chapter, with a description of the marvels of nature that stimulate the poetic imagination. He says that he could list a group of poets who were friends of kings and nobles, and he goes on to list Euripides and Virgil as ancient examples and Dante and Petrarch as modern ones. He represents city life in negative terms in defense of the natural haunts of poets. In his description of what about the city poets avoid, however, he seems to describe what he saw Petrarch as having accepted when he abandoned the solitary life for Milan:

> Decent men detest and abhor their trick of disfiguring their faces with artificial pallor. They detest and abhor this constant strolling about the cities. They detest and abhor this purchase of cheap popularity among idlers, of notoriety among the ignorant, by foul and hideous hypocrisy.

---

[141] Boccaccio 1930, 50–51 Boccaccio 1998, 8.1416–1418 (*Genealogie* 14.9.13).

[142] Boccaccio takes the term *anicula* directly from Apuleius, who also describes the old woman as *delira et temulenta*, which Boccaccio clearly echoes in his description of an old woman as *delirans*. See Apuleius 1996, 292–293 (*Metamorphoses* 6.25).

[143] For a reading that advances this thesis, see Lummus 2011a. On Boccaccio's philosophical and literary engagement with Apuleius, see Candido 2014.

[144] Boccaccio 1930, 54 Boccaccio 1998, 8.1424 (*Genealogie* 14.11.1).

They abhor not merely to ask but even to desire the badges of office, or to haunt the halls of kings, to flatter any man with a head higher than the rest, to be on the track of pontifical robes, for pure idleness and their bellies' sake to flatter poor women into a deposit of money from which they graft, and get by foul means what they could never get on their merits. They detest and abhor with all their hearts this practice of sending souls of usurers to heaven for a price, and assigning them seats in glory according to their contributions.

(Horrent quippe et detestabile ducunt viri spectabiles ficto pallore deformare faciem, et incessu tardo verrere assiduis circutionibus civitates. Horrent atque recusant turpi atque deformi ypocrisi inertis vulgi mercari gratiam laudesque, et ab ignaris monstrari digito. Horrent fasces nedum exposcere, sed optare, aulas ambire regum, aut procerum quorumcunque assentatores fieri, auro pontificum infulas aucupari, ut ventri et inerti ocio latius indulgere queant, blandiri mulierculis, ut deposita subtrahant, pecunia quesituri quod meritis quesisse non poterant. Horrent preterea et totis detestantur affectibus Caturcenses ob pecuniam in celos evehere, et iuxta muneris quantitatem eis exhibere sedes.)[145]

While Boccaccio seems to follow Petrarch's defense of the solitary life over the city, his defense does more to define what a poet must avoid in order to engage ethically with the city. As he claims in the defense of poverty, it is the poet's connection to nature that allows him a privileged perspective on the life of the city. The poet belongs to a separate system of value. Boccaccio sees the accusation of the attackers of poetry as not concerning the "poets' crime of solitude" ("poetarum crimen solitudinis") but rather in the philosophers' own "mind infected by reprehensible ambition" ("infecta mens ambitione damnabili").[146] Since poets do not participate in the negative aspects of the urban heterocosm, they are criticized only because they are different (*discrepantes*).

In the following two sections, Boccaccio addresses two other issues of direct relevance to poets' social utility: the effect of poetry's obscurity and the related accusation that poets are liars. The first of the attackers' claims – that poetry is obscure – contradicts Boccaccio's definition of poetic fables as demonstrative, which he defends by saying that "it is one of the poet's various functions not to rip open the things protected by his fictions" ("inter alia poete officia sit non eviscerare fictionibus pallatia") and that "they are sometimes obscure ... but always understandable if a healthy intellect approaches them" ("non numquam obscuros esse ... sed

---

[145] Boccaccio 1930, 57 Boccaccio 1998, 8.1428 (*Genealogie* 14.11.9–10).
[146] Boccaccio 1930, 57, modified Boccaccio 1998, 8.1428 (*Genealogie* 14.11.8).

extricabiles semper, si sanus ad eos accesserit intellectus").[147] It is the
poet's duty to preserve the meanings hidden by their poetry. The deep
meanings of poetic texts are accessible to those who truly study and
Boccaccio recommends that his detractors study harder: "But I repeat
my advice to those who would like to understand and unravel the ambiguous knots, that they must read, persist, stay up nights, question, and press
in every way on the powers of their brain" ("Et ut iterur dixerim, volentibus intelligere et nexus ambiguos enodare legendum est, insistendum
vigilandumque atque interrogandum, et omni modo premende cerebri
vires").[148] Here Boccaccio takes back up a thread from his second biography of Dante, noting that the obscurity of poetry does not detract from its
utility but adds to it by becoming a stimulus to learning.

Since poetry's detractors believe poetry to be obscure, they consequently
claim that whatever meanings it does have are lies, since – as Boccaccio
responds – they misunderstand them. After a discussion of the meaning of
the adjective *mendaces*, or "lying," Boccaccio claims that there are two
kinds of liar: knowing and ignorant. The first cannot be excused, whereas
the second can be if no fault is found in the liar's ignorance. Pagan poets,
he says, should be excused because they did not know the Christian God
but came close to knowing Christian truth through the natural capacities
of the human mind (*ingenium humanum*). This, he says, may not be
accepted by his attackers as a valid reason because such reasoning does
not make the poets any less liars. He also makes recourse to the commonplace idea that poets are not historians and thus can bend the truth. The
main source of discord between Boccaccio and his attackers, mentioned at

---

[147] Boccaccio 1930, 60, modified Boccaccio 1998, 8.1432 (*Genealogie* 14.12.8–9). Cf. Boccaccio's
words in defense of his *Decameron*: "No word, however pure, was ever wholesomely construed by a
mind that was corrupt … What other books, what other words, what other letters, are more
sacred, more reputable, more worthy of reverence, than those of the Holy Scriptures? And yet there
have been many who, by perversely construing them, have led themselves and others to perdition.
All things have their own special purpose, but when they are wrongly used a great deal of harm may
result, and the same applies to my stories. If anyone should want to extract evil counsel from these
tales, or fashion an evil design, there is nothing to prevent him, provided he twists and distorts
them sufficiently to find the thing he is seeking. And if anyone should study them for the
usefulness and profit they may bring him, he will not be disappointed." ("Niuna corrotta mente
intese mai sanamente parola … Quali libri, quali parole, quali lettere son più sante, più degne, più
reverende, che quelle della divina Scrittura? E sì sono egli stati assai che, quelle perversamente
intendendo, sé e altrui a perdizione hanno tratto. Ciascuna cosa in se medesima è buona a alcuna
cosa, e male adoperata può essere nociva di molte; e così dico delle mie novelle. Chi vorrà da quelle
malvagio consiglio o malvagia operazion trarre, elle nol vieteranno ad alcuno, se forse in sé l'hanno,
e torte e tirate fieno a averlo: e chi utilità e frutto ne vorrà, elle nol negheranno"). Boccaccio 1976,
961; Boccaccio 1995, 799–800 (*Decameron*, Concl.11–14).
[148] Boccaccio 1930, 62, modified Boccaccio 1998, 8.1436 (*Genealogie* 14.12.17).

the start of the thirteenth chapter, is that Virgil has changed the historical course of events in his description of Dido.[149] He responds to this claim by stating that the utility of Virgil's poem, which is "very similar to the truth" ("simillima veritati"),[150] is increased by the way in which he bends the truth: "But, so that he might bring to completion by artifice and veil that which was opportune to his work, he composed a fable that was similar in many ways to the story of Dido." ("Sed, ut artificio et velamento poetico consequeretur quod erat suo operi oportunum, composuit fabulam in multis similem Didonis hystorie").[151] The argument that follows is a further assertion of the value of fiction (*fabula*) over history (*historia*), terms that will be taken up again in Petrarch's translation of the final tale of the *Decameron*.[152]

In a long example of his literary critical skills Boccaccio gives four reasons why Virgil may have modified Dido's true story: because of the epic convention of beginning *in medias res*, Virgil needed a narrative space in which to recount the events that had happened earlier; because he had an underlying moral purpose concealed behind his words that illustrated the role that human passions play in decision making; because he wished to praise Aeneas as founder of the Julian *gens* and so he exaggerated Dido's lasciviousness; and because he intended to praise the glory of Rome. Boccaccio's list of possible reasons behind Virgil's poetic license is indicative of the way he understood the role of poetry in society. The poet's reasoning begins with the necessities of the poem itself, with its form, and passes through the greater moral ideology of the poem to the paradigms that guide its immediate political purpose, then to the greater civic importance of the epic. Form, ethics, and politics are the determining factors of a poet's utility and they allow the poet to bend the truth in order to fulfill his duties.

Finally, Boccaccio moves on to address directly the relationship between poetry and philosophy in the sphere of civic ethics. In chapters 14 and 15, he warns his detractors that one should not condemn what one does not

---

[149] Petrarch is troubled by the non-historicity of Dido in the *Trionfi*. See the *Triumphus Pudicitiae* 11–12 and 154–159 (Petrarch 1996, 228; 254–256). See Simpson 2005, esp. 490–497. On the tradition of interpreting Dido in the Middle Ages, see Desmond 1994.

[150] Boccaccio 1930, 63, modified Boccaccio 1998, 8.1438 (*Genealogie* 14.13.2).

[151] Boccaccio 1930, 67, modified Boccaccio 1998, 8.1446 (*Genealogie* 14.13.12).

[152] About his translation, Petrarch writes: "Whoever asks me whether it is true, that is, whether I have written a history or just a tale, I shall reply with the words of Crispus, 'Let the responsibility fall on the author,' namely my Giovanni" ("Quisquis ex me queret an hec vera sint, hoc est an historiam scripserim an fabulam, respondebo illud Crispi: 'Fides penes auctorem,' meum scilicet Iohannem, 'sit'"). Petrarch 1992, 2.656 (*Seniles* 17.3.5); Petrarch 2004, 3.2220.

understand, nor should one judge things that one does not know. The main question that guides the remaining sections of the defense is whether or not Plato would have expelled the poets from the city. His detractors say that Plato would have rid the city of poets because poetry presents the adulteries of pagan gods and poets persuade their readers to sin. Boccaccio refers to having witnessed a professor of theology at Florence's new university who read the word "poet" in the Gospel according to John and delivered a frenzied tirade against poets, attracting a large audience. The anecdote, and the chapter in general, serves to remind the reader that the defense of poetry is not entirely abstract. Rather, he is defending poetry within a social context, however detached it might seem. Unlike Petrarch, however, Boccaccio represents himself as defending the work of poets from those who would deny it space in the public forum. He has taken on the persona of the excluded outsider. His main concern is the pedagogical influence of men like this professor on the unlearned inhabitants of the city. He is not interested in eliminating the dialogic nature of the community or of the university but with safeguarding such a space for dialogue. In response, Boccaccio proposes that his opponents look more closely at the poems of the ancient Romans, especially the *Aeneid*, in which they will find a great number of moral virtues, which they can follow, since they have not learned how to act by reading the Bible.[153]

Boccaccio asserts that poets can lead men to moral fortitude in a way that can add to the teachings of moral virtue in Christian theology and philosophy. The role of the poet in the political sphere, like that of the teacher and of the shepherd, is to *seduce* honorable men to virtue. Boccaccio explains that poetry's detractors should have done their philological work before accusing poets of being seducers to evil:

> As for the force of this epithet "allurer," which these men hurl at the poets in hope of disparagement, they might have seen that, though Jews hurled it at Christ our Savior when they called him "allurer," yet not for ever was it destined to vilify Him. For these rascal perverters could not rob the word of its pristine force. It may, at times, have a good connotation. Skillful herdsmen may, for example, lure from an infected herd the cattle as yet untainted; much more do cultivated men by their instruction lure away

---

[153] Among the virtues that Boccaccio lists are: Aeneas' exhortation of his friends (*Aeneid* 1.198–207), his ardor to die for his country (2.657–670), his devotion to his father (2.707), his gentleness toward his enemies (3.590), his strength of character (4.279), his generosity and justice at the games at the court of Acestes (5.104), his wisdom during his descent into Hades (6.236), his reaction to the death of Pallas (11.29). All of these virtues are of an ethical nature, and a vast majority of them are about one's interaction with friends and with society.

nobler souls from those foundering under moral disease. Thus, I think, do the great poets most frequently lure the credulous to their improvement.

(Et, ut aliquid, circa vim vocabuli dictum sit, quod tanquam detestabile poetis obiciunt, vidisse debuerant quoniam, et si Christo, Salvatori nostro, a Iudeis obiectum sit – qui illum ignominiose *seductorem* dixere – non tamen semper in malam partem sumendum fore. Nequivere enim illi abutentes infandi homines vim veterem surripuisse; potest enim quandoque in bonam partem sumi *seducere*: nam rem pastoriam ab infectis armentis non dum infectos egritudine boves seduxisse, solertis pastoris est; et sic non numquam eruditi homines generosos animos ab his, qui morbo viciorum laborant, suis seducunt monitis. Quorsum poetas illustres sepissime seducere credulos reor, et eos facere meliores.)[154]

In this passage Boccaccio draws an analogy between the life of Christ, the duty of the shepherd, and the duty of the pedagogue. Poets fall into this same analogy, alongside the learned men to whom Boccaccio is speaking. He continues, in the next chapter, to separate poetry from philosophy and to defend poetry from usurpation by that discipline, claiming that both disciplines are dependent upon Nature and that poetry is not dependent on philosophy.[155] To those who say that it is a sin to read the poets, Boccaccio claims that it has not been recognized by "laws ... prophets, or the holy rulings of the pontiffs" ("non leges ... neque prophete, non sacre pontificum sanctiones"), therefore poetry is a valid alternative to theology for contemplating the "universal truth" ("catholicam veritatem").[156] Boccaccio is not arguing against theology as a mode of contemplation or expression of truth but for poetry as a legitimate discourse, because "we are not all at all times subject to the same inclination, and occasionally some men incline to poetical writers" ("non omnes, nec semper eadem trahimur affectione, et sic non nunquam ad poeticos trahuntur quidam").[157] He is confused by the ways in which other discourses are tolerated by philosophers, whereas poetry is not. People, he says, watch the "wandering clowns doing their low tricks at the corner" ("ioculatores in quadruviis ut plurimum inhonestos ludos agentes"), listen to the entertainers sing their dirty songs at banquets ("hystriones in conviviis turpia canentes"), and tolerate "the buffoons at restaurants, or panderers in the

---

[154] Boccaccio 1930, 77–78 Boccaccio 1998, 8.1465–1466 (*Genealogie* 14.16.8–9). For a suggestive reading of chapters 15 and 16 in terms of Boccaccio's engagement in Ovid-inspired love poetry, see Eisner 2013, 16–19.

[155] On the relationship between Nature and the imagination for Boccaccio, see Lummus 2012b. See also Stone 1998, 141–156.

[156] Boccaccio 1930, 81–82, modified Boccaccio 1998, 8.1472 (*Genealogie* 14.18.5–6).

[157] Boccaccio 1930, 82 Boccaccio 1998, 8.1472 (*Genealogie* 14.18.7).

brothels – yes even let them blaspheme" ("nebulones in popinis, lenones in lupanaribus blasfemantesque").[158] Painters, he says, are allowed to paint any subject in "the palaces of princes and nobles with subjects chosen from the amours of ancient myth, the crimes of gods and men, and all sorts of fabrications" ("in aulis regum et nobilium virorum, amores veterum, deorum scelera hominumque, et quecunque cuiuscunque commenta").[159] The only answer to why poetry is denounced in such a manner while other acts are permitted in the city is that the philosophers, the "new teachers" ("novissimi preceptores") of the university, are blinded by "gnawing envy and ignorance" ("livor edax et ignorantia").[160] In Boccaccio's eyes, the authority of the poet is rejected because it is a threat to the learned classes of the city. In the examples he cites, there is some echo of the defense of the *Decameron* in the author's conclusion, where he defends his licentious language by referencing the obscene speech of the people and the license permitted to painters.[161]

In the response to his attackers Boccaccio does not seek to replace philosophical discourse with poetic discourse but to insert a proper under-standing of poetic discourse into a civic context composed of multiple voices. In this sense it is an alternative to Petrarch's approach, which sought to eliminate philosophical discourse from the political context, so that a single poet could pursue his office without competition. When Boccaccio responds to the philosophers' invocation of Plato's order that poets should be removed from the city, he takes a different approach. He does not claim, as Petrarch had, that poets have always been in collusion with men of power, even if they reside in the countryside, but only that cities have always laid claim to their poets. Although Homer, he says, lived in poverty in the country, seven cities still vie for the right to claim to be

---

[158] Boccaccio 1930, 82 Boccaccio 1998, 8.1472 (*Genealogie* 14.18.9).

[159] Boccaccio 1930, 83 Boccaccio 1998, 8:1474 (*Genealogie* 14.18.9).

[160] Boccaccio 1930, 83, modified Boccaccio 1998, 8:1474 (*Genealogie* 14.18.10).

[161] Cf. Boccaccio's words in defense of his language in the *Decameron*: "Besides, no less latitude should be granted to my pen than to the brush of the painter, who without incurring censure, of a justified kind at least, depicts Saint Michael striking the serpent with his sword or his lance, and Saint George transfixing the dragon wherever he pleases; but that is not all, for he makes Christ male and Eve female, and fixes to the Cross, sometimes with a single nail, sometimes with two, the feet of Him who resolved to die thereon for the salvation of mankind" ("Sanza che alla mia penna non dee essere meno d'autorità conceduta che sia al pennello del dipintore, il quale senza alcuna riprensione, o almen giusta, lasciamo stare che egli faccia a san Michele ferire il serpente con la spada o con la lancia, e a san Giorgio il dragone dove gli piace; ma egli fa Cristo maschio ed Eva femina, e a Lui medesimo che volle per la salute della umana generazione sopra la croce morire, quando con un chiovo e quando con due i piè gli conficca in quella"). Boccaccio 1976, 960; Boccaccio 1995, 799 (*Decameron*, Concl.6).

his place of birth. And although Virgil abandoned Rome and Augustus Caesar was the prince of the world, the towns of Posillipo and Pozzuoli can still boast that they safeguard his tomb. The Mantuans, who lost the right to his ashes when Augustus had them buried near Naples, still revere the field where he was born as if it were a living man. Boccaccio concludes with Petrarch, but only names the places he inhabited before the move to Milan – the Petrarch of the *De vita solitaria* and of the *Posteritati*.[162]

Plato, Boccaccio says, meant that unvirtuous poets should be expelled, not those who guide their cities in their customs, if living, and otherwise by their words. Boccaccio's point is that cities lay claim to the fame of poets precisely because poets have had a significant influence on the foundation of their civilization. He again mentions Homer, whose long-lasting influence is seen in the quotations from the *Iliad* in the *Codex Iustinianus*, and Solon, "who restored a broken and ruined city to civil and moral health" ("qui urbem dissolutam in civilem vitam moresque revocavit").[163] Poets, he concludes, "are not only citizens of their cities and of their state, but the princes and rulers" ("non tantum civitatum, seu sue reipublice, cives esse, sed principes atque magistros").[164] Solon, whom Boccaccio also invoked in the opening of his biography of Dante, is a perfect example of how poets form social bonds among others through language. The poet does not just contemplate the truth but creates it in a tangible historical reality.

In chapter 20, Boccaccio briefly addresses the question of the Muses, which, thanks to Boethius' *De consolatione philosophiae*, were traditionally divided into the honest and dishonest varieties. Boccaccio concludes by equating the Muses of poetry with the Muses of philosophy, and

---

[162] See Boccaccio 1930, 89 Boccaccio 1998, 8.1484 (*Genealogie* 14.19.5): "Francis Petrarch, a man of heaven-sent genius, and the greatest poet of our time, scorned the western Babylon, and ignored the favor of the Pope, for which nearly every Christian longs and contends his utmost – not to say the favor of bonneted cardinals and other princes – and departed to a secluded valley, in an exceptionally lonely part of France, where the Sorga, the greatest of springs, takes its rise. There, in meditation and composition, he spent nearly the whole flower of his youth, content with one servant" ("Franciscus Petrarca, celestis homo profecto et nostro evo poeta clarissimus, nonne, spreta Babilone occidentali atque pontificis maximi benivolentia, quam omnes fere Christiani summopere cupiunt et procurant, et pilleatorum orbis cardinum aliorumque principum, in Vallem Clausam abiit, insignem Gallie solitudine locum, ubi Sorgia, fontium rex, oritur, et ibidem omnem fere floridam juventutem suam, villici unius contentus obsequio, meditando atque componendo consumpsit").

[163] Boccaccio 1930, 90–91 Boccaccio 1998, 8.1488 (*Genealogie* 14.19.12).

[164] Boccaccio 1930, 92, modified Boccaccio 1998, 8.1490 (*Genealogie* 14.19.18).

expunging the comic Muses as false.[165] In the next chapter, Boccaccio closes his defense by addressing the king. As I pointed out above, King Hugh IV operates in the framework of the defense in an entirely rhetorical fashion. Boccaccio's audience is composed of the learned of his time, both the humanists who were following Petrarch's lead in cultivating the recovery of classical antiquity and the caste of priests and scholars of theology who decried poetry's existence. Instead of addressing them directly, however, Boccaccio uses the persona of the Greek king as an outside authority whom his contemporaries would respect. His opening address to the king, in fact, asks for the authority that only a king can give: "But, after your own perusal, when you offer this work to your friends, and it goes forth, by your permission, into the world, it will, I fear, not be weighed in so just a scale by everybody" ("Ceterum, cum iam visum illud in amicorum manus visendum tradideris, et tua licentia prodibit in medium, reor, non equa sic ab omnibus ponderabitur lance").[166] Only the king's charity (*caritas*) and justice (*iustitia*) can impose themselves upon the work's detractors and contradict their *livor*. The distribution of the work at the hands of the king will cause it to be considered in a balanced fashion. He acts as a sort of rhetorical middleman for the resolution of difference.

Although Boccaccio offers the long defense of poetry in Book 14 because he fears that his detractors will not judge him according to the king's balance, it is under the aegis of the king's authority that he offers a pact of peace at the conclusion of the defense. He calls on the same compassion from his first address to the king: "So I would not tire your Highness, nor seem bent on the utter extermination of my opponents; compassion for their ignorance is better even than their destruction, however deserved" ("Et id circo, ne Celsitudini tue tediosus sim, et ne videar hos extra terre terminos fugare velle, cum ignorantie eorum potius compatiendum sit, quam in meritum exterminum procedendum, his finem prestare mens est").[167] Here Boccaccio's persona differs greatly from that of Petrarch in the *Invective* in that he allows for a space in which the poet's office may exist alongside others. Through his defenses, Boccaccio aims to enfranchise poets as intellectuals within a civic context. He uses the king's presence to ensure this peace: "I will therefore pause at this point, and in conclusion do

---

[165] On Petrarch's similar though more aggressive discussion of Boethius' Muses, see the discussion above in the final section of Chapter 3. On Boccaccio's engagement with Boethius, see Schildgen 2000 and Papio 2012.

[166] Boccaccio 1930, 17 Boccaccio 1998, 8.1358–1359 (*Genealogie* 14.1.4).

[167] Boccaccio 1930, 96–97 Boccaccio 1998, 8.1498 (*Genealogie* 14.21.2).

for them, with your indulgence, what of their own accord they would not do: setting aside all the resentment they have earned, and overlooking their weaknesses, I will address to them a friendly word, if by chance I may convert them to a better course" ("et, quod ipsi non facerent, ego ante huius libelli finem tua cum gratia fecisse volo, posuisse scilicet meritam iram omnem, et eorum ignovisse nequitie et eos amicis alloqui verbis, si forsan in consilium melius possim inpellere").[168] The undertones of an ethics based on Christian humility are clear in these last two statements. Boccaccio can only offer peace and conclude his work if the king offers his grace and protection.

The last chapter of the defense is almost palinodic. Although Boccaccio does not entirely take back what he has argued, he begins by calling his attackers "wise men" ("prudentes viri") and by offering "to observe the laws of friendship" ("servare amicitie leges").[169] He does not offer peace from the perspective of the victor but as if their mutual disagreement had reached a stalemate:

> Nevertheless, we have waged war and have come to the point where – with a little bit of glory of the offended despite the great fatigue – for a little bit the desire to win may be entirely repressed and with just laws we can go in peace. Let us go therefore and seize it voluntarily, and let us give rest to our labors. For the spoils of war have been balanced: you take away with you your doctrine, I – as a spoil – a little bit of consolation, and thus enough space is left for peace.

> (Belligeratum tamen est; et eo ventum ut, cum aliquali offensorum gloria, quanquam sudore plurimo, paululum sit omnino vincendi repressa libido et ut equis legibus iri possit in pacem. Vadamus ergo, eamque capessamus ultro, et quietem laboribus demus; librata enim sunt belli premia; nam vos doctrinam, ego refero aliquantulum consolationis in predam, et sic satis loci paci relictum est.)[170]

With typical understatement, Boccaccio describes how his defense has carved out a space for poetry within the city, a space in which the doctrine of the philosophers can exist alongside the natural vocation of the poets. The peace between the two disciplines takes the form of a pact formed after a battle between two states. He requests "by the sacred breast of philosophy" ("per sacrum phylosophie pectus") that the philosophers not conspire again for the complete extermination of the poets: "do not rush

---

[168] Boccaccio 1930, 97 Boccaccio 1998, 8.1498 (*Genealogie* 14.21.2).
[169] Boccaccio 1930, 97, modified Boccaccio 1998, 8.1500 (*Genealogie* 14.22.1, 3).
[170] Boccaccio 1930, 97, modified Boccaccio 1998, 8.1500 (*Genealogie* 14.22.2).

headlong against the poetic name in general, but instead, if you are sane enough, always use distinction where it is opportune" ("ne in totum poeticum nomen adeo dedatis precipites, quin imo, si satis sani estis, distinctione semper, ubi oportuna sit, utamini").[171] The concept of *distinctio* here has a deep cultural relevance that links rhetoric and Scholastic logic with Roman and medieval law. It was the precept of rhetoric by which the meaning of a word was specified, and ambiguity eliminated, and which was central to disputations in Scholastic logic. But it also referred to the contrast of opposing ideas that would take place in a Roman assembly.[172] In the *Institutiones* of Justinian the term was used to indicate that the law made distinctions among the classes of freed-men, among kinds of property, and among the kinds of theft.[173] Boccaccio is speaking to the logical exactness of the philosophers while at the same time employing a concept that was central to law and the civic sphere. He declares to the philosophers that *distinctio* "leads discordant things back into harmony, and, once the clouds of ignorance have been removed, it clarifies the intellect, and leads the imagination where it wishes by a straight path" ("in concordiam discordantia reducit, et, abstersis ignorantie nebulis, intellectum clarificat, et recta quo vult ducit ingenium").[174] He then asks the philosophers to spare the Hebrew and the many venerable pagan poets, but especially, he says, "Christians must be unharmed and immune from injustice; for many poets were or still are from our own numbers" ("Christiani ab iniuriis immunes servandi sunt; plures enim ex nostris poete fuere et adhuc sunt").[175] This statement makes abundantly clear that Boccaccio was defending not only ancient poets but also himself alongside Petrarch, Dante, and the poets of future generations.

The pact of peace is yet another point of contrast between the defenses of poetry offered by Boccaccio and Petrarch. It shows how Boccaccio's poetics followed closely upon an idea of the poet who is engaged for the city, if not in the city. Although he may have begun from Petrarch's ideas,

---

[171] Boccaccio 1930, 99, modified Boccaccio 1998, 8.1502 (*Genealogie* 14.22.7).

[172] For the use of the term *distinctio* in Roman philosophy and natural science, see Cicero, *De finibus*, 1.10.33 and *De natura deorum* 2.5.15. For the rhetorical term, see Cicero, *De Oratore*, 3.48.186 and 3.54.206. In Quintilian, *Institutio oratoria*, 9.3.82 he uses the term to mean "contrast." For the term's importance in Roman law, see Pliny the Younger, *Epistulae*, 8.14.6, where he speaks of the consequences that the present tyranny had education in respect to education during the Republic. See *Codex Iustinianus* 1.3 on the distinctions among free men.

[173] See *Institutiones* 1.12, 2.9, and 4.1. The *Codex Iustinianus* uses the words *differentia* and *distinctio* interchangeably.

[174] Boccaccio 1930, 99, modified Boccaccio 1998, 8.1502–1504 (*Genealogie* 14.22.7).

[175] Boccaccio 1930, 99, modified Boccaccio 1998, 8.1504 (*Genealogie* 14.22.8).

he reformulates the context of the defense and even subverts those points on which he disagrees, with the result of formulating a distinct poetics that is based on a different view of the poet's role in the city. For Boccaccio, the voice of the poet needed to coexist in harmony with the voices of other learned men within a pluralistic civic context, whereas for Petrarch poetry had to replace the current practice of philosophy by other professionals in a civic context ruled by a single will.

*

Boccaccio's ideas on poetry after 1350 undeniably emerge from his relationship with Petrarch. His initial enthusiasm about Petrarch was bound up with his admiration for Dante's *Commedia* and his belief in the public utility of that text. He saw in Petrarch's potential presence in the city as poet laureate of Rome the possibility of posthumously renewing interest in Dante's poem. Upon Petrarch's refusal of that offer and the actions of the city of Florence, which further alienated the poet from them and confirmed his fears about the multitude, Boccaccio had to develop a response, which we have seen progress from the early *Vita di Dante* through the *Genealogie*. Boccaccio's reaction was directed both toward a Florentine audience and toward Petrarch and his admirers. A part of this response is angry and embittered by his personal disappointment with Petrarch's political choices, while another expands Petrarch's notions to include not only Dante and Boccaccio's own works but also an entire array of learning. If Boccaccio rejected Petrarch's political choices, he nevertheless maintained a dedication to including Petrarch's Latin cultural project in its ideal formulation before the move to Milan. Petrarch remains in his imagination the poet laureate of Rome and his friend *Silvanus*. The major modification that Boccaccio brings to Petrarch's ideas on poetry is the stance he takes toward the city and the position therein that he imagines for the poet, as a contemplative who engages with public life even if he stands outside the city. To this cultural ideology we can attribute his cult of Dante and Petrarch, as well as his dedication to the promotion of the liberal arts and vernacular poetry.

The question that I have not answered is whether or not Boccaccio himself was this poet for the city, who acts in benefit of the body politic. He was never recognized as such by his contemporaries, at least not publicly. And with the exception of Salutati, who was in Florence when he died, Boccaccio was not recognized as such by his humanist heirs. Boccaccio's activities as a cultural mediator have often left him elided from the story that he helped to create. He was the champion of Dante who inaugurated the *lecturae Dantis* in Florence, the advocate of Petrarch and his greatest critic, and the patron of the first modern Latin translations of Homer's *Iliad* and *Odyssey*. If he could not have his dream of being recognized as a poet, then he would assign himself the duty of promoting other poets and poetry itself in the city.

If we look back at the *Decameron* through the lens of not only Boccaccio's defense of poetry but also the other books of the *Genealogie*, then we can understand that book as the creation of a poet who is acting for his city. Writing in reaction to the destruction of the plague, Boccaccio offers storytelling as a healing practice through which a new form of being together with others can be born. The book's stories themselves are accessible to a vernacular-speaking readership and audience, just as they open themselves up to what the narrator terms a "loftier, more subtle and truer meaning" ("più sublime e migliore e piú vero intelletto").[176] The book's stories are set in a historically recognizable reality, which is represented from the point of view of a *locus amoenus* beyond the city. The *Decameron* engages with historical reality with a view to social reform and spiritual restoration. Yet Boccaccio himself, as author of the work, ironically disengages himself from a presence in the book itself. He claims no authority over the text and leaves it to the world. In his self-defense in the Introduction to Day 4, he describes his potential impact by imagining himself achieving a nameless fame:

> For whatever happens, my fate can be no worse than that of the fine-grained dust, which, when a gale blows, either stays on the ground or is carried aloft, in which case it is frequently deposited upon the heads of men, upon the crowns of kings and emperors, and even upon high palaces and lofty towers, whence, if it should fall, it cannot sink lower than the place from which it was raised.

> (per ciò che io non veggio che di me altro possa avvenire, che quello che della minuta polvere avviene, la quale, spirante turbo, o egli di terra non la muove, o se la muove, la porta in alto, e spesse volte sopra le teste degli uomini, sopra le corone dei re e degli imperadori, e talvolta sopra gli alti palagi e sopra le eccelse torri la lascia; delle quali se ella cade, più giù andar non può che il luogo onde levata fu.)[177]

---

[176] Boccaccio 1976, 342; Boccaccio 1995, 283 (*Decameron* 3.Concl.18).
[177] Boccaccio 1976, 352; Boccaccio 1995, 290 (*Decameron* 4.Intro.40).

Besides the political aspirations present in this flight of fantasy about his posterity, there is also the sense that Boccaccio as poet and author has identified himself with his work, which he knows will outlast him.

Similarly, at the end of the *Genealogie*, Boccaccio asks that his patron not award him an honor or laurel for his efforts, offering his work to the world in the name of God. Yet he does let slip his desire for recognition at the beginning of Book 14, when he writes of his completion of the enterprise in terms of a sea-voyage coming to an end:

> Now that all is done, and I have, as it were, reached the home or haven which I sought from the beginning, the desire of rest has been growing from the beginning, urging me to leap ashore from the bow, offer due thanks to God for his gift of a safe return, fix the laurel on my triumphant little boat, and at last depart to my long-sought leisure.

> (Quibus sic peractis, quasi in quesitam a principio stationem seu sinum venerimus, suadebat quietis desiderium ut in litus ex navigio prosilirem, et, sacro gratiarum Deo exhibitori rite peracto, laborum victrici cymbe lauros apponere, et inde in exoptatum ocium ire).[178]

If Boccaccio was never publicly honored as a poet, much to his disappointment, he would claim the laurel prize for his greatest achievement. Like Dante, he inscribed his identity as a civic poet within his book. And it will be the *Genealogie* for which Boccaccio is most recognized in the next generation of civic humanists. In it they saw not only the beginnings of the kind of classical learning in which they were themselves engaged but also a way of thinking about poetry as integral to the public sphere.

---

[178] Boccaccio 1930, 15; Boccaccio 1998, 8.1356 (*Genealogie* 14.proem.4).

Epilogue
Coluccio Salutati and the Future of the City of Poetry

What is the result of such an intense series of debates about the office of poetry and the civic function of poets? The easy answer would be to point to civic humanism and the cult of the past that is at the foundation of Renaissance culture – and this is the answer that the tradition of intellectual history has already provided. Individually, each poet's work has a different fate. Mussato's career will be submerged into the pages of history. His use of tragedy as a form of political engagement would be revived in Milan in 1390 by Antonio Loschi, whose *Achilleis* was later attributed to Mussato.[1] He would not be seen as a part of the story of fourteenth-century humanism until the historiographers of early modernity collect his works, which are recovered again by Giosuè Carducci, Roberto Weiss, Guido Billanovich, Eugenio Garin, and others in the nineteenth and twentieth centuries. Dante and Petrarch, and to a lesser extent Boccaccio, would be incorporated into the construction of a Florentine civic identity in the next two generations, with new biographies and political justifications.[2] This, to a great extent, was Boccaccio's desire, although his cultural ideas were far less practical than those of the civic humanists. Boccaccio expressed his hope even in his last extant letter that he would be able to collect Petrarch's *Africa* and *Trionfi* alongside Dante's *Commedia*, with the possible addition of Petrarch's translation of the last tale of the *Decameron*.[3] Petrarch would indeed be refashioned as the antecedent of the humanists of fifteenth-century Florence, but not without a general

---

[1] Loschi's *Achilleis* was printed as a work by Mussato in Osius, Pignorius, and Villanus 1636 and Graevius and Burmannus 1722. See Chevalier 2013, 32–37. The attribution of Loschi's tragedy to Mussato was only disproven in 1832 by Giuseppe Todeschini. Muratori would publish the *Ecerinis* alongside Mussato's histories in 1727, in *Rerum Italicarum Scriptores* 10.2, but would omit the *Achilleis*.

[2] On the biographies of Dante, Petrarch, and Boccaccio, see Bartuschat 2007. On the reception of Dante in fifteenth-century humanist and vernacular culture from Salutati to Alberti, see Gilson 2005, 97–131.

[3] See Boccaccio 1992, 724–737 (*Epistola* 24). On this letter and its context, see Lummus 2017.

resizing of his Latinity, which fifteenth-century humanists saw themselves as having surpassed.[4] The lines of influence that link these poets' efforts to defend poetry to the cultures of fifteenth-century Italy are not direct, nor is it self-evident that the multiple defenses and definitions of poetry of the fifteenth century are in any way the descendants of those of the fourteenth century.

What can be said is that by trying to etch out an institutional place for themselves in their respective cities, these poets also created a status for the study of poetry within a civic space that was devoted to bureaucratic affairs. If they made new epistemological claims for human art, they did so in order to assert the authority of poets and of poetic forms of speech within political structures that had no ready place for them. Since the typical narratives place Coluccio Salutati's defenses of poetry in relation to those of Petrarch and Boccaccio, I would like to turn briefly to one of Salutati's early defenses of poetry in the light of the story just told. Salutati was no poet and, unlike his predecessors, had no personal interest in linking his authority as a civil servant to his engagement with poetry.[5] If this is the case, then how might Salutati's activities in defending ancient poetry be related to his duties as Chancellor of Florence? In order to consider this question, I will focus on one of his early defenses of the value of reading Virgil, written about three years after Boccaccio's death. One of the principal differences between his defense and those of his predecessors derives from his position as a civil servant: he makes no pretense to defend himself as poet through a defense of ancient or modern poetry. Rather he is justifying a practice of reading that has little to do with guaranteeing his role as a professional letter writer. Despite the radical difference in context, he shares with his predecessors the view of poets as interpreters of history. In this light, Salutati's defense may be located in a space between the professional and the private worlds of the man of letters, in which he probes his abilities to interpret history.

Salutati's first defenses of poetry are part of a correspondence, written between 1378 and 1379, with Bolognese Chancellor Giuliano Zonarini, who had asked Salutati how he felt about "the cares of the present time"

---

[4] On the perception of Petrarch's Latinity by later humanists, see Hankins 2012.

[5] On Salutati's defenses of poetry, see Witt 1977, esp. 546–549 on the correspondence with Zonarini discussed below. See also Ullman 1963, 53–70; Lindhardt 1979, 93–151; and Greenfield 1981, 129–145. Although Salutati did not identify as a poet, he did write some Latin verse. See Laureys 2010 on his Latin poetry. For a biography of Salutati, including his defenses of poetry and on the exchange with Zonarini, see Witt 1983, esp. 190–195. On the *De laboribus Herculis*, see Witt 1983, 209–226. See also Witt 2000, 292–337.

("seculi presentis curas") and how he aspired "to the bliss of eternal rest" ("ad beatitudinem eterne quietis").[6] On September 20, 1378, Salutati responds that he, like everyone, is shaken by the good and bad of the world, that he errs, and that he is as weak and ignorant as other men, but that he does not give in to the temptations of fortune. Instead, he places his only hope in God. Salutati portrays himself as vulnerable to the vicissitudes of history, and ignorant of an answer to its course. Yet, he writes in conclusion: "But I do not expect the destruction of the world, which you think is approaching, since you see signs in the sun and moon etc., as you write" ("Orbis vero collisionem, quam, videns signa in sole et luna et cetera, prout scribis, instare putas, non expecto").[7] Were the end to come, however, Salutati says that he would try to bear it, or even more that he would rejoice, as he ends by citing Seneca's *Troades*: "Happy is he who dying sees all things consumed with him" ("Felix est quisquis moriens / Omnia secum consumpta videt").[8] Salutati sent this letter to his friend along with a request that Zonarini obtain for him a codex of Virgil's works. Perhaps expecting to provoke a debate, Salutati begins a brief dispute on poetry when Zonarini subsequently criticizes his request in his next letter, which attacks the value of the ancient Roman poet.

It is important to take note of Zonarini's existential mentality, to which Salutati is responding in this letter and in those that follow. Writing in the fall of 1378, both Chancellors had just seen their cities emerge from an intense struggle with the pope – the so-called War of the *Otto Santi*. During this period, Salutati wrote numerous public missives in which he denied the legitimacy of the papacy and proclaimed Florence as the champion of liberty and of the will of the people. Florence's conflict with the Church, which – for a time – saw the adhesion of Bologna to the Florentine cause, led Pope Gregory XI to impose an interdict in March 1376 that prohibited all religious services in Florence and its territory. As John Najemy has noted, the interdict "confronted Florentines of all social ranks with dilemmas of conscience and loyalty that were not easily resolved," resulting in a "heightened level of religious enthusiasm and emotion."[9] As a response to the sentiment of historical isolation, this enthusiasm manifested itself both as a rejection of the authority of the institutions of the Church and as an assertion of the individual agency to

---

[6] Salutati 1891–1905, 1.294 (*Epistola* 14). Salutati's letters to Zonarini have been partially translated into English in Emerton 1925.
[7] Salutati 1891–1905, 1.297.
[8] Salutati 1891–1905, 1.298. See Seneca 2002, 186–187 (*Troades* 162–163).
[9] Najemy 2008, 152–153.

seek out salvation. From a less existential point of view, it also led to the revolt of the Ciompi, which had begun in the June before Salutati's first letter. Zonarini's question to Salutati, his melancholic attitude toward human affairs, and his expectation of the end of times are linked to extra-institutional religious sentiment provoked by political upheaval. Salutati's exchange about Virgil is entwined within a larger cultural pre-occupation with how to interpret the world of human affairs and the movement of history toward eternity.

In his response to Salutati, Zonarini seems to have maintained a melancholic tone, as before, but also to have mentioned that he found Salutati's response to be "a prudent compendium of theology" ("sapidum theologie compendium").[10] To this compliment, on October 25, 1378, Salutati writes that "whatever I said well, it is from God and his wisdom" ("Quicquid igitur bene dixi, a Deo et eius sapientia est"), denying that he himself was the agent of good advice.[11] Yet Zonarini could not resist criticizing Salutati for his request of Virgil, whom he called a "lying poet" ("vatem mentificum").[12] In the remainder of the letter, Salutati explains why he is a reader of Virgil and why Zonarini should not reprove him for it. Some of his reasons are: (1) Zonarini reads without problem Priscian, Donatus, Job, Seneca, and Cicero, as did the fathers of the Church, such as Augustine and Jerome; (2) one's understanding of the Church fathers is aided by knowing pagan writers, even poets; (3) Salutati admires Virgil's eloquence and profound philosophical thought; (4) in the present age there no longer exists the threat of pagan religion; and so on. These are all familiar ideas.

I would like to focus on how Salutati relates Virgil's poem to revelation and how he represents himself as a reader of poetry. First, Salutati writes:

> I could report for you offhandedly many things from the songs of our Virgil, which are not from the fabrications of fables or from the empty teaching of the pagans, but which you could easily judge to have been drawn from the heights of true theology, whether it be in the nature of truth to emerge among inundations of falsities or whether omnipotent God decided to reveal himself to mortals by witness of all sects and creeds.

> (multa tibi de Maronis nostri carminibus possem discurrendo referre, que non de fabularum commentis aut de gentilium discipline vanitate, sed sumpta de apicibus vere theologie posses facile iudicare, sive proprium sit veritatis inter falsitatum inundationes emergere sive Deus omnipotens se

---

[10] Salutati 1891–1905, 1.300 (*Epistola* 14).   [11] Salutati 1891–1905, 1.300.
[12] Salutati 1891–1905, 1.300.

voluerit mortalibus omnium sectarum et professionum testimonio revelare.)[13]

Salutati here seems to separate Virgil's poetry from fables, or at least to divide its valuable content from the fabulous. In so doing, he implies that they are histories, or partly exemplary of historical truth. The way in which Salutati speaks of the truth in relation to Virgil's poem also indicates that the agent involved is not Virgil but Salutati himself. The verb *referre* indicates the recall from memory through speech or writing, but it literally means "to bring back." It is Salutati, then, who brings back these elements that are taken from "true theology." The interpreter must find and select the truth to bring back. Virgil's poems are useful to Salutati because the truth emerges from a context of falsity, either by nature or by direct will of God. If Salutati is insinuating that Virgil's poems are histories, as Petrarch and Boccaccio had, his interest in them, as will become apparent, is in their unique mimetic quality. The truth is latent and must be sought out, whether in poetry or in life.

Second, Salutati goes on to write that one needs to approach the songs of the ancients with high intentions in order for them to become useful: "but these inventions of the pagans, even the songs of the poets, at which you shudder, if one reads them with a lofty mind, they edify and profit us not a little toward those things which pertain to faith and the readings which you commend in your letters" ("sed hec inventa gentilium ac etiam, quos adeo horres, carmina poetarum, si quis ea alta mente libraverit, non parvum edificant atque prosunt ad ea que fidei sunt et que legenda tuis litteris persuades").[14] The focus here is not on what the texts themselves contain but on what the reader brings to them. The fundamental detachment of ancient poetry from a Christian outlook is overcome by the reader, not – as before – by the poet's ability to re-embody anew the ancient poet's role.

For Salutati, ancient poetry possesses a truth that escapes the intention of the poet. It is the task of the reader or interpreter to elicit this truth from the text. He elaborates on this last point, writing:

> I, a Christian, read Virgil, not as if I will remain in the same place or for a long time, but as I read Virgil I search in a diligent investigation to see if I am able to find something that tends toward honor and best practices. As I leaf through the poetical adumbrations, often on my own, but often with the help of allegory, and not without joy, if I see there is something not

---

[13] Salutati 1891–1905, 1.302.   [14] Salutati 1891–1905, 1.302.

consonant with the truth or stated obscurely, I try to make those statements clear by use of reason. But, when something harmonious with the faith is provided for me to find, even if it is bound up with fictions, I marvel and rejoice, and – since it was allowed for the poet himself to be taught meanings by an enemy – I willingly embrace it and happily make note of it.

(Sic igitur ego christianus Virgilium lego, quod non sim ibidem semper aut aliquandiu permansurus, sed indagine diligenti perscrutor si quid ad honestatem et mores optimos, Maronica legens, valeam reperire, et poeticas adumbrationes mecum sepe per allegorie beneficium non sine iocunditate percurrens, si quid non consonum veritati aut obscure positum video, conor ratione posita declarare. Quando autem aliquid fidei conveniens datur, licet fabulis implicitum, reperire, admiror et gaudeo, idque, cum eiusdem vatis sententia fas sit et ab hoste doceri, libens et letus amplector et noto.)[15]

The enterprise of poetry, for Salutati, is a process of reading and interpretation – of finding meaning, not of producing or communicating it. It is an investigation into the truth, which in poetry, as in life, is often obscure. If Salutati claims that there is truth in the poetry of Virgil, it is not so much to raise the status of that poet in the eyes of Zonarini, as it is to show the Bolognese Chancellor that it is the act of interpretation itself that reveals truth. The authority of ancient poetry is yoked, in large part, to that of the reader, whose access to the truth is not always unobstructed, and whose good judgment – as Salutati mentions in the previous letter – depends upon the grace of God. In conclusion, Salutati writes:

Because if you can, with the powers of your mind and with no notion of the poets, both know Latin and fully understand the many books of the holy fathers, which are filled with the sayings of poets, do not forbid me and everyone else, who enjoy these studies and who have not attained the same height of your mental capacities, to read Virgil. If you enjoy your books, as in the brightest light, allow me, whose eyes do not admit so much light, in the midst of my darkness to look at the stars of the poets, by which the darkness of this night is embellished, and to seek out something among the fables for the edification of the truth and of the faith, for the bitter husk of the tales encloses a sweet and pleasing taste.

(Quod si tu ingenii tui viribus potes sine poetarum noticia aut scire grammaticam aut plurimos sanctorum patrum libros, dictis poetarum refertos, plene cognoscere, non interdicas michi et reliquis, quos vel studia ista delectant vel qui ad illam ingenii tui altitudinem non venerunt, Maronicam lectionem: et si tuis libris, quasi luce clarissima, delectaris, sinas me, qui tantum lumen oculis non admitto, inter tenebras poetarum stellas,

[15] Salutati 1891–1905, 1.304.

quibus illius noctis obscuritas exornatur, aspicere et ad edificationem veritatis et fidei aliquid inter fabulas vestigare, quarum cortex amarus saporem
dulcissime suavitatis includit.)[16]

In juxtaposition to his own stance toward the obscurity of the truth in
ancient poetry, Salutati ironically portrays Zonarini's intellectual security
in the accessibility and transparency of sacred texts. Underlying Salutati's
representation of the difficulty of reading is the obscurity of truth in
general. Salutati resides in a darkness that is only partially illumined by
the lights of the poets. The poets, in fact, only become lights in his
darkness once he has interpreted their works, a process which he describes
in the previous passage in terms of illumining with reason.

In Salutati's next letter to Zonarini, written on May 5, 1379, it becomes
even clearer that the kind of reading he has in mind, and the nature of the
truth that this reading unveils, concerns not only texts but history as well.
This should be unsurprising, since the original subject of the correspondence was an ethical-historical discussion about the cares of this life and of
the preparation for the next. The discussion of poetry's value is embedded
in the subtext of the imminent destruction of the world. At stake is the
question of how individual ethical concerns open up onto ultimate questions about history itself. Salutati begins this second letter in reference to
Zonarini's controversy with a mutual friend, Domenico Silvestri, who had
also written to Zonarini in defense of Virgil. He contrasts their bitter feud,
which was not based on learning, with their own initial friendly contest.
He notes that he would have responded earlier had Zonarini's letter not
"gone astray among my infinite public and private writings" ("inter infinitas meas scripturas privatas et publicas latuisset"),[17] perhaps alluding to
the fact that this matter lies somewhere in between the two spheres. His
concern, in fact, is to defend the philosophy of history that underlies
Virgil's poetry, namely the "revolution of times and events" ("rerum et
temporum circulatio").[18]

The question of the circularity of time in Virgil's poetry concerns the
lines in his fourth eclogue, which Salutati partially cites: "The great line of
the centuries begins anew. Now the Virgin returns, the reign of Saturn
returns; now a new generation descends from heaven on high" ("Magnus
ab integro seculorum nascitur ordo. / Iam redit et virgo, redeunt Saturnia
regna / Iam nova progenies caelo demittitur alto").[19] In the pages that
follow, Salutati draws an analogy between this philosophy of history and

---

[16] Salutati 1891–1905, 1.306.   [17] Salutati 1891–1905, 1.324 (*Epistola* 18).
[18] Salutati 1891–1905, 1.325.   [19] Virgil 1916–18, 48–49 (*Bucolica* 4.6–8).

that of the Old Testament, citing Ecclesiastes 1:9–10 that the past and the future are the same and that "there is nothing new under the sun" ("nichil sub sole novum").[20] Both the Bible and ancient poetry require an able interpreter: "these require therefore a pure reader and a pious interpreter, lest, while we tenaciously cling to the letter that kills, we let go of the life-giving meaning out of ignorance" ("volunt igitur hec purum lectorem et expositorem pium, ne, dum tenaciter inhereamus occidenti littere, vivifi-cantem sensum per ignorantiam dimittamus").[21] He goes on to show how historical circularity is present not only in nature but also in human affairs. By doing so, not only is Virgil's conception of circular history defended by parallels in the Bible, in Nature, and in history, but this analogy between the Old Testament and pagan poetry also allows Salutati to read the relationship between ancient poetry and historical events as typological. Just as the Old Testament prefigures the New Testament and the subse-quent history of mankind, both as a set of institutions and as individual beings, so ancient poetry can illuminate the darkness of history so that the truth becomes more visible to careful interpreters. The real subject of this defense is not so much the ancient poet as it is Salutati himself, as an interpreter of both poetry and history.

Ostensibly a private correspondence about the value of Virgil, these letters to Zonarini show how Salutati links the processes of reading and interpreting to his function as an actor in and interpreter of human affairs as Florence's Chancellor. In the poetry of Virgil, Salutati did not seek refuge from the vicissitudes of history, rather he saw a parallel to his own historical world, which was just as difficult to interpret. In a world of darkness, in which the right path was clothed in ambiguities, Salutati looked to poets like Virgil, whom he viewed as having found a certain kind of truth within a similar darkness. Their poetry honed the modern investigator's abilities to ferret out the truth. A few years later, Salutati would begin a never-completed project in which he would more system-atically seek out a truth in the darkness, analyzing Seneca's tragedies *Hercules furens* and *Hercules oetaeus* and trying to make sense of how the brutal familicide in the one could lead to the apotheosis in the other. Perhaps he thought that if he could hone his interpretative powers on the texts of a philosopher-poet like Seneca, then he could make better sense of the historical world, and understand how the violence of this life could lead to the peace of the next.

---

[20] Salutati 1891–1905, 1.326 (*Epistola* 18). [21] Salutati 1891–1905, 1.326 (*Epistola* 18).

Certain analogies can be drawn between the terms of this defense of poetry and those of the previous two generations. For one, besides a general reliance on similar sources, they all draw analogies between biblical meaning and poetic meaning, so that poetry and theology are parallel. There is also an insistence on poetry as a form of history. Yet Salutati's defenses of poetry and his engagement with poetic texts are categorically different in their scope and function. He is a reader and defends poetry in terms of his role as an interpreter of history. Mussato, Dante, Petrarch, and Boccaccio were poets who saw their function as analogous to that of ancient poets. While reading and right interpretation were a part of their enterprises, their focus was on the production of meaning and their own ability as poets to grasp the truth and to fuse it with exquisite discourse. The authority that Salutati ascribes to Virgil as a poet of history, who was nonetheless unenlightened by Christian revelation, formed the basis of these fourteenth-century poets' claim to a privileged role in society. This role was not inherited by the civic humanists of the next generation, but instead was transferred to their poetic works and to those of their ancient models. This process of living on through their works was a part of the way that Mussato, Dante, Petrarch, and Boccaccio conceived of their own civic roles in relation to posterity, but the future first had to find a place in the present.

Bibliography

PRIMARY SOURCES

Alighieri, Dante. 1996. *De vulgari eloquentia*. Ed. and trans. Steven Botterill. Cambridge: Cambridge University Press.

2003. *The Divine Comedy of Dante Alighieri*. vol. 2. *Purgatorio*. Ed. and trans. Robert M. Durling. Oxford: Oxford University Press.

2007. *Four Political Letters*. Trans. Claire E. Honess. London: Modern Humanities Research Association.

2011. *The Divine Comedy of Dante Alighieri*. vol. 3. *Paradiso*. Ed. and trans. Robert M. Durling. Oxford: Oxford University Press.

2016. *Epistole. Egloge. Questio de aqua et terra*. Nuova edizione commentata delle Opere di Dante. vol. 5. Ed. Marco Baglio, Luca Azzetta, Marco Petoletti, and Michele Rinaldi. Rome: Salerno Editrice.

2018. *Dante, Convivio: A Dual-Language Critical Edition*. Ed. and trans. Andrew Frisardi. Cambridge: Cambridge University Press.

Apuleius. 1996. *Metamorphoses (The Golden Ass), Volume I: Books 1–6*. Ed. and trans. J. Arthur Hanson. Loeb Classical Library 44. Cambridge, MA: Harvard University Press.

Aquinas, Thomas. 1929. *Scriptum super libros Sententiarum Magistri Petri Lombardi*, vols. 1–2. Ed. Pierre Mandonnet. Paris: Lethielleux.

1933–47. *Scriptum super libros sententiarum magistri Petri Lombardi*, vols. 3–4. Ed. Maria F. Moos. Paris: Lethielleux.

1941–45. *Summa theologiae*. 5 vols. Ed. Institutum Studiorum Medievalium Ottaviense (Commissio Piana). Ottawa: Harpeli.

1950. *In duodecim libros Metaphysicorum Aristotelis expositio*. Ed. Raimondo Spiazzi. Turin: Marietti.

Aristotle. 1933. *Metaphysics, Volume I: Books 1–9*. Trans. Hugh Tredennick. Loeb Classical Library 271. Cambridge, MA: Harvard University Press.

Augustine. 1965. *City of God, Volume V: Books 16–18.35*. Trans. Eva M. Sanford and William M. Green. Loeb Classical Library 415. Cambridge, MA: Harvard University Press.

Boccaccio, Giovanni. 1930. "Preface and the Fourteenth and Fifteenth Books of Boccaccio's 'Genealogia Deorum Gentilium.'" Trans. Charles G. Osgood.

In Charles G. Osgood. *Boccaccio on Poetry*. Princeton, NJ: Princeton University Press.

1964–98. *Tutte le opere di Giovanni Boccaccio*. 10 vols. Gen. ed. Vittore Branca. Milan: Mondadori.

1965. *Esposizioni sopra la Comedia di Dante*. Ed. Giorgio Padoan. In *Tutte le opere di Giovanni Boccaccio*. vol 6. Milan: Mondadori.

1974. *Trattatello in laude di Dante*. Ed. Pier Giorgio Ricci. In *Tutte le opere di Giovanni Boccaccio*. vol. 3. Milan: Mondadori.

1976. *Decameron*. Ed. Vittore Branca. In *Tutte le opere di Giovanni Boccaccio*. vol. 4. Milan: Mondadori.

1992. *Epistole*. Ed. Ginetta Auzzas. In *Tutte le opere di Giovanni Boccaccio*. vol. 5.1. Milan: Mondadori.

1995. *The Decameron*. Trans. G. H. McWilliam. 2nd ed. Harmondsworth: Penguin.

1998. *Genealogie deorum gentilium*. Ed. Vittorio Zaccaria. In *Tutte le opere di Giovanni Boccaccio*. vols. 7–8. Milan: Mondadori.

Boethius. 1973. *Theological Tractates. The Consolation of Philosophy*. Trans. H. F. Stewart, E. K. Rand, and S. J. Tester. Loeb Classical Library 74. Cambridge, MA: Harvard University Press.

Cicero. 1914. *On Ends*. Trans. H. Rackham. Loeb Classical Library 40. Cambridge, MA: Harvard University Press.

1923. *Orations. Pro Archia. Post Reditum in Senatu. Post Reditum ad Quirites. De Domo Sua. De Haruspicum Responsis. Pro Plancio*. Trans. N. H. Watts. Loeb Classical Library 158. Cambridge, MA: Harvard University Press.

1933. *On the Nature of the Gods. Academics*. Trans. H. Rackham. Loeb Classical Library 268. Cambridge, MA: Harvard University Press.

1942. *On the Orator: Book 3. On Fate. Stoic Paradoxes. Divisions of Oratory*. Trans. H. Rackham. Loeb Classical Library 349. Cambridge, MA: Harvard University Press.

Del Virgilio, Giovanni. 1933 (for 1931). *Allegorie librorum Ovidii Metamorphoseos*. Ed. Fausto Ghisalberti, "Giovanni del Virgilio espositore delle 'Metamorfosi.'" *Giornale dantesco* 34 (n.s. 4): 3–110 (43–107).

2011. "Ecloga Magistri Iohannis de Virgilio de Cesena missa domino Musatto de Padua poete ad petitionem Rainaldi de Cinciis." In Simona Lorenzini, *La corrispondenza bucolica tra Giovanni Boccaccio e Checco di Meletto Rossi. L'egloga di Giovanni del Virgilio ad Albertino Mussato*. Florence: Olschki. 197–210.

Ferreti, Ferreto. 1908–20. *Historia rerum in Italia gestarum*. In *Le opere di Ferreto de' Ferreti vicentino*. Ed. Carlo Cipolla. 3 vols. Rome: Istituto Storico Italiano.

Horace. 1926. *Satires. Epistles. The Art of Poetry*. Trans. H. Rushton Fairclough. Loeb Classical Library 194. Cambridge, MA: Harvard University Press.

2004. *Odes and Epodes*. Ed. and trans. Niall Rudd. Loeb Classical Library 33. Cambridge, MA: Harvard University Press.

Isidore of Seville. 2004. *Etimologie o origini.* Ed. Angelo Valastro Canale. 2 vols. Turin: UTET.

Justinian. 1895a. *Institutiones.* vol. 1. Ed. Paul Kreuger. *Corpus iuris civilis.* Berlin: Weidmann.

1895b. *Codex Iustinianus.* vol. 2. Ed. Paul Kreuger. *Corpus iuris civilis.* Berlin: Weidmann.

Lactantius. 2005. *Divinarum Institutionum libri septem.* vol. 1. *Books I and II.* Ed. Eberhard Heck and Antonie Wlosok. Munich: K. G. Saur Verlag.

Lucan. 1928. *The Civil War (Pharsalia).* Ed. and trans. J. D. Duff. Loeb Classical Library 220. Cambridge, MA: Harvard University Press.

Mussato, Albertino. 1722. [*Opera*] *Albertini Mussati, Historiographi Paduani, Historiae Augustae De Gestis Henrici VII. Caesaris, libri XVI. De gestis italicorum post Henricum VII, libri XII. Eiusdemque Ludovicus Bavarus ad filium. Haec omnia.* Ed. Johannes G. Graevius and Petrus Burmannus. *Thesaurus Antiquitatem et Historiam Italiae.* vol. 6.2. Leiden.

1999. *Albertini Muxati De obsidione domini Canis Grandis de Verona ante civitatem Paduanam.* Ed. Giovanna M. Gianola. Padua: Antenore.

2000. *Épîtres métriques sur la poésie.* In *Écérinide. Épîtres métriques sur la poésie. Songe.* Ed. and trans. Jean-Frédéric Chevalier. Édition critique, traduction et présentation. Paris: Les Belles Lettres. 29–48.

2006. *Super celebracione sue diei nativitatis fienda vel non.* In *Écérinide. Épîtres métriques sur la poésie. Songe.* Ed. and trans. Jean-Frédéric Chevalier. Édition critique, traduction et présentation. Paris: Les Belles Lettres. 162–168.

2011. *Ecerinis.* In *Humanist Tragedies.* Ed. and trans. Gary R. Grund. I Tatti Renaissance Library 45. Cambridge, MA: Harvard University Press. 3–47.

2012. *Epistola V [Eiusdem ad Iambonum notarium de Andrea super adventu domini Henrici Imperatoris in Italiam].* In *Écérinide. Épîtres métriques sur la poésie. Songe.* Ed. and trans. Jean-Frédéric Chevalier. Édition critique, traduction et présentation. Paris: Les Belles Lettres. 293–295.

Ovid. 1914. *Heroides. Amores.* Trans. Grant Showerman; rev. G. P. Goold. Loeb Classical Library 41. Cambridge, MA: Harvard University Press.

1924. *Tristia. Ex Ponto.* Trans. A. L. Wheeler; rev. G. P. Goold. Loeb Classical Library 151. Cambridge, MA: Harvard University Press.

1926. *Metamorphoses.* Trans. Frank Justus Miller; rev. G. P. Goold. 2 vols. Loeb Classical Library 42–43. Cambridge, MA: Harvard University Press.

1929. *Art of Love. Cosmetics. Remedies for Love. Ibis. Walnut-Tree. Sea Fishing. Consolation.* Trans. J. H. Mozley; rev. G. P. Goold. Loeb Classical Library 232. Cambridge, MA: Harvard University Press.

1931. *Fasti.* Trans. James G. Frazer; rev. G. P. Goold. Loeb Classical Library 253. Cambridge, MA: Harvard University Press.

Persius and Juvenal. 2004. *Juvenal and Persius.* Ed. and trans. Susanna Morton Braund. Loeb Classical Library 91. Cambridge, MA: Harvard University Press.

Petrarch, Francesco. 1938–42. *Le Familiari.* Ed. Vittorio Rossi and Umberto Bosco. 4 vols. Florence: Sansoni.

1953. "Petrarch's Coronation Oration." Trans. Ernest H. Wilkins. *PMLA* 68.5: 1241–1250.

1974a. *Petrarch's Bucolicum Carmen.* Ed. and trans. Thomas G. Bergin. New Haven, CT: Yale University Press.

1974b. *Sine nomine: Lettere polemiche e politiche.* Ed. Ugo Dotti. Rome: Laterza.

1975–85. *Letters on Familiar Matters.* Trans. Aldo S. Bernardo. 3 vols. Baltimore, MD: Johns Hopkins University Press.

1983. *Epistola metrica II.10 – To Zoilus.* (Thomas Bergin, "Petrarch's Epistola metrica II.10: An Annotated Translation"). In *Dante, Petrarch, Boccaccio: Studies in the Italian Trecento in Honor of Charles S. Singleton.* Ed. Aldo S. Bernardo and Anthony L. Pellegrini. Binghamton, NY: Medieval & Renaissance Texts and Studies. 183–229 (188–218).

1988a. "Collatio edita per clarissimum poetam Franciscum Petrarcam rentinum Rome, in Capitolio, tempore laureationis sue." In "La *Collatio laureationis* del Petrarca nelle due redazioni." Ed. Carlo Godi. *Studi petrarcheschi* n.s. 5: 1–58 (29–58).

1988b. "Privilegium laureationis." In Dieter Mertens. *Litterae Medii Aevi: Festschrift für Johanne Autenrieth zu ihrem 65. Geburtstag.* Ed. Michael Borgholte and Herrad Spilling. Sigmaringen: Thorbecke. 236–247.

1992. *Letters of Old Age.* Trans. Aldo S. Bernardo, Saul Levin, and Reta S. Bernardo. 2 vols. Baltimore, MD: Johns Hopkins University Press.

1994. *Lettere disperse, varie e miscellanee.* Ed. Alessandro Pancheri. Parma: Fondazione Pietro Bembo.

1996. *The Revolution of Cola di Rienzo.* 3rd ed. Ed. and trans. Mario Emilio Cosenza. New York: Italica Press.

1999. *De vita solitaria.* Ed. Christophe Carraud. Grenoble: Éditions Jérôme Millon.

2003. *Invectives.* Ed. and trans. David Marsh. The I Tatti Renaissance Library 11. Cambridge, MA: Harvard University Press.

2004. *Epistulae Metricae/Briefe in Versen.* Ed. Otto Schönberger and Eva Schönberger. Würzburg: Königshausen & Neumann.

2004–2010. *Rerum senilium libri.* Trans. Ugo Dotti. Ed. Elvira Nota. 3 vols. Turin: Nino Aragno.

2005. *Invective contra medicum; Invectiva contra quendam magni status hominem sed nullius scientie aut virtutis.* Ed. Francesco Bausi. Florence: Le Lettere.

2014. *Rerum Memorandarum Libri.* Ed. Marco Petoletti. Florence: Le Lettere.

Pliny the Younger. 1969. *Letters, Volume II: Books 8–10. Panegyricus.* Trans. Betty Radice. Loeb Classical Library 59. Cambridge, MA: Harvard University Press.

Quintilian. 2002. *The Orator's Education, Volume IV. Books 9–10.* Ed. and trans. Donald A. Russell. Loeb Classical Library 127. Cambridge, MA: Harvard University Press.

Salutati, Coluccio. 1891–1905. *Epistolario di Coluccio Salutati*. Ed. Francesco Novati. Rome: Istituto Storico Italiano.

Seneca. 2002. *Tragedies, Volume I. Hercules. Trojan Women. Phoenician Women. Medea. Phaedra*. Ed. and trans. John G. Fitch. Loeb Classical Library 62. Cambridge, MA: Harvard University Press.

Servius Grammaticus. 1887. *In Virgilii "Bucolica" et "Georgica" commentarii*. Ed. George Thilo. Leipzig: Teubner.

Statius. 2004. *Thebaid, Volume II: Thebaid: Books 8–12*. Ed. and trans. D. R. Shackleton Bailey. Loeb Classical Library 498. Cambridge, MA: Harvard University Press.

Tacitus. 1925. *Histories. Books 1–3*. Trans. Clifford H. Moore. Loeb Classical Library 111. Cambridge, MA: Harvard University Press.

Virgil. 1916–18. *Eclogues. Georgics. Aeneid: Books 1–6; Aeneid: Books 7–12. Appendix Vergiliana*. Trans. H. Rushton Fairclough; rev. G. P. Goold. Loeb Classical Library 63–64. 2 vols. Cambridge, MA: Harvard University Press.

SECONDARY SOURCES

Albanese, Gabriella. 2003. "La corrispondenza fra Petrarca e Boccaccio." In *Motivi e forme delle "Familiari" di Francesco Petrarca*. Ed. Claudia Berra. Milan: Cisalpino. 39–98.

Albanese, Gabriella. ed. 2014. *Egloge*. In Dante Alighieri, *Opere*. vol. 2. *Convivio, Monarchia, Epistole, Egloge*. Milan: Mondadori. 1593–1783.

2016. "*De Gestis Henrici VII Cesaris*: Mussato, Dante e il mito dell'incoronazione poetica." In *Enrico VII, Dante e Pisa a 700 anni dall morte dell'imperatore e dalla Monarchia (1313–2013)*. Ed. Giuseppe Petralia and Marco Santagata. Ravenna: Longo. 161–202.

2017. "'Poeta et historicus': La Laurea di Mussato e Dante." In *"Moribus antiquis sibi me fecere poetam." Albertino Mussato nel VII centenario dell'incoronazione poetica (Padova 1315–2015)*. Ed. Rino Modonutti and Enrico Zucchi. Florence: SISMEL, Edizioni del Galluzzo. 3–45.

Albanese, Gabriella and Paolo Pontari. 2016. "Il notariato bolognese, le Egloge e il Polifemo dantesco. Nuove testimonianze manoscritte e una nuova lettura dell'ultima egloga." *Studi Danteschi* 81: 13–130.

2017. "Il cenacolo ravennate di Dante e le 'Egloge': Fiduccio de' Milotti, Dino Perini, Guido Vacchetta, Pietro Giardini, Menghino Mezzani." *Studi Danteschi* 82: 311–427.

Albanese, Gabriella and Paolo Pontari. ed. 2018. *L'ultimo Dante e il cenacolo ravennate : catalogo della mostra, Ravenna, Biblioteca Classense, 9 settembre–28 ottobre 2018*. Ravenna: Longo.

Alessio, Gian Carlo, ed. 2004. *Il mito nella letteratura italiana*. vol. 1. *Dal Medioevo al Rinascimento*. Brescia: Morcelliana.

Allegretti, Paola. 2004. "Un acrostico per Giovanni del Virgilio." *Studi Danteschi* 69: 289–294.

2010. "Dante 'Tityrus annosus' (*Egloghe*, IV.12)." In *Dante the Lyric and Ethical Poet: Dante lirico e etico*. Ed. Zygmunt G. Barański and Martin McLaughlin. London: Legenda. 168–208.

Ambrosini, Riccardo. 2002. "Canto XVII." In *Lectura Dantis Turicensis: Paradiso*. Ed. Georges Güntert and Michelangelo Picone. Florence: Franco Cesati Editore. 243–264.

Anderson, Benedict. 2006. *Imagined Communities: Reflections on the Origin and Spread of Nationalism*. Rev. ed. London: Verso.

Annett, Scott. 2013. "'Una veritade ascosa sotto bella menzogna': Dante's *Eclogues* and the World Beyond the Text." *Italian Studies* 68: 36–56.

Antonelli, Roberto. 2002. "Canto XXVII." In *Lectura Dantis Turicensis: Paradiso*. Ed. Georges Güntert and Michelangelo Picone. Florence: Franco Cesati Editore. 429–439.

Arduini, Beatrice. 2015. "Boccaccio and His Desk." In *The Cambridge Companion to Boccaccio*. Ed. Guyda Armstrong, Rhiannon Daniels, and Stephen J. Milner. Cambridge: Cambridge University Press. 20–35.

Arena, Valentina. 2007. "Roman Oratorical Invective." *A Companion to Roman Rhetoric*. Ed. Jon Hall and William Dominik. Malden, MA: Blackwell. 149–160.

Ariani, Marco. 2015. "Canto XXIV: Mistica degli affetti e intelletto d'amore." In *Cento canti per cento anni. III: Paradiso*. Ed. Enrico Malato and Andrea Mazzucchi. 2 vols. Rome: Salerno Editrice. 2.698–722.

Armstrong, Guyda. 2015. "Boccaccio and Dante." In *The Cambridge Companion to Boccaccio*. Ed. Guyda Armstrong, Rhiannon Daniels, and Stephen J. Milner. Cambridge: Cambridge University Press. 121–138.

Armstrong, Guyda, Rhiannon Daniels, and Stephen J. Milner, eds. 2015a. *The Cambridge Companion to Boccaccio*. Cambridge: Cambridge University Press.

Armstrong, Guyda, Rhiannon Daniels, and Stephen J. Milner, 2015b. "Boccaccio as Cultural Mediator." In *The Cambridge Companion to Boccaccio*. Ed. Guyda Armstrong, Rhiannon Daniels, and Stephen J. Milner. Cambridge: Cambridge University Press. 3–19.

Arnaldi, Girolamo. 1976. "Il primo secolo dello Studio di Padova." In *Storia della cultura veneta*. vol. 2. *Il Trecento*. Ed. Gianfranco Folena. Vincenza: Neri Pozza Editore. 1–18.

Ascoli, Albert Russell. 1991. "Petrarch's Middle Age: Memory, Imagination, History, and the 'Ascent of Mount Ventoux.'" *Stanford Italian Review* 10: 5–43.

2008. *Dante and the Making of a Modern Author*. Cambridge: Cambridge University Press.

2009. "Blinding the Cyclops: Petrarch after Dante." In *Petrarch and Dante: Anti-Dantism, Metaphysics, Tradition*. Ed. Zygmunt G. Barański and Theodore J. Cachey, Jr. Notre Dame, IN: University of Notre Dame Press. 114–173.

2010. "Dante and Allegory." In *The Cambridge Companion to Allegory*. Ed. Rita Copeland and Peter T. Struck. Cambridge: Cambridge University Press. 128–135.

2011. "Petrarch's Private Politics: *Rerum Familiarum Libri* 19." In *A Local Habitation and a Name: Imagining Histories in the Italian Renaissance*. New York: Fordham University Press. 118–158.

Ascoli, Albert Russell and Unn Falkeid, eds. 2015. *The Cambridge Companion to Petrarch*. Cambridge: Cambridge University Press.

Azzetta, Luca and Andrea Mazzucchi, eds. 2014. *Boccaccio editore e interprete di Dante. Atti del Convegno internazionale di Roma, 28–30 ottobre 2013, in collaborazione con la Casa di Dante in Roma*. Rome: Salerno.

Baglio, Mario. 2013. "'Avidulus glorie': Zanobi da Strada tra Boccaccio e Petrarca." *Italia medioevale et umanistica* 54: 343–395.

Baldan, Paolo. 1996. "Pentimento ed espiazione di un pubblico lettore (Boccaccio e la *Commedia* dantesca)." In *Bufere e molli aurette: Polemiche letterarie dallo Stilnovo alla "Voce."* Ed. M. G. Pensa. Milan: Guerini. 21–35.

Banella, Laura. 2017. *La Vita nuova del Boccaccio. Fortuna e tradizione*. Rome: Antenore.

Barański, Zygmunt G. 1997. "Notes on Dante and the Myth of Orpheus." In *Dante Mito e Poesia*. Ed. Michelangelo Picone and Tatiana Crivelli. Florence: Franco Cesati Editore. 133–154.

2000. *Dante e i segni: Saggi per una storia intellettuale di Dante Alighieri*. Naples: Liguori.

2001. *"Chiosar con altro testo": Leggere Dante nel Trecento*. Florence: Cadmo.

2002. "Canto XXII." In *Lectura Dantis Turicensis: Paradiso*. Ed. Georges Güntert and Michelangelo Picone. Florence: Franco Cesati Editore. 339–362.

2005. "Dante Alighieri: Experimentation and (Self-)Exegesis." In *The Cambridge History of Literary Criticism*. Ed. Alastair J. Minnis and Ian Johnson. vol 2. *The Middle Ages*. Cambridge: Cambridge University Press. 561–582.

2007. "The Ethics of Ignorance: Petrarch's Epicurus and Avveroës and the Structures of the *De Sui Ipsius et Multorum Ignorantia*." In *Petrarch in Britain: Interpreters, Imitators, and Translators over 700 Years*. Ed. Martin McLaughlin, Letizia Panizza, and Peter Hainsworth. Oxford: Oxford University Press. 39–59.

2009. "Petrarch, Dante, Cavalcanti." In *Petrarch and Dante: Anti-Dantism, Metaphysics, Tradition*. Ed. Zygmunt G. Barański and Theodore J. Cachey, Jr. Notre Dame, IN: University of Notre Dame Press. 50–113.

2017. "On Dante's Trail." *Italian Studies* 72.2: 1–15.

Barański, Zygmunt G. and Martin McLaughlin, eds. 2010. *Dante the Lyric and Ethical Poet: Dante Lirico e etico*. London: Legenda.

Barański, Zygmunt G. and Theodore J. Cachey, Jr., eds. 2009. *Petrarch and Dante: Anti-Dantism, Metaphysics, Tradition*. Notre Dame, IN: University of Notre Dame Press.

Barolini, Teodolinda. 1984. *Dante's Poets: Textuality and Truth in the "Comedy."* Princeton, NJ: Princeton University Press.

1992. *The Undivine Comedy: Detheologizing Dante.* Princeton, NJ: Princeton University Press.

2014. "Aristotle's *Mezzo,* Courtly *Misura,* and Dante's Canzone *Le dolci rime*: Humanism, Ethics, and Social Anxiety." In *Dante and the Greeks.* Ed. Jan M. Ziolkowski. Washington, DC: Dumbarton Oaks. 163–179.

2015. "*Amicus eius*: Dante and the Semantics of Friendship." *Dante Studies* 133: 46–69.

Baron, Hans. 1955. *The Crisis of the Early Italian Renaissance: Civic Humanism and Republican Liberty in an Age of Classicism and Tyranny.* 2 vols. Princeton, NJ: Princeton University Press.

1968. *From Petrarch to Leonardo Bruni: Studies in Humanistic and Political Literature.* Chicago: University of Chicago Press.

1985. *Petrarch's "Secretum": Its Making and Its Meaning.* Cambridge, MA: Medieval Academy of America.

Barsella, Susanna. 2004. "The Myth of Prometheus in Boccaccio's *Decameron.*" *Studia Humanitatis: Essays in Honor of Salvatore Camporeale.* Ed. Walter Stephens. *MLN* 119 (supp. 1): 121–141.

2006. "A Humanistic Approach to Religious Solitude (*De otio religioso*)." In Victoria Kirkham and Armando Maggi. *Petrarch: A Critical Guide to the Complete Works.* Chicago: University of Chicago Press. 197–208.

2010. *In the Light of the Angels: Angelology and Cosmology in Dante's Divina Commedia.* Florence: Olschki.

Bartuschat, Johannes. 2007. *Les "Vies" de Dante, Pétrarque et Boccace en Italie (XIVᵉ–XVᵉ siècles): contribution à l'histoire du genre biographique.* Ravenna: Longo.

Bausi, Francesco. 2005. Introduzione. In Francesco Petrarch. *Invective contra medicum; Invectiva contra quendam magni status hominem sed nullius scientie aut virtutis.* Ed. Francesco Bausi. Florence: Le Lettere. 9–22.

Benedictow, Ole J. 2004. *The Black Death 1346–1353: The Complete History.* Woodbridge: Boydell.

Beneš, Claire E. 2011. *Urban Legends: Civic Identity and the Classical Past in Northern Italy, 1250–1350.* University Park: Pennsylvania State University Press.

Bergin, Thomas. 1983. "Petrarch's *Epistola metrica* II.10: An Annotated Translation." In *Dante, Petrarch, Boccaccio: Studies in the Italian Trecento in Honor of Charles S. Singleton.* Ed. Aldo S. Bernardo and Anthony L. Pellegrini. Binghamton, NY: Medieval & Renaissance Texts and Studies. 183–229.

Bernardo, Aldo S. and Anthony L. Pellegrini, eds. 1983. *Dante, Petrarch, Boccaccio: Studies in the Italian Trecento in Honor of Charles S. Singleton.* Binghamton, NY: Medieval & Renaissance Texts and Studies.

Bertelli, Sandro and Davide Cappi, eds. 2014. *Dentro l'officina di Giovanni Boccaccio. Studi sugli autografi in volgare e su Boccaccio dantista.* Vatican City: Biblioteca Apostolica Vaticana.

Billanovich, Giuseppe. 1947. *Petrarca letterato*. vol. 1. *Lo scrittoio del Petrarca*. Rome: Edizioni di Storia e Letteratura.

1949. "La Leggenda dantesca del Boccaccio: Dalla lettera di Ilaro al *Trattatello in laude di Dante*." *Studi Danteschi* 28: 45–144.

Billanovich, Guido. 1958. "'Veterum vestigia vatum' nei carmi dei preumanisti padovani. Lovato Lovati, Zambono di Andrea, Albertino Mussato e Lucrezio, Catullo, Orazio (*Carmina*), Tibullo, Properzio, Ovidio (*Ibis*), Marziale, Stazio (*Silvae*)." *Italia medioevale e umanistica* 1: 155–243.

1976. "Il preumanesimo padovano." In *Storia della cultura veneta*. vol. 1. *Dalle origini al Trecento*. Ed. Gianfranco Folena. Vincenza: Neri Pozza Editore. 19–110.

Billanovich, Guido and Guglielmo Travaglia. 1942–54. "Per l'edizione del 'De Lite inter Naturam et Fortunam' e del 'Contra casus fortuitos' di Albertino Mussato." *Bollettino del Museo civico di Padova* 31–43: 279–295.

Biow, Douglas. 2002. *Doctors, Ambassadors, Secretaries: Humanism and Professions in Renaissance Italy*. Chicago: University of Chicago Press.

Black, Robert. 2001. *Humanism and Education in Medieval and Renaissance Italy: Tradition and Innovation in Latin Schools from the Twelfth to the Fifteenth Century*. Cambridge: Cambridge University Press.

Boitani, Piero. 2000. "Those who will call this time ancient: The Futures of Prophecy and Poetry. *In Memoriam* Howard H. Schless." In *Medieval Futures: Attitudes to the Future in the Middle Ages*. Ed. John A. Burrow and Ian P. Wei. Woodbridge: Boydell Press.

Boli, Todd. 1988. "Boccaccio's *Trattatello in laude di Dante*, Or *Dante Resartus*." *Renaissance Quarterly* 41.3: 389–412.

Bologna, Corrado. 1993. *Tradizione e fortuna dei classici italiani*. 2 vols. Turin: Einaudi.

2010. "Dante e il latte delle Muse." In *Atlante della letteratura italiana*. vol. 1. *Dalle origini al Rinascimento*. Ed. Sergio Luzzatto and Gabriele Pedullà. Turin: Einaudi. 145–155.

Booth, Alan D. 1980. "Allusion to the 'Circulator' by Persius and Horace?" *Greece & Rome*, 27.2: 166–169.

Bortolami, Sante. 1995. "Da Rolandino al Mussato: tensioni ideali e senso della storia nella storiografia padovana di tradizione 'repubblicana.'" In *Il senso della storia nella cultura medievale italiana (1100–1350)*. Pistoia: Centro Italiano di Studi di Storia e d'Arte. 53–86.

Branca, Vittore. 1975. *Giovanni Boccaccio: Profilo biografico*. Florence: Sansoni.

Branca, Vittore and Giorgio Padoan, eds. 1967. *Dante e la cultura veneta*. Florence: Olschki.

Braund, Susanna Morton. 2004. Introduction. In *Juvenal and Persius*. Loeb Classical Library 91. Cambridge, MA: Harvard University Press. 1–39.

Breen, Katharine. 2010. *Imagining an English Reading Public, 1150–1400*. Cambridge: Cambridge University Press.

Brotto, Giovanni and Gasparo Zonta. 1922. *La facoltà teologica dell'Università di Padova*. vol. 1 *Secoli XIV e XV*. Padua: Tipografia del Seminario.

Brownlee, Kevin. 1984. "Why the Angels Speak Italian: Dante as Vernacular Poet in *Paradiso* XXV." *Poetics Today* 5.3: 596–610.

1991. "Pauline Vision and Ovidian Speech in *Paradiso* 1." In *The Poetry of Allusion: Virgil and Ovid in Dante's "Commedia."* Ed. Rachel Jacoff and Jeffrey T. Schnapp. Stanford, CA: Stanford University Press. 202–213.

Brucker, Gene A. 1969. "Florence and Its University, 1348–1434." *Action and Conviction in Early Modern Europe.* Ed. T. K. Rabb and J. F. Seigel. Princeton, NJ: Princeton University Press. 220–236.

1977. *The Civic World of Early Renaissance Florence.* Princeton, NJ: Princeton University Press.

Bruni, Francesco. 1990. *Boccaccio: L'invenzione della letteratura mezzana.* Bologna: Il Mulino.

Burckhardt, Jacob. 1929. *The Civilization of the Renaissance in Italy.* Trans. S. G. C. Middlemore. London: Harrap.

Cachey, Jr., Theodore J. 2009. "Between Petrarch and Dante: Prolegomenon to a Critical Discourse." In *Petrarch and Dante: Anti-Dantism, Metaphysics, Tradition.* Ed. Zygmunt G. Barański and Theodore J. Cachey, Jr. Notre Dame, IN: University of Notre Dame Press. 3–49.

2014. "Cartographic Dante: A Note on Dante and the Greek Mediterranean." In *Dante and the Greeks.* Ed. Jan M. Ziolkowski. Washington, DC: Dumbarton Oaks. 197–226.

Caferro, William. 2013. "Petrarch's War: Florentine Wages and the Black Death." *Speculum* 88.1: 144–165.

2018a. *Petrarch's War: Florence and the Black Death in Context.* Cambridge: Cambridge University Press.

2018b. "The Visconti War and Boccaccio's Florentine Public Service, 1351–53." In *Boccaccio and His World.* Proceedings of the Third Triennial Meeting of the American Boccaccio Association. Duke University, September–October 2016. Ed. Valerio Capozzo, Martin Eisner, and Timothy Kircher. *Heliotropia* 15 (special issue): 111–131: http://www.heliotropia .org/.

Calì, Carmelo. 1893. "Due epistole di Albertino Mussato a Giovanni da Vigonza, secondo un nuovo codice." *Rivista Etnea di lettere, arti e scienze* 1: 21–24.

Candido, Igor. 2014. *Boccaccio umanista: studi su Boccaccio e Apuleio.* Ravenna: Longo.

Carducci, Giosuè. 1900. "Della Ecerinide e di Albertino Mussato." In *Albertino Mussato. Ecerinide.* Ed. Luigi Padrin. Bologna: Ditta Nicola Zanichelli. 251–283.

Carrai, Stefano. 2006. "Pastoral as Personal Mythology in History (*Bucolicum Carmen*)." In Victoria Kirkham and Armando Maggi. *Petrarch: A Critical Guide to the Complete Works.* Chicago: University of Chicago Press. 165–177.

Casadei, Alberto. 2013. *Dante oltre la "Commedia."* Bologna: Il Mulino.

2014. "Sull'autenticità dell'*Epistola a Cangrande.*" In *Ortodossia ed eterodossia in Dante Alighieri: atti del convegno di Madrid (5–7 novembre 2012).* Ed.

Carlota Cattermole, Celia de Aldama, and Chiara Giordano. Madrid: Ediciones de La Discreta. 803–825.

2019. *Dante. Altri accertamenti e punti critici.* Milan: FrancoAngeli.

Cecchini, Enzo. 1985. "Le epistole metriche del Mussato sulla poesia." In *Tradizione classica e letteratura umanistica: per Alessandro Perosa.* vol. 1. Ed. Roberto Cardini, Eugenio Garin, and Lucia Cesarini Martinelli. Rome: Bulzoni Editore.

Celenza, Christopher S. 2004. *The Lost Italian Renaissance: Humanists, Historians, and Latin's Legacy.* Baltimore, MD: Johns Hopkins University Press.

Cherchi, Paolo. 2018. "The Inventors of Things in Boccaccio's *De genealogia deorum gentilium.*" In *Petrarch and Boccaccio: The Unity of Knowledge in the Pre-Modern World.* Ed. Igor Candido. Berlin: De Gruyter. 244–269.

Chevalier, Jean-Frédéric, ed. 2000. Albertino Mussato. *Écérinide. Épîtres métriques sur la poésie. Songe.* Édition critique, traduction et présentation. Paris: Les Belles Lettres.

Chevalier, Jean-Frédéric, 2004. "Le couronnement d'Albertino Mussato ou la renaissance d'une célébration." *Bulletin de l'Association Guillaume Budé* 2: 42–55.

2006. "Le statut de l'élégie autobiographique au début du *Trecento*: Albertino Mussato et le modèle des *Tristes* d'Ovide." *Studi umanistici piceni* 26: 149–168.

2010. "Albertino Mussato o la figura del poeta esiliato: edizione di un centone autobiografico dai *Tristia* di Ovidio." *Studi umanistici piceni* 30: 111–131.

2012. "Les épîtres métriques d'Albertino Mussato (1261–1329): une autobiographie politique?" *La lyre et la pourpre: Poésie latine et politique de l'Antiquité tardive à la Renaissance.* Ed. Nathalie Catellani-Dufrène and Michel Jean-Louis Perrin. Rennes: Presses universitaires de Rennes. 281–296.

2013. "Neo-Latin Theatre in Italy." *Neo-Latin Drama in Early Modern Europe.* Ed. Jan Bloemendal and Howard Norland. Leiden: Brill. 25–101.

Chiarenza, Marguerite Mills. 1983. "Time and Eternity in the Myths of Paradiso XVII." In *Dante, Petrarch, Boccaccio: Studies in the Italian Trecento in Honor of Charles S. Singleton.* Ed. Aldo S. Bernardo and Anthony L. Pellegrini. Binghamton, NY: Medieval & Renaissance Texts and Studies. 133–156.

Chiavacci Leonardi, Anna. 1988. "'Le bianche stole': il tema della resurrezione nel *Paradiso.*" In *Dante e la Bibbia.* Ed. Giovanni Barblan. Florence: Olschki. 249–271.

Ciampi, Mario. 2009. *Il pensiero politico di Dante Alighieri nella critica del Novecento.* Rome: Drengo.

Coggeshall, Elizabeth A. 2012. "Dante's Friends." Ph.D. dissertation, Stanford University.

Combs-Schilling, Jonathan. 2015. "Tityrus in Limbo: Figures of the Author in Dante's *Eclogues.*" *Dante Studies* 133: 1–26.

Contini, Gianfranco. 1970. "Dante come personaggio-poeta della *Commedia.*" In *Un'idea di Dante.* Turin: Einaudi. 33–62.

Copeland, Rita. 1991. *Rhetoric, Hermeneutics, and Translation in the Middle Ages: Academic Traditions and Vernacular Texts.* Cambridge: Cambridge University Press.

2002. "Pre-Modern Intellectual Biography." In Helen Small, ed. *The Public Intellectual.* Oxford: Blackwell. 42–61.

Copeland, Rita and Ineke Sluiter, eds. 2009. *Medieval Grammar and Rhetoric: Language Arts and Literary Theory, AD 300–1475.* Oxford: Oxford University Press.

Coppi, Ettore. 1886. *Le università italiane nel Medio Evo.* 3rd ed. Florence: Loescher & Seeber.

Cornish, Alison. 2000. *Reading Dante's Stars.* New Haven, CT: Yale University Press.

2011. *Vernacular Translation in Dante's Italy: Illiterate Literature.* Cambridge: Cambridge University Press.

Crescini, Vincenzo. 1885. "Note e appunti." *Giornale degli eruditi e dei curiosi* 5: 125–128.

Crouzet-Pavan, Élisabeth. 2010. "Il sogno di Roma: Petrarca e Cola di Rienzo." In *Atlante della letteratura italiana.* vol. 1. *Dalle origini al Rinascimento.* Ed. Sergio Luzzatto and Gabriele Pedullà. Turin: Einaudi. 188–193.

Curtius, Ernst Robert. 1953. *European Literature and the Latin Middle Ages.* Trans. Willard R. Trask. Princeton, NJ: Princeton University Press.

D'Entrevès, Alessandro P. 1952. *Dante as a Political Thinker.* Oxford: Clarendon Press.

Davies, Jonathan. 1998. *Florence and Its University during the Early Renaissance.* Leiden: Brill.

Davis, Charles T. 1957. *Dante and the Idea of Rome.* Oxford: Clarendon Press.

Dazzi, Manlio. 1964. *Il Mussato preumanista (1261–1329): L'ambiente e l'opera.* Vicenza: Neri Pozza Editore.

1967. "Due note dantesche: I. Dante e Mussato. II. Per una illustrazione della 'Commedia.'" In *Dante e la cultura veneta.* Ed. Vittore Branca and Giorgio Padoan. Florence: Olschki. 303–305.

De Keyser, Jeroen. 2013. "The Descendants of Petrarch's *Pro Archia.*" *Classical Quarterly* 63.1: 292–328.

De Marchi, Pietro. 2002. "Canto XXIV." In *Lectura Dantis Turicensis: Paradiso.* Ed. Georges Güntert and Michelangelo Picone. Florence: Franco Cesati Editore. 373–389.

De Robertis, Teresa, Carla Maria Monti, Marco Petoletti, Giuliano Tanturli, and Stefano Zamponi, eds. 2013. *Boccaccio autore e copista.* Florence: Mandragora.

Dell'Oso, Lorenzo. 2017. "Per la formazione intellettuale di Dante: i cataloghi librari, le tracce testuali, il 'Trattatello' di Boccaccio." *Le tre corone. Rivista internazionale di studi su Dante, Petrarca, Boccaccio* 4: 129–161.

Demetz, Peter. 1958. "The Elm and the Vine: Notes toward the History of a Marriage Topos." *PMLA* 73.5/1: 521–532.

Denley, Peter. 1983. "The Social Function of Italian Renaissance Universities: Prospects for Research." *CRE Information* 62: 47–58.

    1988. "Academic Rivalry and Interchange." *Florence and Italy: Renaissance Studies in Honor of Nicolai Rubinstein.* Ed. Peter Denley and Caroline Elam. London: Committee for Medieval Studies, Westfield College. 193–208.

    1991. "The Collegiate Movement in Italian Universities in the Late Middle Ages." *History of Universities* 10: 29–91.

Desmond, Marilyn. 1994. *Reading Dido: Gender, Textuality, and the Medieval Aeneid.* Minneapolis: University of Minnesota Press.

Di Salvo, Andrea. 1996. "Il Signore della Scala: percezione e rielaborazione della figura di Cangrande I nelle testimonianze del secolo XIV." *Rivista Storica Italiana* 108.1: 36–86.

Dotti, Ugo. 2001. *Petrarca civile: alle origini dell'intellettuale moderno.* Rome: Donzelli.

Eisenhauer, Robert. 2007. *Archaeologies of Invective.* New York: Peter Lang.

Eisner, Martin G. 2011. "The Return to Philology and the Future of Literary Criticism: Reading the Temporality of Literature in Auerbach, Benjamin, and Dante." *California Italian Studies* 2. 1: https://escholarship.org/uc/item/4gq644zp.

    2013. *Boccaccio and the Invention of Italian Literature: Dante, Petrarch, Cavalcanti, and the Authority of the Vernacular.* Cambridge: Cambridge University Press.

    2014. "In the Labyrinth of the Library: Petrarch's Cicero, Dante's Virgil, and the Historiography of the Renaissance." *Renaissance Quarterly* 67.3: 755–790.

    2021. *Dante's New Life of the Book: A Philology of World Literature.* Oxford: Oxford University Press.

Emerton, Ephraim. 1925. *Humanism and Tyranny: Studies in the Italian Trecento.* Cambridge, MA: Harvard University Press.

Facchini, Bianca. 2014. "A Philosophical Quarrel among *Auctoritates*: Mussato's *De lite inter Naturam et Fortunam* and its Classical and Medieval Sources." *Italia medieoevale e umanistica* 55: 71–102.

    2017. "Albertino Mussato: ultime riflessioni sulla poesia." In *"Moribus antiquis sibi me fecere poetam." Albertino Mussato nel VII centenario dell'incoronazione poetica (Padova 1315–2015).* Ed. Rino Modonutti and Enrico Zucchi. Florence: SISMEL, Edizioni del Galluzzo. 141–158.

    2020. "Lucan and Virgil: From Dante to Petrarch (and Boccaccio)." *International Journal of the Classical Tradition* 27: 1–22: https://link.springer.com/article/10.1007%2Fs12138-018-0482-x.

Fachard, Denis. 2002. "Canto XVI." In *Lectura Dantis Turicensis: Paradiso.* Ed. Georges Güntert and Michelangelo Picone. Florence: Franco Cesati Editore. 231–242.

Fanelli, Giovanni. 1980. *Firenze.* Bari: Laterza.

Fenzi, Enrico. 2005. "Petrarca a Milano: Tempi e modi di una scelta meditata." In *Petrarca e la Lombardia. Atti del Convegno di Studi (Milano, 22–23 maggio 2003).* Rome: Antenore.

2011. "Per Petrarca politico: Cola di Rienzo e la questione romana in *Bucolicum Carmen* V, *Pietas pastoralis.*" *Bollettino di italianistica* 1: 49–88.

Feo, Michele. 1991. "Il Poema epico latino nell'Italia medievale." In *I linguaggi della propaganda. Studio di casi: medioevo, rivoluzione inglese, Italia liberale, fascismo, resistenza.* Milan: Edizioni scolastiche Bruno Mondadori.

Ferrante, Joan M. 1984. *The Political Vision of the* Divine Comedy. Princeton, NJ: Princeton University Press.

Ferri, Sabrina. 2015. *Ruins Past: Modernity in Italy, 1744–1836.* Oxford: Voltaire Foundation.

Filosa, Elsa. 2013. "To Praise Dante, to Please Petrarch (*Trattatello in laude di Dante*)." In *Boccaccio: A Critical Guide to the Complete Works.* Ed. Victoria Kirkham, Michael Sherberg, and Janet Levarie Smarr. Chicago: University of Chicago Press. 213–220.

2014. "L'amicizia ai tempi della congiura (Firenze 1360–61): 'A confortatore non duole capo.'" *Studi sul Boccaccio* 42: 195–220.

Folena, Gianfranco, ed. 1976. *Storia della cultura veneta.* vol. 1. *Dalle origini al Trecento.* Vincenza: Neri Pozza Editore.

Frasso, Giuseppe. 2015. "Canto XXVII: Invettiva e profezia." In *Cento canti per cento anni. III. Paradiso.* Ed. Enrico Malato and Andrea Mazzucchi. 2 vols. Rome: Salerno Editrice. 2.787–811.

Freccero, John. 1986. *Dante: The Poetics of Conversion.* Cambridge, MA: Harvard University Press.

Frugoni, Chiara. 2008. *L'affare migliore di Enrico: Giotto e la cappella Scrovegni.* Turin: Einaudi.

Fumagalli, Edoardo. 2002. "Canto XXV." In *Lectura Dantis Turicensis: Paradiso.* Ed. Georges Güntert and Michelangelo Picone. Florence: Franco Cesati Editore. 391–404.

Furlan, Francesco and Stefano Pittaluga, eds. 2016. *Petrarca politico.* Milan: Ledizioni.

Galletti, Alfredo. 1912. "La ragione poetica di Albertino Mussato e i poeti teologi." In *Scritti varii di erudizione e di critica in onore di Rodolfo Renier (con xx tavole fuori testo).* Turin: Fratelli Bocca. 331–359.

Galli, Quirino. 1974. "L'*Ecerinis* di Albertino Mussato tra laudario e sacra rappresentazione." *Misure critiche* 4.10–11: 31–47.

Gallo, Donato. 1998. *Università a Padova dal XIV al XV secolo.* Trieste: Edizioni LINT.

Gargan, Luciano. 1971. *Lo studio teologico e la biblioteca dei domenicani a Padova nel Tre e Quattrocento.* Padua: Antenore.

Garin, Eugenio. 1954. *Medioevo e Rinascimento: Studi e Ricerche.* Bari: Laterza.

1957. *L'educazione in Europa (1400–1600): Problemi e programmi.* Bari: Laterza.

Garin, Eugenio. ed. 1958. *Il pensiero pedagogico dello Umanesimo.* Florence: Giuntine/Sansoni.

Gianola, Giovanna. 1987. "Le 'divinae personae' nell'epica del primo Trecento: Albertino Mussato, Pace da Ferrara (e Dante)." In Marco Pecoraro, *Studi in onore di Vittorio Zaccaria.* Milan: Unicopli. 65–88.

1988. "Tra Padova e Verona: il Cangrande di Mussato (e quello di Dante)." In *Gli Scaligeri, 1277–1387: Saggi e schede pubblicati in occasione della mostra storico-documentaria allestita dal Museo di Castelvecchio di Verona (giugno–novembre 1988)*. Ed. Gian Maria Varanini. Verona: Mondadori.

1992. "L'*Ecerinis* di Albertino Mussato tra Ezzelino and Cangrande." In *Nuovi studi ezzeliniani*. Ed. Giorgio Cracco. Rome: Istituto storico per il Medio Evo. 537–574.

1999. Introduzione. In Albertino Mussato, *Albertini Muxati de obsidione domini canis grandis de Verona ante civitatem Paduanam*. Ed. Giovanna Gianola. Padua: Antenore. xxv–cxc.

Gilson, Simon. 2005. *Dante and Renaissance Florence*. Cambridge: Cambridge University Press.

2013. "Modes of Reading in Boccaccio's *Esposizioni sopra la Comedia*." In *Interpreting Dante: Essays on the Traditions of Dante Commentary*. Ed. Paola Nasti and Claudia Rossignoli. Notre Dame, IN: University of Notre Dame Press. 250–282.

Ginsberg, Warren. 2002. *Chaucer's Italian Tradition*. Ann Arbor: University of Michigan Press.

Gittes, Tobias Foster. 2002. "St. Boccaccio: The Poet as Pander and Martyr." *Studi sul Boccaccio* 30: 125–157.

2008. *Boccaccio's Naked Muse: Eros, Culture, and the Mythopoeic Imagination*. Toronto: University of Toronto Press.

2015. "Boccaccio and Humanism." In *The Cambridge Companion to Boccaccio*. Ed. Guyda Armstrong, Rhiannon Daniels, and Stephen J. Milner. Cambridge: Cambridge University Press. 155–170.

Gloria, Andrea. 1888. *Monumenti della Università di Padova (1318–1405)*. Padua: Tipografia del Seminario.

Godi, Carlo. 1988. "La *Collatio laureationis* del Petrarca nelle due redazioni." *Studi petrarcheschi* n.s. 5: 1–58.

Graevius, Joannes G. and Petrus Burmannus, eds. 1722. *Thesaurus antiquitatum et historiarum Italiae*. vol. 6, pt. 2. Leiden.

Grassi, Ernesto. 1988. *Renaissance Humanism: Studies in Philosophy and Poetics*. Binghamton, NY: Medieval & Renaissance Texts and Studies.

Greene, Thomas M. 1982. "Petrarch 'Viator': The Displacements of Heroism." *Yearbook of English Studies* 12 (Heroes and the Heroic Special Number): 33–57.

Greenfield, Concetta Carestia. 1981. *Humanist and Scholastic Poetics, 1250–1500*. Lewisburg, PA: Bucknell University Press.

Gross, Karen Elizabeth. 2009. "Scholar Saints and Boccaccio's *Trattatello in laude di Dante*." *MLN* 124.1 (Italian Issue): 66–85

Gullace, Giovanni. 1989 (for 1986). "Medieval and Humanistic Perspectives in Boccaccio's Concept and Defense of Poetry." *Mediaevalia* 12: 225–248.

Güntert, Georges and Michelangelo Picone, eds. 2002. *Lectura Dantis Turicensis: Paradiso*. Florence: Franco Cesati Editore.

Hankins, James. 1995. "The 'Baron Thesis' after Forty Years and Some Recent Studies of Leonardo Bruni." *Journal of the History of Ideas* 56.2: 309–338.

2012. "Petrarch and the Canon of Neo-Latin Literature." In *Petrarca, l'Umanesimo e la civiltà europea: Atti del Convegno Internazionale, Firenze, 5–10 dicembre 2004*. Ed. Donatella Coppini and Michele Feo. 2 vols. Florence: Le Lettere. 905–922.

Hawkins, Peter S. 1992. "Self-Authenticating Artifact: Poetry and Theology in *Paradiso* 25." *Christianity and Literature* 41.4: 387–394.

Hobbins, Daniel. 2003. "The Schoolman as Public Intellectual: Jean Gerson and the Late Medieval Tract." *American Historical Review* 108.5: 1308–1335.

Hollander, Robert. 1969. *Allegory in Dante's "Commedia."* Princeton, NJ: Princeton University Press.

1976. "Dante as Theologus-Poeta." *Dante Studies* 94: 91–136.

1977. *Boccaccio's Two Venuses*. New York: Columbia University Press.

1997. *Boccaccio's Dante and the Shaping Force of Satire*. Ann Arbor: University of Michigan Press.

2007. Commentary to *Paradiso*. Dartmouth Dante Project. https://dante .dartmouth.edu.

2010. "Marsyas as *figura Dantis: Paradiso* 1.20." *Electronic Bulletin of the Dante Society of America*. 27 April. www.princeton.edu/~dante/ebdsa/hollander 042710.html.

2013. "Boccaccio's Divided Allegiance (*Esposizioni sopra la 'Comedia'*)." In *Boccaccio: A Critical Guide to the Complete Works*. Ed. Victoria Kirkham, Michael Sherberg, and Janet Levarie Smarr. Chicago: University of Chicago Press. 221–231.

Honess, Claire E. 1997. "Feminine Virtues and Florentine Vices: Citizenship and Morality in *Paradiso* XV–XVII." In *Dante and Governance*. Ed. John Woodhouse. Oxford: Clarendon Press. 102–120.

2006. *From Florence to the Heavenly City: The Poetry of Citizenship in Dante*. London: Legenda.

2013. "'Ritornerò poeta...': Florence, Exile, and Hope." In *Se mai continga...: Exile, Politics and Theology in Dante*. Ed. Claire E. Honess and Matthew Treherne. Ravenna: Longo.

Hooper, Laurence E. 2012. "Dante's 'Convivio,' Book 1: Metaphor, Exile, 'Epochē.'" *MLN* 127.5: S86–S104.

Hortis, Attilio. 1879. *Studj sulle opere latine del Boccaccio*. Trieste: Libreria Julius Dase Editrice.

Houston, Jason. 2010. *Building a Monument to Dante: Boccaccio as Dantista*. Toronto: University of Toronto Press.

2012. "Boccaccio at Play in Petrarch's Pastoral World." *MLN* 127.1 (Italian issue supplement): S47–S53.

Hyde, John K. 1966. *Padua in the Age of Dante*. Manchester: Manchester University Press.

Iannucci, Amilcare A., ed. 1993. *Dante e la "bella scola" della poesia: Autorità e sfida poetica*. Ravenna: Longo.

Inglese, Giorgio. 2015. *Vita di Dante: Una biografia possibile*. Rome: Carocci.

Kay, Sarah. 2006. "Original Skin: Flaying, Reading, and Thinking in the Legend of Saint Bartholomew and Other Works." *Journal of Medieval and Early Modern Studies* 36.1: 35–74.

2017. *Animal Skins and the Reading Self in Medieval Latin and French Bestiaries*. Chicago: University of Chicago Press.

Keen, Catherine. 2003. *Dante and the City*. Stroud: Tempus.

Kircher, Timothy. 2006. *The Poet's Wisdom: The Humanists, the Church, and the Formation of Philosophy in the Early Renaissance*. Leiden: Brill.

Kirkham, Victoria. 1992. "The Parallel Lives of Dante and Virgil." *Dante Studies* 110: 233–253.

1993. *The Sign of Reason in Boccaccio's Fiction*. Florence: Olschki.

2006. "Petrarch the Courtier." In Victoria Kirkham and Armando Maggi. *Petrarch: A Critical Guide to the Complete Works*. Chicago: University of Chicago Press. 141–150.

Kirkham, Victoria and Armando Maggi. 2006. *Petrarch: A Critical Guide to the Complete Works*. Chicago: University of Chicago Press.

Kirkham, Victoria, Michael Sherberg, and Janet Levarie Smarr, eds. 2013. *Boccaccio: A Critical Guide to the Complete Works*. Chicago: University of Chicago Press.

Kohl, Benjamin G. 1998. *Padua under the Carrara, 1318–1405*. Baltimore, MD Johns Hopkins University Press.

Kriesel, James C. 2009. "The Genealogy of Boccaccio's Theory of Allegory." *Studi sul Boccaccio* 36: 197–226.

2018. *Boccaccio's Corpus: Allegory, Ethics, and Vernacularity*. Notre Dame, IN: University of Notre Dame Press.

Kristeller, Paul Oskar. 1944–45. "Humanism and Scholasticism in the Italian Renaissance." *Byzantion* 17: 346–374.

Lanza, Lidia. 2000. "Albertinus Mussatus." In *Compendium Auctorum Latinorum Medii Aevi (500–1500)*. vol. 1, pt. 2. Florence: SISMEL, Edizioni del Galluzzo. 108–110.

Larner, John. 1990. "Traditions of Literary Biography in Boccaccio's *Life of Dante*." *Bulletin of the John Rylands University Library of Manchester* 72: 108–117.

Laureys, Marc. 2010. "La poesia latina di Coluccio Salutati." In *Coluccio Salutati e l'invenzione dell'umanesimo. Atti del convegno internazionale di studi. Firenze, 29–31 ottobre 2008*. Ed. Concetta Bianca. Rome: Edizioni di Storia e Letteratura. 295–314.

Le Goff, Jacques. 1993. *Intellectuals in the Middle Ages*. Trans. Teresa Lavender Fagan. Oxford: Blackwell.

Ledda, Giuseppe. 2015. "Canto XV: Dante e Cacciaguida nel cielo di Marte: I modelli, il martirio, la città." In *Cento canti per cento anni. III. Paradiso*. Ed. Enrico Malato and Andrea Mazzucchi. 2 vols. Rome: Salerno Editrice. 1.430–458.

Lee, Alexander. 2018. *Humanism and Empire: The Imperial Ideal in Fourteenth-Century Italy.* Oxford: Oxford University Press.

Lindhardt, Jan. 1979. *Rhetor, Poeta, Historicus.* Studien über rhetorische Erkenntnis und Lebensanschauung im italienischen Renaissancehumanismus. Leiden: Brill.

Locati, Silvia. 2006. *La rinascita del genere tragico nel Medioevo: L'Ecerinis di Albertino Mussato.* Florence: Franco Cesati Editore.

Lombardo, Luca. 2014. "Oltre il silenzio di Dante: Giovanni del Virgilio, le Epistole metriche di Mussato e i commentatori danteschi antichi." *Acta Histriae* 22.1: 17–40.

2017. "L'edizione critica delle 'Epistole' metriche di Albertino Mussato: il testo, i temi, le fonti (con un'appendice 'dantesca')." In *"Moribus antiquis sibi me fecere poetam." Albertino Mussato nel VII centenario dell'incoronazione poetica (Padova 1315–2015).* Ed. Rino Modonutti and Enrico Zucchi. Florence: SISMEL, Edizioni del Galluzzo. 89–106.

2018. "Un'epistola dantesca di Albertino Mussato." *L'Alighieri* 51.1: 37–62.

Looney, Dennis. 2006. "The Beginnings of Humanistic Oratory: Petrarch's Coronation Oration (*Collatio laureationis*)." In Victoria Kirkham and Armando Maggi. *Petrarch: A Critical Guide to the Complete Works.* Chicago: University of Chicago Press. 131–140.

Lorenzini, Simona. 2011. *La corrispondenza bucolica tra Giovanni Boccaccio e Checco di Meletto Rossi: L'egloga di Giovanni del Virgilio ad Albertino Mussato.* Florence: Olschki.

Lummus, David. 2011a. "Boccaccio's Three Venuses: On the Convergence of Celestial and Transgressive Love in the *Genealogie Deorum Gentilium Libri.*" *Medievalia et Humanistica* 37: 65–88.

2011b. "Dante's *Inferno*/Critical Reception and Influence." In Critical Insights: *The Inferno.* Ed. Patrick Hunt. Pasadena, CA: Salem Press. 63–81.

2012a. "Boccaccio's Hellenism and the Foundations of Modernity." *Mediaevalia* 33: 101–167.

2012b. "Boccaccio's Poetic Anthropology: Allegories of History in the *Genealogie deorum gentilium libri.*" *Speculum* 87.3: 724–765.

2013a. "The Changing Landscape of the Self (*Buccolicum Carmen*)." In *Boccaccio: A Critical Guide to the Complete Works.* Ed. Victoria Kirkham, Michael Sherberg, and Janet Levarie Smarr. Chicago: University of Chicago Press. 155–169.

2013b. "Edoardo Sanguineti's New Dante." In *Edoardo Sanguineti: Literature, Ideology and the Avant-Garde.* Ed. Paolo Chirumbolo and John Picchione. Italian Perspectives 26. London: Legenda. 40–55.

2014. "Review Essay: Boccaccio." *Medieval Review* 14.02.01: https://scholarworks.iu.edu/journals/index.php/tmr/article/view/18509.

2015. "The *Decameron* and Boccaccio's Poetics." In *The Cambridge Companion to Boccaccio.* Cambridge: Cambridge University Press. Ed. Guyda Armstrong, Rhiannon Daniels, and Stephen J. Milner. Cambridge: Cambridge University Press. 65–82.

2017. "Placing Petrarch's Legacy: The Politics of Petrarch's Tomb and Boccaccio's Last Letter." *Renaissance Quarterly* 70 (2017): 435–473.

Luzzatto, Sergio and Gabriele Pedullà, eds. 2010. *Atlante della letteratura italiana*. vol. 1. *Dalle origini al Rinascimento*. Turin: Einaudi.

McLaughlin, Martin. 1995. *Literary Imitation and the Italian Renaissance*. Oxford: Clarendon Press.

Malato, Enrico and Andrea Mazzucchi, eds. 2015. *Cento canti per cento anni. III. Paradiso*. 2 vols. Rome: Salerno Editrice.

Marangon, Paolo. 1997. *Ad Cognitionem Scientiae Festinare: Gli studi nell'Università e nei conventi di Padova nei secoli XIII e XIV*. Ed. Tiziana Pesenti. Trieste: Edizioni LINT.

Marchesi, Simone. 2001. "'Sic me formabat puerum': Horace's *Satire* I,4 and Boccaccio's Defense of the *Decameron*." *MLN* 116.1: 1–29.

2006. "Petrarch's Philological Epic (*Africa*)." In Victoria Kirkham and Armando Maggi. *Petrarch: A Critical Guide to the Complete Works*. Chicago: University of Chicago Press. 113–130.

Marcozzi, Luca. 2002. *La biblioteca di Febo: mitologia e allegoria in Petrarca*. Florence: Cesati.

2015. "Canto XVI: Il declino di Firenze e il trionfo del tempo." In *Cento canti per cento anni. III: Paradiso*. Ed. Enrico Malato and Andrea Mazzucchi. 2 vols. Rome: Salerno Editrice. 1.459–489.

Marcus, Millicent Joy. 1979. *An Allegory of Form: Literary Self-Consciousness in the "Decameron."* Saratoga, CA: Anma Libri.

Marino, Lucia. 1980. "Prometheus, or the Mythographer's Self-Image." *Studi sul Boccaccio* 12: 263–273.

Marsh, David. 2003. Introduction. In Petrarch, *Invectives*. Ed. and trans. David Marsh. The I Tatti Renaissance Library 11. Cambridge, MA: Harvard University Press. vii–xx.

2015. "Petrarch's Adversaries: The *Invectives*." In *The Cambridge Companion to Petrarch*. Ed. Albert Russell Ascoli and Unn Falkeid. Cambridge: Cambridge University Press. 167–176.

Martellotti, Guido. 1977. Nota critica. In Petrarch, *De vita solitaria*. Ed. Guido Martellotti. Turin: Einaudi. x–xi.

Martines, Lauro. 1963. *The Social World of Florentine Humanists, 1390–1460*. Princeton, NJ: Princeton University Press.

Martinez, Ronald L. 2006. "*The Book without a Name*: Petrarch's Open Secret (*Liber sine nomine*)." In Victoria Kirkham and Armando Maggi. *Petrarch: A Critical Guide to the Complete Works*. Chicago: University of Chicago Press. 291–299.

2015. "The Latin Hexameter Works: *Epystole, Bucolicum carmen, Africa*." In *The Cambridge Companion to Petrarch*. Ed. Albert Russell Ascoli and Unn Falkeid. Cambridge: Cambridge University Press. 87–99.

Mazza, Antonia. 1966. "L'inventario della *Parva Libraria* in Santo Spirito e la biblioteca del Boccaccio." *Italia medioevale e umanistica* 9: 1–74.

Mazzotta, Giuseppe. 1979. *Dante, Poet of the Desert: History and Allegory in the "Divine Comedy."* Princeton, NJ: Princeton University Press.

1993a. *Dante's Vision and the Circle of Knowledge.* Princeton, NJ: Princeton University Press.

1993b. *The Worlds of Petrarch.* Durham, NC: Duke University Press.

2000. "Boccaccio: The Mythographer of the City." In Jon Whitman, ed. *Interpretation and Allegory: Antiquity to the Modern Period.* Leiden: Brill. 349–364.

2006a. "Humanism and the Medieval Encyclopedic Tradition." In *Interpretations of Renaissance Humanism.* Ed. Angelo Mazzocco. Leiden: Brill, 2006. 113–124.

2006b. "Petrarca e il discorso di Roma." In *Petrarca, canoni, esemplarità.* Ed. Valeria Finucci. Rome: Bulzoni. 259–272.

2009. "Petrarch's Dialogue with Dante." In *Dante the Lyric and Ethical Poet: Dante Lirico e etico.* Ed. Zygmunt G. Barański and Martin McLaughlin. London: Legenda. 177–194.

Megas, Anastasios Ch. 1969. *Albertini Mussati Argumenta tragoediarum Senecae Commentarii in L.A. Senecae tragoedias fragmenta nuper reperta.* Cum praefatione, apparatu critico, scholiis edidit. Thessalonica: N. Nikolaïde.

Mertens, Dieter. 1988. "Petrarcas 'Privilegium laureationis.'" In *Litterae Medii Aevi: Festschrift für Johanne Autenrieth zu ihrem 65. Geburtstag.* Ed. Michael Borgholte and Herrad Spilling. Sigmaringen: Thorbecke. 225–247.

Mésoniat, Claudio. 1984. *Poetica theologia: La "Lucula noctis" di Giovanni Dominici e le dispute letterarie tra '300 e '400.* Rome: Edizioni di Storia e Letteratura.

Milner, Stephen J. 2015. "Boccaccio's *Decameron* and the Semiotics of the Everyday." In *The Cambridge Companion to Boccaccio.* Ed. Guyda Armstrong, Rhiannon Daniels, and Stephen J. Milner. Cambridge: Cambridge University Press. 83–100.

Minnis, Alastair J. 1988. *Medieval Theory of Authorship: Scholastic Literary Attitudes in the Later Middle Ages.* 2nd ed. Philadelphia: University of Pennsylvania Press.

2000. "*Quadruplex Sensus, Multiplex Modus*: Scriptural Sense and Mode in Medieval Scholastic Exegesis." In Jon Whitman, ed. *Interpretation and Allegory: Antiquity to the Modern Period.* Leiden: Brill. 231–256.

Minnis, Alastair J. and Ian Johnson. 2005. *The Cambridge History of Literary Criticism.* vol 2. *The Middle Ages.* Cambridge: Cambridge University Press.

Minnis, Alastair J., A. Brian Scott, and David Wallace, eds. 1988. *Medieval Literary Theory c.1100–c. 1375: The Commentary Tradition.* Oxford: Oxford University Press.

Mocan, Mira. 2015. "Canto XXIII: Vedere la 'vera luce' nel cielo delle stelle fisse. Il trionfo di Cristo e di Maria." In *Cento canti per cento anni. III: Paradiso.* Ed. Enrico Malato and Andrea Mazzucchi. 2 vols. Rome: Salerno Editrice. 2.671–697.

Modesto, Filippa. 2015. *Dante's Idea of Friendship: The Transformation of a Classical Concept.* Toronto: University of Toronto Press.

Modonutti, Rino. 2017. "Le orazioni nelle 'Storie' di Albertino Mussato." In *"Moribus antiquis sibi me fecere poetam." Albertino Mussato nel VII centenario dell'incoronazione poetica (Padova 1315–2015)*. Ed. Rino Modonutti and Enrico Zucchi. Florence: SISMEL, Edizioni del Galluzzo. 125–140.

Modonutti, Rino and Enrico Zucchi, eds. 2017. *"Moribus antiquis sibi me fecere poetam." Albertino Mussato nel VII centenario dell'incoronazione poetica (Padova 1315–2015)*. Florence: SISMEL, Edizioni del Galluzzo.

Moevs, Christian. 2005. *The Metaphysics of Dante's Comedy*. Oxford: Oxford University Press.

2009. "Subjectivity and Conversion in Dante and Petrarch." In *Petrarch and Dante: Anti-Dantism, Metaphysics, Tradition*. Ed. Zygmunt G. Barański and Theodore J. Cachey, Jr. Notre Dame, IN: University of Notre Dame Press. 226–259.

Montuori, Francesco. 2015. "Canto XVII: Le parole dell'esilio tra l'eterno e il tempo." In *Cento canti per cento anni. III: Paradiso*. Ed. Enrico Malato and Andrea Mazzucchi. 2 vols. Rome: Salerno Editrice. 1.491–530.

Moschetti, Andrea. 1927. "Il 'De lite inter Naturam et Fortunam' e il 'Contra casus fortuitos' di Albertino Mussato." In *Miscellanea di studi critici e ricerche erudite in onore di Vincenzo Crescini*. Cividale del Friuli: Tip. Fratelli Stagni. 567–599.

Muratori, Ludovico A., ed. 1727. *Rerum Italicarum Scriptores*. vol. 10.2. Milan.

Musto, Ronald G., ed. 1996. Introduction. Petrach, *The Revolution of Cola di Rienzo*. New York: Italica Press. xiii–xxii.

Najemy, John M. 2008. *A History of Florence, 1200–1575*. Malden, MA: Blackwell.

Novati, Francesco. 1881. "Poeti veneti del Trecento." In *Archivio Storico per Trieste, l'Istria e il Trentino*. vol. 1. Ed. S. Morpurgo and A. Zenatti. Rome: Direzione proprietaria. 130–141.

Olson, Kristina. 2014. *Courtesy Lost: Dante, Boccaccio, and the Literature of History*. Toronto: University of Toronto Press.

2016. "Shoes, Gowns, and Turncoats: Reconsidering Cacciaguida's History of Florentine Fashion and Politics." *Dante Studies* 134: 26–47.

Ong, Walter J. 1958. *Ramus, Method, and the Decay of Dialogue*. Cambridge, MA: Harvard University Press.

Onorato, Aldo. 2005. "Albertino Mussato e magister Ioannes: la corrispondenza poetica." *Studi medievali e umanistici* 3: 81–127.

Osgood, Charles G. 1930. *Boccaccio on Poetry, Being the Preface and Fourteenth and Fifteenth Books of Boccaccio's "Genealogia Deorum Gentilium."* Princeton, NJ: Princeton University Press.

Osius, Felix, Laurentius Pignorius, and Nicolaus Villanus, eds. 1636. *Albertini Mussati Historia Augusta Henrici VII Caesaris et alia quae extant omnia*. Venice.

Padoan, Giorgio. 1978. "Il Boccaccio 'fedele' di Dante." In *Il Boccaccio, le Muse, il Parnaso e l'Arno*. Florence: Olschki. 229–246.

Paolazzi, Carlo. 1983. "Petrarca, Boccaccio e il *Trattatello in laude di Dante*." *Studi Danteschi* 55: 165–249.

Papio, Michael. 2009. "Introduction: Boccaccio as *Lector Dantis*." In *Boccaccio's Expositions on Dante's Comedy*. Trans. Michael Papio. Toronto: University of Toronto Press. 3–38.

2012. "Boccaccio: Mythographer, Philosopher, Theologian." In *Boccaccio in America*. Ed. Elsa Filosa and Michael Papio. Ravenna: Longo. 123–142.

Park, Katharine. 1985. *Doctors and Medicine in Early Renaissance Florence*. Princeton, NJ: Princeton University Press.

Pastore Stocchi, Manlio. 1966. "Dante, Mussato e la tragedia." In *Dante e la cultura veneta: atti del convegno di studi organizzato dalla Fondazione "Giorgio Cini."* Florence: Olschki. 251–262.

1987. "Il 'Somnium' di Albertino Mussato." In Marco Pecoraro, *Studi in onore di Vittorio Zaccaria*. Milan: Unicopli. 41–63.

2004. "Giovanni Boccaccio. La 'Genealogia deorum gentilium': una novità mitografica." In *Il mito nella letteratura italiana*. vol. 1. *Dal medioevo al Rinascimento*. Ed. Gian Carlo Alessio. Brescia: Morcelliana. 229–246.

Pastore Stocchi, Manlio. ed. 2012. Dante Alighieri, *Epistole, Ecloge, Quaestio de aqua et terra*. Medioevo e Umanesimo 117. Rome: Antenore.

Pecoraro, Marco. 1987. *Studi in onore di Vittorio Zaccaria*. Milan: Unicopli.

Pertile, Lino. 2010. "Le *Egloghe* di Dante e l'antro di Polifemo." In *Dante the Lyric and Ethical Poet: Dante Lirico e etico*. Ed. Zygmunt G. Barański and Martin McLaughlin. London: Legenda. 153–167.

Perugi, Maurizio. 2002. "Canto XXIII." In *Lectura Dantis Turicensis: Paradiso*. Ed. Georges Güntert and Michelangelo Picone. Florence: Franco Cesati Editore. 363–371.

Petoletti, Marco, ed. 2015. *Dante e la sua eredità a Ravenna nel Trecento*. Ravenna: Longo.

Petoletti, Marco. 2016. Nota introduttiva. Nota ai testi. In Dante Alighieri, *Epistole, Egloge, Quaestio de aqua et terra*. Nuova edizione commentata delle Opere di Dante. vol. 5. Ed. Marco Baglio, Luca Azzetta, Marco Petoletti, and Michele Rinaldi. Rome: Salerno Editrice. 491–514.

Picone, Michelangelo. 2005. "Il tema dell'incoronazione poetica in Dante, Petrarca, e Boccaccio." *L'Alighieri* 25: 1–26.

Pirovano, Donato. 2015. "Canto XXVI: 'A la riva' del 'diritto' amore." In *Cento canti per cento anni. III: Paradiso*. Ed. Enrico Malato and Andrea Mazzucchi. 2 vols. Rome: Salerno Editrice. 2.747–786.

Porta, Giuseppe, ed. 1979. *Cronaca dell'Anonimo Romano: Vita di Cola di Rienzo*. Milan: Adelphi.

Prandi, Stefano. 2015. "Canto XXV: 'Ritornerò poeta.'" In *Cento canti per cento anni. III: Paradiso*. Ed. Enrico Malato and Andrea Mazzucchi. 2 vols. Rome: Salerno Editrice. 2.723–746.

Raffa, Guy. 1996. "Dante's Mocking Pastoral Muse." *Dante Studies* 114: 271–291.

Raimondi, Ezio. 1970a. *Metafora e storia. Studi su Dante e Petrarca*. Turin: Giulio Einaudi Editore.

1970b. "L'aquila e il fuoco di Ezzelino." In *Metafora e storia. Studi su Dante e Petrarca*. Turin: Giulio Einaudi Editore. 123–146.

1970c. "Una tragedia del Trecento." In *Metafora e storia. Studi su Dante e Petrarca*. Turin: Giulio Einaudi Editore. 147–162.

Rashdall, F. Hastings. 1936. *The Universities of Europe in the Middle Ages*. Ed. F. M. Powicke and A. B. Emden. New ed. 3 vols. Oxford: Oxford University Press.

Reggio, Giovanni. 1969. *Le Egloghe di Dante*. Florence: Olschki.

Regnicoli, Laura. 2013. "Codice diplomatico di Giovanni Boccaccio. 1. I documenti fiscali." *Italia medioevale et umanistica* 54: 1–80.

Ricci, Pier Giorgio. 1947. "Il Petrarca e Brizio Visconti." *Leonardo* 16: 337–345.

1955. "Nota critica alle *Invective*." In *Francesco Petrarca: Prose*. Ed. Guido Martellotti. Milan: Riccardo Ricciardi. 1171–1172.

1974. "Le tre redazioni del Trattatello in laude di Dante." *Studi sul Boccaccio* 8: 197–214.

Ricci, Pier Giorgio. ed. 1978. Francesco Petrarch, *Invective contra medicum*. Appendix by Bartolo Martinelli. Rome: Edizioni di storia e letteratura.

Rico, Francisco. 1974. *Vida u obra de Petrarca*. vol. 1. *Lectura del Secretum*. Padua: Antenore.

2012. *Ritratti allo specchio: Boccaccio, Petrarca*. Rome: Antenore.

Rippe, Gérard. 2003. *Padoue et son contado (X^e–XIIIe siècle): Société et pouvoirs*. Rome: École française de Rome.

Ronconi, Giorgio. 1976. *Le origini delle dispute umanistiche sulla poesia (Mussato e Petrarca)*. Rome: Bulzoni Editore.

2017. "Echi dell'incoronazione poetica di Albertino Mussato in Dante e Giovanni del Virgilio." In *"Moribus antiquis sibi me fecere poetam." Albertino Mussato nel VII centenario dell'incoronazione poetica (Padova 1315–2015)*. Ed. Rino Modonutti and Enrico Zucchi. Florence: SISMEL, Edizioni del Galluzzo. 47–62.

Sandal, Ennio, ed. 2006. *Dante e Boccaccio*. Padua: Antenore.

Sanguineti, Edoardo. 1992. *Dante reazionario*. Rome: Editori riuniti.

Santagata, Marco. 1996. Introduzione. In *Francesco Petrarca: Canzoniere*. Ed. Marco Santagata. Milan: Mondadori. xix–cii.

Sarolli, G. Roberto. 1971. *Prolegomena alla "Divina Commedia."* Florence: Olschki.

Schildgen, Brenda Deen. 2000. "Boethius and the Consolation of Literature in Boccaccio's *Decameron* and Chaucer's *Canterbury Tales*." In *The Decameron and the Canterbury Tales: New Essays on an Old Question*. Ed. Leonard Michael Koff and Brenda Deen Schildgen. Madison, NJ: Fairleigh Dickinson University Press. 102–127.

Schnapp, Jeffrey T. 1986. *The Transfiguration of History at the Center of Dante's "Paradise."* Princeton, NJ: Princeton University Press.

1995. "Tragedy and the Theater of Hell." In *"Libri poetarum quattor species dividuntur": Essays on Dante and "Genre."* Ed. Zygmunt G. Barański. *The Italianist* 15 (suppl. 2): 100–127.

2003. "Petrarch's New Antiquity." In *Zeit und Text: Philosophische, kulturanthropologische, literarhistorische un linguistische Beiträge.* Ed. Andreas Kablitz, Wulf Österreicher, and Rainer Warning. Munich: Fink Verlag. 236–245.

Schönberger, Otto and Eva Schönberger. 2004. Einleitung. In Francesco Petrarch, *Epistulae Metricae/Briefe in Versen.* Ed. Otto Schönberger and Eva Schönberger. Würzburg: Königshausen & Neumann.

Scott, John. 2004. *Understanding Dante.* Notre Dame, IN: University of Notre Dame Press.

Setton, Kenneth M. 1976. *The Papacy and the Levant, 1204–1571.* 4 vols. Philadelphia: American Philosophical Society.

Simpson, James. 2005. "Subjects of Triumph and Literary History: Dido and Petrarch in Petrarch's *Africa* and *Trionfi.*" *Journal of Medieval and Early Modern Studies* 35.3: 489–508.

Singer, Julie. 2011. *Blindness and Therapy in Late Medieval French and Italian Poetry.* Cambridge: D. S. Brewer.

Singleton, Charles S. 1956. *Dante Studies 2: Journey to Beatrice.* Cambridge, MA: Harvard University Press.

Siraisi, Nancy G. 1973. *The Arts and Sciences at Padua: The Studium of Padua before 1350.* Toronto: Pontifical Institute of Mediaeval Studies.

Small, Helen, ed. 2002. *The Public Intellectual.* Oxford: Blackwell.

Smarr, Janet Levarie. 1982. "Petrarch: A Virgil without a Rome." In *Rome in the Renaissance.* Ed. P. A. Ramsey. Binghamton, NY: Medieval & Renaissance Texts and Studies. 133–140.

1986. *Boccaccio and Fiammetta: The Narrator as Lover.* Urbana: University of Illinois Press.

1987. "Ovid and Boccaccio: A Note on Self-Defense." *Mediaevalia* 13. 247–255.

Staüble, Antonio. 2002. "Canto XV." In *Lectura Dantis Turicensis: Paradiso.* Ed. Georges Güntert and Michelangelo Picone. Florence: Franco Cesati Editore. 219–229.

Steinberg, Justin. 2007. *Accounting for Dante: Urban Readers and Writers in Late Medieval Italy.* Notre Dame, IN: University of Notre Dame Press.

2013. *Dante and the Limits of the Law.* Chicago: University of Chicago Press.

2014. "Response" to "Professional Dantology and the Human Significance of Dante Studies" by William Franke. *Diacritics* 42.4: 72–74.

Stierle, Karlheinz. 2002. "Canto XXVI." In *Lectura Dantis Turicensis: Paradiso.* Ed. Georges Güntert and Michelangelo Picone. Florence: Franco Cesati Editore. 405–418.

Stone, Gregory B. 1998. *The Ethics of Nature in the Middle Ages: On Boccaccio's Poetaphysics.* New York: St. Martin's Press.

Strodach, George Kleppinger. 1933. "Latin Diminutives in –ello/a- and –illo/a: A Study in Diminutive Formation." *Language* 9.1: 7–98.

Sturm-Maddox, Sara. 2009. "Dante, Petrarch, and the Laurel Crown." In *Petrarch and Dante: Anti-Dantism, Metaphysics, Tradition.* Ed. Zygmunt G. Barański and Theodore J. Cachey, Jr. Notre Dame, IN: University of Notre Dame Press. 290–319.

Tavoni, Mirko. 2015a. "Che cos'è la poesia? Chi è poeta" In Mirko Tavoni, *Qualche idea su Dante.* Bologna: Il Mulino. 295–334.

2015b. "Linguistic Italy." In *Dante in Context.* Ed. Zygmunt G. Barański and Lino Pertile. Cambridge: Cambridge University Press.

Trinkaus, Charles. 1970. *In Our Image and Likeness: Humanity and Divinity in Italian Humanist Thought.* 2 vols. Chicago: University of Chicago Press.

1979. *The Poet as Philosopher: Petrarch and the Formation of Renaissance Consciousness.* New Haven, CT: Yale University Press.

Ullman, Berthold L. 1963. *The Humanism of Coluccio Salutati.* Padua: Antenore.

Usher, Jonathan. 2007. "Monuments More Enduring Than Bronze: Boccaccio and Paper Inscriptions." *Heliotropia* 4: 21–50: www.heliotropia.org/.

2009. "Petrarch's Diploma of Crowning: The *Privilegium laureationis.*" In *Italy and the Classical Tradition: Language, Thought and Poetry 1300–1600.* Ed. Carlo Caruso and Andrew Laird. London: Duckworth.

Vecce, Carlo. 2015. "Canto XXII: San Benedetto e il 'mondo sotto li piedi.'" In *Cento canti per cento anni. III: Paradiso.* Ed. Enrico Malato and Andrea Mazzucchi. 2 vols. Rome: Salerno Editrice. 2.642–670.

Veglia, Marco. 2006. "*Ut medicina poesis.* Sulla 'terapia' del *Decameron.*" In *Petrarca e la medicina. Atti del Convegno di Capo d'Orlando (27–28 giugno 2003).* Ed. Monica Berté, Vincenzo Fera, and Tiziana Pesenti. Messina: Centro Interdipartimentale di Studi Umanistici. 201–228.

2014. *La strada più impervia: Boccaccio fra Dante e Petrarca.* Rome: Antenore.

Veglia, Marco. ed. 2015–16. Atti del Convegno "Boccaccio politico." University of Bologna, July 19–21, 2013. In *Heliotropia* 12–13: www.heliotropia.org.

Velli, Giuseppe. 1992. Introduzione. In Giovanni Boccaccio, *Tutte le opere di Giovanni Boccaccio.* vol. 5.1. Ed. Ginetta Auzzas. Milan: Mondadori. 377–402.

2006. "A Poetic Journal (*Epystole*)." In Victoria Kirkham and Armando Maggi. *Petrarch: A Critical Guide to the Complete Works.* Chicago: University of Chicago Press. 277–290.

Villa, Claudia. 2009. *La protervia di Beatrice.* Florence: Edizioni del Galluzzo.

2010. "Il problema dello stile umile (e il riso di Dante)." In *Dante the Lyric and Ethical Poet: Dante Lirico e etico.* Ed. Zygmunt G. Barański and Martin McLaughlin. London: Legenda. 138–152.

Vinay, Gustavo. 1949. "Studi sul Mussato I: Il Mussato e l'estetica medievale." *Giornale storico della letteratura italiana.* 126: 113–159.

Wallace, David. 1997. *The Chaucerian Polity: Absolutist Lineages and Associational Forms in England and Italy.* Stanford, CA: Stanford University Press.

2002. "Humanism, Slavery and the Republic of Letters." In Helen Small, ed. *The Public Intellectual.* Oxford: Blackwell. 62–88.

Weiss, Roberto. 1949. *Il primo secolo dell'umanesimo: Studi e testi*. Rome: Storia e letteratura.

1986. "Mussato." In *Dizionario Critico della Letteratura Italiana, diretto da Vittore Branca*. 2nd ed. 4 vols. Turin: UTET. 237–239.

Westwater, Lynn Lara. 2006. "The Uncollected Poet (*Lettere disperse*)." In Victoria Kirkham and Armando Maggi. *Petrarch: A Critical Guide to the Complete Works*. Chicago: University of Chicago Press. 301–308.

Whitman, Jon, ed. 2000. *Interpretation and Allegory: Antiquity to the Modern Period*. Leiden: Brill.

Wicksteed, Philip H. and Edmund Gardner. 1902. *Dante and Giovanni del Virgilio, Including a Critical Edition of the Text of Dante's "Ecloghae Latinae" and of the Poetic Remains of Giovanni del Virgilio*. London: Constable.

Wilkins, Ernest H. 1953. "Petrarch's Coronation Oration." *PMLA* 68.5: 1241–1250.

1955. *Sudies in the Life and Works of Petrarch*. Cambridge, MA: Mediaeval Academy of America.

1956. *The "Epistolae Metricae" of Petrarch: A Manual*. Rome: Edizioni di Storia e Letteratura.

1958. *Petrarch's Eight Years in Milan*. Cambridge, MA: Mediaeval Academy of America.

1959. *Petrarch's Later Years*. Cambridge, MA: Mediaeval Academy of America.

1961. *Life of Petrarch*. Chicago: University of Chicago Press.

Witt, Ronald G. 1977. "Coluccio Salutati and the Conception of the *Poeta Theologus* in the Fourteenth Century." *Renaissance Quarterly* 30.4: 538–563.

1983. *Hercules at the Crossroads: The Life, Works, and Thought of Coluccio Salutati*. Durham, NC: Duke University Press.

2000. *In the Footsteps of the Ancients: The Origins of Humanism from Lovato to Bruni*. Leiden: Brill.

2015. "The *Poeta-Theologus* from Mussato to Landino." *The European Legacy* 20.5: 450–461.

Wojciehowski, Dolora A. 1995. *Old Masters, New Subjects: Early Modern and Poststructuralist Theories of Will*. Stanford, CA: Stanford University Press.

Woodhouse, John, ed. 1997. *Dante and Governance*. Oxford: Clarendon Press.

Yocum, Demetrio S. 2013. *Petrarch's Humanist Writing and Carthusian Monasticism: The Secret Language of the Self*. Medieval Church Studies 26. Turnhout: Brepols.

Zabbia, Marino. 2012. "Mussato, Albertino." *Dizionario Biografico degli Italiani*. vol. 77. Rome: Istituto della Enciclopedia Italiana. 520–524.

Zaccaria, Vittorio. 1998a. Introduzione. In Giovanni Boccaccio, *Tutte le opere di Giovanni Boccaccio*. vol. 7. Milan: Mondadori. 7.13–42.

1998b. Nota al testo. In Giovanni Boccaccio, *Tutte le opere di Giovanni Boccaccio*. vol. 8. Milan: Mondadori. 8.1592–1599.

2001. *Boccaccio Narratore, Storico, Moralista, e Mitografo*. Florence: Olschki.

Zak, Gur. 2010. *Petrarch's Humanism and the Care of the Self.* Cambridge: Cambridge University Press.

    2015. "Boccaccio and Petrarch." In *The Cambridge Companion to Boccaccio.* Ed. Guyda Armstrong, Rhiannon Daniels, and Stephen J. Milner. Cambridge: Cambridge University Press. 139–154.

    2016. "The Ethics and Poetics of Consolation in Petrarch's *Bucolicum carmen.*" *Speculum* 91.1: 36–62.

Zardo, Antonio. 1884. *Albertino Mussato: Studio storico e letterario.* Padua: Tipografia del Seminario.

Ziolkowski, Jan M., ed. 2014. *Dante and the Greeks.* Washington, DC: Dumbarton Oaks.

Index

CAMBRIDGE STUDIES IN MEDIEVAL LITERATURE

www.ingramcontent.com/pod-product-compliance
Ingram Content Group UK Ltd.
Pitfield, Milton Keynes, MK11 3LW, UK
UKHW020454010325
455719UK00016B/573